ROUSSEAU'S OCCASIONAL AUTOBIOGRAPHIES

Rousseau's Occasional Autobiographies

Susan K. Jackson

Ohio State University Press
Columbus

Library of Congress Cataloging-in-Publication Data

Jackson, Susan K.
    Rousseau's occasional autobiographies / Susan K. Jackson.
        p.   cm.
    Includes bibliographical references and index.
    ISBN 0–8142–0565–8 (alk. paper)
    1. Rousseau, Jean-Jacques, 1712–1778—Biography.   2. Authors,
French—Biography—History and criticism.   3. Autobiography.
I. Title.
PQ2043.J33   1991
848′.509—dc20
    [B]   91–34284
                                                                              CIP

Text and jacket design by Donna Hartwick.
Type set in Garamond by The Composing Room of Michigan, Grand Rapids, MI.
Printed by Versa Press, East Peoria, IL.

Contents

Preface

One occupational hazard of spending too much time in close quarters with Rousseau's autobiographies is the risk we run of catching his incapacity for spontaneous self-irony and, by way of compensation, carrying self-irony to ludicrous extremes. It is partly to have done with the demons of fluctuating tone and excruciating self-awareness that I offer the following accounting for the way this book has turned out.

Earlier versions were not nearly so concerned as this one with multiplying and elongating the moments of Rousseau's coming to write about himself. My exorbitant fascination with the question of how anyone could bring herself or himself to do such a thing nonetheless extends as far back as, Rousseau abetting, I can now remember. Painful or pleasurable, anything but affectively neutral, talking publicly about himself is one thing to which Rousseau's autobiographical texts never quite seem to come naturally. The defiant "moi. Moi seul" of the preamble to the *Confessions* only echoes less endearingly the antiphonal asides of the "Préface" to *Narcisse* ("Il faut malgré ma répugnance que je parle de moi") and the *Lettres à Malesherbes* ("J'aime trop à parler de moi").

Striking a chord, Rousseau's labored beginnings remind me of growing up in a household where what seemed like thousands of mirrors were clearly off limits and designated as ornaments to be looked at, not into. Enshrining the master bathtub in damning testimony to the character flaws of former owners, a *galerie de glaces* furnished the *occasion pro-*

chaine of sins committed by my brother and me on the watches of unwitting babysitters. Was there really a self or two in the house? At the time of these early reconnaissance missions, we had no way of knowing that for me, as a girl growing up in the fifties, the question would turn out to be moot; there was, in any event, no self worth talking about. Cut to Mr. Barclay's Friday afternoon ballroom dancing classes, where the fox-trot and cha-cha provided incidental music for further lessons in living right, which involved crossing our legs at the ankles, turning to the gentleman on our left, and beseeching him to give us a full accounting of his interests. By the time we had figured out the part about the ankles well enough to "know" full well what was on our partners' minds, it was too late to break the habit of our discreet, other-directed inquiries. Since boys were in short supply, the tallest girls were sometimes recruited to cross over, with the result that, on the dance floor at least, I still always lead a little. But when it came time for small talk, we single-sex couples were strictly on our own—allowed to chat, as I recall, but required by the master script only to mark time with both pairs of ankles crossed.

To the published confidences of women like Hélène Cixous I am grateful for validating and easing my discomfiture, and for nudging this book about perennial comings to self-inscription over the final conceptual hurdle. Cixous's "Sorties" evoke the inextinguishable resonances in any woman's writing of the momentous "déchirement qu'est pour la femme la prise de la parole orale—'prise' qui est effectuée comme un arrachement, un essor vertigineux et une lancée de soi, une plongée." This feeling is not entirely lost on the Rousseau of the *Confessions,* who mourns the innumerable missed occasions for speaking up and out from the depths of his being that someone less constitutionally slow-witted than Jean-Jacques would have known how to seize. Except that he of supreme faith in staircase wit (as, among other things, an indelible trait of his own character) thinks finally to take his revenge on real life. To his *Confessions* falls the task of driving a differential wedge between past and present, and of positing a former lifetime of failure to express his self in conversational context. Rousseau's act to end all acts of self-inscription aspires to remember and remedy without commemorating the former failure.

My heart goes out more spontaneously to the earlier Rousseaus of less grandiose and single-minded ambitions for writing off the recurring wrench of coming to writing as a one-time investment in permanent selfhood. For the women of my generation, that wrench has become less uniformly traumatic since I first stared in disbelief at the interminable spaces allotted on my college applications for "personal" essays. But the fear and exhilaration of crossing the line have never entirely gone away, whether the transgression consists in sneaking enough of a peek at the mirror to recall that I am for all practical purposes still there or, more usually, in improvising an alternative to Mr. Barclay's scenario where we girls would assume responsibility for formulating our own questions.

But taking responsibility has little to do with the pathetic isolationism of Rousseau's sometimes wanting to befriend the truth to the point where there would be no further need for the help and support of real friends. I thank my teachers at Ohio State and my colleagues at Duke and Boston Universities for nurturing and challenging this project at every stage along the way. To Ron Rosbottom goes special gratitude for staying cheerfully and effectively on the case long beyond the endpoint of official obligations. At a critical moment, a Junior Fellowship from the Humanities Foundation at Boston University made time for sustained reading and thinking. I am lucky beyond measure to have parents who strongly encouraged those two activities when I was inclined to get by with less, and who understood when I eventually leapt to the opposite extreme of taking their encouragement over-seriously. I wish finally to acknowledge that portions of chapter 3 previously appeared as an article entitled "Text and Context of Rousseau's Relations with Diderot" in *Eighteenth-Century Studies.*

To Hannah and Nathaniel, I am indebted for their keeping things always slightly out of control and in perspective. For them and for the room to grow in fits and starts, I dedicate this book to Richard.

Introduction

On the Occasional

. . . j'écris moins l'histoire de ces éve[ne]mens en eux-mêmes que celle de l'état de mon ame, à mesure qu'ils sont arrivés. Or, les ames ne sont plus ou moins illustres que selon qu'elles ont des sentimens plus ou moins grands et nobles, des idées plus ou moins vives et nombreuses. Les faits ne sont ici que des causes occasionnelles.

Rousseau, "Ebauches des *Confessions*"

Sans ces causes occasionnelles un homme né très sensible ne sentiroit rien, et mourroit sans avoir connu son être.

Rousseau, *Confessions*

B etween 1765 and 1770, Jean-Jacques Rousseau wrote the *Confessions,* which, published posthumously in the two volumes of 1782 and 1789, have been widely credited with "inaugurating the genre [of autobiography] in its modern form."[1] Of these events in publishing history, literary historians after Rousseau's own heart have consented to make a more or less unprecedented and precedent-setting *grande occasion.* The tendency to commemorate Rousseau's would-be first of a kind "portrait d'homme"[2] as a pivotal turning point in the evolution of Western letters is, understandably, most pronounced in the French tradition. Georges May, for example, takes a turn at celebrating an "occasion" already named in the pioneering work of Georges Gusdorf: "Tout indique . . . que le succès du livre [les *Confessions*] fut l'occasion de la première vraie prise de conscience collective de l'existence littéraire de l'autobiographie. Comme l'écrit G. Gusdorf: 'De cette occasion mémorable datent les lettres de noblesse de l'autobiographie en France et dans les principales cultures européennes.' "[3] But the dossier does not lack for influential Anglo-Saxon voices of corroboration. Francis R. Hart's "Notes for an Anatomy of Modern Autobiography," the critical text in English most often cited with Gusdorf's as having decisively rekindled interest in autobiographical studies, also gives the nod, albeit less categorically, to

1

Rousseau: "On the . . . controversial assumption that modern autobiography began two centuries ago, I shall limit these applications to Rousseau and his successors."[4] By "Rousseau," Hart means, first and foremost, the *Confessions* and, to a lesser degree, their successors in Rousseau's posthumous corpus. The later *Dialogues: Rousseau juge de Jean-Jacques* and unfinished *Rêveries* are texts generally esteemed to have extended Rousseau's remarkably obsessive, even Sisyphean[5] preoccupation with self-inscription virtually up until the moment of his death in 1778.

My aim in this book is to extend the period of that preoccupation in the opposite direction. I want to reconceptualize the *Confessions* as several and by no means the first in a series of occasional autobiographies that Rousseau began writing as early as 1752. Within Rousseau's own œuvre, there is a protohistory to autobiography that readers persuaded or put off by the *Confessions'* emphatic claims to absolute originality have found easy to ignore or leave latent. The enterprise of bringing that protohistory into sharper relief is favored at this time by a critical climate of skepticism where historically fetishized beginnings and honorifics like "father of autobiography" are concerned. And the reconfiguration of Rousseau's corpus to accommodate the protohistory poses no real challenge to the *Confessions'* unquestioned literary value, or even to their standing as a particularly rich repository of autobiographical thinking. On the contrary, I will argue that acknowledging the parameters and durable pertinence of Rousseau's earlier comings to write about himself can only enhance the intelligibility and interest of the *Confessions,* especially the relatively underread and underappreciated second volume.

But I will first clarify my use of the term "occasional" to epitomize the autobiographical adventure in Rousseau, and I will start by taking a look at the current state of autobiographical studies. How better, in fact, to begin to rewrite the beginning than nourished by a discourse that is now positioned self-consciously at the "beginning of the end" of autobiography. What has been shown by felicitous pairings like that of Diderot's *Jacques le fataliste* with the nouveau roman holds for autobiography as well: the contours of a given genre emerge less clearly in the heyday of enthusiastic proliferation than at the two mutually illuminating extremes when the genre either has not yet acceded to the status of a second nature or has evolved to the point where that status becomes, once again, open to suspicion.

Of the genre—modern autobiography—that the *Confessions* are widely reputed to have launched, Elizabeth Bruss writes almost retro-spectively: "We have grown so accustomed to this kind of introspective activity that it is difficult for us to appreciate its fragility."[6] For Bruss, facing up to fragility and to the eventual demise and essential premises of autobiography is a matter of acknowledging the ways in which "auto-biographical" cinema does not and cannot conform to any time-honored scriptural model. Critics may disagree as to how quickly, inevitably, or irretrievably that model is receding into obsolescence; they may have ideological reasons for speeding the process along or, alternatively, downplaying its scope and significance; and they may be more or less interested in squaring a flurry of theoretical postmortems with a flourish-ing practice of life writing that still goes, however insouciantly or inno-vatively, by the name of autobiography. But few would dismiss Bruss's basic finding in "Eye for I" that autobiography narrowly enough defined to be replicable, discussable, and valued is looking more and more un-mistakably like a historically contingent phenomenon. In the era and aura of poststructuralism, there has been a sizable outpouring of agreement when it comes to describing and assigning root causes to that contingen-cy. A persistent pattern of cultural imbrication has emerged, from which it is increasingly difficult to want to abstract autobiography as such, in and of itself, or for all times. The autobiographical activity of the past two centuries is specifically recognized to go hand in hand with a collective commitment to proceeding as though there were some a priori basis in fact to the cultural and linguistic constructs of self (*autos*) and life (*bios*).

Only at its most naively wishful would autobiography pretend not to be emboldened at the outset by the availability of these constructs or enabling in turn of "historical ideologies of selfhood and the processes of our storytelling." Even in the disruptive process of bringing to light some traditionally female alternatives to mainstream autobiography, Sidonie Smith does not deny her women writers a sense of self or preclude them from plotting the course of a life. Rather, she reads their texts for signs of discomfiture with a particular "hegemonic conception of selfhood"[7] and for instances of deviation from prevailing plotlines. But, whether re-placed by the camera or displaced through a countervalorized "connec-tedness,"[8] the old imperial "I" of autobiography runs a similar risk of exposure as only one option among others. These new uncertainties as to "what," among other things, the self might be are compounded by even deeper-seated suspicions as to the "how" or preconditions of its being anything at all. The stress of autobiographical studies has come to fall more exclusively than ever before on the problematical third term of *graphē,* or writing. Self and life, however conceived, are in consequence dislodged from the realm of aprioristic, immediately accessible, and universally valid referential certainties or "independent sovereignties."[9] It is only as ends or belated by-products that, thus humbled, *autos* and *bios* are granted readmission to a newly dominant interplay between prescriptions writ large and impersonal and the writing read as specifically constitutive of this or that "take" on autobiography.

"The self, then, is a fiction and so is the life," concludes James Olney,[10] his matter-of-factness belying the enormity of the implications were we to espouse them wholeheartedly and unflinchingly. To these two, he might have proceeded to add a third fictional assumption on which autobiography has traditionally rested and relied. An essential connection has been assumed to exist between *autos* and *bios* and to be likewise uncontaminated or not necessarily contaminated by any prior act of writing. In this scheme of things, self and life are held to be mutually influencing, affirming, and informing. The life provides a suitable arena for the progressive unfolding and coming to consciousness of a self at least partially responsible for whatever direction that life will have taken or imprint it will have left. But the relationship has proven to be not quite symmetrical: the practice of modern autobiography has tended to privilege the more exorbitant and deeply cherished of the two fictions, the self, in whose name and service life stories most often purport or turn out to have been told. Gusdorf makes the point: "[Autobiography's] deepest intentions . . . are directed toward a kind of apologetics or theodicy of the individual being."[11] And Olney confirms it by releasing the notion of *bios* from any absolute obligation to the potentially digressive or distracting diachrony with which *bios* is most often and automatically associated. When the concept of *bios* is expanded to connote not only the usual "course of a life seen as a process rather than a stable entity" but "the unique psychic configuration that is this life and no other,"[12] life moves from being merely and potentially embraceable by the ideology of selfhood into that ideology's direct embrace.

The priorities Gusdorf and Olney spell out are, however, already implicit in one of life writing's perennial, remarkably resilient linguistic tics. I am thinking of how inevitably life writers—biographers and autobiographers alike—slip into the habit of converting selected events of their subject's lived experience into so many "occasions" of individual character. Implicit in this discreet reconceptualization is the assumption that selfhood reveals itself—what and *that* it is—most unmistakably through the nominal subject's responses to specific situations in which other subjects, including the reader, might have reacted differently. Mere events alone could not convey this double sense of "self" as universal, aprioristic virtuality and as an unquestioned birthright or entitlement of the particular subjects at hand. On the contrary, left to other devices of writing, events might easily fall into a configuration of causes and effects so airtight as to squeeze the self entirely out of the picture. Nor does the democratic ideology of modern selfhood wish to be misrepresented as holding the most "eventful" life or life lived in greatest proximity to in-controvertibly earthshaking events to be, sui generis, the most interest-ing or illuminating. It must all come down to whatever the self manages to make of whatever occasions the life writer arranges to throw the sub-ject's way.

But in order to sustain attention and suspend disbelief, the "self" must be furnished with some probable cause for intervention, some occa-sion requiring nothing less than a further gesture of self-actualization. Multiplying such occasions over the course of an entire life means that, for the time it takes to write or read the record of that life, doubts as to the self's empirical existence and to the essential goodness of its existing can be held in abeyance. The trick lies both in getting the life into line with the self and in getting the dynamics of the relationship just right. Ideally, the gap between *autos* and *bios* is closed in ways that naturalize and domesticate the narrative mode of self-inscription, but serve ulti-mately to put the self not so much on permanent display as in the more noteworthy position of responding, and deigning to respond, to repeated solicitations. Such are the aims and the compelling advantages of what we might overemphatically call, considering how routinely it has been de-ployed, the "occasional strategy" of autobiography.

Among the life writers who have come to celebrate the occasions of their selfhood, Giambattista Vico is one whose candidacy for the title of first modern autobiographer has been suggested by Michael Sprinker as a possible alternative to Rousseau's.[13] Rehearsing the early failures of his third-person "I" to make a mark in conventional academic circles, Vico nonetheless hastens to add: "He however blessed all these adversities as so many occasions for withdrawing to his desk, as to his high impregnable citadel, to meditate and to write further works."[14] Questions as to who really got there first aside, the coupling of Vico's project with Rousseau's remains doubly pertinent. Vico's intuition or inscription of a self characteristically prone to opportunistic writing is, as we shall see, one that the author of the *Confessions* might easily have seconded, were it not for the overwhelming resistance to any such thought that lies revealingly at the heart of Rousseau's greater, and lesser, modernity. But Vico's *Life* is no match for the *Confessions* when it comes to self-consciously singling and spelling out the occasional strategy per se as the global principle of its own—and, by extension, any autobiography's—composition.

The entirety of my theoretical addendum to Olney can, in fact, be coaxed out of the tension between the two epigraphs to this introduction. "[J]'écris moins l'histoire de ces éve[ne]mens en eux-mêmes que celle de l'état de mon ame, à mesure qu'ils sont arrivés." On the one hand, the "Ebauches" lead with a devaluing of "éve[ne]mens en eux-mêmes," which turns emphatically to the advantage of the essential self or "ame" identified as the upcoming story's real protagonist (1:1150). The writer in pursuit of a fuller accounting than that of conventional memoirs vows not to misrepresent the events of his life as an unbroken, self-sustaining continuum of causes and effects. He will instead render selected events as so many opportunities for renewed involvement by his surplus of self in what becomes in consequence a two-tiered "histoire." Yet, the "faits" unmasked here as nothing but "causes occasionnelles" come back to haunt the actual text in progress of the *Confessions,* at the juncture of Jean-Jacques's paradigmatically fortuitous encounter with Mme de Warens: "Sans ces causes occasionnelles un homme né très sensible ne sentiroit rien, et mourroit sans avoir connu son être" (1:104). Madeleine Anjubault Simons's is an eloquent distillation of the formula that underwrites a host of further episodes in the *Confessions:* "Une latence du cœur, une rencontre d'apparence fortuite."[15] Having become doubly restrictive, our cumulative proposition now reads: *but for the only occasional, were it not for the only occasional,* the self would remain unknowable in its specificity, but also and more intolerably "unfelt" or insusceptible of empirical verification through inner assent.

What makes the two halves of the proposition not quite compatible is the disappearance from the *Confessions* proper of the "I" that the

"Ebauches" will have caught ("j'écris moins l'histoire de ces éve[ne]mens en eux-mêmes . . . ") in the act of writing. The question thus arises as to what difference, if any, the act of inscription will have made in Rousseau's ability to "know his being." Rescuing the antiphonal passage of the "Ebauches" from the cutting-room floor allows us to see how arbitrarily the *Confessions* relegate the interplay between *autos* and *bios* to a past history—now simply, passively recorded—where self-actualization needed only and especially for the subject Jean-Jacques to have known Mme de Warens. We can appreciate how tightly, in the *Confessions* as written, the occasional strategy adheres to a system of beliefs where mere words are adjudged to be less of a factor than they might have been (and even less of a factor than "faits"), and where the meeting grounds of *autos* and *bios* in occasions of character are willfully presumed to belong to the order of things.

It is thus all the more paradoxical and potentially enlightening to have to trace Rousseau's key notion of "causes occasionnelles" and its implied other, general causes, to the promptings of an already written source. The notion of the "occasional" had, of course, been around as though forever; it had figured prominently in theories of human behavior at least since the Ancients deified OCCASIO and put her on a par with Pallas and Jove in calculations of the individual's chances for success. All the mental and physical prowess in the world would go for naught in the absence of opportunities to exercise or test it. So claimed Ausonius, the moral of his epigram on OCCASIO being that wisdom (Pallas) and power (Jove) are thus rightly invested in the seeing and seizing of such occasions—few and far between, difficult to discern, and always already evanescent—as the niggardly goddess deigns to mete out.[16] This practical morality struck a chord with Rousseau's contemporaries in the philosophical camp. OCCASIO presides understandably over a separate entry in the *Encyclopédie,* which outfits her, in the best tradition of iconographical overdetermination, with the several accessories of her imminent escape: "un pié en l'air & l'autre sur une roue, . . . un [*sic*] voile de la main gauche."[17] The Encyclopedists were beleaguered by the authorities, hypersensitive to their times of less than equal opportunity, and convinced that the spread of enlightenment would depend on their ability to devise effective strategies of opportunistic vulgarization. They had every reason to make a provisional virtue of judiciously picking one's spots for speech and action, even when the better part of valor—and ego-

protection—consisted less in rising rashly to the occasion than in knowing enough to flee "l'occasion de faillir."[18]

For his part, however, and "in spite of his animadversions against the
'subtleties' of abstract metaphysics," Rousseau proved more "sympathetic" than his fellow Encyclopedists "to the broad metaphysical tradition which strove to discover a rational meaning in the structure of
reality as a whole."[19] And his eventual quarrel with the philosophical
movement was—to some degree, at least—religious. On these bases, it is
easy to see why the pragmatics of occasionality we have just sketched left
Rousseau unsatisfied and open to the suggestively totalizing scheme of
causality that had been propounded by the eminent neo-Cartesian philosopher and theologian Nicolas de Malebranche (1638–1715). By all accounts, the works of Malebranche figured prominently in the course of
remedial reading to which Jean-Jacques applied himself during the Cham-
béry years of his mid-twenties. Scholarship has confirmed that the
"magasin d'idées" stockpiled by Jean-Jacques in the throes of sympathetic reading paid off handsomely for the self-styled *autodidacte* in a
lifetime of easy recall and periodic returns to the sources he names: "*la
Logique* de Port-royal, l'*Essai* de Locke, Mallebranche, Leibnitz, Des-
cartes, etc." (1:237). The entirety of the "Profession de foi du vicaire
savoyard," Rousseau's most systematically developed credo, is now commonly assumed to reflect and inflect "la notion, malebranchiste, de
l'ordre" (4:1338), even though Rousseau's text typically makes no absolutely clinching gesture to confirm his indebtedness.

I am convinced that, had Rousseau's *cahiers de lecture* survived, they
would testify, as the First Discourse does obliquely, to his having been
especially taken by Malebranche's binary scheme of causality. Decades
later, with his refrain of the "only occasional," the autobiographer would
echo and appropriate that causal scheme or essential precipitate of
"Malebranchisme" down to which the *Encyclopédie* likewise distilled
the eight-hundred-odd pages of Malebranche's *De la recherche de la vérité.*[20] The question presumed to have given rise to philosophical occasionalism was that of how the body (passive, unthinking extension) and
soul (active, unextended thinking) could interact, "correspond without
communication" (Rousseau's wording in the First Discourse), or exert
the kind of mutual influences that are readily available to observation in
defiance both of Cartesian principles and of orthodox theology (3:118).
"If ideas could be produced, caused or in any way brought about by

things (bodies) outside the mind, then that would be an undeniable example of interaction between two created existents."[21] In an effort to bring rationalism into line with faith, Malebranche retorted that what looked misleadingly like interactions were only apparent, the causal connections a mere mirage, the correspondence necessarily mediated at every juncture by the undeniable third term of divine causality.

Italicizing, the *Encyclopédie* insists: "Selon Malebranche, *Dieu est le seul agent; toute action est de lui; les causes secondes ne sont que des occasions qui déterminent l'action de Dieu,*" and goes on to elaborate: *"c'est que le corps ne peut être mu physiquement par l'ame, ni l'ame affectée par le corps; ni un corps par un autre corps; c'est Dieu qui fait tout en tout par une volonté générale."* The essentially pejorative term "cause occasionnelle" would thus have been brought into play by Malebranche for the express purpose of putting down the upstarts (body and soul) to which it refers and, by extension, enhancing the ubiquity and prestige of their polar opposite, the general cause. Following Malebranche, the "occasional" can be conceived only as the "only occasional." For without the incessant intervention of general causes, seen as the Creator's perennial prerogative, the dysfunctional composites that are human beings would literally be at a loss to keep body and soul together. Malebranche's cosmic script calls for every movement of mind and matter to give pause, placing the workings of the universe in a state of suspended animation that nothing less than a further act of creation on God's part can rectify or transcend. However, as Leibniz and the Encyclopedists recognized, human free will is only the most obvious casualty of doctrinaire "Malebranchisme"; for the Divinity as well, there is something compromising and demeaning about the circumstance of being always on call, expected to respond at the drop of a hat, knowable primarily through the reliability of services rendered on command to finite substances. Malebranche's God is at once otherworldly, hyper-interventionist, *and* utterly dependent on worldly, especially human, activity to make His presence known.

But for the only occasional—these structural tensions of mutual dependency are already implicit in Malebranche and will have survived Rousseau's radical break with the substance of his erstwhile mentor's message. That break may be among the best-kept secrets of the Enlightenment's increasingly insistent secular humanism; it is nonetheless spectacular, even Promethean. Rousseau exploits the letter of Malebranche's philosophy in order to precisely and perversely defy its spirit. Events and empirical subjects are relegated by Rousseau's theory of autobiography to the respective, mutually inaccessible points of Malebranche's body and soul. Getting from one point to the other becomes a matter of passage through the new general cause of the human self. And it is, in consequence, that self—*his* soul!—that Rousseau promotes to the pinnacle of the causal caret. The terminology, enabling conceptual configuration, and volatile equilibrium of Malebranchism are transplanted intact to the scene of the *Confessions,* but with the crucial difference that Rousseau reassigns to his or any self what had formerly been God's monopoly on general causality.

"Dans le paradis de Jean-Jacques, Dieu lui-même s'effacera discrètement, pour laisser place à Jean-Jacques."[22] This admission, which compellingly inflects Pierre Maurice Masson's insistence on the role and sincerity of Rousseau's religious convictions, rings especially true in the light of heretical displacements effected by Rousseau in the formulation of his autobiographical project. By virtue of slipping, under cover of orthodox theocentricity, into a place custom-made for God, individual character accedes to His hypothetical autonomy and basks, inexhaustible, in the afterglow of His prestige and permanence—*and* becomes subject in turn to the constraints on His (exercise of) omnipotence. What if Jean-Jacques had never happened on Mme de Warens's doorstep? "Quoique cette sensibilité de cœur qui nous fait vraiment jouir de nous soit l'ouvrage de la nature et peutêtre un produit de l'organisation, elle a besoin de situations qui la développent. Sans ces causes occasionnelles . . . " (1:104). There is room in Rousseau's latter-day occasionalism for fluctuation among a fairly wide range of intellectual and affective responses to the occasional. The positive charge that he attaches to occasions in an immediate context of gratitude for the chance to have known Mme de Warens by no means diminishes his capacity to feel that other occasions may be, at best, necessary nuisances and, at worst, serious threats to the self's independence of action. Interestingly enough, the dangerous new ideology of individual powerlessness that Bruss reads into the present-day cinematic swerve on autobiography[23] lies already latent in this potential for occasions to loom too large within the framework established by the founding texts of a full-blown cult of self.

Indeed, Rousseau's deified self becomes vulnerable to eventual de-motion at the very moment of taking God's place *and* coming to differ in an important and profoundly humanistic way from the Malebranchean deity. Of the superhuman "simplicity of God's ways," Malebranche had made the most conclusive evidence of His otherworldly wisdom and the most compelling explanation for the apparent limits on His power.[24] Not that He was incapable of creating other, more intrinsically perfect worlds than ours. But the laws of causality governing those worlds would inevitably have exceeded the all-embracing principle of occasionalism in their complexity. As an author of codicils and corollaries, that Creator would have too closely resembled the human soul, whose variability *our* author risks making it his business to exalt in the "Ebauches." "Or, les ames ne sont plus ou moins illustres que selon qu'elles ont des sentimens plus ou moins grands, des idées plus ou moins vives et nombreuses." Rousseau not only links the value of the individual self directly to the quality *and* quantity of its ideas, but he takes the further step of projecting countervalorized complexity onto the temporal axis: "J'écris moins l'histoire de ces éve[ne]mens en eux-mêmes que celle de l'état de mon ame, à mesure qu'ils sont arrivés." Thus implicated in an albeit superior history, the self becomes subject to change and to a possible loss of transcendent self-identity.

But Rousseau knows to guard against that possibility. What his text resists—by interposing an "état" or buffer zone between the "histoire" and the "ame" and through the added precaution of singularizing the replacement, "un état," for a welter of "éve[ne]mens"—is the collapse of his essential "I" into interchangeability with any one in particular of the intermediate states through which the grammatical shifter of the first person pronoun will have passed. The autobiographer is evidently preoccupied with keeping the self involved, evolving, and yet off limits to irrecuperable contingency or fragmentation. That preoccupation resurfaces in Rousseau's recourse to plural titles: *Confessions, Dialogues, Rêveries.* Each imagines plurality to inhere most fundamentally not in the self or even in the life, but in the act of (confessional, or dialogic, or oneiric) writing. Self-inscription is susceptible to infinite multiplication and conceivable in a wide variety of modes. But it must ultimately fail in any one attempt, however well-intentioned at the time, to contain and bring an otherworldly surplus of self down to earth. Seized after the fact as so many discrete and doomed occasions of self-inscription, Rousseau's *Confessions* and *autres écrits autobiographiques* combine to further the cause of protecting the self against demeaning abuses of localizable search and seizure.

But Rousseau came more extensively *and* literarily prepared than has thus far been acknowledged to his sense of self and to mindfulness of the need to prevent his self from falling into the traps of occasionality. The *Confessions'* scenario of selfhood derives and deviates not only from textbook Malebranchism but also from Rousseau's firsthand experience as an inveterate and increasingly self-conscious author of "occasional" texts. The texts we will read in chronological order here all belong to the middle years of his literary career, 1750–62. That period, which Clément calls "la plus féconde de sa vie,"[25] is most often plotted as Rousseau's triumphant disengagement from mainstream eighteenth-century intellectualism and discovery of his own philosophical voice. Robert Ellrich elaborates: "During the middle period, starting with the momentous publication of the First Discourse and ending with the condemnation of *Emile,* Rousseau wrote and published the great discursive works on which his international reputation was to rest." But Ellrich proceeds from this commonplace to the darker side of Rousseau's success, as evidenced by "self-protective fantasies of androgyny"[26] that keep cropping up in lesser-known minor works from the same period. There is some incidental, even significant overlapping between Ellrich's chosen corpus and the one I think it important to reconstitute here. The difference is that Ellrich's criteria for inclusion are essentially thematic. My readings address those works and only those to which the epithet "occasional" incontrovertibly applies, either automatically and on the basis of standardized literary usage or because Rousseau himself made a point of invoking it.

To quality for consideration here, a text does not need to stand alone. I begin, in the margins of some minor *and* major works, with a pair of prefaces (to *Narcisse* and to *Julie*) and a pair of dedications (to *Le Devin du village* and to the Second Discourse). Each of these texts exemplifies what is referred to in English usage as "occasional" writing and what French calls œuvres de circonstance. In each instance, we will be dealing with a text written, in greater or lesser conformity with a reconstructible general consensus as to how such occasions were to be handled, on the occasion of another (primary) text's accession to print. The liminary exercises of prefacing and dedicating may well have become perfunctory in the minds and practice of Rousseau's contemporaries.

These versions of occasional writing could, however, take a stand vis-à-vis a lingering tradition of using œuvres de circonstance only or primarily to immortalize the anniversaries and exploits of the high and mighty. The potential existed for prefacers and dedicators to commemorate the occasions of their own careers by way of significant and self-conscious departure from that tradition. Rousseau did exercise this option, most pointedly by twice declining to write a dedication to the French king, whose patronage might have consigned him to a lifetime of exalting the other. But he did not stop at this tacit, more or less traceless disruption of the cause-effect connection between primary texts and their inevitable ancillaries. Rather, he went on to compound and complicate the vague hubris of self-validation by arranging for the most conventionally other-directed (dedication) and object-centered (preface) of discourses to accommodate that nearest and dearest of subjects, himself. At some point occasional writing became synonymous and interchangeable in Rousseau with self-inscription: autobiography (according to Olney's broader definition of *bios*) gravitated predictably to œuvres de circonstance and became just as predictably identifiable as the dominant impulse or outcome of whatever œuvres de circonstance Rousseau came to write.

Not that any member of this first, liminary subset of Rousseau's occasional autobiographies leaps headlong and heedless of what it is supposed to be doing into its preoccupation with self. The prefaces *do* preface, and the dedications dedicate. Generic specificity, that impersonal place from which the prefatory or dedicatory discourse comes, enables (the perception of) such self-revelatory deviations from standard practice as the dialogism of the *Préface de Julie.* But generic specificity also encodes the enterprise of self-portraiture in the terms of the occasion as inherited. We might ask, When is a preface to *Narcisse* not a preface to *Narcisse?* and answer, with Rousseau, When it is not simply a portrait of the artist, but a portrait of the artist as non-narcissistic prefacer of the First Discourse. Rather than shut the door behind his self, the apprentice autobiographer keeps working on, against, with, and through the givens of threshold discourses in ways that are as productive of eventual meaning as of immediate tensions. Far from making tabulae rasae of titles and topoi, Rousseau's in situ self-portraits reveal him to have a greater sensitivity to the heuristic function of commonplaces than is sometimes thought compatible with his legendary iconoclasm. The move to self-inscription is never made once and for all; rather, it is perennially rewritten to and from the literary moment. My readings will savor the diversity of these liminal texts but also highlight their commonality as pressure points of give and take between the occasional and the transcendent, and as precedents for further autobiographical activity along the same lines.

Indeed, from these margins of other texts, we will follow Rousseau's practice of self-inscription—one foot in, one foot out, the practically freestanding *Préface de Julie* shows the way—to the heart of two autonomous works, the *Lettres à Malesherbes* and *Le Lévite d'Ephraïm*. We could easily find our own reasons for putting a stamp of "occasionality" on the four personal *Lettres* Rousseau wrote in direct response to cues furnished by his addressee, or on the biblical paraphrase he purportedly wrote to pass the time of a carriage ride into exile following the condemnation of *Emile*. More significantly, however, the writer insists on the "occasional" nature of both texts, apologizing as follows to Malesherbes: "Quoi que j'aime trop à parler de moi, je n'aime pas en parler avec tout le monde, c'est ce qui me fait abuser de l'occasion quand je l'ai et qu'elle me plait" (1:1142). The eventual reader of *Le Lévite* is enjoined in turn to give careful consideration to "l'occasion dans laquelle elle [cette bagatelle] a été faite" (2:1207). The *Lettres* and *Le Lévite* share with the earlier, more narrowly occasional texts an acute awareness of how inhibiting and enabling the specifications of genre can be in the positing and particularizing of a self. The epistolary context makes all the difference to one version, the in-betweenness of a self-styled "poème en prose" to the other. What nonetheless sets these two relative latecomers to Rousseau's occasional corpus apart is the fact that they postdate the momentous decision to mount some full-scale memoirs, the eventual *Confessions*. A life story already in the works had the effect of shifting the burden of content and occasional causality as conceptualized by Rousseau from textual to existential antecedents. Both works are thought to owe their existence to specific threats of natural (the *Lettres*) or unnatural (*Le Lévite*) death. Both allude less incidentally or obliquely than their predecessors to the facts of Rousseau's biography—however much the *Confessions* may protest that, except in its inception, *Le Lévite* has nothing whatsoever to do with Jean-Jacques. And their role of makeshift replacements for memoirs that, under the circumstances, might never get written makes a difference: the *Lettres* and especially *Le Lévite* reprivilege the narrative mode of self-portraiture, which the preface to *Narcisse* had explicitly renounced ten years earlier.

One beneficial outcome of reconstituting the set of Rousseau's occasional autobiographies and including the *Confessions* has thus to do with heightening our sensitivity to the arbitrariness of the "whole life" approach espoused within the pages of the authorized autobiography. We will also be positioned to appreciate the lengths to which the author and his successors would go to hide that arbitrariness, and the other unpursued possibilities, from view. In Rousseau's case, however, that amounts to camouflaging possibilities already pursued in the texts of our protohistory. The *Confessions'* second volume does mention these occasional sketches, but only referentially and as unrelated items in an accruing, parsimoniously annotated bibliography of "other works by the same author." Vague symptoms of a closer, intertextual connection and of the *Confessions'* deeper indebtedness to occasional antecedents are there for the discerning. Remarkably, for example, the *Confessions* have nothing but nice things, although almost never the "right" nice things, to say about each of the occasional texts we will read, even those of most dubious literary value (*Le Lévite*) or rhetorical effectiveness (the dedication to Geneva). Each preface or dedication is moreover considered on its own merits, independently of the primary text whose margins it usually inhabits. Carried to extremes, this practice has meant that a mere dedicatory epistle (but one that turns out to have happened upon the crucial autobiographical strategy of *auto-avilissement*) can receive ten times more coverage in the *Confessions* than its earthshaking enclosure, the *Discourse on Inequality.* In short, Rousseau hovers time and again on the brink of acknowledging the tokenism involved in his conferring preautobiographical status only on the *Lettres à Malesherbes.* For to single out the *Lettres* is to ignore their belonging to an impressive body of likewise "personal" writings. Knowing this, we do not have to look to other authors or models of autobiography for challenges to the *Confessions'* claims to absolute originality or paradigmatic status.

This body of occasional texts could not, however, be acknowledged as such, much less read autobiographically, by the *Confessions,* because it posed an obstacle to *their* investment in direct apprehension of a living, breathing somebody named Jean-Jacques. The author's self-image was further invested for the short term in denial that who this Jean-Jacques really was had much of anything to do with his having happened for a time to write books. "Not that he was ever a 'professional' writer,"[27] claims Ronald Grimsley, playing along. But of course, notwithstanding all his posturing as an "occasional" writer, Rousseau remains a man whose life story might easily have been as specifically and unhesitatingly centered as Vico's on his "particular development as a man of letters."[28] Therein lies the best reason to overlook Rousseau's hesitations and take a second look, through the prism of occasional self-portraiture, at the relatively "disappointing" second volume of the *Confessions.*

In chronicling the adult, literary life of Jean-Jacques, Rousseau has seemed to many readers to retreat from the essentially modern and richly suggestive stance of Volume 1 into that of an uninspiring memorialist or one-dimensionally paranoid apologist. As landmark events proliferate and conspire with everyday occurrences to configure a universal "plot" against Jean-Jacques, the *Confessions* do an increasingly sporadic job of inviting us to plumb psychological depths. But, as my readings will show, the unconscious dimension is neither absent from Volume 2, nor all that simple, nor meant simply to be carried over intact from the extensive auto-analyses of Volume 1's formative years. It is, rather, the case that the unconscious dimension is no longer uniquely traceable to the psyche of a civilian. The depths are, to a significant degree, given over to the already written occasional self-portraiture against which the *Confessions* shape up self-protectively (and without whose muffled promptings they would have shaped up differently). We need to take as seriously as he does Rousseau's claiming not to have any personal memory of anything he has once committed to paper (1:351). For, recalling imperfectly both what really happened and what he wrote at the time about what happened, the *Confessions* commemorate both, in incessant testimony to the inherent forgetfulness of self-inscription. Whatever Rousseau writes in praise of this or that occasional anteceden turns out to be only the tip of an iceberg and the surest warning sign to be on the lookout for yet another version of the returning repressed. Each occasional text in turn comes back to haunt, leaving the imprint of its situation-specific anxieties and insights on whichever region of the *Confessions* will have dropped its name.

The result is a patchwork of intertextualities, which the *Confessions'* apparently seamless global narrative covers imperfectly, but to the eventual advantage of "autobiographical intentionality per se." In his forceful argument against a mimetic explanation for stylistic pluralism in the *Confessions,* Louis A. Renza has proposed that this pluralism is more likely Rousseau's way of "guarding . . . his self-identity, from slipping into whatever norms of self-reference he is aware of, however subliminally, at the time of writing."[29] But the later *Confessions* are exempted from straining so visibly and virtuosically after stylistic diversity, and for the very reason that there are at least as many bad approximations of Rousseau already available for the self to engage and transcend in Volume 2 as opportunities for clandestine *texte-à-texte* with "only occasional" alter egos. In this respect, the *Confessions* continue and compound Rousseau's long-standing proclivity for painting himself in figura. This self-portraiture of the in figura variety takes off from the positing of hypothetical resemblances to famous others with whom there can, however, be no absolute identification. It had been a staple of Rousseau's occasional writing from the moment of his first choosing, in the "Préface" to *Narcisse*, to toss himself back and forth from the clutches of Narcissus to the more welcome embraces of Socrates and, surprisingly, Echo. Other more or less astounding avatars, from the Roman Lucretia to the biblical Benjamin, had followed at irregular intervals, no two alike and no one enough like Rousseau's essential self to close down the process of self-inscription.

It is thus by releasing the *Confessions* from the impossible obligation to tell all that we can best do justice not only by their heretofore neglected sources, but by a newly compelling composite of the adult Jean-Jacques as author of an entire gallery of in figura self-portraits. Moreover, by following up on the autobiographer's vague hints at intertextuality, we can also know the strength of Rousseau's abiding commitment to situating the self always just beyond the reach of (this or that) writing. In the aftermath of failed *Confessions,* felicitous failure would be written just as indelibly into the *Dialogues.* Those anxiety-ridden sequels to autobiography are, like the *Rêveries,* beyond the scope of this book. They nonetheless suggest that Rousseau may have anticipated my rereading of the *Confessions* as less scrupulous than they might have been in footnoting their sources. Making a major offense of plagiarism and misattribution, the *Dialogues* also place the reluctant "man of letters" on an equal footing with the "real man" and play them off against each other as rival claimants to the name of Jean-Jacques. Failure nonetheless comes as an afterthought to the *Confessions* and *Dialogues,* both of which follow to the bittersweet end from an equal and opposite commitment to the more straightforward rhetorical success of getting the self written right and exhaustively once and for all. The *Rêveries* tend, by contrast, toward putting this conflict of interests behind them. What attunes them more close-ly to the earlier, less self-consciously ambitious instances of occasional autobiography is the *Rêveries'* rediscovery of satisfaction and value in writing wholeheartedly to, and away from, particular moments. How fit-tingly the tenth promenade trails off, to be continued, with a reminis-cence on the fiftieth anniversary of Rousseau's first meeting with Mme de Warens. For, with a final relaxation of extraneous tensions accumulated en route, Rousseau's autobiographical project returns, as to a matrix of infinite rebeginnings, to that most characteristic, inspiring, and volatile of tensions, between the universal transcendent and the only occasional.

1

Echoing *Narcisse:*
The Self-Portraitist as Prefacer

Je me suis piqué à rompre la glace.

Montaigne

Of all Rousseau's comings to write about himself, the densest and most disarming occurs at the outset of the preface he published in 1753 with his comedy *Narcisse ou l'amant de lui-même.* There is simply no wading in at one's own pace to this liminal text, whose first page alone hits the well-intentioned reader with wave after wave of false starts and apparent affronts to logic and truth. Self-inscription makes a preemptive strike: three sentences into a fairly standard preface, we are advised that, lacking courage to say anything further about *Narcisse,* the writer is therefore writing and obliged to write about himself. "Ce n'est donc pas de ma piéce, mais de moi-même qu'il s'agit ici" (2:959). We must first adjust, then, to accepting self-centered in lieu of prefatory discourse, although why the one should follow so logically and necessarily from the other remains a mystery. But almost before we can think to object that Rousseau could be writing on any number of other subjects or writing nothing at all, the objection becomes moot. The erstwhile preface changes topics a second time. Having dislodged "ma piéce," "moi-même" is itself dislodged by an impersonal, loosely related *question d'Académie,* the one to which Rousseau's prize-winning *Discours* of 1750 had responded, paradoxically, in the negative: "Si le rétablissement des sciences et des arts a contribué à épurer les mœurs." And, inasmuch as it requires

19

the remaining fifteen pages of text to exhaust that question, we auto-
biographfiends[1] are left to wonder whether Rousseau's first announced
foray into self-inscription is more accurately characterized as groundless
and precipitous or as short-lived.

The key to overcoming this bewilderment and appreciating the text
for what Rousseau's topic sentence rightly claims it to be—a rigorously
grounded and sustained exercise in self-portraiture—lies in giving full
weight to the occasion apparently eschewed of prefacing *Narcisse*. At no
point does the self-portrait entirely exit the orbit prescribed by the two
titles or foci of "Préface" and *Narcisse*. Rather, the "here" or venue of
Rousseau's writing is *and* remains a preface, even beyond the two instances of refocalization on "moi-même" and on "la question que j'exam-
inois il y a quelques années" (2:959). Implicit recourse to a specifically
prefatory logic first gets the writer safely to the point of substituting
"moi-même" for "ma piéce"; subsequent reexamination of the *question
d'Académie* takes the form of a belated preface in all but name to the First
Discourse.

But where does that leave "moi-même" as an object of knowledge? A
self unsupported by autobiography's crutch of chronology and off limits
to direct apprehension becomes knowable primarily through evidence of
its likes and dislikes. "Je ne sais ce que je suis: bon, méchant, spirituel,
sot. Ce que je sais parfaitement, ce sont les choses qui me font peine ou
plaisir, que je désire ou que je hais."[2] Stendhal's generalization is tellingly
exemplified here by the prefacer qua prefacer's choosing covert prefacing of one text (the *Discours*) over doing his straightforward prefatory
duty by another (*Narcisse*). And *that* choice begins to make sense only
when we consider that abandoning the play by no means amounts to
getting the Narcissus topos out of the textual system once and for all. On
the contrary, the initial move to expropriate *Narcisse* has the opposite
effect of exposing the self to fresh accusations of narcissism. An anxious
self-portraitist recommits his text to improvising complex lines of defense, *and* authentic inquiry. The non-preface to the First Discourse is
thus penned in partial fulfillment of Rousseau's unspoken wish to escape
from narcissism, as projected onto his past life and immediate intellectual
environs, and into positive identification as a full-fledged philosopher and
second coming of Socrates. But the writer's anxieties go deeper still, to
the heart of his present, antisocial activity of writing and his notoriety as
an author of occasional texts. To what extent can he be reassured by an

eighteenth-century understanding of prefacing as the next closest thing
to "required" writing? We will return to that question after elaborating
on the points raised thus far about the aptly named and affiliated "Préface" to *Narcisse*.

SELF-PORTRAITURE VERSUS AUTOBIOGRAPHY

I should first make it clear that, following Rousseau's lead, this chapter understands the categories of self-portraiture and autobiography to be
mutually exclusive and informing. To Michel Beaujour's *Miroirs d'encre,*
I am indebted for the apt distinction ("L'autoportrait se distingue de l'autobiographie par *l'absence* d'un récit suivi")[3] and for the general topography of literary self-portraiture that subtends and nourishes my
reading of the "Préface." That topography has the distinct advantage of
embracing and normalizing the paradoxes of a "self-centered" discourse
with no self to speak of at the center. The several extended absences
from Rousseau's text of the first person singular pronoun *are* compatible
with self-portraiture, as is a paucity of predicates and epithets so striking
that of himself Rousseau says directly only: "Je suis grossier." And that, in
a footnote, by way of contrast with his "adversaires" and with "la po-
litesse de mon siécle," and by comparison with some historical alter egos,
"les Macédoniens de Philippe" (2:960).

Of course, no modern-day barbarian could know enough to number
himself among the barbaric conquerors of Ancient Greece. There can be
no apprehending even the most culturally marginal self except through
the mediation of cultural categories. No scriptural equivalent exists, in
other words, for the experience of standing in an otherwise empty room
before a full-length mirror. In the aftermath of an initial "panique stérili-
sante,"[4] self-portraiture invariably, if unhappily, operates on this assumption, to which modern autobiography has nonetheless managed to
partially blind us. The concept of the (always exemplary) life provides
autobiography with a secret formula: a reason for being, a timeline, and a
natural starting point. For want of a single analogous conceptual support
of equal potency and persuasiveness, self-portraiture remains all but inconceivable as ex nihilo project, and the self-portraitist remains incapable of knowing where to begin or even how to begin "at the beginning."
"L'autoportrait est d'abord un *objet trouvé* auquel l'écrivain confère une
fin d'autoportrait en cours d'élaboration."[5] It is only the most tautological
of self-portraits—one thinks of Jacques Prévert's opening line: "Je suis

comme je suis"[6]—that does not somehow begin *in medias res.* No exception to Beaujour's rule, Rousseau does not simply declare at the outset of some freestanding text: "c'est de moi-même qu'il s'agit ici." Nor could he, unless he already had some reason and topics for discussion at the ready. Some impersonal space needs to have been made available for subsequent remodeling by the self-portraitist in (pursuit of) his own image. "Here" is already somewhere specific: Rousseau will have taken up temporary residence in the margins of *Narcisse* and availed himself of the *lieu commun* of prefacing.

In hindsight, the *Confessions* plot this crucial point of the self-portraitist's knack for creative use of public space in the narrative terms of Jean-Jacques's behavior at the play's premiere. There is reason to doubt that the evening happened exactly as told and so to conjecture that the autobiography does a better job of commemorating the writer's experience than of remembering the spectator's.[7] The telling hinges, in any event, on topography. Watching *Narcisse* anonymously from the audience at the Comédie Française, our hero is at once bored and "surpris et touché de l'indulgence du public" (1:387). The situation recalls those that Beaujour finds most fertile and consistently thematized in self-portraiture: the writer feels suddenly and unexpectedly alone in the crowd, dislocated, out of sync with his surroundings, problematically placed with respect to his own cultural context.[8] Jean-Jacques, as unable to sit still as a restless child or bumptious savage ("je ne pus tenir jusqu'à la fin"), exits the theater early, as Rousseau will have unceremoniously abandoned the prefacing of *Narcisse.* But rather than to the four walls of his rooms or to some South Sea island, Jean-Jacques retreats—no sooner out than back in—to another eminently public space: "sortant du spectacle, j'entrai au caffé de Procope où je trouvai Boissi et quelques autres, qui probablement s'étoient ennuyés comme moi" (1:387–88). This facility, accessed as through a revolving door, ends up serving Jean-Jacques to perfection as a makeshift theater for an impromptu one-man show.

Where he might have *joué aux échecs,* Jean-Jacques plays up and at *l'échec* (or failure) of *Narcisse,* and to an audience of one:

> Là je dis hautement mon *peccavi,* m'avouant humblement ou fierement l'auteur de la Piéce, et en parlant comme tout le monde en pensoit. Cet aveu public de l'Auteur d'une mauvaise Piéce qui tombe fut fort admiré et me parut très peu pénible. J'y trouvai même un dédomagement

d'amour-propre dans le courage avec lequel il fut fait, et je crois qu'il y
eut en cette occasion plus d'orgueil à parler qu'il n'y auroit eu de sote
honte à se taire. (1:388)

Presumed to be likewise "ennuyés," the café's other clients are not, however, consulted "en cette occasion." They are called only to witness passively, as though still at the other theater of the Comédie, a performance
staged primarily for the benefit of the protagonist. Putting oneself to tests
of character, in both the moral and literary senses of the word, discovering the stuff of which one is made—these are precisely the ends and
means of self-portraiture as methodologically rooted in, for example, the
Exercices spirituels of Loyola.[9] Self-portraiture depends on, cherishes,
even seeks out (or will in hindsight have sought out) the mediation of
such exercises. Temporarily assuming self-portraiture's frustration with
the impossibility of unmediated self-knowledge, the *Confessions* fail,
symptomatically, to choose between the adverbial epithets "humblement" and "fierement." What the phrase "humblement ou fierement"
evokes is the uneasy coexistence of Christian and Classical world views
at the heart of Rousseau's Western culture; what the phrase spells out is
the paradox of the self-portraitist's going in to get out. However resistant
to inscription in any one among the prevailing orders of signification, he
nonetheless relies on the codes and categories of those very orders to
measure the force of his resistance. At the all but inconceivable intersection of pride and humility, Jean-Jacques is denied direct and certain access to "his own" emotions ("Cet aveu me *parut* très peu pénible"), and
barred from acting simultaneously as spectator and protagonist ("J'y
trouvai même un dédomagement d'amour-propre dans le courage avec
lequel *il fut fait*"). His first person singular nonetheless alternates between those two sites, to the exclusion of a third-party audience reduced
to overhearing his confession. Of this "type d'auditoire," writes Beaujour,
"il ne pouvait être question pour la rhétorique classique, qui suppose le
face-à-face entre destinateur et destinataire."[10]

Therein lies the really guilty secret of self-portraiture, one whose
anguish, as we shall see, the "Préface" knows more intimately than the
ostensibly other-directed *Confessions.* The autobiography makes much
ado about acknowledging the "sin" twice removed of Jean-Jacques's having authored and failed to acknowledge *Narcisse* ("Là je dis hautement
mon *peccavi*"). Misplaced verbal excess provides the only clue to a sub-

sequent compounding of sin in Jean-Jacques's antisocial, even oxymoronic speech act of confessing publicly to himself. But, however
unwittingly, the solipsistic protagonist takes his cue from the self-portraitist: in the conversion of prefatory space, as in that of the café or
privileged eighteenth-century locus of conversation, the erstwhile prefacer will have displaced the reader as communicant and so perverted
rhetoric's socially oriented and acceptable ends of edification and persuasion. There, as here, "tout l'édifice rhétorique de la persuasion se défait,
pour se reformer selon une configuration inédite."[11] Jean-Jacques seeks
to change no minds and says of the play only what "tout le monde"
already thinks. The café scene throws the bombast of Rousseau's writing
prefatory rhetoric out of his "Préface" into even higher relief: "pourvu
que je convainque mes adversaires, je me soucie très peu de les persuader; en travaillant à mériter ma propre estime, j'ai appris à me passer
de celle des autres" (2:959). So too does a scene from the play *L'Amant
de lui-même* that has been criticized by Jacques Scherer for a like-
minded departure from "l'usage."[12] In that scene, Valère, Rousseau's Narcissus in modern dress, soliloquizes "hautement" and at length on a
painted portrait of himself in drag, oblivious to the presence of his fian-
cée, Angélique (2:998–99). Indeed, it is the specter of a self-preoccupied
Narcissus and of society's disapproving witness that always comes back
to haunt self-portraiture, even when the topos must be retrieved from
farther afield. With the reduction of the reader to an admiring and all but
impotent Echo comes the risk of revenge (as exercised by Angélique in
the play and by the reviewers who condemned the preface as "out-
rée").[13] The Christian analog of that risk, as already interiorized by Rousseau, is authorial guilt. If self-portraitists must find a way to answer "no"
to Jacques Borel's question, "Narcisse écrit-il?",[14] they must also, even
now, continue to ask it.

Autobiographies, in contrast, short-circuit the issue of narcissism by
marshaling in advance their alibis of social usefulness. One thinks of the
"prémiére piéce de comparaison pour l'étude des hommes" that is promised by the preamble to the *Confessions.* Only in anticipation of formulating such a promise can the preamble begin by advertising "le seul
portrait d'homme, peint exactement d'après nature et dans toute sa vérité, qui existe et qui probablement existera jamais" (1:3). Even today, a
long historical view links the proliferation of life stories with society's
having passed on from "rulers" to "the common man" the right to a

certain healthy narcissism.[15] But no such clean bill of health is automatically conferred on authentic self-portraits. With no tale to tell, no human interest to exploit, and no experiences to share or lessons for living to derive therefrom, Rousseau sets himself up in the "Préface" for inevitable comparisons with Valère, a protagonist "bien occupé," like himself, "de son portrait" (2:998).

FROM "MA PIÉCE" TO "MOI-MÊME": Prefatory Logic and the Emergence of the Subject

How or by what logic Rousseau manages to set his self up as the vanishing point of discourse is another story, which requires our going back beyond the preface's topic sentence to its opening salvo: "J'ai écrit cette Comédie à l'âge de dix-huit ans, et je me suis gardé de la montrer, aussi long-tems que j'ai tenu quelque compte de la réputation d'Auteur. Je me suis enfin senti le courage de la publier, mais je n'aurai jamais celui d'en rien dire. Ce n'est donc pas de ma piéce, mais de moi-même qu'il s'agit ici." The problem is obvious: logic comes as an exorbitant afterthought to the narrative context. The adverb *donc* sticks out like the proverbial sore thumb; a derisory fetish of the cogito forces the issue of a clean break with narrative and with *Narcisse.* To join Rousseau in making what looks like a premature leap of and into logic, we need more to go on than the highly polished surface of his prose explicitly and summarily delivers. But beyond that, the ripple effect of *donc*'s prestige makes the topic sentence *seem*—but with what force—to read, if not "ma piéce," then "moi-même." It is as though, however impertinent this thought in the abstract, the field of possibilities for discourse were exhaustively rendered by the two topics "ma piéce" and "moi-même."

Paraphrasing the question that Philippe Sollers sees the Mallarmé of *Igitur* putting to the Cartesian cogito,[16] we might well ask: Who or what is this *donc* in the sentence "ce n'est donc pas de ma piéce, mais de moi-même qu'il s'agit ici"? Psychohistoricism focuses on the likely suspect of an individual so hell-bent from the beginning on self-presentation that he chomps at the bit of prefacing and imperfectly masks his desire with the appearances of logic. No wonder that Lester Crocker can scarcely repress a smile[17] at the apologetic posture into which that individual retreats at the outset of the following paragraph: "Il faut, malgré ma répugnance, que je parle de moi" (2:959). But pure-state self-portraiture is too absorbed by the here and now to hazard or invite such claims to referential understanding. "Il n'y a pas d'autoportrait qui ne soit celui d'un écrivain en tant qu'écrivain."[18] And regardless of what caprices may be laid at the doorstep of Rousseau the man, the writer is better characterized, for the moment, as opportunistic. Rousseau talks himself out of prefacing in the colloquial sense, but also in the sense that "moi-même" accedes to the discourse not out of nowhere but in accordance with a widespread, culture-specific understanding of how prefaces operate.

As a rule, setting the self apart entails opposition to the other, through recourse to the time-honored categories of subject and object. That *Narcisse* should here be conceived as other to "moi-même" and that the object qua object should call the subject into play as the only alternative follow from a discrepancy, troubling to eighteenth-century minds, between the ideal of prefacing and the reality. Prefacing at best would constitute the paradigmatic instance of object-centered discourse: there can be no casting about for something to discuss when the preface owes its existence and every allegiance to a unique, adjacent, and very palpable textual object. The *Encyclopédie* entrusts prefaces with "facilitating the intelligibility"[19] of whatever it is that follows. As implemented by real-life authors, this noble aim of shedding light on the object competes, however, with the discordant aim of presenting the object in the best possible light. Its merits are enumerated and extolled, its apparent defects excused.[20] Prefaces tell us not only how to read but why we should.

In the process of forging this unholy and untenable alliance between philosophy and rhetoric, prefacing creates further confusion between subject and object. "Les préfaces sont un autre écueil," claims Voltaire in his facetious advice to authors, as though evoking some new, secularized occasion of that worst of all sins, amour propre: "Le *moi* est haïssable, disait Pascal. Parlez de vous le moins que vous pourrez, car vous devez savoir que l'amour-propre du lecteur est aussi grand que le vôtre. Il ne vous pardonnera jamais de vouloir le condamner à vous estimer. C'est à votre livre à parler pour lui, s'il parvient à être lu dans la foule".[21] Voltaire has more drastic measures in mind than censoring instances of the first person singular pronoun; his final prescription calls for fleeing the occasion, for total abstinence from prefacing. The problem evoked is one of inevitable narcissistic investment by even a self-effacing subject in an object presumed by all concerned to be an extension of her or his self. Love me, love my book. That subject becomes in consequence the individual least well qualified to know either what the object is or where the object

leaves off and the subject begins. Similarly, the *Encyclopédie* article "Préface" warns against the temptation to pervert prefacing's "caractere particulier" with a (perforce self-serving) *apologia pro libro suo.*[22] Already,
then, as Rousseau launches his preface to *Narcisse,* "everyone" sees
through the apparent object-centeredness of prefacing to a more or less
spectral subject.

In receipt of the subject-object polarity, Rousseau both plays out and
puts an emphatic end to its narcissistic subversion. On the one hand, his
rendering of the familiar "how-this-book-came-to-be-written-and-
published" storyline rehearses the object's increasing engulfment by a
self-preoccupied subject. Without stepping all the way out of character,
prefacing crosses the fine line into autobiography, or "how I came to
write and publish"; the two verbs become, for all practical purposes, in-
transitive. The inaugural proposition, "J'ai écrit cette Comédie à l'âge de
dix-huit ans," could have gone either way, toward further days in the life
of the play *or* of the author. That the latter seems at first a remote possibility is a tribute to the implications of the title "Préface." To feel the
full confirming force of the impersonal deictic "cette [Comédie]" is to
rediscover the preface as one-way pointer.

Already, though, in recounting the equivalent durations of the play's
secret pre-history and of the prefacer's prior obsession with literary lau-
rels, the conclusion of that same sentence raises more insistently the
option of autobiography. Even when its confessional content is abstracted, the phrase "aussi long-tems que j'ai tenu quelque compte de la
réputation d'Auteur" reads as more than a convenient chronological indicator, one for which such other possibilities as "for *n* years" or "for an
incredibly long time" might have been substituted with the same effect.
Whereas simple addition could have placed the play's composition in
1730, objective or real time has yielded to subjective time as absolute
ground for the figure of the play's suppression. But beyond that, Rousseau's conceding a point—"j'ai tenu quelque compte de la réputation
d'Auteur"—that his readers know him to have never before conceded in
so many words has the paradoxical effect of reversing the figure-ground
relation. The prefacing subject rears, as always, its ugly head, but more
defiantly than in a "normal" preface. "Not so fast there," we are moved to
interject. "So you *did* aspire to be a famous writer . . . "—even as a relentless textual machine presses on to the next balanced and likewise
disconcerting period.

"Je me suis enfin senti le courage de la publier, mais je n'aurai jamais celui d'en rien dire." Here the play gets even shorter shrift: that it has been published is hardly news to readers who would otherwise not be reading it. More noteworthy by far is the announcement of the subject's accession to a greater, if not limitless, courage. An absolutely decisive turn would seem to have been taken in the direction of autobiography, with its presumed emphasis on "l'histoire de [l]a personnalité."[23] Indeed, the focus of the prefacer's statements about himself has moved progressively inward: from professional life, to feelings about professional life, to the life of feelings. For these feelings, however, there is no sure accounting. An otherwise categorical conclusion—"je n'aurai jamais celui d'en dire un seul mot"—hopelessly blurs the boundaries between engulfing subject and engulfed object. To what degree is terminal aphasia an attribute of a (not really very courageous) author? To what extent is it induced by a (simply awful, or somehow threatening, or otherwise unspeakable) play?

Rousseau thus demonstrates the prefacer's congenital subjectivity and the preface's inability to know its object, but with the important difference that he concurrently tells a tale of narcissistic *dis*investment. Reversing the familiar scenario, he displaces backward from the moment of publication the period of the aspiring author's living with his manuscript in a state of narcissistic confusion. *Narcisse* will formerly have been hoarded as treasure and talisman against potential injury to a narcissism operationally defined as authorial ambition. What Rousseau contains and puts behind him is prefacing per se, or rather, prefacing as he and his readers know it to be a drowning pool of amour propre. Not prefacing *Narcisse* becomes the necessary and sufficient condition of a new autonomy for "ma piéce" (non-me) and, in consequence, for "moi-même." Object and subject emerge from a paroxysm of pre-prefacing as viable and inevitable alternatives. What remains to be scripted is some new, more pure and acceptable version of object relations.

NARCISSUS UNCHAINED

Rousseau's tale of getting *Narcisse* and narcissism out of his system is modeled on physical excretion. His revision of prefatory logic illustrates, in Julia Kristeva's terms, the "simple logic of *excluding filth*, which, promoted to the level of defilement, founded the 'self and clean' of each social group if not of each subject."[24] To the play designated (by pronouns—*la, en*—only) as unspeakable waste product and taboo topic devolves the ambiguous status of any excremental object. Victimized by the subject's sadistic indifference ("All that is not me is dirty"[25]), it is nonetheless cherished, if only for the sense of self and omnipotence its otherness confers (All that is not dirt is "moi-même").

Breaking its self-imposed silence, the "Préface" goes on, however, to generalize about the category of texts to which "cette petite Comédie" belongs: "Ce sont des enfans illégitimes que l'on caresse encore avec plaisir en rougissant d'en être le pére, à qui l'on fait ses derniers adieux, et qu'on envoie encore chercher fortune, sans beaucoup s'embarrasser de ce qu'ils deviendront" (2:963). Referential readings have seized on this extended metaphor and translated it into an early admission of Rousseau's guilt at having fathered and abandoned Thérèse Levasseur's children. But the text's own translation of anal into interpersonal categories raises a more immediate problem: at the moment of reconceptualizing waste matter as the "enfans" of the next generation, the subject brushes up against his own mortality. Having been reinscribed in a universal cycle of birth and death from which no "on" can so easily or cavalierly take his leave, the "object" of an embarrassed caress—in this instance, *Narcisse* —loses a portion of its otherness and comes to exert a more permanent and troubling fascination on the self.

The extended metaphor is just one of the ways in which the "Préface" reverses the process of expropriating, fetishizing, and trivializing the Narcissus topos as *Narcisse.* The net results of this partial reversal are to make Narcissus topical and to make repositioning the self with respect not to the play but to the topos the single most urgent item of new business on the self-portraitist's agenda. But the preface must first set the agenda, and Rousseau's opening line works already to release Narcissus from containment in his prior incarnation as Valère. The *Confessions* would later expose that opening line as a bald-faced lie: "ce ne fut qu'à Chamberi que j'executai ce projet en écrivant *l'Amant de lui-même.* Ainsi quand j'ai dit dans la préface de cette pièce que je l'avois écrite à dixhuit ans, j'ai menti de quelques années" (1:120). Since eighteen is the age attributed to Narcissus in most versions of the myth,[26] and no age is ever attributed to Valère, the lie reveals that the possibility of bypassing *Narcisse* and hazarding a direct return to the mythological pool was crossing Rousseau's mind even as he began to write.

The lie leaves the author of the *Confessions* remarkably unfazed. The autobiographer in fact proceeds to number the preface among "mes bons écrits" (1:388). His positive endorsement recognizes the erstwhile self-portraitist's inscription in a different, more elastic order of truth and, in the process, reasserts the *Confessions'* referential hegemony. As Beaujour reminds us, self-portraiture always stretches the limited and limiting "truth" of autobiography by raiding the public storehouses and reaching back beyond the biological birth of the subject for images, analogies, and contexts. In self-portraiture, the memory that serves is not individual, but collective and cultural: "l'autoportrait tend . . . à évider et à contester la mémoire de l'individu empirique en la dispersant dans les *topoi* contestés de sa culture."[27] And, from time immemorial, the particular field in which the preface's typically tentacular opening line takes the liberty of depositing Rousseau had been magnetically charged and hotly contested. The sheer volume and variety of Louise Vinge's compendium, *The Narcissus Theme in Western European Literature up to the Early 19th Century,*[28] demonstrate to what extent Freud and Kohut must be counted as latecomers to a long and rich tradition of reading Ovid's poem allegorically. By the time they came along to posit a pathology, the *Encyclopédie* had already appended a modern-sounding cautionary tale on "les effets funestes de l'amour-propre"[29] to such earlier interpretations of the Narcissus myth as the Fall of Man, the snare of representation, and the frigidity of the lady love. And by the time Rousseau took a second turn at the topos, eighteenth-century characterology had long since made a permanent fixture of Narcissus as general type, albeit primarily of physical narcissism like Valère's.

In the sway of global "justifications référentielles,"[30] autobiography must downplay the cultural memory of self-portraiture and appear to like nothing better than denouncing past lies and setting the personal record straight. And in this instance, the *Confessions* act with exemplary efficiency: by the time they get through their three installments of *Narcisse*'s pre-publication history, the prefacer will have been caught stretching the truth on every count. Not only was the play actually written later than he claims, but in the heyday of his lusting after "la réputation d'Auteur," Jean-Jacques made every effort not to hide *Narcisse* but to get it published. After seizing the first available opportunity to show it to one of his idols, Marivaux, "qui eut la complaisance de la retoucher," he engaged in "sept ou huit ans" of fruitless negotiations with the Italians (1:287, 387).

And in the "caffé de Procope," he broke his vow of eternal silence even before the "Préface" could formulate it.

To this self-consciously autobiographical remembering of a personal history, self-portraiture opposes a memory that is not only cultural but intratextual.[31] The "Préface" remembers accordingly to unchain Narcissus even as an apparently opaque barrier goes up in the blank space between preface and play. That barrier looks at first to be insurmountable. Having made a formal declaration of independence, formerly prefatory discourse continues to inhabit the margins of the adjacent text as if by chance; the "Préface" comes and goes as freely as would some unseen and unseeing tenant in a kind of *liber duplex.* Well beyond the moment of abdicating his prefatory responsibilities, Rousseau continues to exercise the prefacer's prerogative of merely pointing at a next-door neighbor he never names or helps us to know as text. And yet, read in turn, the "Préface" does not so entirely absorb our attention as to erase the still-fresh memory of a *titre* that supplies "cette petite Comédie" with a title and with a disapproving subtitle, *l'amant de lui-même.* If not *lui-même,* then . . . "moi-même." An unmistakable echo of the subtitle's last word thus haunts the moment of the preface's ostensibly turning a deaf ear on "ma piéce." *Narcisse* comes back from expropriation to underwrite, mediate, and mock the belated self-reflexivity of the preface and the belated self-absorption of the prefacer. Rousseau risks finding himself, after all, in a house of mirrors and in direct confrontation with himself as Narcissus. With a glassing over of our opaque barrier, the prefacer's stance comes to derive, thus always already violating the absolute of self-absorption, from that of a mythological alter ego selectively frozen in an attitude of perverse fascination.

The mirror that stands ready to ground and generate Rousseau's self-imagery goes unacknowledged in the "Préface." "Narcisse peut même subtiliser les glaces," writes Luce Irigaray[32] in rueful recognition of the fact that the phallologocentric social order's investment in self-identity extends to the further refinement of pretending to do it (representation, identity, self-sameness) without mirrors. Rousseau's unrelenting pursuit of unmediated identity is rightly famous for such feats of legerdemain; Jean Starobinski rephrases the rule of "transparence" or non-mediation in asking: "Où sont les miroirs autour de Jean-Jacques?"[33] Exceptionally, however, the self-portraitist's mirror does finally materialize in the

Confessions, right after Rousseau confesses to having lied about his play's date of composition. "C'est à peu près à ce tems-ci que se rapporte un événement peu important en lui-même, mais qui a eu pour moi des suites. . . . " (1:120) Loose chronological linkage notwithstanding,[34] the event has everything to do with keeping the Narcissus topos alive, even as, at the anecdotal level, fire rages through the outbuildings and threatens to send Mme de Warens's main house up in flames. Jean-Jacques, his adrenalin pumping, joins in the effort to rescue her furnishings: "J'étois si troublé que je jettois indifferemment par la fenetre tout ce que me tomboit sous la main, jusqu'à un gros mortier de pierre qu'en tout autre tems j'aurois eu peine à soulever." Only an anonymous, disincarnated voice dissuades our latter-day Hercules from performing what the text next proposes as an even more superhuman feat: "j'étois prêt à y jetter de même une grande glace, si quelqu'un ne m'eut retenu." In real life, Jean-Jacques will have been brought to his senses: had he saved the mirror according to his lights, it would no doubt have been smashed to pieces. But the more we get to know the self-portrait of Rousseau's "Préface," the more paradigmatically Jean-Jacques will seem to be poised on the brink of Montaigne's double-entendre: "Je me suis piqué à rompre la glace." However subliminally, Rousseau knows that to make a self-portrait, one has not to spirit mirrors away, but to make and break them. The enterprise requires tacit acceptance of a falling away from total and totalizing representation into reliance on shards like the Narcissus topos. Self-exposure to the jagged edges of these shards endows with a new vulnerability the subject willing to divert such partial representations toward sincerely epistemological ends. Only by taking this risk of self-knowledge and refusing to stand transfixed can the subject pride himself (the other meaning of *se piquer*) on distinguishing his voice from the one to which Madame's mirror (*Confessions*) and a whole century's blissfully ignorant narcissism ("Préface") owe their intactness.

HERE AND NOW: The Prefacer as Philosopher

The self of Rousseau's preface is thus no sooner isolated than subjected to a battery of tests for residual narcissism. Warming to the task, Rousseau centers the paragraph of his starting over on an aggressive retreat from rhetoric:

Il faut, malgré ma répugnance, que je parle de moi; il faut que je con-
vienne des torts que l'on m'attribue, ou que je m'en justifie. Les armes
ne seront pas égales, je le sens bien; car on m'attaquera avec des plaisanteries, et je ne me défendrai qu'avec des raisons: mais pourvu que je
convainque mes adversaires, je me soucie très peu de les persuader; en
travaillant à mériter ma propre estime, j'ai appris à me passer de celle
des autres, qui, pour la plûpart, se passent bien de la mienne. Mais s'il ne
m'importe guéres qu'on pense bien ou mal de moi, il m'importe que
personne n'ait le droit d'en mal penser, et il importe à la vérité que j'ai
soutenue, que son défenseur ne soit point accusé justement de ne lui
avoir prêté son secours que par caprice ou par vanité, sans l'aimer et
sans la connoître. (2:959)

The words tumble out, defiant and yet no less reliant on belief in the
mutual incompatibility of rhetoric and philosophy. Witness the untenable position that prefatory discourse attempts to stake out in the no-
man's-land of selling *and* making sense. What better forum than this
"Préface" for making the point of mutual interference. At least one contemporary reader, a certain Du Maunoir, went on record as having taken
the bait: "Et M. Rousseau qui fait plus gloire d'être Philosophe que Rhé-
teur, entre bien dans ce sens quand il dit: *on m'attaquera avec des plaisanteries*. . . . "[35] Forced to choose and fully cognizant of the antisocial
implications of choosing against rhetoric, Rousseau stacks the deck so
that the outcome derives "logically" from a hierarchical inequality of the
two categories. That (philosophy) which Rousseau exempts from reductive naming emerges as the morally superior alternative to a rhetoric
projected onto his "adversaires," rendered facile, and reduced to a lowest
common denominator of "plaisanteries." Avatars of Rousseau's humorists
would, of course, go on to figure prominently in the rogues' gallery of
narcissists whom Freud both envies and condemns for their blissful disengagement or "narcissistic consistency with which they manage to keep
away from their ego anything that can diminish it."[36] In their only apparent other-directedness, Rousseau's "all the others" as rhetoricians are
likewise blinded and blinding; they constitute the really narcissistic cho-
rus from which our would-be philosopher here makes a first move to
disengage himself.

A footnote drives home the point in more prosaic terms, citing his
adversaries' refusal to read each other's arguments, the narcissistic
wounds they suffer when Rousseau answers one in apparent preference

to the others, and, by way of reductio ad absurdum, the incredibly insuf-
ferable parochialism of the Leipzig Faculté de Philosophie. No matter that
Rousseau may not be citing verbatim the German sermon that begins "à
peu près de cette maniére":

> *Mes fréres, si Socrate revenoit parmi nous et qu'il vît l'état florissant*
> *où les sciences sont en Europe? que dis-je en Europe? en Allemagne;*
> *que dis-je en Allemagne? en Saxe; que dis-je en Saxe? à Leipsic; que*
> *dis-je à Leipsic? dans cette Université. Alors saisi d'étonnement, et pén-*
> *étré de respect, Socrate s'assieroit modestement parmi nos écoliers; et*
> *recevant nos leçons avec humilité, il perdroit bientôt avec nous cette*
> *ignorance dont il se plaignoit si justement.* (2:960–61)

As we have seen, self-portraiture cares little for the accuracy of individual
memory. What counts is that these latter-day intellectual Narcissi should
be caught in the act of reducing the macrocosm to a neighborhood puddle
and inviting Socrates himself to join them in a self-congratulatory peek.
The general rule of which Paul Zweig reminds us holds here: "Narcissus is
never ourselves, he is always the other one who cannot see us."[37]

But in our self-portraitist's mirror, the profile of Narcissus quickly
comes into the clearer, more distinct and dangerous focus of an alter ego.
Rousseau is visibly haunted by the "rhétorique un peu surchauffée"[38] of
his own First Discourse. The erstwhile author of the infamous "pros-
opopée de Fabricius," among other rhetorical flourishes, echoes the hard-
est to dismiss of his critics' charges: "Ils prétendent que je ne crois pas un
mot des vérités que j'ai soutenues" (2:961). Small wonder that Rousseau's sincerity had been placed in doubt by a performance given under
competitive conditions, and only reprised outside the pressure to write
more artfully than anyone else on an assigned topic. Narcissus thus becomes the other *and* the former self who stands accused of hiding behind
the impenetrable defenses of rhetoric. In contrast, the Rousseau of the
"Préface" no longer wants any part of defying Tiresias's prophecy and
living forever by avoiding the self-knowledge of a latter-day Socrates.
From that misunderstood philosopher, second only to Christ in his appeal to generations of in figura self-portraitists,[39] comes the reassurance
that soliloquizing in the crowd in no way precludes putting oneself on
the line. But in order to clinch the case for identification with Socrates,
Rousseau cannot merely continue "as usual" to seek "the truth"; any
claim he might advance on this score would prove insufficiently "con-

vincing." He must instead seek the further reassurance that would come from confirming the *meta*philosophical hypotheses of his abstinence from rhetoric and immunity from narcissism. He needs "to ensure, at least once in his life, that what he outwardly professes he inwardly believes with his entire being."[40] Let others shore up their egos; he will expose his to the test devised in the paragraph's final lines: can he lay claim to the attribute of philosopher? The question calls for an operational definition and can be answered in the affirmative only if he can be shown to "love" truth truly and truly "know" it. Not as he might, projecting narcissistically, have loved *Narcisse.* But, rather, according to a different anthropomorphic model of object relations that narcissism—there is no simply walking away from the topos—suggests as a way of naming the alternative.

The prefatory context remains equally suggestive. How better to demonstrate a singular capacity for object relations with ideas than by undertaking to rid the immediate environs of rhetoric and to restore them to philosophical purity? No matter how many pamphlets and letters may already have retraced the arguments of the First Discourse, prefacing that text presents a unique challenge and opportunity for distinction. Insofar as the medium emerges as part and parcel of the message, critics like Fréron have overestimated the degree to which Rousseau's preface merely rehashes here "ce qu'il a déjà dit tant de fois."[41] What, how, and even *that* he prefaces become the measures of the otherwise elusive man. Lest he seem to have set himself a simple task, no lesser cultural authority than the *Encyclopédie* declares its difficulty, citing the high failure rate of Rousseau's fellow prefacers and the highly rhetorical "essence" of prefacing: "Il n'y a rien qui demande plus d'art, & en quoi les auteurs réussissent moins pour l'ordinaire."[42] To succeed without art where others have failed and where he too may easily fail becomes the implicit plan of action for which the stage is already set. Exit *Narcisse,* or art incarnate. Against all odds, the preface looks beyond its "natural" object, the one it is bound to (love), for one more worthy of its attentions. Far be it from our truth-lover to let even the most conventional of conventions, prefacing's obligatory marriage of convenience, dictate his own priorities and predilections—except, of course, insofar as these last can be conceived only as deviations from convention.

Enter "moi-même." Having been released from prior obligations and from the referential constraints of autobiography, the subject of self-portraiture nonetheless accedes to absolute freedom only for the fleeting instant of its emergence. It cannot go off the cultural menu except into silence. The writer remains free, however, to appropriate whatever vestiges of the personal or impersonal past he wants to make pertinent, topical, epistemologically crucial. To the extent that prefacers are in the business of presenting or *pres*enting other texts, Rousseau's about-face gets at the heart of self-portraiture. Rather than lapse into silence, his discourse relapses into what emerges as prefacing with a difference, prefacing in all but name. Nowhere identified as such, the First Discourse cedes its concrete objectivity to a body of ideas. Rousseau will not have engendered but rather discovered these ideas, and made them his out of love for them. And he will have done so only after the fact and by dint of the superhuman fidelity of which his doing dirt to *Narcisse* constitutes a compelling counterproof. In his diction, the would-be philosopher exercises extreme caution, giving us "[l]e parti que j'ai pris" and "[l]es vérités que j'ai soutenues" (2:961) in lieu of the customary "book that I authored." With no such book in sight, he appears at least to have nothing to sell. Since discussion will focus on ideas already in the public domain rather than on an adjacent, still untested, and needy source, the chances are reduced of his aiming to please or getting caught up again in the vicious circle of narcissistic investment. Unacknowledged preface meets unacknowledged primary text in a philosophical alternative to the cult of authorship.

And it is no accident that Rousseau here seems to play the chivalrous defender to a "truth" that he blames his century's rampant authorial amour propre for placing in acute distress. His new lease on prefacing is coded throughout in the willfully anachronistic abstractions of the classical lexicon: "vertu," "gloire," and especially "honneur." This last term pops up everywhere, in places "of honor" and in passing, its frequency suggestive of a diagnosis that his text leaves us well placed to make in Rousseau's stead. For, however exhaustively surveyed or reflective of eighteenth-century realities, intellectual narcissism does not, finally, exhaust the topos. Immunity from intellectual narcissism is purchased by (upward) displacement of Rousseau's discourse into what seems to him a Platonic sphere only because he does not see the signposts ("vertu," "gloire," "honneur") welcoming him to the neighboring town of moral narcissism. "Dès qu'il faut renoncer à quelque satisfaction," writes André Green, "le narcissique moral se porte volontaire," not so much masochistic as simply ascetic, beyond the pleasure-pain dynamic.[43] As if on cue, our self-portraitist reports having steeled himself against the seductive charms of literary exercises: "j'ai sacrifié à la paix de mon cœur les seuls plaisirs qui pouvoient encore le flatter" (2:973). The terms of Rousseau's retreat from rhetorical relations ("s'il ne m'importe guéres qu'on pense bien ou mal de moi, il m'importe que personne n'ait le droit d'en mal penser") are likewise consistent with the clinical profile of moral narcissists. He shares their fundamental desire not for esteem, but for the peace of mind that comes only from reassurance as to their unconditional right to be esteemed. As though already playing out the scene of analysis, Rousseau projects onto us unseen analysts his "désir d'*amour inconditionnel*": tell me that I am still absolutely lovable: I can do without (or, rather, I cannot make do with) your telling me that you love me.[44] Du Maunoir's juridical metaphor gets it just right: "M. Rousseau alors imite ces plaideurs qui négligent le jugement d'un premier siége, parce qu'il leur en faut un dont il n'y ait plus d'apel."[45]

The "Préface" thus plays out the sequel to a story launched as such in the *Confessions,* and houses raw data for an eventual third volume. Were it to be spun all the way out, that story would tell of Rousseau's reading and rereading the topos of narcissism selectively, in order to stay always one step ahead of his own and society's accusatory finger. Jean-Jacques is said, in the *Confessions,* to have written his play about a dim-witted physical narcissist for the express purpose of proving that he (Jean-Jacques) was not "bête" (1:120). He wanted there to be no mistaking him for the identical twin or spitting image of the Narcissus whose name sometimes means just that, "stupid or heavy."[46] Rousseau's preface will in turn have been scripted to exempt him from the Enlightenment's "new" narcissism of overweening pride in intelligence and intellectual achievement. In the name of what, thinking the territory of narcissism to be wholly delimited by the Cartesian polarity of body and mind, the prefacer cannot say directly in any complete sentence. The moral narcissist remains free to personalize the lexicon of "honneur," pending analysis or, in his lifetime, the discovery that peace with always insatiable honor is never achieved except through such repeated renunciations of life as make that peace the moral equivalent of death. Already, the "Préface" spells an end to the death in life or doomed experiment of Rousseau's *réforme morale* and heralds a return to the "plaisirs" of literary exercises: "dans les langueurs qui m'accablent, et sur la fin d'une carriére pénible et douleureuse,

j'ai osé les reprendre quelques momens pour charmer mes maux"
(2:973).

But there is much more to the present exercise or test for narcissism
than a tightrope walk through terminology and partial definition.
Through the global project of reclaiming prefatory space for philosophy
alone, Rousseau seeks to reverse the emphatic *unité de lieu* of *Narcisse*
itself. As for the play that Rousseau had set entirely in the apartment of
Valère, it systematically lures the members of an ostensibly healthy supporting cast into the nets of narcissism. Marton is the resident humorist;
Cléonte/Léandre, the man who would be loved "for himself"; Lisimon,
the father who would act, intransigently, "in character";[47] Angélique, the
wounded lover to whom, at the appropriate moment, Valère rightly de-
fers: "Je vais vous céder la place" (2:1002); and Lucinde, the sister whose
family resemblance to Valère is duly noted: "C'est une petite veine du
sang fraternel" (2:1008). Only Valère's manservant, Frontin, manages to
escape for a time into the neighborhood watering spots.

By way of earning his own right to escape from the narcissistic
crowd, Rousseau now sticks as closely as possible to the prefatory ideal of
enhancing intelligibility. The *Encyclopédie* prescribes the first order of
business for the "avertissement qu'on met au-devant d'un livre" as that
of instructing "le lecteur de l'ordre & de la disposition qu'on y a observé
[*sic*]."[48] And Rousseau takes that business seriously and literally, to the
temporary exclusion of all else. Rather than argue on behalf of his absent
Discours, he painstakingly rehearses its arguments, starting at the beginning ("Il s'agissoit de savoir si le rétablissement des sciences et des arts a
contribué à épurer nos mœurs" [2:964]) and proceeding point by point,
for the space of eight pages, to the recognizable finish line of remarks on
the subject of academies (2:972). After some initial hemming and haw-
ing, he loses "himself" for pages on end, but only apparently, in a tableau
of the immoral macrocosm on the basis of which it will eventually be
decided whether his portrait belongs *in* it. The underlying issue is not so
much "who I am" as "where I am." That crucial issue of positioning the
writing subject is kept alive by apparently random alternation between
first- and third-person, personal and impersonal, singular and plural pronouns. And it is privileged from the first moment of Rousseau's substituting "nos mœurs" for the Academy's original wording, "les mœurs."
Thanks to that personal touch, both reader and writer are provisionally
implicated in the topos of a consequently more than academic question.

For his part, the writer resurfaces having demonstrated himself to be in full possession of ideas no longer close at hand but, rather, now in his heart. Not the least encouraging of signs consists, I would wager, in the relative sobriety of his present prose as contrasted with that of the *Discours* itself. Shorn of their most gaudy rhetorical excesses, Rousseau's ideas now stand on their own merits. Of the essence here is knowing, knowing in extenso what in fact he truly did or did not say. It is onto his nemeses, the narcissistic rhetorician-humorists and authors of self-protective one-liners, that Rousseau projects his own former crime of prosopopoeia. They are charged with putting into his mouth a reductive twelve-line résumé of the *Discours* that he begins by citing and disavow-ing: "Voilà ce que mes adversaires ont très-bien réfuté: aussi jamais n'ai-je dit ni pensé un seul mot de tout cela, et l'on ne sauroit rien imaginer de plus opposé à mon sytême que cette absurde doctrine qu'ils ont la bonté de m'attribuer" (2:964). Of course, there is no reasoning without rhe-toric, least of all here, where the text practically denounces its own re-course to prosopopoeia, to antithesis ("on ne saurait rien imaginer de plus opposé"), to reductio ad absurdum ("cette absurde doctrine"). But to speak discursively in terms that might someday name figures of speech is to create the illusion of reinventing those figures from scratch, just as the overall discourse appears to happen with spontaneous sincerity on what some stickler might insist on reserving the right to call "prefacing."

Nor does the philosopher-prefacer's modest but manageable project of putting the house of the *Discours* in its true order preclude his si-multaneously seeking to convince us that truth also inhabits each of the rooms he revisits. Rousseau negotiates a chance not only to prove himself but to prove himself right. Having preempted *Narcisse,* the preface none-theless reserves the right to treat its anointed object as though it too were a play, that is, susceptible to prefacing after the fact and on the basis of reception by live audiences. Knowing what he knows about reader response to the *Discours* allows Rousseau to take accurate aim at points of real contention. To settle even the dispute as to what was truly said, we shall, after all, have to reread the *Discours,* to say nothing of *Narcisse.* Rousseau's depriving the play of a fair hearing only encourages us to do the opposite. However our reading turns out—either the prefacer's word cannot be trusted, or the playwright has in fact penned an abomination—this no-lose opportunity for exercising morbid curiosity seems too good to pass up. Could even the most shameless of narcissistically invested authors hope to do a better job of selling not one book but two?

The inspired idea of submitting the "Préface" to purificatory rites necessarily exceeds Rousseau's (or anyone's) powers of literal implementation. Within the bounds of possibility, he can, however, derive a measure of self-satisfaction from having done a philosophical job of prefacing. At the very least, he can point with pride at the way his non-preface fulfills the promises made about its "ordre" and "disposition" by the sort of second-degree preface that gets it going: "Je suivrai pour cela, selon ma coutume, la méthode simple et facile qui convient à la vérité. J'établirai de nouveau l'état de la question . . . " (2:963). To the extent that the writer ends up doing what the prefacer says he will, a verifiable convergence will have been scripted, at least for this magic moment stolen from real life, between words and deeds. The writing subject remains demonstrably true to himself, whatever the referential accuracy of the parenthetical "selon ma coutume," which further unifies "moi-même" in violation of self-portraiture's exclusive commitment to the here and now. The "Préface" thus qualifies as a reasonable facsimile of what Beaujour terms "l'unité référentielle et imaginaire de la maison perdue."[49]

AFTER THE FALL: Self-Portraiture's Impossible Dream House of Primary Narcissism

However it turns out, self-portraiture is always driven by the challenge of fashioning a verbal construct whose specifications would as nearly as possible match those of temples lost in time. It is out of nostalgia for sites no longer on the map of waking life that the subjects of self-portraiture seek asylum. And Rousseau's nostalgia shines through a cynical footnote that scoffs at his former, benighted hero-worship of philosophers:

> Toutes les fois que je songe à mon ancienne simplicité, je ne puis m'em-
> pêcher d'en rire. Je ne lisois pas un livre de Morale ou de Philosophie,
> que je ne crusse y voir l'ame et les principes de l'Auteur. Je regardois
> tous ces graves Ecrivains comme des hommes modestes, sages, ver-
> tueux, irréprochables. Je me formois de leur commerce des idées an-
> géliques, et je n'aurois approché de la maison de l'un d'eux que comme
> d'un sanctuaire. Enfin, je les ai vus; ce préjugé puéril s'est dissipé, et
> c'est la seule erreur dont ils m'aient guéri. (2:962)

He now knows better than to confuse the real-life philosophers he has encountered with the true essence of philosophy: "La science prise d'une manière abstraite mérite toute notre admiration. La folle science des hommes n'est digne que de risée et de mépris" (2:965). No one will catch him pretending that the angels of yesteryear are not fallen. "But a fearfull example we have of the danger of self-love in the fall of the Angells; who intermitting the beautiful vision, by reflecting upon themselves, and admiration of their owne excellency, forgot their dependence upon their creator."[50] George Sandys's gloss of Ovid pertains, except insofar as it is "la vérité des choses," rather than the Creator of orthodox Christianity, that Rousseau's angelic philosophers are scorned for loving too intermittently. It is from the deity of "souveraine intelligence" that they will have averted their gaze downward, and it is the image of divine Truth that, in their self-preoccupation, they will have neglected to pursue and cultivate wholeheartedly. How suggestively Rousseau semanticizes the name of Valère's leading lady, Angélique. The playwright had imagined even this paragon of unconditional love to react when wounded and to do a convincing imitation of sadistic indifference. What the self-portraitist replays here is the scene of his protagonist's devastating awakening to the ideal other's capacity for narcissism. At least duplicitous, "great" authors do not necessarily practice the virtues they preach; they live, like everyone else, in houses and not as gods in temples.

Rebuilding the temple of truth after the fall and enshrining his true self as celebrant-god at the center is what Rousseau's "Préface" is all about. There is no scarcity of raw materials, only none especially set aside and consecrated for housing the self, the whole self, and nothing but the self in undivided and unmitigated splendor. In this respect as well, the title "Préface" lays down the working conditions of self-portraiture. The same Encyclopedia article that endows "la préface" with "son goût, son caractere particulier qui la fait distinguer de tout autre ouvrage" proves unable to define that "goût" and "caractere," except by recourse to a litany of antitheses: "Elle n'est ni un argument, ni un discours, ni une narration, ni une apologie."[51] Actual prefaces are all of the above; they accommodate argument, speechifying, narration, and apology in varying proportions and cannot help but bear the stamp of that which they preface. So too does Rousseau's public rooming house of self-portraiture, which can only strain toward rezoning as a one-room *maison particulière* for the self.

At the root of this permanent housing crisis is impossible longing for a self not only at one but at one with the macrocosm. Out of nostalgia for what we might anachronistically call primary narcissism, our self-portraitist sets his sights on the edenic dream house of the mother. In a further *Narcisse*-related allegory, the *Confessions* locate that dream house near and yet so far from the space of actual self-portraiture. According to the autobiography, writing *Narcisse* will have been Jean-Jacques's way of coping with what is diagnosed in all but name as a narcissistic wound. Mme de Warens had recruited one of her relatives, a M. d'Aubonne, to administer a vocational aptitude test to our hero. The results were devastating: Jean-Jacques was deemed to be "un garçon de peu d'esprit, sans idées, presque sans acquis, très borné en un mot à tous égards" and, consequently, fit at best for a lifetime sinecure as "Curé de village" (1:113). When d'Aubonne later took revenge, by writing a comedy, against the cuckolded husband who had driven him out of Annecy, Jean-Jacques was inspired to take his own revenge against d'Aubonne: "[Cette piéce] me plut et me fit naitre la fantaisie d'en faire une pour essayer si j'étois en effet aussi bête que l'Auteur l'avoit prononcé" (1:120).

The first of these two episodes is implicitly patterned on the moment in the Narcissus myth when his mother, Liriope, consults the seer Tiresias. We are set up for d'Aubonne's intervention by the evocation of a prior state of untroubled bliss and unlimited promise. Crucial to the perpetuation of this state is Jean-Jacques's being together with the surrogate mother in the very house that fire will presently threaten to consume. Time is suspended. So too, for the duration of Maman's wondering indecisively how to "place" or "house" Jean-Jacques such that the social order will in turn embrace the entirety of his self, are the threats of contingent action and impoverishing individuation: "Tout en folâtrant Maman m'étudioit, m'observoit, m'interrogeoit, et bâtissoit pour ma fortune force projets dont je me serois bien passé" (1:112). Our narcissist "quails before the least real achievement, and yet his potential for expansion is infinite."[52] How lucky for him that the ecosystem is self-sustaining: "Heureusement que ce n'étoit pas le tout de connoitre mes penchans, mes gouts, mes petits talens, il falloit trouver ou faire naitre les occasions d'en tirer parti, et tout cela n'étoit pas l'affaire d'un jour" (1:112).

This moment might also be qualified as "pre-scriptural." The fallen order of self-portraiture, which makes the best of a bad (post-narcissistic) situation, is reversed by Maman's supposing the self to be already knowable otherwise than through the mediation of particular tests. Postponing the tests or staving off "occasions" becomes the essential safeguard of Jean-Jacques's oneness with the world and unwitting megalomania. At one with his (virtual) self and invulnerable in Maman's eyes to direct translation into social categories, Jean-Jacques, alias "Petit," is nothing because he might be everything, and vice versa: "enfin tout alloit au gré de mes désirs, grace à la bonne opinion qu'elle avoit de moi" (1:112). He has the run of a dream house coextensive, for all he knows, with the world at large; he has no sense of self, only a sense of almost infinite well-being.

The autobiography typically corrupts Jean-Jacques's "jouissance" with foreknowledge that it cannot last. But if the mother's house is from the first accessible only through the pathways of nostalgia, our hero is nonetheless shocked into appreciating ex post facto the catastrophe inherent in a simple, unannounced change of venue. As though to drop a hint about her duplicitous belonging to the narcissistic microcosm and to the social order, the text suddenly names as "Mad^e de Warens" the mother who sends her unsuspecting son out, as from the womb, to be tested. "Mad^e de Warens m'envoya chez [M. d'Aubonne] deux ou trois matins de suite, sous pretexte de quelque commission, et sans me prévenir de rien" (1:112). Unselfconsciously assuming himself still to be in the maternal sphere, Jean-Jacques delights in the conversations with d'Aubonne, which he has no way of recognizing as so many occasions of self-portraiture. It is telling of the *Confessions'* attempt at (re)creating an authentic state of primary narcissism that the authorized version, "J'étois enchanté de lui," deletes the further precision of the Neuchâtel manuscript: "jétois enchanté de lui croyant qu'il l'étoit de moi" (1:113, 1284). For want of a self-concept and of a reason not to confuse d'Aubonne with the mother, Jean-Jacques is momentarily excluded and exempted from thinking in terms of what the "parent" may or may not be thinking of him.

All that will change, however. Whereas his oral activity had formerly been confined to kissing the mother's hands and mouth, Jean-Jacques is now called upon to speak for himself. In self-portraiture, there turns out to be "no place like home," only the proliferation of topoi that the culture, in the person of d'Aubonne, repeatedly proposes for Jean-Jacques's consideration. When prompted to join d'Aubonne in speaking "de niaiseries et de toutes sortes de sujets" (1:112), our hero can only assume that the house rules still hold, that he has nothing to prove and no reason for rhetoric. And yet, the inhospitable macrocosm begins in his own backyard. Rather than accept Jean-Jacques's self unconditionally, d'Aubonne inventories it in accordance with a culturally approved checklist. On all counts—"esprit . . . idées . . . acquis"—Jean-Jacques fails to measure up even to the promise of his own "physionomie" (1:113). Deeply divided against himself by the paradigmatic body/mind polarity that the culture puts at the tester's disposal (and by who knows what other more superficial stab wounds), the self is not entirely rejected by the system, only systematically diminished and marginalized. D'Aubonne recommends that Jean-Jacques set his sights on a curacy. Formerly a citizen of the world, he is thus relegated to a "village" and, worse still, to a chance at professional mediocrity.

The culture shock attendant on expulsion from the mother's house is the shock of culture per se. The *Confessions* proceed to establish that shock as both inevitable and recurrent. It turns out that our hero might have known better: d'Aubonne's judgment replicates that, long since recounted, of the first master to whom Jean-Jacques was apprenticed: "Ce fut la seconde ou troisiéme fois que je fus ainsi jugé; ce ne fut pas la derniére, et l'arrêt de M. Masseron a souvent été confirmé" (1:113). Remembering all the other times, the autobiographer comes close to putting his finger on the paradigmatic "mémoire" of his occasional self-portraiture: "elle rappelle de préférence les surprises, les méprises et les échecs d'un apprentissage, la résistance aux lieux communs, à la rhétorique, ainsi que le passage de l'autonome au systématique, et inversement."[53]

With each new eviction from places that have the deceptive look and feel of the mother's house, Rousseau will in time have learned to manage his own occasions of self-portraiture. Looking ahead, we might appreciate that each occasional text over which we will linger follows from a forbidden spatial antecedent and/or antecedent wound to Rousseau's narcissism. For the "Dédicace" to the *Second Discours,* the walled city of Geneva does what the termination of his life's most nurturing intellectual relationship does for the *Préface de Julie.* The *Lettres à Malesherbes* are written in response to a reductive portrait penned by the *destinataire, Le Lévite d'Ephraïm* in the course of flight into exile from the chateau of surrogate parents, the Maréchal and Maréchale de Luxembourg. With varying degrees of conscious commitment to the actual enterprise of self-portraiture, Rousseau thus commemorates the conditions of this one, picking his spots less randomly than it might otherwise seem. In fact, even the *Confessions* now find themselves positioned to take an extended break from narration and delve into the paradoxical recesses of Jean-Jacques's character (1:113–16). Rousseau's real imitation of and revenge against d'Aubonne consists in wresting from him (and from all the others) this measure of control over the scheduling of occasional self-portraiture.

But Rousseau will let no such occasion pass without an attempt at partial return to the mother's house and an ironic sneer at the futility of any such attempt. "The edenic image of primary narcissism is perhaps a defensive negation elaborated by the neurotic subject when he sets himself under the aegis of the father."[54] Julia Kristeva's conjecture fits the case of Rousseau's ambivalence. Even before trying out the makeshift quarters of his "Préface," he gives Valère/Narcisse an only temporary pass to primary narcissism. Having come in from the garden (or Garden?), Valère is disappointed by the contingent image that greets him in his mirror on this particular morning: "Comment me trouves-tu ce matin? Je n'ai point le feu dans les yeux; j'ai le teint battu; il me semble que je ne suis pas à l'ordinaire" (2:983). That with which Valère falls hopelessly in love is not, then, himself, but rather a portrait of himself dressed as a woman. Although there turns out to be no extant model, the portrait touches a chord by conjuring up the otherwise inaccessible realm of an utterly intact, undifferentiated, and unlimited self. Valère's blindness somehow looks less like that of Narcissus than like that of the seer Tiresias, uniquely privileged among mortals to have lived as man *and* woman. Of course, Valère's ill-conceived infatuation makes him the butt of innumerable jokes. In a household from which the maternal figure is conspicuously absent, he cannot be allowed to persist in his folly any longer than it takes for the supporting cast to get off their several rounds of zingers. "Valère ne peut les comprendre," writes Jacques Scherer in the debit column of his critical balance sheet, "et se trouve ainsi exclu d'un dialogue qui devient artificiel dans la mesure où il y participe passivement" (2:1865). At the risk of taking the play too seriously, we might, however, read the protagonist's unfitness for the stage as making the precise point of an exultant bisexuality or narcissistic otherworldliness that he would share, pending mortal wounds, with d'Aubonne's insouciant interlocutor. The "narcissistic honeymoon"[55] cannot last; Valère must submit to the cure of finding out who *he* really is, listen to Angélique's verbal portrait of *him*self, take it like a man, and get married. Glimpsed fleetingly in the androgynous portrait of the comedy, the *soi* that Béla Grunberger, controversially, postulates and places on a par with the trinity of *moi, surmoi,* and *ça*[56] must be reduced to the proportions of *moi.* Only divine intelligence can grasp the *soi* instantaneously and in its entirety. And there is no use writing to Him: He already knows.

NARCISSUS OR ECHO? Writing and the Alibi of Prefacing

The preface echoes, both by confining self-inscription to the margins of a comedy and by revising the initial estimate of its object downward from "moi-même" to "moi." But that is the least of the slippage that occurs in the incremental interval between what passes for a statement of fact—"Ce n'est donc pas de ma piéce, mais de moi-même qu'il s'agit ici"—and the next sentence's defensive posturing—"Il faut, malgré ma répugnance, que je parle de moi." The subject's assuming responsibility (" je parle") for a discourse just now attributed to the impersonal reflexive "il s'agit" sends up yet another signal of distress. A person is currently preoccupied with putting words on paper who might be otherwise engaged, and to more socially useful ends. That this same writer will proceed to renounce even the pretenses of rhetoric only compounds his crime of failure to do his civic duty. Without explicitly targeting writers, Sandys sets a trap for the subcategory of Narcissi who "likely sequester themselves from publique converse and civill affaires, as subject to neglects and disgraces, which might too much trouble and deject them."[57] Indeed, it is one thing to look away, self-preoccupied, from the Creator, but doubly criminal, in an eighteenth century on the cusp between God and Man, to disserve both by taking time out to verbalize the act of creating. What I said earlier about self-portraiture's "moments stolen from real life" takes on new, more dire and literal meaning. Our culture can forgive almost anything except the "seules fautes irrémisibles" of "la retraite, l'oisiveté, le retrait."[58] For, were everyone to follow suit, there would be no one to perpetuate the race, mind the store, keep the fires burning in the temple, or even love us neighbors.[59] Writers who spend time writing, especially with no end in sight, are left with a lot of explaining to do.

And Rousseau does explain, lustily and at length. The preface's penultimate paragraph overflows into a bravura recitation of the narcissistic man of letters' indictable offenses:

S'ils [ceux qui sont si ardens à chercher des reproches à me faire] s'ap-
perçoivent jamais que je commence à briguer les suffrages du public, ou
que je tire vanité d'avoir fait de jolies chansons ou que je rougisse
d'avoir écrit de mauvaises Comédies, ou que je cherche à nuire à la
gloire de mes concurrens, ou que j'affecte de mal parler des grands
hommes de mon siécle pour tâcher de m'élever à leur niveau en les
rabaissant au mien, ou que j'aspire à des places d'Académie, ou que
j'aille faire ma cour aux femmes qui donnent le ton, ou que j'encense la
sotise des Grands, ou que cessant de vouloir vivre du travail de mes
mains, je tienne à ignominie le métier [de copiste de musique] que je
me suis choisi et fasse des pas vers la fortune, s'ils remarquent en un mot
que l'amour de la réputation me fasse oublier celui de la vertu, je les
prie de m'en avertir, et même publiquement, et je leur promets de jetter
à l'instant au feu mes Ecrits et mes Livres, et de convenir de toutes les
erreurs qu'il leur plaira de me reprocher. (2:973–74)

How stirring it must have been for Rousseau to reread these cathartic
lines, which so lavishly elaborate on the initial elimination of *Narcisse,*
leaving no stone unturned in the relentless pursuit of narcissism's every
heinous crime and petty offense. His one-sentence paragraph sweeps the
literary landscape in an apparently successful attempt to round up all the
potential offenders in himself. His logic, however, remains radically sacrificial: the "auteur" is elected to suffer in the name of civic "vertu," but in
the writer's stead. Providing that he forswears the perks, the preening,
and the pique associated with having written, and even as he forswears
them, this writer can continue in the here and now to write.

The would-be ascetic is betrayed at every turn by the material lux-
uriance of his own prose. Nothing better epitomizes the writer's retreat
from the rhythms of real life than a sentence that defies our reading it
without coming up for air. So too, under the circumstances, the writer's
high-handedly rejecting "l'amour de la réputation" echoes the mythological boy's brutal, even inhuman rejection of the nymph Echo, otherwise
known as *fama.* But Rousseau knows full well that there will be plenty of
echoing of this text by those to whom he refuses to talk in it. The sacrifice
of authorial ambition is more easily made than masked. For, at the point
of inviting us to burn both "mes Ecrits" and "mes Livres"—in the event,
that is, that Rousseau ever strays from the straight and narrow—the text
really plays with fire. We need only to make something of the difference
between process (writing) and product (authorship) to see that the two

are really variations on the single theme of narcissism. And we might well wonder in consequence whether vainglory were not the less socially undesirable alternative to the "in-vain-ness" of writing. But no matter. Having convinced himself that the "author" as fall guy will take the rap, the real brains behind this "écrivaillerie coupable"[60] unabashedly plots an unlimited future life of crime: "En attendant, j'écrirai des Livres, je ferai des Vers et de la Musique, si j'en ai le talent, le tems, la force et la volonté" (2:972).

But how did Rousseau get himself to this point, if not aided and abetted once again by the prefatory context? He does need help: the solitary pleasure or asceticism of writing figures among those vices to which he cannot ordinarily bring himself to admit publicly. As hazarded in a personal letter to Mme de Francueil, Rousseau's earliest systematic attempt at rationalizing the abandonment of Thérèse's children is telling in ways that the *Confessions* are not of an unspeakably self-indulgent desire to write at all costs: "[E]t si j'étois contraint de recourir au metier d'auteur comment les soucis domestiques et le tracas des enfans me laisseroient ils dans mon grenier la tranquillité d'esprit nécessaire pour faire un travail lucratif?"[61] Whatever care is taken to couch the rhetorical question in terms of economic necessity, it nonetheless sets the writer's attic retreat apart as a site uncontaminated by organic or social life. The guilt that traverses this and all comparable sites is more obliquely acknowledged by the "Préface." It argues, as the *Lettre à d'Alembert* will do more emphatically, that any time spent by corrupt individuals in a theater is that much time made unavailable for the enactment of their own criminal tendencies. Rousseau thus projects onto the theater-going public an "inactivity" of which he manages to make a relative social good. Not that the supplier of spectacles like *Narcisse* gives an entirely accurate accounting for his own time of writing. He goes so far as to claim: "Je m'estimerois trop heureux d'avoir tous les jours une Piéce à faire siffler, si je pouvois à ce prix contenir pendant deux heures les mauvais desseins d'un seul des Spectateurs" (2:973). But Rousseau stops short for the moment of linking their theater to his attic. Nowhere does he explicitly state the obvious: to deliver on his own tall order, he would be obliged to write around the clock, and then some.

At an even greater remove from guilty pleasure, the *Confessions* deploy an untranslatable pun to legitimate or naturalize writing done specifically in the name of prefacing *Narcisse*. What needs to be explained away is the seeming contradiction of Jean-Jacques's having pulled his comedy off the stage (after a single two-night run) and into print. "[C]omme il étoit sûr que la piéce, quoique glacée à la réprésentation soutenoit la lecture, je la fis imprimer, et dans la Préface qui est un de mes bons écrits, je commençai de mettre à découvert mes principes un peu plus que je n'avois fait jusqu'alors" (1:388). The adjective *glacée* is only partially rendered in English as "spoilt" and "insipid." Lost in these translations is the notion that each new "re-presentation" in the theater only mirrors an already written or frozen text, to the exclusion of writing in the present. In performance, *Narcisse* remains as absolutely repetitive as the mythological boy's watery gaze, as impervious to outside linguistic intervention and chilling to the other's desire as his posturing beside the pool. When Valère speaks, everybody else, including Jean-Jacques, can only listen. But the decision to publish changes everything. The autobiographer throws his claims about the play's readability and his nomination of "la Préface" as "un de mes bons écrits" so close together as to make reading one and writing the other virtually interchangeable. What the play is assumed to support and even require is the further linguistic act of reading that is writing a preface. As the *Encyclopédie*'s etymological note reminds us, speech per se lies at the root, *fari*, of prefacing.[62]

Vis-à-vis a play stigmatized as narcissistic, prefacer Jean-Jacques will thus have assumed what amounts, in all but name, to the posture of Echo! He finds himself in precisely the situation of the all but forgotten other "who could neither hold her peace when others spoke, nor yet begin to speak till others had addressed her."[63] The pendulum having swung to the opposite extreme, the writer addressed by *Narcisse* "must" have broken the silence that the theatrical context had formerly imposed on the spectator. To be sure, he will have gone the nymph one better: where she can only position herself strategically and "await the sounds to which she may give back her own words,"[64] Rousseau can, by simply publishing *Narcisse,* take a more active role in creating his own opening for discourse. And he can, in fact, monopolize the right to speak. Exercising complete artistic control, the recording artist does double duty as the sound engineer in charge of echoing his own play. "La voix même reprise à Echo," notes Luce Irigaray in the course of a revisionist visit to Plato's cave.[65]

Any doubts that Rousseau's mental map of the Narcissus topos extends to the Echo episode are dispelled by a cursory reading of his play. What makes the comedy fly—or would have, had Rousseau had a lighter touch—is recourse to the residue of Ovidian wit in a conventional dramatic principle of echoing. All the characters—except Valère, who is rightly excluded on the grounds of pathological deafness—are given to repetition with an eventual difference of the preceding speaker's final words:

> Angélique: Ah si c'est un défaut, quelle vertu plus charmante un homme pourroit-il apporter dans la société!

> Marton: Sur—tout, dans la société des femmes. (2:980)

> Valère: Le respect. . . .

> Lisimon: Oh! le respect consiste à m'obéir et à ne me point gêner. (2:989)

In the process of this ironic glossing, as in self-portraiture, language itself becomes the common ground of individual and individualizing speech. Echoing serves dramatic irony as well; the supporting cast jokes with the audience at Valère's expense and answers "truthfully" his inquiries as to the identity of the portrait's model:

> Valère: . . . Parle-moi sincérement. L'original est-il aussi aimable que le portrait?

> Frontin: Comment; aimable! savez-vous, Monsieur, que si quelqu'un pouvoit approcher de vos perfections, je ne trouverois qu'elle seule à vous comparer. (2:985–86)

When he is accused later in the same scene of making lewd insinuations about the mystery woman or "fille anonyme," Frontin explicitly identifies the echoing of Valère as the motor that drives the play:

> Valère: Ces idées que tu m'en a données. . . .

> Frontin: Ne voyez-vous pas que vous me les fournissiez vous-même? (2:987)

In this modernization of the myth, Frontin has no choice but to speak and to echo the discourse of his master: the servant's job is always on the line. The same socioeconomic necessity that Rousseau later invoked in the letter to Mme de Francueil rationalizes the curse of echoing that had been visited on the mythological nymph by the goddess Juno's injunction.

But how much more convincingly can the desire to speak be authorized and dissociated from Narcissus when it is literary convention that all but condemns Rousseau to the other role of echoing *Narcisse.* To the writer obsessed with the guilty secret of his own writing, the title "Préface" offers at least the semblance of an airtight alibi. For, in the eighteenth century, nothing comes closer than prefacing to the status of required writing. Any preface worth the name marks the occasion of some major work's accession to print. To the eighteenth-century preface fell the further responsibility of *making* the occasion. Any would-be book remained defective so long as its "corps" lacked for a "préface": "[U]n livre imprimé, relié, sans préface, est-il un livre? Non sans doute: il ne mérite point encore ce nom; c'est une manière de livre, livre sans brevet, ouvrage de l'espèce de ceux qui sont livres, ouvrage candidat, aspirant à le devenir, et qui n'est digne de porter véritablement ce nom, que revêtu de cette dernière formalité; alors le voilà complet."[66] The assumption that there would be something unseemly or too presuming[67] about the body's venturing forth partially unclad becomes a persistent refrain of prefacers who—for form's sake, or so they claim—only go through the motions of slapping a prefatory fig leaf onto their manuscripts. No doubt, some authors did view prefacing as a pensum, especially given the no-win rhetorical situation described by Voltaire. But others evidently did not; in keeping with Zweig's first law about the otherness of Narcissus, a self-styled reluctant prefacer will, from time to time, call his colleagues on *their* lack of reluctance: "Some authors are so fond of a Preface that they will write one when there be nothing in it but an apology for itself."[68] William Congreve comes close here to denouncing the self-indulgence of a writing for writing's sake. For the defense, prefatory tradition provided a complex of ready-made arguments that tended toward associating the vices of narcissism with failure to preface.

Writers of manuscripts who exempt themselves from scripting this rite of passage into authorship can be faulted, on the one hand, for laziness or downright boorishness. They may be seen not to have made the effort to read as the other or to meet the public halfway. They may be cited for noncompliance with their duty of bridging whatever gaps of intelligibility might otherwise hinder public access to the primary text. Alternatively, these same writers may be charged with projecting their own sense of self-sufficiency so entirely onto the unprefaced manuscript as to find it already perfectly intelligible—in need, as we say, of no introduction. It may be harder than Voltaire's advice suggests to get away with attempting to let textual bodies speak for themselves. In either case, prefacing appropriates the values of hard work and public-spiritedness, which writing per se would seem to flaunt. Better to go cheerfully about one's prefatory chores than to simulate either narcissistic indifference to text and reader or trans-narcissistic[69] investment in the text's perfect wholeness.

For his part, in doubling back to preface the wrong text, Rousseau does not so thoroughly discredit the activity as to make the prefatory alibi of writing entirely unusable. Nowhere, in fact, does his self-portrait's residual dependency on prefatory precedent come through more clearly than in the phrasing of his purportedly fresh start. Where have we heard something very like the claim "Il faut, malgré ma répugnance, que je parle de moi," if not in the course of prefaces like Marivaux's to *La Voiture embourbée:* "Or donc Lecteur, puisqu'il faut une préface, en voici une."[70] To this echo or unconscious allusion,[71] the text remains indebted for getting it going again. Thus empowered, Rousseau heads off in the direction of the apocalyptic book burning with which he needs to flirt, but against which "required" writing in the present would finally steel itself.

And yet, Narcissus the writer grimaces still, refusing to vacate Rousseau's looking glass altogether. We have thus far gone along with the assumption that, however difficult to portray, the self does in fact exist somewhere, beyond the pale of discourse and not merely as a figment of our and the writer's imagination. What if this were not the case? What if cultural interference only interfered with our knowing there to be no self anywhere but between these lines?[72] The question—to the extent that anything can—torments Valère. Under conditions of limited visibility, he sees himself in figura as Don Juan—to the point of unconsciously replaying with his father the celebrated "have-a-seat" scene from Molière's comedy (2:989). And until the final judgment of amour propre is handed down in no uncertain terms, Valère knows himself only as inexplicably and irretrievably fickle:

> "Que j'éprouve de bisarrerie dans mes sentimens! Je renonce à la pos-
> session d'un object charmant et auquel, dans le fond, mon penchant me
> raméne encore. Je m'expose à la disgrace de mon pére pour m'entêter
> d'une belle, peut-être indigne de mes soupirs, peut-être imaginaire, sur
> la seule foi d'un portrait tombé des nues et flatté à coup sûr. Quel ca-
> price! Quelle folie!" (2:999)

The greatest scandal to Valère's mind is that of the ease with which he can change it, as though there were no center of gravity there, nothing to be grasped except an infinite potential for change. What kind of self is it that can be moved by a bolt out of the blue to go off on a tangent or send his servant on wild goose chases? What kind of self so thoroughly and unpredictably subverts its own vested interest in constancy? In the hands of a better philosopher than dramatist, dramatic irony ups the ante for us spectators, knowing as we do that the love object is in fact both Valère "himself" and "imaginaire."

Nor, it would appear, does Valère's self-diagnosis entirely miss the mark. In full possession of the facts of the case, analyst Angélique none-theless echoes the patient's soliloquy, citing *bizarrerie* and *caprice* as the first signs of Valère's narcissism: "C'est une petite personne bizarre, ca-pricieuse, éventée, étourdie, volage, et surtout d'une vanité insupporta-ble" (2:1001). Against this scenic backdrop, the precise wording of the challenge that Rousseau sets for himself in the "Préface" takes on greater relief: "il importe à la vérité que j'ai soutenue, que son défenseur ne soit point accusé justement de ne lui avoir prêté son secours que *par caprice* ou par vanité, sans l'aimer et sans la connoître" (emphasis added). In focusing on the nature of the would-be philosopher's attachments, we have thus far neglected the other, equally important criterion of their strength. We have skipped lightly over the surface of that which in Rous-seau's composite profile of Narcissus seems strangely unmindful of the myth. Could any more steadfast soul be conceived than the one who remains riveted to the death on the banks of his pool? No, and yes.

Compared with the poetic justice of the babbling Echo's plight, the boy's final metamorphosis into a flower seems much less well motivated. But it provides a fitting denouement insofar as it inscribes capriciousness

or capacity for radical change at the very heart of Narcissus's stead-
fastness—and nowhere more indelibly. For the ground rules of represen-
tability, in Rousseau's and our common culture, call not for unmitigated
and always provisional or suspect sameness, but for repetition at discrete
(and discreet) intervals. Fittingly, in the play's comic anticlimax, Valère's
self-knowledge comes as a relief and a reward for his having weathered
the interval of questing after the imaginary self and jealously reattached
himself to Angélique. The Rousseau of the *Confessions* knows full well
that where self-sameness is the object and identity the message, such
intervals must be engineered and experienced, at least subliminally. "Je
me répéte," he claims meta-autobiographically, "on le sait; il le faut"
(1:414). The second "le" is ambiguously referential: it proclaims the twofold necessity of repetition and of the unconscious perception thereof.
Echo, in other words, disappears, to be replaced by an unseen echo
chamber or unspoken principle of echoing.

In that respect, prolonging into "quelques années" the interval between Discourse and Preface serves the cause of a self that will be seen to
have withstood a more rigorous than usual test of time: "The infinite
rippling of commentary is agitated from within by the dream of masked
repetition."[73] *Narcisse* is, of course, relegated by the self-portraitist to
another lifetime: "Je n'ai pas toujours eu le bonheur de penser comme je
fais" (2:962). The "Préface" does not go so far as to make its chosen self-
image coextensive with Rousseau's biography. But even in submitting
that image to a more modest test of durability, Rousseau resurrects the
temporal axis and plays some of his self-portrait by the rules of autobiography, that is, against the grain. His text is overwhelmed by the temptation to get referential and to get more from the instant than the
frightening instantaneousness of self-portraiture. Rousseau's is not, after
all, that "'propre' de la femme" that Hélène Cixous postulates as "sa ca-
pacité de se déproprier sans calcul."[74] Instead, Rousseau seizes this opportunity to acknowledge by the phrase "par caprice" the possibility of
his having entered the Academy's contest on a whim and improvised his
answer on the spur of the moment. If, for all anyone knows, that answer
has nothing to do with anything but the localized circumstances of its
elaboration, why not script an ex post facto defense that might double as
a defense of the embattled self-concept? Why not put the inspiration of a
former moment in the proper perspective of an only occasional catalyst
to the general cause of philosophy?

And yet, the solution to Rousseau's crisis of identity compounds it: the text that undertakes to rescue the Discourse as pretext and pre-text from "occasional" status is itself occasional. In so many ways an ally, prefacing turns out to be the self's worst enemy as well. By going ahead with the contingency plan of prefacing *Narcisse,* Rousseau gives the enemy without and within new grounds for pressing Fréron's charges of opportunism, the moral equivalent of capriciousness: "il paraît qu'il n'a publié sa comédie que pour avoir occasion de répéter dans une longue Préface ce qu'il a déjà dit tant de fois" (2:1862). It is all well and good to say once more what "I" have already said, but this is not the first time either that "I" will have capriciously spoken on the slightest pretext, or, as Grimm puts it, "sans aucun sujet."[75] A sense of self-identity does emerge from this second, procedural repetition, but at what expense, insofar as it renders the self essentially opportunistic. In what verges on oxymoron, the qualifier contradicts the substantive and poses a clear threat to its ontological status. Is there any such animal as an opportunist, or are there only boundless opportunities for opportunism? Contingency begins to look like the only absolute. No wonder that the less fundamentally troubling question of "vanité" all but monopolizes the preface's expanded moment of forgetting that the solipsism really at work here is that of writing. "Il s'agit," after all. The title "Préface" speaks volumes in Rousseau's stead about writing's infinite scorn for the "experience" it treats as so much fodder and for the moments it milks as though there were no tomorrow, or yesterday. Whatever good it seems to do, writing cannot *be* otherwise than as an orgy of opportunism. And at some level, the writer knows about working through the possibility of referential grounding only to cast the (writing) self adrift and back into question.

If that is the bad, indigestible news of self-portraiture, at least it is news. No brain-dead Narcissus, Rousseau will have dared to get his feet wet. In those lines of his text that do not simply retrace a self-protective "retour au pays natal" are inscribed the force and the vulnerability of a provisional "subjectivité ouverte."[76] At the very least, Rousseau will have learned from this experiment in self-portraiture that the experience, but not the precise experiment, is infinitely repeatable, and that laboratory conditions can be replicated in any occasional text. To wit, the dedications and the other prefaces we will be reading in the next two chapters.

For their part, sensing a lack of direct competition, the *Confessions* can find more than a little in the "Préface" to cheer according to their own lights. Once the moment of crisis has passed, our reading cannot help but seem like much ado about nothing. For all our head-spinning, we have little to show in the way of precipitates, only a lingering dizziness, and that too will pass. Can Rousseau ever really have doubted for a single instant that he was born to write, to philosophize, and to reconfigure the history of Western philosophy? Putting the inset map of the "Préface" into perspective means for the *Confessions* delighting in the resemblance of real life to one of mainstream autobiography's favorite stories, the one we might call "eventual success": "dans la Préface qui est un de mes bons écrits, je commençai de mettre à découvert mes principes un peu plus que je n'avois fait jusqu'alors" (1:388). This forging of a clear and continuous path to philosophical maturity leaves so much momentary messiness and so many fleeting insights by the wayside. The autobiographer's official storyline accounts neither for the former narcissistic crisis nor for the several moments when—in the café de Procope and in the mother's house—the present autobiography itself echoes the topography of response to that crisis. The autobiographer acts finally as though the progressive unfolding in time of always already extant truth were, then and now, the only name of the game. We will never know which of the philosophical principles in question Rousseau might not have discovered for himself without benefit of opportunistically writing his way into every mirrored corner of the Narcissus topos. Nor will we know what conceptual gaps a decision not to publish *Narcisse* might have left in texts like the *Lettre à d'Alembert* and the Second Discourse, or even whether these texts would have been written. What we will have known momentarily—because self-portraiture does not finally shut out third-party readers so much as inveigle them into participating as "sujet de l'énonciation" in the text's elaboration[77]—are the sinuous and sinlined pathways of approach to writing about the self. How impoverishing of those approaches are the autobiography's perspective and the brief words of self-congratulation offered there for a job well done, as far as it goes. The "Préface" points beyond the *Confessions'* unsatisfying referential assurances to the third of Rousseau's *Lettres à Malesherbes* and especially to the *Rêveries du promeneur solitaire.* In the distant aftermath of Valère's coming in from the garden, the solitary botanist therefore sallies forth to explore and exploit new occasions of self-inscription in the cosmos. "Me voilà donc seul sur la terre, n'ayant plus de frere, de prochain, d'ami, de société que moi-même" (1:995).

2

Rededications:
Auto-avilissement and Autobiography

Si je hais les tyrans, je hais plus les flatteurs.
Voltaire, *Brutus*

Et le Pére des Dieux même ne se plait à l'hommage des mor-
tels que parce qu'ils ne sont point forcés de le lui offrir.
Rousseau, *La Mort de Lucrèce*

Hegel remarks somewhere that all facts and personages of
great importance in world history occur, as it were, twice. He
forgot to add: the first time as tragedy, the second as farce.
Marx, *The Eighteenth Brumaire of Louis Bonaparte*

From the inspired perversity of prefacing the wrong text, we move on with Rousseau to the slightly perverse anachronism of dedicating any text whatsoever. Where the dedicatory epistle was concerned, enlightened, self-respecting authors of the eighteenth century were well advised by experts like Voltaire and Marmontel to exercise newly available options of letting the occasion pass or proceeding with extreme caution. Nor did Rousseau himself make a habit of courting favor, a seeming prerequisite to scripting a resumption of rhetorical relations in the dedicatory mode. But the combined weight of these warnings did not stop Rousseau from making 1755 his year of the dedication. In that year, he published both of the only two dedicatory epistles he ever finished: his opera *Le Devin du village* was addressed to fellow author Charles Duclos, and his Second Discourse to the Republic of Geneva. For third-party readers, these epistles retain a bare minimum of intrinsic appeal. The one to Duclos is three sentences short and remarkable only in its choice of dedicatee; the one to the Republic is unbearably long-winded and, as far as I can tell from its fulsome and wildly fluctuating tones, unreadable.

What thus becomes all the more remarkable is the amount of attention lavished by the *Confessions* on resurrecting, pairing, appropriating, and making sense of these two eminently forgettable moments of Rousseau's literary career. The dedications furnish the key coordinates on the basis of which the entire second half of Book 8 can be graphed as a downward slope. And that plotting turns out to be a matter neither of referential necessity nor of authorial whim. It is, rather, an oblique expression of indebtedness to the second dedication, as differentiated from the first and extended obsessively into the unfinished occasional tragedy *La Mort de Lucrèce*. In dialogue with those texts, the autobiography discovers the end and means of its own single-minded commitment to self-identity at any price. From the impossible dream of dedication without self-abasement, Rousseau will have salvaged self-abasement per se as the autobiographical strategy most conducive to indelible selfhood. Various avatars of Lucretia abetting, Book 8 thus replays the emergence of the modern antihero and his gradual Pyrrhic victory over the resistance of more classically heroic or neoclassically acceptable self-images. More riveting in this instance than Rousseau's liminary texts themselves is the centrality to Western thought of his eventual glosses on them. We will concentrate on reading those glosses for evidence of "le pouvoir qu'il a de transformer ses échecs en réussites"[1] and vice versa. But we will first look at the ways in which conventional wisdom of the Enlightenment made dedication into a surprisingly crucial litmus test of individual character and consigned any latter-day attempt to dedicate to automatic failure.

CAVEAT AUCTOR: Dedication as Auto-avilissement

"Temples are to be dedicated to the gods," said Aristides, circa 400 B.C., "and books to good men."[2] In eighteenth-century France, that truth was becoming less self-evident, at least where books and good men were concerned. It is precisely between still required (prefatory) and newly optional (dedicatory) liminary exercises that Marivaux's preface to *La Voiture embourbée* (1714) draws the line: "A l'égard de l'épître dédicatoire, c'est une formalité qu'il [le livre imprimé] est libre de retrancher ou d'ajouter. Or donc, Lecteur, puisqu'il faut une préface en voici une."[3] Marivaux thus captured or helped to create a moment of transition between one set of norms or expectations (integral to books, dedications might, by an exercise of free will, be subtracted) and another (unnecessary, they might be added). En route to becoming archaic, the dedicatory epistle remained, for the moment, notable either by its presence or by its absence.

By mid-century, however, philosophers were united in denunciation of the link between literary dedication and an increasingly obsolete and despised system of literal patronage. Fontenelle had put it succinctly in his *Jugement de Platon:* "Il faut que celui à qui s'adresse l'épître dédicatoire paye ou protège."[4] There could be no pretending the dedicatory exchange to be modeled on the neoclassical ideal of rational, reciprocal, instantaneously reversible *jugement* between social equals. Instead, the operative model, on which the uneven distribution of wealth and power was seen to have left an indelible stamp, is that of an asymmetrical, mutually degrading exchange: flattery for favors, words for food. Dedicatory discourse not only demeaned the flatterer and masked his resentments, but, favorably received, it exposed the enormity of the flattered party's amour propre. Dedication restaged, inevitably, the encounter of La Fontaine's fox and crow.[5]

Voltaire's remarks on the practice of dedication become, in the article "Auteurs," a thinly veiled pretext for attacks on clerical hypocrisy, but his diatribe only gains in clarity and venom by the association. "L'épître dédicatoire n'a été souvent présentée que par la bassesse intéressée à la vanité dédaigneuse." This allegory play of vices degenerates into a pot-luck dinner: "On ne sait pas que la plupart des dédicaces, en Angleterre, ont été faites pour de l'argent, comme les capucins chez nous viennent présenter des salades, à condition qu'on leur donnera pour boire."[6] Voltaire thus evokes a tradition of venal transactions that had reached its apogee (or nadir) in seventeenth-century England with the flourishing tradesmen known as falconers. Assisted by so-called mongrels, these falconers roamed the countryside armed with samples of a forthcoming book and multiple separate copies of a dedicatory page where only the dedicatee's name had been left blank.

> [Upon arrival] at the mansion of a local magnate, the mongrel, who carried a hand press, filled in the name of the particular noble, and the book was presented as dedicated to him alone. Having extracted from him all the recompense possible, the two proceeded to a new district in pursuit of some other knight or nobleman who might, in like manner, fall victim to flattery.[7]

The animal names, mongrel and falconer, symptomize the contagious dehumanization of flattery, whose self-abasing practitioners seek to gain some measure of revenge by baiting hooks with choice words or luring

their unsuspecting victims into verbal traps. Voltaire makes the same
point by his pertinent analogy with the quid pro quo of food for drink.
Having reduced the dedicatory epistle to its crassest common denominator, he relies on perspicacious readers to see through his subsequent expression of relief that "Les gens de lettres, en France ignorent
aujourd'hui ce honteux avilissement: et jamais ils n'ont eu tant de noblesse dans l'esprit, excepté quelques malheureux qui se disent *gens de
lettres* dans le même sens que des barbouilleurs se vantent d'être de la
profession de Raphael, et que le cocher de Vertamont était pöete."[8]

Condorcet echoes the sentiment, and the key word, "avilissement":
"Les gens de lettres ont renoncé à ces épîtres dédicatoires qui avi-
lissaient l'auteur, même lorsque l'ouvrage pouvait inspirer l'estime ou le
respect."[9] He further suggests that nothing less than the aspired-after dig-
nity and autonomy of intellectual pursuits would be jeopardized by the
prostitution of publishing epistles dedicatory. Any self-respecting man of
letters who voluntarily indulged in that kind of letters stood to set back
not only the progress of his own book but also that of a new meritocracy
with the *philosophes* themselves at its pinnacle. It is, in short, of the
dedication's still noteworthy absence that the *philosophes* made a measure of authorial character and—insofar as the term is not anachronistic—class-consciousness. Truly self-interested writers and those in
greater solidarity with their own peers than with the peers of the realm
chose, with good reason, not to dedicate. The eighteenth century had
come to see the time-honored dedicatory topos of "mea mediocritas"[10]
as formalizing redundantly a humiliation endemic to the enterprise. Even
vacating the topos in favor of some other version of dedication would
produce no substantive promotion of the writing self. Or so it would
seem.

Dedicatory space is often (not always) a meeting ground for
"bassesse intéressée" and "vanité dédaigneuse," opines Voltaire, himself
an inveterate penner of dedications. And Voltaire was not alone in failing
to follow the lead of Pierre Bayle, who had sworn off dedicatory discourse on principle: "I have so often ridiculed dedications that I must not
risk any."[11] It is precisely the presumption of so many clearly defined
pitfalls that would appear to have provided a challenge and piqued the
ambition of those who fancied themselves—French would use the verb
"se flatter" here—equal to the task of striking a mutually acceptable tone
and doing dedications up right. Voltaire's warnings against dedication

may not be totally disinterested: any fellow writer who dedicated and managed to get away with it could be counted as a new enemy or object of envy.

The article "Auteurs" is correspondingly short on constructive suggestions. Voltaire's protégé Marmontel went on, however, to catalog a finite number of vitiated dedicatory strategies and to sketch a plan of escape from the impasse of *auto-avilissement.* Published in the same year, 1755, as Rousseau's two dedications, Marmontel's practical advice to would-be dedicators is developed in a series of articles for the *Encyclopédie* that begins by consigning the *épître* itself to a kind of archaic, marginal formalism: "Ce terme n'est presque plus en usage que pour les lettres écrites en vers & pour les dédicaces des livres."[12] The familiar, prosaic *lettre* more nearly captures the contemporary spirit with which Marmontel's next article seeks to infuse the *épître dédicatoire* itself. He first evokes an edenic, if short-lived, *état de nature,* from which he sees the epistle dedicatory to have fallen into degradation: "Il faut croire que l'estime & l'amitié ont inventé l'*épître dédicatoire,* mais la bassesse & l'intérêt en ont bientôt avili l'usage: les exemples de cet indigne abus sont trop honteux à la Littérature pour en rappeler aucun."[13] Marmontel thus joins forces with Voltaire and Condorcet in situating the notion of *avilissement* at the heart of his critique; he makes into a historical process their essence of an authorial posture.

Marmontel refuses to dirty his hands by citing any one offending text. Rather, he invites his readers to test his lucid generalizations against their own experience. He appeals particularly to a public of potential dedicatees who, however insatiable their natural appetites for flattery, must certainly balk at the recycled, unappealing forms in which it is being served up to them:

> [N]ous croyons devoir donner aux auteurs un avis qui peut leur être utile; c'est que tous les petits détours de la flaterie sont connus. Les marques de bonté qu'on se flate d'avoir reçues, & que le Mécene ne se souvient pas d'avoir données; l'accueil favorable qu'il a fait sans s'en appercevoir; la reconnoissance dont on est si pénétré, & dont il devroit être si surpris; la part qu'on veut qu'il ait à un ouvrage dont la lecture l'a endormi: ses ayeux dont on fait l'histoire souvent chimérique; ses belles actions & ses sublimes vertus qu'on passe sous silence pour de bonnes raisons; sa générosité qu'on loue d'avance, &c. toutes ces formules sont usées, & l'orgueil qui est si peu délicat, en est lui-même dégoûté. *Monseigneur,* écrit M. de Voltaire, à l'électeur Palatin, *le style des dédi-*

*caces, les vertus du protecteur, & le mauvais livre du protégé, ont sou-
vent ennuyé le public.*[14]

Significantly, Marmontel's first-mentioned "détour" ("Les marques de
bonté qu'on se flate d'avoir reçues . . . ") brings the ambiguous reflexive
se flatter into play. The deviousness denounced in passing is that of making other-directed flattery a seemingly safe investment in self-flattery by
association. As Marmontel's answering clause ("& que le Mécene ne se
souvient pas d'avoir données") declares emphatically, the strategy back-
fires: authors "flatter" or delude no one but themselves when they aspire
after the illusory compensations of reflected glory. At the mercy of
uncooperative dedicatees, they have nothing to gain and everything to
lose.

What surfaces here is a mutual aggression that Marmontel stops just
short of declaring endemic to dedicatory discourse per se. Let the authors beware whom Marmontel assumes to assume that dedicatees will
continue to take the same bait indefinitely. Complacent recourse to a
handful of commonplaces can mean only that, in reality, the flatterers feel
nothing but scorn for their addressees and take them for dupes on the
order of La Fontaine's crow. How else is Marmontel to account for his
contemporaries' failure to invent a more restrained or otherwise un-
restrained dedicatory discourse? Repetition threatens, however, to expose the commonplaces for what they are and to awaken in dedicators'
erstwhile dupes the self-consciousness formerly off limits to their amour
propre. These slumbering giants are bound to catch on, sooner or later,
to an unmistakable deviation between the "portraits flattés" they read
and themselves as models. "Maître Corbeau" could no doubt be tricked a
second time into dropping his cheese, but probably not by a fox content
to reprise verbatim his fellow trickster's former effusions. Recognizing
the conventions, dedicatees will disdain to recognize themselves, and so
repay the authors' tacit *mépris* with a scorn susceptible of more overt
and devastating expression. In the aftermath of psychological reciprocity
(scorn for scorn) reasserted at the expense of all civility and in the absence of real social equality, authors risk finding themselves further back
even than square one. As Jean Starobinski puts it, in his article "Sur la
flatterie": "[Q]ue le flatteur se montre excessif ou maladroit, et le mépris
lui est rendu, l'agression se retourne contre lui, d'autant plus dangereuse
qu'elle lui vient d'un puissant. Tout se passe comme si l'énergie agressive

naissait, chez le destinataire de la flatterie, en raison de l'impossibilité d'accepter ou d'habiter l'image trop embellie qu'on lui propose de lui-même."[15] The moral becomes all the more inescapable when, in the dotage of dedication, rhetorical excesses are flagged by those of redundancy.

In the same vein, Diderot's translation of Shaftesbury's *An Inquiry into Virtue and Merits* completes the scenario whereby unsuspecting addressees of flattery are provoked, paradoxically, into coming to grips with unsolicited self-knowledge: "Nor are the greatest favourites of Fortune exempted from this task of self-inspection. Even flattery itself, by making the view agreeable, renders us attentive this way, and ensnares us in the habit. . . . " That portion of the English author's text is rendered in the following, even more menacing terms by Rousseau's sometime mentor, Diderot, whom we know specifically to have mediated the Genevan's encounter with Shaftesbury: "D'ailleurs, les maîtres du monde & les mignons de la fortune ne sont pas exempts de cette inspection domestique. Toutes les impostures de la flatterie se réduisent la plupart du temps, à leur en familiariser l'usage, & ses faux portraits à les rappeler ce qu'ils sont en effet."[16] And provided it were distasteful enough, the realistic self-image triggered as an aftershock by a flattering image might well prod its subject into defensive recriminations against the offending flatterer.

What dedicators had, then, to avoid was ensnaring their prey only in the habit of "self-inspection" and being caught in flagrante delicto of setting transparent traps. There was a need to short-circuit the process whereby dedications inadvertently force-fed the Socratic message "Know Thyself" to *destinataires* who, in their reluctance, might like as not kill the messenger. One possible, if already conventional, response to the problem of unpalatable conventions is suggested by Marmontel's quotation from a dedicatory epistle by Voltaire. *"Monseigneur,* écrit M. de Voltaire, à l'électeur Palatin, *le style des dédicaces, les vertus du protecteur, & le mauvais livre du protégé, ont souvent ennuyé le public.* " Metadedicatory discourse along these lines sought to allay suspicions and ward off scorn by translating the author's explicit awareness of flattery everywhere in the environs into assurances of his own congenital incapacity to flatter. Rousseau's youthful freestanding verse epistles to Messieurs Bordes (1741) and Parisot (1742) exploit this topos. Both come at "sincere," "well-deserved" praise of the addressee from the angle of the poet's failure to make his way in the world. If only his rigorous

Genevan education had not forever precluded Rousseau from stooping to deal in the (counterfeit) French currency of *louanges:*

> Mais moi qui connois peu les usages de France,
> Moi, fier républicain que blesse l'arrogance,
> Du riche impertinent je dédaigne l'appui,
> S'il le faut mendier en rampant devant lui,
> Et ne sais applaudir qu'à toi, qu'au vrai mérite.
>
> "Epître à M. Bordes" (2:1130)

> Ah s'il faloit un jour absent de ma patrie
> Traîner chez l'Etranger ma languissante vie
> S'il falloit bassement ramper auprés des Grands
> Que n'en ai-je appris l'art dès mes plus jeunes ans?
>
> "Epître à M. Parisot" (2:1137)

Marmontel no doubt recognized that such assurances do not really exempt the author from the blindness he ascribes to other flatterers and their dupes and that, in any case, redundancy was again at work undermining the perception of authenticity. He does not pursue this avenue any further. Rather, Marmontel subordinates the issue of sincerity to the other desired outcome of authorial self-respect. What he proposes in his own name would look very much like a retreat to the neoclassical model of reciprocal *honnêteté,* if the prerogative to pass final judgment were not now displaced onto the reading public: "Il ne reste plus qu'une façon honnête de dédier un livre: c'est de fonder sur des faits la reconnoissance, l'estime, ou le respect qui doivent justifier aux yeux du public l'hommage qu'on rend au mérite."[17]

The specter of flattery so haunts Marmontel's prescriptions that they all but bracket the dedicatee's role as reader/respondent. Whether second persons see themselves in or even see the images linked to their names must matter not at all if authors are to be immunized with maximal certainty against ulterior or profit motives. Any dedicatory discourse that was acknowledged to be the least bit transactional would be tainted by the notorious precedents of bribing interlocutors into future favors or buying silence with respect to past services not really rendered. Better that authors should seem to forgo any attempt at instituting a mutual-admiration society of two and concentrate instead on giving third-party referees the wherewithal to pronounce the discourse devoid of flattery. It is by writing dedications that a public in possession of the facts would have been pleased or proud to write in their stead that Marmontel's authors would "distinguish" themselves as *honnêtes,* reintegrate themselves into a community of equals, and make the best possible case for rehabilitating dedicatory discourse.

More important to this enterprise than any absolute value of the dedicatee's "mérite" were that the discourse observe throughout and thoroughly document a due sense of proportionality. There could be no failing to furnish the empirical evidence on the sole basis of which "mérite" had been inferred and was being submitted for confirmation by other like-minded observers. No allowance could be made for feelings left unspoken, implicit, enigmatic, inchoate; the now familiar option of "a brief expression of love or esteem for a person close to the author"[18] remained inconceivable. Nor could there be any dedicating out of private, asocial, idiosyncratic feelings like guilt, passionate love, or partisan zeal, which would tend, just as surely and subversively as flattery, to inflate the discourse. To deviate from the approved list of rational or already rationalized responses ("la reconnoissance, l'estime ou le respect") would be to court public ridicule in lieu of or in addition to a dedicatee's individual scorn. What we mean today by real honesty or depth of emotion thus counted for less than adequacy and transmissibility and for as little as a dedicatee's true identity. As played in accordance with these essentially aesthetic rules, the dedicatory game might, in some instances, warrant retransposition into the heroic register only vaguely evoked by Marmontel's use of the term "hommage." But only where the "facts" in question amounted to truly noble deeds would authors be allowed (and required by a decisive respect for proportionality) to mimic the poet-chroniclers of classical Antiquity in their parallel nobility. Conversely, modest praise would entirely befit the more modest exploits—first and foremost, services to the author—characteristic of modern-day dedicatees. By his emphasis on conformity to universal standards of seemliness, Marmontel humbled the literary exercise in order that authors might be rescued from making a public spectacle of *auto-avilissement.*

The oblique, skin-deep self-presentation of epistles dedicatory would thus steer clear of autobiographical excess, or accept the consequences. This was no place to put Rousseau's eventual motto "*Intus, et in Cute*" (1:5) into practice, no place for authors to let their hair all the way down, or for readers to catch them in the act. Present-day readers are bound to be disappointed if they turn to the mainstream of eighteenth-century French dedications "just to see personal feelings, which have been kept in check in the effort to be objective or conciliatory, break through, as if the author found relief in forgetting everything except his [or her] own convictions or hopes or fears."[19] The difference that a twentieth-century compiler has posited between (utterly impersonal) dedicated and (highly personalized) dedicatory texts remained, by and large, only relative: "Many an author who never wore his heart on his sleeve put it into his dedication, and through the medium of this humble literary instrument we have received revelations of feeling, messages of love, reverence, and loyalty, which we could ill afford to lose."[20] Rousseau's contemporaries rarely forgot everything; what they saw fit to put into their dedications was heartfelt up to a point, or faintly reminiscent of the heartfelt; a self-protective *pudeur* held in check any urges toward demonstrably reckless abandon.

Rousseau cannot have been unaware of psycho-political baggage that was widely thought to encumber the very decision to dedicate and the choice of dedicatory strategies. He must have remarked his contemporaries' collective recoiling before the horror of *avilissement* and the premium they were placing on abstention. And since he was less inclined than Marmontel to table the question of sincerity, Rousseau had further reason to recoil. In the preface to *Narcisse* he had repudiated "vile et basse flatterie, soins séducteurs, insidieux, puériles" in no uncertain terms—not so much because flattery could not work as because it did, but only to corrupt the "cœur" of the flatterer irreversibly and to shrink his "ame" (2:968).

DEDICATION AS LÈSE MAJESTÉ: From the Heights of Heroism . . .

It is by his unconventional choices of dedicatees that Rousseau first hoped to have inured his soul against this shrinkage. The "Préface" had promised specifically that he would leave no written record of having courted the "femmes qui donnent le ton" or showered praise on "la sotise des Grands" (2:974). The pride he took, provisionally, in having lived up to the letter of that promise gives us a first way of accounting for the relative fanfare with which Rousseau's two dedications are ushered, in tandem, into Book 8 of the *Confessions:* "Je dédiai ma Piéce [*Le Devin du village*] à M. Duclos qui l'avoit protégée et je déclarai que ce seroit ma seule dédicace. J'en ai pourtant fait une seconde avec son consentement; mais il a du se tenir encore plus honoré de cette exception que si je n'en avois fait aucune" (1:382). The brief epistle to Duclos is in fact centered on the unkept promise of singularity:

A Monsieur Du Clos,
Historiographe de France, l'un des Quarante de l'Académie Fran-
çoise, et des Inscriptions et Belles-Lettres.

Souffrez, Monsieur, que vôtre nom soit à la tête de cet Ouvrage, qui sans vous n'eut jamais paru. Ce sera ma prémiére et unique Dédicace. Puisse-t'elle vous faire autant d'honneur qu'à moi.

Je suis de tout mon cœur,
MONSIEUR,
Votre trés humble et trés Obéissant Serviteur,
J. J. Rousseau (2:1095)

This skeletal rendition seems content to make a few modest stabs at modernizing and personalizing the dedicatory form letter. Singling out Duclos, Rousseau instills value in what passes for a once-in-a-lifetime, never-to-be-repeated gesture. He makes his own singularity—his sympathy, really, for the philosophic stance—a matter of characteristic reluctance to dedicate. Smoothly and respectfully turned, the compliment does not attract undue attention; fulfilling his avowed desire to dedicate leaves the dedicator already fully sated. Yet the text remains remarkably top-heavy with titles and weighed down at the last by formulaic assurances of vasselage. Marmontel would have approved the explicit (and verifiable) evocation of Duclos's good offices in getting the play staged but might have stopped short of endorsing genuflexion as an appropriate posture of gratitude. And Marmontel surely would have counseled against the *Confessions'* equation of those good offices with the *bête noire* of "protection." It is, after all, to a friend and fellow author, connected but not enthroned, that Rousseau addressed this strange amalgam of fulsome, measured, and faintly self-serving phrases.

But it is just this intrinsically disproportionate mix of old- and new-style dedication that makes Rousseau's text more telling for what it avoids than for what it says. The dedication *not* written, the dedication in lieu of which Rousseau addresses Duclos, would have honored Louis XV. Lèse majesté between the lines is overdetermined by a title page recall-

ing that *Le Devin* had twice been successfully staged "DEVANT LEURS
MAJESTES" (2:1093), by a neoclassical tradition making dedication of
plays to the monarch particularly automatic, and by the wording that
distinguishes Duclos as "historiographe *de France*" from a long line (including Racine) of *historiographes du roi.* The message becomes that of
Rousseau's deliberate choice to cast himself as the "trés humble et trés
Obéissant Serviteur" of someone other than Louis.

So near and yet so far: Rousseau flirts with the amply illustrated precedent of using nominal dedicatees to mediate eventual access of the
discourse to the ultimate seat of power. Many a dedicator had rehearsed
the exploits of royal consorts, offspring, ministers, and the like as a way of
setting the stage for the main attraction of heaping praise on their il-
lustrious relation.[21] But here, fealty to Duclos remains unswerving and
untranscended; art will not imitate the one and only dedicatee's having
gone between Rousseau and Louis. Singularity of address thus has less to
do with a blanket exclusion of all other comers from Rousseau's liminary
pages than with the pointed rejection in perpetuity of a sole "natural"
claimant.

What the occasional text in this instance commemorates—and the
Confessions remember, making it the narrative apogee of Book 8—is the
author's heroic refusal of a royal pension: "Au centre, comme sur un large
palier, *ralentendo,* on assiste au triomphe du *Devin du Village* devant la
Cour. 'Moment critique', et tentation précise: Rousseau acceptera-t-il
d'être présenté au roi, d'être pensionné? Il refuse, pour des raisons plus
ou moins pures, et il jouit orgueilleusement de sa gloire et de sa vertu"
(1:1425). Whatever "démarches auto-punitives"[22] were certainly involved in Rousseau's actual refusal to appear before the king have left no
trace in the dedication. Saying no to flattery, the dedicator goes on record
as having said no to the favors that, in the throes of the court's "vifs
transports d'admiration" for *Le Devin* (1:379), Louis would have conferred on the playwright. There is something not only covertly defiant
but already autobiographical-by-omission about this use of an occasional
text to mark not some red-letter day in the monarch's life but, rather, one
of Rousseau's own proudest moments. "Humbled" before and only before his friend, he can take lasting pride both in the occasion and in the
harmless show of humility that provides a permanent record of inocula-
tion against any real *avilissement.*

Unlike Marmontel, however, Rousseau cannot dissociate self-respect from an essential component of sincerity. It is to truthfulness, *his* truthfulness, that the specter of flattery poses the more immediate threat. And over truthfulness any dedication might cast a pall, by allowing readers to presume that the author had in mind at every moment of writing his opera the desire to please or not entirely displease some specific outside reader.

We might well read the dedication to Duclos as the proximate cause of the author's hastening to follow with a somewhat mean-spirited and off-putting "Avertissement." "Quoyque j'aye approuvé les changemens que mes amis jugérent à propos de faire à cet Interméde, quand il fut joué à la Cour et que son succés leur soit dû en grande partie," warns Rousseau, "je n'ai pas jugé à propos de les adopter aujourd'huy, et cela par plusieurs raisons" (2:1096). To be dispelled, emphatically, is the suspicion that Duclos's election as dedicatee has in any way compromised the integrity of the author's original text. Rousseau denies literal collaboration as a way of denying concessions to the pleasure of any intended reader other than himself. The last and most compelling of his "plusieurs raisons" drives home the point: "n'ayant fait cet ouvrage que pour mon amusement, son vrai succés est de me plaire. Or personne ne sait mieux que moi comment il doit être pour me plaire le plus" (2:1096).

Differentiating the signed and printed *Devin* from the version performed in the theater, Rousseau extends the message of his dedication to the point of partially dis-honoring a dedicatee already demoted to the status of "friend" among others. Not only does no trace persist anywhere in *Le Devin* of former efforts to court royal favor, but primary responsibility for those misguided efforts—seen significantly as undermining the work's "unité" (2:1096)—lies entirely with the worldly-wise Duclos et al. Onto them, Rousseau projects the *savoir-flatter* from which he continues to seek exemption, in testimony to persistent doubts that the dedicatory mentality can honestly be confined to proper dedications. He "confesses" his own past complicity in schemes to placate Louis and goes out of his way to devalue the pleasure or incur the displeasure of even a relatively benign dedicatee. Clearly, Rousseau's relief at having resisted the temptation of royal patronage in the nick of time is matched by anxiety that this heroic gesture may have dealt an only symbolic blow to the radical insincerity of any and all addressed discourse in a society of unequals. The slimmest of dedications thus becomes an occasion for disquieting and defensive postmortems. How can Rousseau know for sure that his denials of desire to win favor are emitted from a vantage point of absolute lucidity?

Years later, at the moment of writing *Du contrat social,* he was still trying to reassure himself and to consolidate the heroism of the *Devin* episode. It is with his own brief career as a dedicator in mind that Rousseau sketched biographies of one of the *Contract*'s designated whipping boys, Grotius, and his translator, Barbeyrac. From the safety of the sidelines, Rousseau enjoys watching these other dedicators squirm and their integrity suffer in consequence:

> Grotius refugié en France, mécontent de sa patrie, et voulant faire sa cour à Louis XIII, à qui son livre est dédié, n'épargne rien pour dépouiller les peuples de tous leurs droits et pour en revétir les rois avec tout l'art possible. C'eut bien été aussi le goût de Barbeyrac, qui dédioit sa traduction au Roi d'Angleterre George I. Mais malheureusement l'expulsion de Jacques II qu'il appelle abdication, le forçoit à se tenir sur la réserve, à gauchir, à tergiverser, pour ne pas faire de Guillaume un usurpateur. Si ces deux écrivains avoient adopté les vrais principes, toutes les difficultés étoient levées et ils eussent été toujours conséquents; mais ils auroient tristement dit la vérité et n'auroient fait leur cour qu'au peuple. Or la vérité ne mene point à la fortune, et le peuple ne donne ni ambassades, ni chaires, ni pensions. (3:370–71)

This transparently parallel life of Grotius recalls Genevan refugee Rousseau's refusal to follow suit with a later Louis. But it also evokes, in the guise of the good road not taken by Grotius, the second and really *dernière* of Rousseau's *épîtres dédicatoires.* By offering his Second Discourse "A LA REPUBLIQUE DE GENEVE" (3:111), Rousseau could believe to have completed and complemented his message of nondedication to the French king. Election of the republic perpetuates rejection of the monarch. The silent treatment accorded a party ready, able, and willing to pay informs and is informed in turn by the subsequent choice of a dedicatee, Geneva, in no position—ontologically (as a nonperson) or politically (as "the people")—to dispense favors. Where previously he had withheld a stigma of insincerity, Rousseau now places a stamp of sincerity on the text proper of the Second Discourse.

No wonder that, following the *Contract*'s counter example, the *Confessions* couple the two roughly contemporaneous Rousseau dedications in an intertext so binding that each ends up honoring the other's honoree. Duclos's stature is enhanced by the exclusive company he comes to keep, Geneva's by its singular fitness to confer that stature and to "force" Rousseau into breaking his vow never to dedicate again. Something of the classical ideal of honors conferred reciprocally but at a distance incompatible with base bartering is thus displaced from intra- to interdedicatory space. By simultaneously exposing the two sides of a single coin, the *Confessions* show Rousseau to have exhausted the possibilities for unproblematical, politically correct use of dedicatory space. The moment is complete unto itself, completely heroic, and fleeting.

. . . To the Depths of Auto-avilissement

By first evoking the dedication to Geneva out of turn, the *Confessions* also pose a tantalizing question. What exactly can Rousseau have found to say and in what tones within the ten-page epistle that contrasts so unmistakably with the three lines of dedication to Duclos? The answer that the *Confessions* withhold suspensefully I shall take for granted. Rousseau's second and final *épître dédicatoire* reads like so hyperbolic an exercise in flattery that one contemporary reader was moved to declare its excesses unprecedented: "Il n'est pas naturel de confondre sa Dédicace avec les Dédicaces ordinaires. . . . Quoiqu'il y ait dans la suite de ce long narré bien des faits qui conviennent effectivement à l'Etat que M. Rousseau a en vuë, le plus grand nombre n'est guères relatif qu'à l'*Utopie,* et l'Auteur s'est plu à suivre une espèce de verve qui l'entraînoit, plutôt qu'à dépeindre les objets dans leur exacte réalité" (3:1288). The title of his organ (*La Bibliothèque impartiale*) notwithstanding, no one would be tempted to take Formey's for an impartial assessment. Still, it was echoed by Genevans, like former *premier syndic* Jean-Louis Du Pan, who had trouble recognizing themselves in so flattering a group portrait: "Vous avés suivi dans l'epitre dedicatoire les mouvemens de votre cœur, et je crains que l'on ne trouve que vous nous flatés trop. Vous nous representés tels que nous devrions etre et non pas tels que nous sommes."[23] Among our contemporaries, Jean-Daniel Candaux pulls no punches in alluding to "une dédicace à la République de Genève, où la louange, par son emphase, atteint aux limites de la flagornerie: il n'y est question que de la douceur et de la bonté des magistrats, les Citoyens y sont tous vertueux, instruits, sensés, etc." (3:clxxxiii). And Starobinski reminds us of what Rousseau seems to have forgotten since the epistles to Bordes and Parisot: nowhere were such excesses less apt to go undetected or unquestioned than in Rousseau's (and his critic's) hometown: "Les Genevois aiment les manières tranquilles" (3:xlix).

We can only speculate about the sense of Rousseau's self-delusion or strategic planning. Did he think, in idealizing Geneva, to render sincere homage to what, in the infinite nostalgia of exile in Parisian deserts, he really saw? In that case, what comes across as miscalculated *honnêteté* might be traced to a more far-reaching nostalgia for dedication in the heroic register. Repeated assurances in the *épître* that the Genevans' is a happier lot than the Ancients' (3:113–14, 119) would belie a problematical attempt, on the part of a self-styled Genevan, to resurrect the oratory of Antiquity. The resulting mixed message would read: Live with the moderation of Moderns; read this as larger-than-life Ancients. Or did Rousseau intend, more deviously, to exhort, even chide his addressees into closing the gap between their ideal and real selves? Whether or not it was tendered, that bait was taken—in what spirit it is impossible to determine—by Du Pan: "Nous devons tous profiter des sages preceptes qu'elle [l'épître dédicatoire] contient et travailler de concert à procurer le bonheur de notre Patrie."[24] Was Rousseau's unsolicited advice to change nothing really aimed at bringing their Geneva into closer conformity with his?

Or was the hidden agenda, as R. A. Leigh assumes, more specifically subversive still? Was the gap Rousseau wished to see closed that between the magistratical oligarchy and a "people" addressed separately and treated to a deliberately hollow-sounding celebration of the status quo?[25] Is Geneva as "best of all possible worlds" really meant to seem as ripe for reform as Voltaire's Westphalia? Or was Rousseau bent from the first on provoking the good (but not great) citizenry (3:117) into acknowledging his own superior brand of citizenship? Was it to be deplored—or, perhaps, perversely hoped—that the Genevans would repudiate the "vrai Patriote" whose "zéle ardent et légitime" and "tendre affection" could only get the better of him? Rousseau in fact concludes by endowing himself with the Christ-like generosity "d'un homme qui n'envisage point de plus grand bonheur pour lui-même que celui de vous voir tous heureux" (1:120–21). Is there a method to the madness of the *épître*'s self-evident sycophancy? Are we dealing here with the prodigal son as such, as Livy-come-lately, as *juge-pénitent,* as political agitator, or as self-anointed martyr?

The *épître*'s own impossible eclecticism and instability of tone preclude none of the possibilities just sketched. The mere fact that "tender" and "zealous" versions of Rousseau rub shoulders in a single sentence makes it futile to try to pin him down to any one affective register or established mode of dedication on the sole basis of the performance itself. More accessible and interesting by far are Rousseau's postmortems. That they exist and are so protracted is already noteworthy, given the obvious alternative for an important author of never giving a mere dedication, once delivered, a second thought. But Rousseau did, and his ongoing enterprise of self-portraiture was permanently inflected by the choice he made for himself among the plethora of possible readings of the *épître.*

To the author of the *Confessions* it comes to matter less whether or what, in dedicating, he stooped to conquer than that he stooped at all—and never quite straightened up again. In the aftermath of dedication, there would be no reascending directly into the heavens from which Jean-Jacques, "auprès de la divinité," is said to have emitted the immediately preceding broadcast of the Second Discourse (1:388–89). The text of presentation to the graphically exalted "MAGNIFIQUES, TRES HONORES ET SOUVERAINS SEIGNEURS" of Geneva (3:111) becomes, in contrast, a kind of rite of initiation into *auto-avilissement.* Even as the *philosophes* warned against it, Rousseau was making a connection between *auto-avilissement* and autobiography. He was recognizing paradoxical ways in which gratuitous servility can be self-serving. And he was exploring the still relatively uncharted depths of modern antiheroism. This, at least, is the sense of having dedicated that the *Confessions* go to considerable lengths to promote and to press through the narrative filter of Book 8's final ten pages. Rededication to *auto-avilissement* underwrites the episodic account where Rousseau tells of writing the *Discours:* returning, dedication in hand, to the city of his birth; reveling for four months in the welcome extended there; reconverting to Calvinism and regaining his rights of citizenship; returning to France; and eventually abandoning plans for permanent resettlement in Geneva (1:389–400).

Even at the level of manifest content, the emphases of this account are startling. What Rousseau's Pléiade editors have noted vis-à-vis the entirety of Book 8 has special relevance for its waning moments: "L'étonnant est qu'une si petite place soit accordée aux 'idées', en ces années qui durent être vouées à de très nombreuses lectures et à la méditation du 'triste et grand système' dont un premier exposé sera donné dans le

Discours sur l'Inégalité" (1:1425). In a paradigmatic reversal of figure and ground, the writing and reception of Rousseau's dedication to Geneva come in for more extensive chronicling than those of the Second Discourse itself. If the two stories parallel each other in raising and dashing Jean-Jacques's hopes for favorable reception of the respective texts, only the dedication's story has a suspenseful unfolding. No sooner is the *Discours* composed and the hopeful sign of Diderot's approval noted than an answering clause of the same sentence delivers the bad news: "De ces méditations resulta le *Discours sur l'inégalité,* ouvrage qui fut plus du gout de Diderot que tous mes autres Ecrits, et pour lequel ses conseils me furent le plus utiles, mais qui ne trouva dans toute l'Europe que peu de lecteurs qui l'entendissent, et aucun de ceux-là qui voulut en parler" (1:389). A single additional sentence fleshes out this outline of vertical fall.

In contrast, the dedication's fate is left hanging for the duration of Jean-Jacques's stay in Geneva. Acknowledgement of its composition heralds his arrival: "Avant mon départ de Paris j'avois esquissé la dédicace de mon *Discours sur l'inegalité.*" But, uncirculated, the dedication is quickly forgotten, and remains forgotten for three festive pages: "Arrivé dans cette ville [Genève] je me livrai à l'enthousiasme républicain qui m'y avoit amené" (1:392). So effusively do the Genevans welcome Jean-Jacques and in such total forgiveness of past transgressions such as his conversion to Catholicism, that, at this point in the narrative, one can well imagine that someone other than Rousseau might have pocketed or at least toned down his *épître dédicatoire.* The biblical prodigal, on whose story Jean-Jacques's is provisionally modeled, had likewise rehearsed a full-blown speech of contrition: "*Mon* père, j'ai péché contre le ciel et contre toi;/Et je ne suis plus digne d'être appelé ton fils; traite-moi comme l'un de tes domestiques."[26] But when it comes time in the Bible for actually delivering the speech, the final clause, with its embrace of servanthood, is preempted; the son is forever precluded by (gratitude for) his father's premature embrace from delivering the self-deprecatory punch line. Expectations are raised by the biblical parallel that a Rousseau "[f]êté, caressé dans tous les états" (1:392) will also have swallowed his prepared text or at least those parts of his text rendered obsolete and too obsequious by the city fathers' having already rolled out the red carpet and killed the fatted calf.

Instead, as though mindless of their "running down the road"[27] to avoid a native son's humiliation, Jean-Jacques forges ahead as planned with his dedication. He refuses not only to heed the general warnings of Marmontel and company but to espouse the orthodox repentance that has been defined, on the basis of Jesus's parable, as "the capacity to forego pride and accept graciousness."[28] A golden opportunity for the authentic, unselfconscious humility of silent wonder at the other's spontaneous, unfathomable, and inimitable generosity goes unexploited, and conspicuously so. It is as though Jean-Jacques saw the city fathers only as rivals in *auto-avilissement,* as though they were taunting him to outdo their *Imitatio* and to exceed their example of running a self into the ground. For Jean-Jacques, there could be no tacit compliance with an unanticipated state of grace from which his own *mediocritas* might be inferred, incidentally, as a corollary of the other's exaltation. The occasion called, rather, for reappropriating and brandishing that *mediocritas* as his alone. He would make it public through dedication itself and explicit in such extraneously self-flagellatory versicles as: "si les égaremens d'une folle jeunesse me firent oublier durant un tems de si sages leçons, j'ai le bonheur d'éprouver enfin que quelque penchant qu'on ait vers le vice, il est difficile qu'une éducation dont le cœur se mêle reste perdue pour toujours" (3:118).

As though to explain our returning hero's apparent willingness to risk all in order to have his say, Kenneth E. Bailey reads between the biblical lines:

> We *could* assume that [the prodigal's failure to finish his prepared speech] indicates a self-interest which says, "This is better than I expected. Why not take all I can get? I'll keep silent and accept. If he will give me sonship, who cares about being a workman?" Certainly this is not what the omission signifies. Given the prodigal's previous mind-set, sonship has certain distinct disadvantages. If he accepts sonship, he will have to live with his brother and be fed from his brother's property. He will again be under the total authority of his father. He will be denied the self-satisfaction of having "earned his own way."

Rather than forgo that last self-satisfaction, the Jean-Jacques who would dedicate thus parts company with the prodigal and reverts to the "perverted pride" of explicit insistence "that he is 'too humble' for sonship."[29]

It would seem, then, that there is a victory to be snatched from the

Genevans by dedication to them, and that it consists in perfecting the well-known reversal whereby a godless semblance of Christian humility is fetishized as a "phallus held high."[30] Rousseau was certainly no stranger to the detours of Augustinian theology ("God humbled Himself in order to be exalted") or to the corollaries of a discreetly neo-Promethean psychology ("Augustine knew well that humility itself could become an 'exploit'").[31] At one point in the *épître,* for example, Rousseau cannot resist exalting the humility of his father, Isaac, whom the author sees in his mind's eye "vivant du travail de ses mains, et nourissant son ame des Verités les plus sublimes" (3:118). And yet, the *Confessions'* saga of the *épître dédicatoire* does not end here or, for that matter, in precisely the kind of paradoxical redemption scripted by Augustine. Being "saved," especially insofar as that would entail reliance on the caprices of external ratification, comes to matter much less to Rousseau than the more modest and modern, if still difficult, aim of being "himself."

Conversion to the cult of self-identity takes time, however, and the prodigal of orthodox Christianity is not the only or even the most nostalgically mourned casualty of this conversion. The *Confessions* let go much more easily of the prodigal than of the aspirations to a straightforwardly heroic self-image that are left over from the dedication to Duclos. Meandering his way through a kind of talking cure, Rousseau puts up massive initial resistance to his compatriots' antiheroic misreadings of the second *épître.*

The prodigal Jean-Jacques has by now returned to Paris, having left advance copies of his dedication behind. It was not well received, according to the *Confessions,* by the dedicatees ("Cet effet ne me fut pas favorable" [1:395]). What most shocks and disappoints Jean-Jacques and seems still to catch Rousseau off guard is the failure of all but a few Genevans to write back, and those few's failure to respond in kind. He seems to think that one good, heartfelt *épître* deserved others just like it and just as imbued as his with "un vrai zèle de cœur" (1:395). Instead, Jean-Jacques's sincere expression of "pur patriotisme" has somehow managed to lend itself to one version or another of misinterpretation. It has been mistaken either for a mere literary exercise on the safe, Marmontel model or, worse, for an atavistically flattering assault on the dedicatees' amour propre. A first set of readings, which Rousseau judges to be disproportionately low on affect, is exemplified by Chief Magistrate Chouet's "honnête" but "froide" letter and the "quelques complimens" penned by "des particuliers." But, as though it meant to flatter and not gratuitously, this selfsame *épître* will also have provoked the defensive overreactions of "enmity" in the Petit Conseil and jealousy "dans la bourgeoisie" (1:395). What Rousseau says to have scandalized "tous ceux qui la remarquérent" is the Genevans' so-called "indifférence." He evidently means to fault his dedicatees for unwillingness or inability to differentiate his from the run-of-the-mill dedications that had made either timid tea-party conversation or mutually degrading travesties of sincere emotion.

It is, of course, beyond the power of the *épître* itself to outlaw this indifference. In particular, whatever traces zeal may have left in texts that somehow strike their models as having exceeded realistic portraiture are indistinguishable from the traces of a conscious desire to flatter. Readers familiar with Rousseau's tragedy *La Mort de Lucrèce* will be struck—with what pertinence we shall see shortly—by the coincidence between Jean-Jacques's unmet demands and those placed on Lucrèce by her confidante Pauline. After urging her mistress to lead a less austere existence, Pauline claims to have acted selflessly: "Si mon zéle a pu vous déplaire du moins n'en blamez pas les motifs" (2:1025). Omniscience, in the case of the tragedy, allows us to discover that what Pauline arbitrarily calls "zéle" amounts, in fact, to the base and passionate self-interest of a co-conspirator in Lucretia's eventual rape. In the case of the dedication, by contrast, sincerity remains undecidable and, in effect, less than decisive. Not knowing what to think, the Genevans may think the worst, and worse still, think only of themselves. Even to recognize Rousseau's zeal would be to want to denounce the portrait itself as flattering, whatever the portraitist's intent. But by this point in the *Confessions,* Rousseau has obviously dropped all pretense of concern for the accuracy of the portrait qua portrait. He cares only that as a self-portrait it has proven doubly inadequate: it is neither recognizable enough as an exercise in individuation nor equal to the task of portraying its subject in sufficiently unequivocal terms. That Rousseau's "vrai zèle" and the "bassesse intéressée" denounced by Voltaire can be called to account for one and the same increment of the artist in the artist's rendering constitutes, for the would-be self-portraitist, the really scandalous and inevitable "indifférence."

For Rousseau wants, finally, to be recognized as a subject and to control his self-image, whatever that takes. Following the lead of Masson, we might confront Rousseau with the evidence of warm, even effusive letters of praise for his *épître,* "car les remerciements du Conseil furent aussi élogieux et courtois qu'un gouvernement très conservateur pouvait se les permettre."[32] But any such efforts would run counter to what emerges finally as the autobiographer's chosen path. By the time we think to catch him or convince him to leave well enough alone, Rousseau has already rededicated himself, with a vengeance, to *auto-avilissement*. In defiance of at least some empirical evidence, he makes a spectacle of snatching humiliating defeat from the jaws of partial, unsatisfactory victory. A piquant anecdote puts an emphatic end to the indeterminacy of mixed reviews. Rousseau drives to new extremes the point of the dedication's utter failure among its elected *destinataires* and submits Jean-Jacques to a gratuitous reprise of ridicule: "Je me souviens que dinant un jour à Clichy chez Mad^e Dupin avec Crommelin Resident de la République et avec M. de Mairan, celui-ci dit en pleine table que le Conseil me devoit un présent et des honneurs publics pour cet ouvrage, et qu'il se deshonoroit s'il y manquoit. Crommelin, qui étoit un petit homme noir et bassement méchant, n'osa rien répondre en ma présence, mais il fit une grimace effroyable, qui fit sourire Mad^e Dupin" (1:395). The earlier, matter-of-fact report of Europe's invisible silence before the Second Discourse pales before this miming of failure by a *grimace* both horrifying and laughable. The dinner-table scene, which Rousseau might easily not have remembered or evoked, does not so much illustrate "indifférence" (or lack of "honneurs publics") as hurtle by it, in apparent submission to some irresistible gravitational pull. The Frenchwoman's enigmatic smile makes a debasing mockery even of the honor/dishonor polarity and allows the Genevan *diablotin* to smirk with impunity and in perpetuity at his countryman.

Even when allowances are made for what the autobiographer knew better than the new citizen about the subsequent deterioration of his relations with the Genevan notables, there is something strangely complacent about this wallowing in the grotesque Grand Guignol of mutual *avilissement*. Or there would be, had the autobiographer not followed with a bottom line: "Le seul avantage que me procura cet ouvrage [l'épître dédicatoire] outre celui d'avoir satisfait mon cœur fut le titre de Citoyen qui me fut donné par mes amis, puis par le public à leur exemple, et que j'ai perdu dans la suite pour l'avoir trop bien mérité" (1:395). The *Confessions* have settled finally not only on a tone (of sardonic laughter at Jean-Jacques's misfortunes), but on the theme of identity.

To hear Rousseau tell it, he might just as well have dispensed with the entire body of the dedication and proceeded directly to the complimentary closing ("Vôtre très humble et très-obéissant serviteur et Concitoyen" [3:121]), which makes the point of his citizenship by emphatic contrast with the otherwise identical closing ("Votre trés humble et trés Obéissant Serviteur") to the Duclos dedication (2:1095). Or more economically still, Rousseau might have contented himself with having his name and title coupled on the *Discours*'s title page, where they were guaranteed relief both by the initially anonymous publication of his First Discourse "Par un Citoyen de Genève" (3:1) and by the norm of more numerous and highfalutin "mentions honorifiques dont les personnages importants faisaient suivre leur noms" on title pages (3:1285).[33] His doing neither has resulted not simply in a regrettable, qualitative difference like that between his epistle and the Genevans' letters, but in so exaggerated a quantitative disproportion of expended to received verbiage as to invite laughter. Either the dedicatory enterprise itself was ridiculously excessive, or its one-word pay-off ("Citoyen") was tragicomically paltry. Even what elsewhere passes for an enormous gain is here belittled before the fact: the *dédicace* will have managed only to confer on Jean-Jacques a new identity, which, radiating outward from the subject, gains gradual public acceptance. As Starobinski puts it: "Le titre de Citoyen de Genève n'est plus une périphrase mais une apposition" (3:1285). Foreshadowing relentlessly, these same lines reflect, however, on the vulnerability of any such identity to the ravages of time and public opinion. A seemingly decisive victory deteriorates into a radical paradox of nonconformity between titles and true merit, between one's own and others' versions of identity.

AUTO-AVILISSEMENT AND AUTOBIOGRAPHY

There, in a nutshell, is the problem of self-identity that the *Confessions,* as would-be monument to the character of Rousseau, confront at every turn. The autobiographer, whose secular immortality had long since been assured, worried not about "being forgotten," but about "being remembered as someone he himself would recognize."[34] As formulated by Gregory L. Ulmer, the question haunting Rousseau and his spiritual descendants ups the ante of immortality: they come to wonder obsessively "how, once they have attracted the attention of the crowd, they may preserve their 'true' identity, as distinct from the legend created in the perception of others."[35] The misunderstandings they strive to foreclose are those arising from attempts at getting beyond self-promotion to self-definition. Ulmer argues convincingly that only the early, unknown Rousseau may be wholly inscribed in the tradition of the Greek Herostratus, who so monomaniacally and enviously thirsted after fame that he settled for the notoriety of burning the temple of Modesty on the occasion of Alexander the (really) Great's birth. Rousseau's later, self-reflexive writings are credited by Ulmer with taking the tradition in a decisively modern direction.

This "defamiliarization or 'swerve' "[36] went largely unrecognized by those of Rousseau's contemporaries who continued to the death to taunt him with the name of "Erostrate." The preface to *Narcisse* could not make those contemporaries forget what kept being reconstrued as the flagrant opportunism of the First Discourse. "Indeed, his attack on the arts and sciences bears an allegorical resemblance to Herostratus's destruction of the beautiful temple."[37] Rousseau's eye-catching, iconoclastic entry into the Dijon Academy's essay contest had forever endowed his philosophical edifice with a foundation whose seeming shakiness could be recalled on the occasion of each further addition. R. A. Leigh, for one, reminds us of the sobriquet's staying power: "Lors des troubles de Genève, et surtout à partir de la publication des *Lettres de la Montagne* [en 1764], on appliqua volontiers à JJ lui-même, dans les milieux politiques orthodoxes, le surnom d'Erostrate."[38]

But Rousseau himself did not sit still forever for such in figura portraits. He moved beyond the desire for fame that the Greek arsonist has come to embody—somewhat misleadingly, as though that desire were not really the single most compelling motive of all classical art. Rousseau was never entirely cured of the Herostratan envy he most often evinces by transparent projection onto his "enemies." But he nonetheless proceeded, without a clean bill of health, to set himself the additional tasks of fashioning a durable self-image and making that image impervious to envy. Satisfaction of his desire for "honneurs publics" was as unsatisfactory to him as it remains for his spiritual descendants among us. Once granted, fame is not enough; it is "for ourselves" that we persist in wanting to be known. "The key to the modern applicability of the Herostratus factor . . . is the translation of reputation (fame) into identity. In the modern crisis of self, any identity will do so long as it can be determined that it is our identity, hence that selfhood is possible, just as for Herostratus any reputation would do so long as he had one."[39]

Ulmer cites the meta-autobiographical postface to Book 8 of the *Confessions,* and sees it as encapsulating the new crisis invented by Rousseau in the aftermath of setting his world on fire: "puisqu'enfin mon nom doit vivre, je dois tâcher de transmettre avec lui le souvenir de l'homme infortuné qui le porta, tel qu'il fut réellement, et non tel que d'injustes ennemis travaillent sans relâche à le peindre" (1:400). Ulmer does not, however, insist enough on the timeliness of these remarks, which are theoretically valid for the entirety of the *Confessions* but made with special pertinence both to the events just told in Book 8 and to the context of their telling. If, henceforth, Rousseau's "nom doit vivre," this certainty of afterlife derives specifically from his first, prize-winning *Discours* and among the broader, theater-going public, from the *succès de scandale* of *Le Devin du village.* But the autobiographer's rededication to the pursuit of identity also comes within striking distance of his afterthoughts on the dedication to Geneva: "Le seul avantage que me procura cet ouvrage . . . fut le titre de Citoyen qui me fut donné par mes amis, puis par le public à leur exemple, et que j'ai perdu dans la suite pour l'avoir trop bien mérité" (1:395). Rousseau's formula sketches the problem of preserving identity in the face of external (envious) efforts to undermine it. But it also exemplifies a solution privileged by the *Confessions.* The parting of the ways between identity and legend is appropriately rendered as paradoxical, for paradox ranks high among the "fool's inversions."[40] And it is likewise telling that Rousseau downplays the value even of identity, as though that were the best way possible to lull the green-eyed monster into a false sense of indifference.

Indeed, the selfhood to which these lines show the way is predicated on volunteering early and often to play the fool, on wresting the weapon of ridicule from the other, seizing envy's initiative, and burying oneself beneath more ridicule than the other could ever conceive of dishing out. Thoroughgoing autohumiliation provides the kind of preemptive strike that discourages biographical challenges to the autobiography. As a strategy of self-preservation, self-mockery aims at reducing the mockers to silence or, better yet, luring them into the vociferously impotent echoing of an antihero's text on which it becomes all but impossible to improve. And so, far from embellishing or ennobling the "facts," Rousseau will go out of his way to render them farcical. He will exploit the comic potential of various misadventures as a means to exercising artistic control over his self-image.

Among these "comical catastrophes,"[41] Ulmer lists the particularly "successful" failure of Jean-Jacques to shine before the committee of Genevan ministers that had been assembled to hear his abjuration of Catholicism and profession of faith:

> Cette attente m'effraya si fort qu'ayant étudié jour et nuit pendant trois semaines un petit discours que j'avois préparé, je me troublai lorsqu'il fallut le réciter au point de n'en pouvoir pas dire un seul mot, et je fis dans cette conférence le rolle du plus sot écolier. Les Commissaires parloient pour moi, je répondois bêtement *oui* et *non*: ensuite je fus admis à la communion et réintégré dans mes droits de Citoyen: je fus inscrit comme tel dans le rolle des Gardes que payent les seuls Citoyens et Bourgeois. (1:393)

Indeed, on the heels of extensive, ceremonial build-up, Jean-Jacques's inability to rise to so momentous an occasion might easily have been rendered as pure tragedy. Instead, all's well (but hardly heroic) that ends in comic anticlimax: an utter inconvertibility of input ("je répondois bêtement *oui* et *non*") into output ("ensuite je fus admis à la communion") underwrites what becomes a kind of *conversion manquée* or mock conversion. In this comic variant, the prodigal's unprovoked inability to deliver his prepared text becomes laughable, even laughably inconsequential. The "moment" itself is trivialized; the paragraph in which it is buried lapses into discussing the most mundane logistics of a projected move back to Geneva. And what might have been an experience of tragic alienation (one thinks of Diderot's nun) is converted into a particularly well-choreographed instance of prophylactic self-ridicule on the part of a formerly "besotted schoolboy."

Who would think to take issue with so laughable a contribution to the lore?—or, for that matter, with Rousseau's "memory" of feasting on Jean-Jacques's misfortunes at Mme Dupin's? How appropriately his *épître dédicatoire* provides the opening for this further gravitation of the potentially sublime toward the ridiculous. By virtue simply of writing that *épître*, Rousseau will have willfully espoused the *avilissement* that was widely held to be the inevitable posture of evitable dedication. He will have found the perfect forum for self-ridicule. But he will have found it unwittingly, thinking to avoid the inevitable, to defy the odds, to wax heroic and to be recognized as having waxed heroic. The dedication thus becomes, on his and our rereading, the textual site par excellence of confusion and incompatibility between old ends (fame) and new means (humiliation), themselves prophetic of new but unrecognized ends (self-identity). In the *épître*'s cacaphony or "indifférence," the two voices of the heroic and the antiheroic Rousseaus converge momentarily and vie to be heard; "louange" verging on "flagornerie" is delivered "avec emphase"; Roman *virtu* meets and meets its match in neo-Christian humility. Beyond the imagination of our conventionally wise theoreticians, a possibility emerges from this discordant duet for untold excesses of groveling to gratify and fortify the ego. *Auto-avilissement* extrapolated from its dedicatory context and rededicated to autobiography can work to position the self beyond the reach of its would-be persecutors. The anachronistic "hommage" he thought to have delivered may well have done Jean-Jacques's heart good. For Rousseau, the more lasting satisfaction lies in coming to know what he never admits directly: smirk though they may, detractors of his dedication have long since been beaten to the punch by the dedication's own shameless, even defiant sycophancy. He "asks for it" now, and, in retrospect, asked for it then. At some level, the autobiographer knows memory to be the "primary integrative force of the personality,"[42] especially the kind of memory that writing trumps up to trick past and present selves into mutual conformity. Acting on this knowledge, Rousseau introduces the pivotal dinner-table pantomime with an otherwise gratuitous nod to memory: "Je me souviens. . . . "

The *Confessions*' lingering over the dedicatory cover letter thus attests to its role in setting their own agenda and tone. The place of the enclosure or Second Discourse in Rousseau's œuvre had long since been assured and acknowledged: the *Institutions politiques* whose outline he recalls having "digested" in Geneva (1:394) are a logical outgrowth and obvious sequel. The *épître*'s ongoing importance remained less obvious and, for the autobiographer, more immediately relevant. In fact, explicit references to the *épître* only scratch the surface of that relevance. It turns out that the fait accompli of having dedicated can be called to account for virtually everything that "happens" to Jean-Jacques from the moment of departure for Geneva to the conclusion of Book 8. With no advance warning of their meta-autobiographical itinerary, the *Confessions* take us one more time all the way down the road of *auto-avilissement* to the partial clearing of identity. And not without some nostalgic backward glances at the high road of Augustinian redemption or at the still higher road of Roman heroism. But in order to appreciate how far and how emblematically Jean-Jacques—and a supporting cast charged, as ever, with acting out the author's residual anxieties[43]—will have fallen, we shall have to bring a third text into play.

ROUSSEAU'S LIVES AS LUCRETIA

To that text, a little known, incomplete prose tragedy entitled *La Mort de Lucrèce,* the *Confessions* allude explicitly only once, to say that it was begun during the Genevan sojourn—that is, in the suspenseful interval of deferment between the writing and reading of the *dédicace.* In a posthumous edition of Rousseau's complete works (1792), Gabriel Brizard published, under the title *Courts fragmens de Lucrèce, tragédie,* all that he could decipher from a manuscript in pencil, since lost. Discovery in this century of a second, presumably later manuscript has led to publication of what appear to be two complete acts and a tantalizing series of fragments (2:1871–82). Rousseau takes no official note of abandoning the project, in part because his motives in doing so are implicit in those alleged for its formulation: "je méditois . . . un plan de Tragedie en prose, dont le sujet qui n'étoit pas moins que Lucrece ne m'ôtoit pas l'espoir d'atterrer les rieurs, quoique j'osasse laisser paroitre encor cette infortunée, quand elle ne le peut plus sur aucun Theatre françois. Je m'essayois en même tems sur Tacite, et je traduisis le prémier Livre de son histoire qu'on trouvera parmi mes papiers" (1:394).

Any hope of getting a tragic Lucretia staged was already doomed in Rousseau's eyes by the general laws of successful dramaturgy he enunciated in his *Lettre à d'Alembert:* "Un auteur qui voudrait heurter le goût général composerait bientôt pour lui-même."[44] Prevailing taste was indeed against him: in eighteenth-century France, the plight of Lucretia had become the property of the comic repertoire and a "popular subject for parody." Inventorying the repertoire gives Ian Donaldson grounds for concurring with Rousseau and with his editor Jacques Scherer that "French audiences may have been predisposed to regard the story lightheartedly."[45] And removing any direct reference to the rape from the working title of his "Tragédie" may well have been Rousseau's way of attempting to circumvent "the prevalent assumption that rape was inherently comic."[46] It still remains to be seen what it was exactly that Rousseau's contemporaries found so amusing about a Roman matron whose name (and the generic *une Lucrèce*) had long since become synonymous with spotless female virtue, courage, and exemplary conjugal fidelity.

How could they make a laughingstock of this woman, whose heroic suicide following her rape by Sextus Tarquin, son of the reigning tyrant, had
first been chronicled by Livy and so often since commemorated ico-
nographically?[47]

The tragic Lucretia's partial demise stems in part from Augustine's
skeptical critique of her suicide. "There is no possible way out," reasons
Augustine. "If she is adulterous, why is she praised? If chaste, why was she
put to death?"[48] Surely it was not her conscience that Lucretia consulted
in taking such desperate (and sinful) measures, but rather—and this the
Augustinian mentality finds abhorrent and unassimilable—her reputation
in the eyes of others.[49] Unless, of course, the measures *were* appropriate
and a reliable indicator of her complicity, even pleasure, in the so-called
"rape."

It was evidently at this latter alternative that Rousseau's contemporaries sniggered: "Lucretia's suicide, so far from being proof of her innocence, is now [in the 1630s, when Jacques du Bosc wrote *L'Honneste
Femme*] seen to be a tacit confession of her moral corruption."[50] Rousseau, in turn, saw his contemporaries as envious and uncomprehending
of a virtue at once so austere and so little exemplified by their own
mores. The Rousseau who would, in self-defeating defiance of those
mores, have staged *La Mort de Lucrèce* intended, so he says, to "atterrer
les rieurs." But how? For as long as we do not actually read the extant
acts, we can assume that his would have been the Roman, the heroic, the
haughty stance. Far from courting ridicule, the translator of Tacitus
would have championed Lucretia and sent her forth to crush the sar-
casms of his enemies, as one might crush an insect between one's fingers.
And better yet, in making a spectacle and an exemplum of her virtue, the
playwright would himself have reprised the role of Junius Brutus, whom
history had honored with the titles "Brutus the Liberator" and "Father of
the Roman Republic." That Brutus, it will be recalled, seized the occasion
of Lucretia's suicide to thrust off the persona of a harmless simpleton (or
"dullard") in which he had previously cloaked his political insurgency.
By awakening the Roman populace to their collective violation by foreign
despots, he had succeeded in rallying them to an essentially conservative
revolt.[51]

It was in the guise of a not yet irretrievably humbled Brutus that
Rousseau had launched his *épître dédicatoire*: "Convaincu qu'il n'appartient qu'au Citoyen vertueux de rendre à sa Patrie des honneurs qu'elle

puisse avouer, il y a trente ans que je travaille à mériter de vous offrir un hommage public: et cette heureuse occasion suppléant en partie à ce que mes efforts n'ont pû faire, j'ai cru qu'il me seroit permis de consulter ici le zéle qui m'anime, plus que le droit qui devroit m'autoriser" (3:111). In a bold reversal of figure and ground, primary text and dedication, the *Discours* thus becomes Rousseau's Lucretia, his pretext (and pre-text) for patriotic address, supposedly thirty years in the making, to his compatriots. The Dijon Academy's second essay contest moves down the chain of causality to become the only occasional cause of an occasional cause, the *Discours,* which in turn only precipitates the "hommage public" that Rousseau claims to have made his life's single driving ambition. Had Rousseau pulled off a reversal that strains credibility, the Genevans would have recognized his civic zeal to replicate and resonate with that of Brutus. Their rapture would have matched that of Lucretia's "bourgeois" husband, Collatinus, in the final finished scene of the unfinished tragedy. There, it takes only a foretaste of eloquence to come to win Collatinus over to the Republican cause: "O Brutus, ta voix agite mon ame, et je me sens pénétré du feu celeste qui brille dans tes regards. Oui, que Rome soit libre! Quelle puissance peut resister à ton zéle et quel cœur lâche hésiteroit à le partager?" (2:1041).

But Brutus's oratorical victory is short-lived; Rousseau's calculating, envious courtisan of a Collatinus is slated—Brutus predicts as much (2:1042)—to betray the Republican cause, like some latter-day Judas. By way of confirmation, a fragment from some later act places Brutus and co-conspirator Lucretius under house arrest (2:1043). The tragedy would evidently have strayed sooner or later into the New Testament. Its outlines alone end up mocking Rousseau's inability to bring off or to sustain the role of the Roman Brutus in his dedication; we are left with the shadings of a Christ-like antihero. Rousseau's Brutus is given, symptomatically, to Providentialist turns of phrase: "Les Dieux ont voulu que Rome portat une fois le joug de la servitude pour apprendre à la conoitre et par consequent à la détester" (2:1039).

But the transformation of Brutus pales by comparison with that of Rousseau's Lucretia: she will, by the close of Act 1, have lost all but the remnants of her former Roman austerity. And in the process of bringing her down to earth, Rousseau will have devised a less direct and defiant strategy for "squashing the scoffers" than the frontal assault suggested by the *Confessions.* In immediate subversion of his avowed aim, the playwright wastes no time recalling that the heroine and her would-be assailant were, at one time, engaged to be married. To hear Sextus's ally Pauline tell it in the scene of exposition, Lucretia's father, the "inflexible" Lucretius, "rompit un mariage qui devoit faire le plus ardent de ses vœux" (2:1025). Needless to say, nothing of the kind occurs in the Roman source. Rousseau's flight of fancy opens wide the possibilities for bringing Lucretia too far down to earth. An eighteenth-century audience versed in the conventions of parental interference might well infer that Sextus and Lucretia, so-called rapist and victim, are best played as star-crossed lovers.

To be sure, successful modernization required the kind of love interest that Voltaire deplored, even though he usually bowed to public pressures.[52] On the occasion of publishing his own tragedy about Brutus's later expoits, Voltaire acknowledged: "Des critiques judicieux pourraient me demander pourquoi j'ai parlé d'amour dans une tragédie dont le titre est *Junius Brutus,* pourquoi j'ai mêlé cette passion avec l'austère vertu du sénat romain et la politique d'un ambassadeur." Voltaire then went on to plead the extenuating circumstances of prevailing taste. Likewise, in her "immensely long, digressive, inventive, and popular romance," *Clélie* (1654–60), Mlle de Scudéry had made "clandestine, passionate" lovers of Lucretia and Brutus, whose "chaste affair" is "finally terminated in a melodramatic nocturnal scene in Lucretia's garden at Collatia."[53] But Rousseau's other shoe has yet to fall; it does in Scene 5, when we learn conclusively from a Brutus as wise in affairs of the heart as in affairs of state that, unbeknownst to herself, Lucrèce does remain enamored, even adoring of the tyrant Sextus (2:1032). There is henceforth no question but that Rousseau has settled on the all but inconceivable love interest *most* perversely calculated to stimulate—*not* to silence— the catcalls of Lucretia's detractors. Why, we must ask, has he dragged the tragedy of an impeccable heroine down into the morass of still often unprovable date rape?

The strategy is, of course, identical to the one deployed in bringing Jean-Jacques himself down off the pedestal from which no other enemy could then, belatedly, topple him. He who laughs first thinks already to laugh last, and best. The theatrical project's execution belies its Roman sources: a tragicomic Lucrèce would not so much "crush" as court and so short-circuit ridicule. The playwright's precautionary measures anticipate the autobiographer's, especially insofar as Lucretia's *avilissement* remains, at the textual endpoint of his tragedy, unredeemed. Having set the stage not for a replay of Livy but for a Christian variant, Rousseau failed to follow through even to that alternative apotheosis. Only in imagination can we leap to the hypothetical moment when, in death, Lucrèce might have assumed the enormity of her own and her fellow Romans' guilt, leaving Church Father Brutus to declaim her eulogy and spread the apostolic gospel of a new salvation. Unless, of course, Brutus would have been proven wrong: did he misread Lucrèce as sinning in her heart? We will never know; nor will we know the exact nature of the impasse that precluded Rousseau from bringing his tragedy full circle to the *mort* announced by its title. Perhaps he was stymied by the problem of marrying the Classical and Christian traditions—a major problem, admittedly, in the *épître dédicatoire,* and one to which the *Confessions* bear discreet witness by segregating Jean-Jacques's readings of the Gospels (1:392) and of the Roman historians (1:394). Or perhaps, that problem really moot, it was his Christian contemporaries' more devastatingly "basses et sotes interpretations" (1:392) of Jesus Christ that paralyzed any movement toward 180-degree reversal of his heroine's fortunes. Rousseau may have come to know that the already finished business of endowing Lucretia with a new identity was the only end to which he could realistically aspire.

In any case, his lapsing into silence speaks volumes, as does the fact that Lucrèce, and not Brutus, lives on in the *Confessions* as the autobiographer's alter ego of choice. If the autobiographer abandons "her" story a second time, it is not without appropriating both the story itself and the means of its telling. In explicit confirmation of subterranean, in figura self-portraiture, the same *Confessions* that called Lucretia "cette infortunée" (1:394) reassign the epithet, six pages later, to Jean-Jacques. He becomes "l'homme infortuné" (1:400) whose life story must do the kind of telling all that privileges worst-case scenarios if the rumormongers are to be put out of business and his self-image steeled against their attacks. For Rousseau, as for the Lucrèce whose express desire to be forgotten by history veritably reeks of dramatic irony (1024), there can be no going back to a state of pre-Herostratan anonymity. He can only throw himself on the pyre from which the phoenix of fame may yet be reborn as identity.

But the sharing of an epithet is the least of Rousseau's slippage from the heights of Brutus's heroism into identification with Lucretia. En route to this conclusion, the autobiographical account of Jean-Jacques's return to Geneva already does a thorough job of dragging the Lucretia topos down into grotesquely modern depths. The *Confessions* press the actors of Jean-Jacques's real life into staging what might appropriately be entitled "the three farces of Lucretia." And the farcical trilogy is precisely what a Rousseau more thoroughly disabused of his prior ambitions might have seen fitter to write than a tragedy.

Symptomatically, the primary motivation invoked elsewhere for this journey, patriotic zeal, is trivialized here: Rousseau cites only his consenting to the *cause occasionnelle* of an invitation to accompany his friend Gauffecourt, who had business in Geneva (1:390). Feeling too ill to forgo the nursing services of his companion, Thérèse, Jean-Jacques brings her along. Having done so becomes a source of eternal chagrin: "Je dois noter ce voyage comme l'époque de la prémiére expérience qui jusqu'à l'age de quarante deux ans que j'avois alors, ait porté atteinte au naturel pleinement confiant avec lequel j'étois né, et auquel je m'étois toujours livré sans réserve et sans inconvenient" (1:390). Given this ominous and somewhat suspicious prelude—has Jean-Jacques's path not already been strewn with disillusions?—we comprehend much more quickly than he the imploring Thérèse's reason for not wanting to be left alone in the carriage with Gauffecourt. He, Jean-Jacques's so-called friend, has, from the outset of the voyage, seized every available opportunity to seduce her.

There is a perfect and obvious parallel between the narrative outlines of this story ("mon ami M. de Gauffecourt . . . travailloit depuis notre départ à corrompre une personne . . . qui appartenoit à son ami" [1:390]) and that fragment of *La Mort de Lucrèce* that, unattributed to any speaker, declares: "Le Vertueux Sextus s'efforce de corrompre la femme de son ami [Collatin]" (2:1044). It is what the *Confessions* say in the interstices that makes the comic difference. Rather than by some dashing *jeune premier* and darling of the masses, their Sextus is played by "mon ami M. de Gauffecourt, âgé de plus de soixante ans, podagre, impotent, usé de plaisirs et de jouissances"—in short, by a literally *boîteux diable.* The object of his seduction or Lucretia figure, on whose enviable "attraits" and "charmes" (2:1024) the tragedy had insisted, here becomes "une personne qui n'étoit plus ni belle ni jeune" (1:390).

Played to the hilt of grotesquery, the seduction of Thérèse takes the form of solicitation. Gauffecourt sinks so low as to "lui presenter sa bourse," and when that fails, he deploys pornographic literature ("un livre abominable . . . des figures infames") to get her in the mood. How comically righteous is the indignation that moves her to the extreme measure of throwing "son vilain livre par la portiére." As for the climactic tête-à-tête in chambers, there is nothing in Rousseau's real life to match the dramatic tension of Sextus's inability to manage such a meeting by the end of Act 2. The Roman tyrant is still rehearsing in the fragment of a soliloquy that, with all the pomposity of an *épître dédicatoire,* sings the praises of Lucrèce's "beauté céleste" and the unworthiness of the singer's own "infame cœur" (2:1045). Gauffecourt's path is, by contrast, unencumbered; already "le prémier jour," he takes advantage of Jean-Jacques's retiring with "une violente migraine" (the sort of violence from which tragic heroes were, of course, miraculously immune) to make his move. And, bypassing even the pretense of civilized courtship, Gauffecourt resorts to "des tentatives et des manœuvres plus dignes d'un satyre et d'un bouc que d'un honnête homme" (1:390).

The symbolism of Jean-Jacques's descending even from "un carrosse bourgeois" to walk and Thérèse's desiring to join him there is unmistakable: through insistence on physical infirmity and animal instincts, the tragedy of Lucretia has sunk below comedy into farce. Of his reaction to learning the truth, Rousseau writes: "Je tombai des nues" (1:390). But it is not so much our hero who "falls from the clouds" as the entirety of the drama that reserves for him the plum role of the cuckolded burgher Collatinus, elsewhere blinded by political ambition, here simply, stupidly blind. Given a more auspicious setting, this King of Fools might, like Brutus, have risen above the prevailing *abrutissement* and thought to expose and expostulate on the cadaver of Lucretia. When *not* in Rome, Jean-Jacques chooses instead, "pour ne pas exposer Thérèse," to repay Gauffecourt's hypocritical *avilissement* in kind: "Le malheureux me cachoit sa turpitude . . . je me vis forcé de lui cacher mon mépris, et de receler au fond de mon cœur des sentimens qu'il ne devoit pas connoitre" (1:391). In fact, the one whom Rousseau will have waited until these *Confessions* to avenge is not his Lucretia (Thérèse) but himself *as* Lucretia: "Douce et sainte illusion de l'amitié, Gauffecourt leva le premier ton voile à mes yeux. Que de mains cruelles l'ont empêché depuis lors de retomber!" (1:391). The *Confessions* do not so much put an end to Jean-Jacques's former bad faith as put the finishing touches on it. To hear the "moral" into which Rousseau seductively coaxes his story of attempted seduction, Gauffecourt's real crime (as opposed to the one he merely intended) would consist in the irreparable "rape" of Jean-Jacques's "naturel pleinement confiant" (1:390).

Are we then to read *La Mort de Lucrèce* as trivially autobiographical or superficially based on an event in the life of the real-life Rousseau? I think it much more likely that the passage exemplifies Rousseau's characteristic tendency toward "le réinvestissement de la fiction dans le vécu,"[54] and that a tragedy available for exemplary trivialization by the autobiography took the lead in mediating memory of the "event." For one thing, as we shall see, what "happens" next in the *Confessions* could be credited just as easily and arbitrarily as Gauffecourt's betrayal with inspiring the already written tragedy that holds sway over both episodes. And in its actual unfolding, that betrayal seems not in the least to have fazed its self-styled victim. The *Correspondance* and *Confessions* are full of expressions of undying enthusiasm for "le bon homme" Gauffecourt (1:468); he is charged here and only here with first destroying Jean-Jacques's illusions about friendship: "Quelle surprise! quel serrement de cœur tout nouveau pour moi! Moi qui jusqu'alors avois cru l'amitié inséparable de tous les sentimens aimables et nobles qui font tout son charme, pour la prémiére fois de ma vie je me vois forcé de l'allier au dédain, et d'ôter ma confiance et mon estime à un homme que j'aime et dont je me crois aimé!" (1:390–91). Stretching the facts of his immediate response gives Rousseau leeway to chronicle the corruption of pure, lofty, mutual sentiment in terms of dedicatory *avilissement.* In memory of the *épître* that, begun in Paris, underwrites the journey, the *Confessions* tell covertly of the dedication's fall from *honnêteté* into flattery, and of the conspiratorial cover-up that consists in pretending the model of reciprocity ("un homme que j'aime et dont je me crois aimé") still to be operative and positively charged. The "bas" and "honteux" (1:390) stratagems of seduction to which Gauffecourt resorts exaggerate and expose the essential asymmetry and veniality of the flattery-for-favors exchange. Having taken bribery one worse, from words for money to money for sex, he goes even further (and closer to dedication) in counting on a text replete with shameful/disgusting images ("figures infames") to arouse or flatter the senses of its *destinataire.* Thérèse's tossing the book no doubt prefigures Genevan rejection of the *épître* and so makes a travesty of trauma. That trauma is kept for the moment at arm's length: the *Confessions* safely victimize Jean-Jacques and ensconce Rousseau, whose "realistic" portraits are as belittling of Thérèse/Lucrèce as of Gauffecourt/Sextus, in the locus of scornful skepticism.

But that changes, although the topos does not, with a parting of the ways: "A Lyon je quittai Gauffecourt pour prendre ma route par la Savoye" (1:391). The journey's second stage, a last-ever visit to Mme de Warens, extends our reading of the life through the dual filter of *La Mort de Lucrèce* and of the *épître dédicatoire* and reconstitutes the sources of the departed Gauffecourt's shame as those of Jean-Jacques's own guilt. "Je la revis . . . ," writes Rousseau, suspensefully, of his beloved Maman, "dans quel état, mon Dieu! quel avilissement! que lui restoit-il de sa vertu prémiére? Etoit-ce la même Mad^c de Warens jadis si brillante à qui le Curé Pontverre m'avoit adressé? Que mon cœur fut navré! Je ne vis plus pour elle d'autre ressource que de se dépayser" (1:391). If "vertu" is hardly the first of Maman's attributes to come to mind on the basis of previous portraits, context continues to hold sway over fidelity to "fact." From Thérèse, Maman now takes over the role of Lucretia, as Brutus and Collatinus might have seen her after the rape. Whereas the Thérèse-Gauffecourt couple had been depicted, in absolute terms, as already old and infirm, past the point of love or being lovable, Mme de Warens's "avilissement" comes as a shock. Memory of a former incarnation makes of Jean-Jacques's visit (and of the remainder of Book 8) a kind of *matinée chez la Princesse de Guermantes*. The text specifies the threat that, even in the absence of tragic contingencies, the passage of objective time poses to selfhood. The question explicitly framed is the paramount question of self-identity: "Etoit-ce la même Mad^c de Warens?"

A fragment of *La Mort de Lucrèce* asks in strikingly similar terms, whether of Lucretia or of the virtue she incarnates, "Nos cœurs ont bien de la peine à l'aimer pure, brillante et parée encore de tous ses charmes; lui serons-nous plus fidelles quand les taches qu'elle aura receues nous auront disposés à la moins regretter?" (2:1043). By way of partially assuaging the guilt of his own neglectfulness, Rousseau invents grounds for believing that the desire to give Mme de Warens a change of scene ("la dépayser") will have been realized symbolically through the writing of the tragedy she seems, for the moment, to have inspired. But the *Confessions* know better than to refrain from regressing through the topos to the flattering preliminaries. It falls to Jean-Jacques to do a discreet imitation of Gauffecourt's comic variations on Sextus Tarquin's seductions: "Je lui réiterai vivement et vainement les instances que je lui avois faites plusieurs fois dans mes lettres. . . . Je lui fis encore quelque legere part de ma bourse" (1:391). Mme de Warens remains unmoved— albeit for less lofty reasons than a Lucretia attached not to her "pension" (1:391) but to "mon Epoux . . . mon Pére . . . mes Enfans" (2:1024). And so, whereas Rousseau had unceremoniously snatched the tragic heroine's pedestal out from under Thérèse, Mme de Warens is privileged to under- go a modicum of apotheosis. As though giving "herself" to Jean- Jacques/Sextus, she takes from her finger a euphemistic "dernier bijou" and places it on that of Thérèse, "qui la remit à l'instant au sien en baisant cette noble main qu'elle arrosa de ses pleurs" (1:391). The burlesque and tragic Lucretias are thus fused in a freeze-frame; *avilissement* becomes, at the last, paradoxically ennobled and ennobling.

From Maman's apotheosis, the two-timing Jean-Jacques is, however, frozen out. Then, if ever, writes a remorseful Rousseau, "c'étoit . . . le moment," the occasion to be seized: "Il falloit tout quitter pour la suivre, m'attacher à elle jusqu'à sa derniére heure, et partager son sort quel qu'il fut" (1:391). Instead, "Je n'en fis rien. . . . [j]e gémis sur elle"—or made a halfhearted pass at writing a tragedy with her in mind—"et ne la suivis pas" (1:392). So near, and yet so very far. For a still-guilty Jean-Jacques, there will be no identifying, except in spirit and in a trumped-up letter of dedication, with the heroically opportunistic Junius Brutus. Witness the modern autobiography's derisory attempts to reproduce the almost mag- ical narrative copula—defiled Lucretia-Rome revenged—at the heart and soul of the haunting Roman legend. Not for want of trying, the auto- biography's Rousseau makes a hollow mockery of Brutus's former ability to preside over the direct, simultaneous translation of personal tragedy into political discourse and action. The only connection the *Confessions* are up to forging is syntactic; they announce, fast on the heels of failure to follow Maman, that "avant mon départ de Paris j'avois esquissé la dédi- cace de mon *Discours sur l'inegalité*" (1:392). The Catholic Mme de Warens means nothing to the Calvinist Genevans, nor they to her; dedica- tion to them bespeaks a sinful lack of dedication to her. In testimony to the tragicomic fragmentation of modern life, the *Confessions* have now twice told the story of Lucretia without endowing it with any redeeming social value. And in the process, a Jean-Jacques who falls indifferently into the roles of Collatinus and Sextus Tarquin has twice faltered on the brink of readmission into the heroic sphere of action frequented by Brutus. The reflex to reverse directions and divert these farces of Lucretia toward straightforward heroism on the Antique model has already slowed perceptibly in the interval between what masquerades as a dastardly betrayal of sacred friendship and what Rousseau admits to despising about the lukewarm lover in himself.

It remains only for Rousseau to espouse the crisis of identity as his own and to replace the existential inevitability of *avilissement* with the autobiographical strategy of *auto-avilissement*. The shock of visiting Maman is repeated when Jean-Jacques, back in Paris, receives an unexpected visit from his old friend Venture, "qui vint me surprendre un beau matin, lorsque je ne pensois à rien moins" (1:398). An invitation is explicitly tendered to link this third and final spectacle of physical and moral deterioration with that of Mme de Warens. It is "cette femme angélique" whom the young Jean-Jacques had first neglected in his *engouement* (1:125) for Venture, and who "maintenant n'étoit guéres moins changée que lui" (1:398). Here, too, identity is the issue, its emerging preeminence underscored by the formerly decisive role of Venture in the young Jean-Jacques's obsessive quest for fame and fortune. It is the chameleon Venture, Venture the successful social climber, whose "grand mérite" and "rares talens" had kindled our hero's ambition and envy (1:133). And it is in flattering imitation of *his* Alexander, the self-styled "Venture de Villeneuve," that our hero as mock-heroic Herostratus had adopted the anagrammatic pseudonym "Vaussore de Villeneuve" and undertaken, with humiliating results, to pass himself off as a teacher and composer of music (1:147–50). Of this formerly dazzling Venture, there remains no perceptible trace: "Qu'il me parut changé! Au lieu de ses anciennes graces je ne lui trouvai plus qu'un air crapuleux, qui m'empêcha de m'épanouir avec lui. . . . Je le vis presque avec indifférence. . . . " (1:398). Venture thus becomes a sort of backwards Brutus, his trajectory the reverse of the Roman hero's emergence from the shadows of self-imposed imbecility: "la débauche avoit abruti son esprit" (1:398).

Or, rather, that *may* be the case. The hypothesis of Venture's objective transformation occupies a middle ground between those of an equally radical transformation on the part of the subject Jean-Jacques and a universal, inescapable deterioration of all being in time: "Ou mes yeux n'étoient plus les mêmes, ou la débauche avoit abruti son esprit, ou tout son prémier éclat tenoit à celui de la jeunesse qu'il n'avoit plus" (1:398). The alternative is, nonetheless, only apparent: the sight of Venture universalizes *and* personalizes the mockery that death-in-life makes of human ambitions and so devalues momentary "éclat." Julia Kristeva knows Rousseau's horror: "The corpse, seen without God and outside of science, is the utmost of abjection. It is something rejected from which one does not part, from which one does not protect oneself as from an *object*."[55] Everyman, every *man*, is a Lucretia, his posthumous reputation subject to the infinite caprices and devices of historical revisionism; only the wise fool knows, like Rousseau, if not to stave off physical death, at least to write his self into a perpetual state of *auto-avilissement* as a hedge against the "indifférence" of non-identity.

Playing the madeleine to Jean-Jacques's Marcel, Venture's visit eventually triggers an avalanche of "durable" memories and reconstitutes recorded memory as fundamentally integrative of the autobiographical self. But the *Confessions* passage is not content merely to recall the "transports desormais perdus pour moi" (1:399) of the young Jean-Jacques's amorous adventures; it also previews a forthcoming orgy of *auto-avilissement*. In Book 9, these same "transports" will stage a "retour tardif et funeste" (1:399): infatuation with Sophie d'Houdetot—married, already involved elsewhere, and young enough to be his daughter—will give Jean-Jacques the opportunity to outdo the outrageous seduction of Thérèse by Gauffecourt. Rousseau will wax sarcastic at his own expense, and even—is there no bottom to this barrel?—at the expense of what become his delusions of *avilissement*: "n'allai-je pas me fourrer dans la tête que l'amour desormais si peu convenable à mon age, à mon maintien, m'avoit avili aux yeux de Mad^e d'Houdetot . . . " (1:442). Thanks to the same kind of historical revisionism that has made a travesty of Lucretia's seduction, Book 9 will not merely remember one of Jean-Jacques's pasts (with Sophie), but rewrite those more distant ("tous ces ravissans délires d'un jeune cœur" [1:398]) in the comic register.

More than anything else, this self-protective knowledge of "folie" (1:442) or silliness to come permits Book 8 to end on an upbeat or optional grace note. Having played out the three farces of Lucretia, the *Confessions* make a last-ditch effort to vindicate the dedication to Geneva and salvage the honor of the dedicator. Success as a hero is no longer crucial, thanks to the assurance of an undisputed prior claim on the territory of antiheroism. There being nothing left to lose and paradise lost to be regained, Rousseau takes a stab at having both a recognizable and a reputable identity. "The abject is edged with the sublime."[56] Hence the "pure" pleasure (1:399) Rousseau derives from recounting the so-called "affaire Palissot." Onto the person of Palissot, author of an anti-philosophical "divertissement" entitled *Le Cercle ou les Originaux,* Rousseau projects his own former sins and sorrows of dedication. In *Le Cercle* Palissot had invented a character, Blaize Nicodème, in unmistakable if relatively innocuous satirical imitation of Rousseau. Imputations of Rousseau's obsession with fame and of his ruthless opportunism were already legend when Blaize chimed in: "Hé! qu'importe, si par là [ses paradoxes] je me suis fait une réputation? Pensés-vous, lorsque j'ai débuté que je n'aye pas ri moi-même de me trouver des Partisans. . . . J'ai débité toutes ces belles choses sans les croire, dans l'idée qu'un Philosophe devoit penser, parler, écrire et même s'habiller autrement que le Vulgaire. J'ai refusé jusqu' à de l'argent pour ne ressembler à personne."[57] At this stage in the *Confessions,* Palissot's attacks are woefully behind the times. Reputation is no longer the issue; it costs Rousseau little enough to contribute to Palissot's notoriety. Nor does it matter that *Le Cercle* makes a belated mockery of Rousseau's pretentious sincerity, of his highly touted personal *réforme,* and of his refusal of a royal pension. As exempted even from Rousseau's own selective revisionism, these highlights of Book 8 will have weathered the storm of satire, thanks to a fatal miscalculation on Palissot's part.

In staging his "divertissement" for the Polish king Stanislas, who had vigorously argued against the conclusions of Rousseau's First Discourse, Palissot "crut apparemment faire sa cour, en jouant dans ce Drame un homme qui avoit osé se mesurer avec le Roi la plume à la main" (1:399). But, by the *Confessions'* calculations, the would-be courtier has underestimated a king both "généreux" and quickly moved to righteous indignation.[58] Rousseau's Stanislas promptly threatens, as his real-life counterpart eventually did, to have Palissot banished from the Royal Academy. Applying the general lessons of Marmontel, d'Alembert (who may well have initiated these reprisals on Rousseau's behalf) deemed the punishment fitting "quand un auteur, assez vil pour prostituer ainsi sa plume, se pare de la protection prétendue qu'un grand roi lui accorde."[59] For his part, Jean-Jacques argues in the *Confessions'* "vive priére" that Palissot should be pardoned and that all traces of the affair should be excised from the "registres de l'Académie."

And well Rousseau might take advantage of this rare opportunity to imagine what it might have been like to play God the Son for the duration. Feeling nothing but pity for the obviously envious Palissot puts

Jean-Jacques for the short term in an enviable position: "Tout cela fut accompagné tant de la part du Roi que de celle de M. de Tressan de témoignages d'estime et de considération dont je fus extrémement flatté, et je sentis en cette occasion que l'estime des hommes qui en sont si dignes eux-mêmes produit dans l'ame un sentiment bien plus doux et plus noble que celui de la vanité" (1:399). Having been serendipitously elevated in royal eyes and named to the most elite of mutual admiration societies, Rousseau basks, through no fault of his own, in the deferred, heady, uncomplicated pleasures that neither nondedication to Louis nor dedication to Geneva had procured.

Or does he? Was it Jean-Jacques or was it Palissot who got the response of unmitigated disgust that Rousseau's dedication to Geneva really deserved? Do the *Confessions,* by their discreet idealization of Stanislas's response, endow with factitious "pureté" a pleasure really attained through the detours of aggressive-defensive projection? Could Rousseau's Palissot, for all his self-aggrandizing sycophancy, be nothing more than a sacrificial straw man? At a considerable temporal remove, the *Confessions* work to foreclose this possibility of projection. By way of ex post facto self-congratulation for Rousseau's having held to his promise of no further dedications, Book 8 points the simple moral that there is more to be gained by forgiving foolish mortals than by joining in their no-win dedicatory games. But it was *La Mort de Lucrèce* that followed immediately on the heels of the *épître* to Geneva. And *La Mort de Lucrèce* leaves otherwise unresolved and haunting of Rousseau's first person the anxiety provoked by dedication's still fresh and guilty secrets.

ONCE A FLATTERER . . .

It takes a flatterer to know one. Or so it would seem from a meditation on flattery more thorough and subtle in Rousseau's occasional tragedy than in all the explicit theorizing of his contemporaries. That meditation is the playwright's primary contribution to modernization of the Lucretia topos, however suggestively he may have rewritten the roles of Lucretia and Brutus. Those two major players are hopelessly overshadowed by the quantitatively larger roles that the extant text reserves for their underlings, all of whom combine forces in what gradually takes shape as a counter-conspiracy to seduce Lucretia. The historico-legendary political conspiracy to overthrow the Tarquins remains, in contrast, strikingly undermanned. Whereas Republican leader Brutus does not even appear until Scene 5 and can count only Lucretius among his proven allies on stage, Sextus Tarquin is amply aided from the outset. His cause is served not only by the blindly ambitious Collatinus and by his own confidant, the *affranchi* Sulpitius, but even, as we learn belatedly and with abhorrence, by the confidante to whom Lucrèce will already have bared her soul in Scene 1, Pauline. Reassigning the name of Corneille's Christian heroine to a duplicitous servant makes marginalization and degradation of the heroic a fait accompli in a play where, as Jacques Scherer puts it, "Les confidents jouent . . . un rôle important. . . . De longues scènes leur sont dévolues et les personnages principaux, qui cherchent le secret, sont obligés de passer par leur intermédiaire, ce qui provoque inévitablement un ralentissement de l'action" (2:1871). The action does next to nothing to advance the Republican cause. But even the rape/suicide, which Montesquieu's history of Rome had trivialized as a paradigmatically "only occasional" cause,[60] is subjected in turn to seemingly interminable delays. This regression through hitherto "unrevealed" behind-the-scenes manipulations is both logical and profoundly moral: apparently obsessed with the *bas-fonds* of his *monde à l'envers,* Rousseau lingers longer there than either good drama or a lifelong distaste for servile flattery would dictate. In unfulfilled anticipation of dueling to the death in singular combat with Sextus, his Lucrèce is surrounded and besieged by an entire irregular army of courtiers in friends and lovers' clothing.

Between Rousseau's invented plot and the one he inherited from Antiquity, there is a telling fragility of integration. As though echoing the unmanageable reconciliation of heroic with flattering dedication, the playwright twice resorts, when the dastardly Sulpitius spies Brutus and Lucretius from afar, to those *liaisons de fuite* on which proper tragedies frowned (2:1031, 1036–37). It seems that the air Brutus breathes would be contaminated by even passing intercourse with the members of the enemy camp, whose collective vileness and unmitigated me-firstism come out detail by disgusting detail. The opening moment of Scene 2 is particularly melodramatic and is commemorative of Rousseau's *épître.* To Lucrèce, messenger Sulpitius explains that he has come to "[v]ous avertir, Madame, de la prochaine arrivée du Prince et de votre Epoux et vous remettre une Lettre de sa part." In response, Lucrèce asks for clarification of the ambiguously referential possessive: "De la part de qui?" (2:1027). She asks as though it made a difference that the letter comes not from

Sextus, the reigning "courtisan vulgaire," but from the husband, Collatin, whose "humanité" and "passions douces et modérées" (2:1026) Lucrèce has just defensively extolled to Pauline. As it happens, the "Lettre" bids Lucrèce make ready to receive the prince to whose favor Collatin has inextricably tied his own ambitions. It reveals nothing other than the courtier in Collatin: "Faites-lui donc préparer un logement convenable et songez en recevant l'héritier de la Couronne que c'est de lui que dépend la fortune de vôtre Epoux" (2:1027). With no real antidote in sight, contagious flattery runs rampant through the environs, as do the tell-tale verbs *flatter* and *se flatter*.

As further revelations of *bassesse intéressée* follow in quick succession, a relentless recurrence of those verbs symptomizes Rousseau's preoccupations of the moment just as reliably as had the pathological "honneur" of his preface to *Narcisse*. No sooner have we learned in Scene 3 that Pauline has betrayed Lucrèce out of love for Sulpitius (2:1028), than Sulpitius's Scene 4 soliloquy reveals his contempt for the "love object" he is merely stringing along as a means to gratify his own *arriviste* ambitions: "il faut la [Pauline] flater d'une union chimérique, jusqu'à ce qu'avec son secours Lucréce séduite et Sextus satisfait laissent pour ainsi dire à ma discrétion le choix de mes récompenses" (2:1031). Even this scorn for the gullible Pauline pales by comparison with the contempt that Sulpitius betrays in "friendly" tête-à-tête with the princely avatar of the dedication's MAGNIFIQUES, TRES HONORES ET SOUVERAINS SEIGNEURS. The confidant flatters (2:1034) his master's hopes of amorous conquest only in order that he, Sulpitius, may someday rule Rome from behind the scenes. It falls logically to Rousseau's "affranchi," still imprisoned and advantaged by a slave mentality, to demystify his "dedication" to lord, lady, and lover, and to posit the mutual neediness on which literary dedication feeds:

[V]ous n'ignorez pas que dans nôtre condition les vices de nos maitres nous servent de dégrés pour monter à la fortune, et que c'est en excitant leurs passions que nous parvenons à contenter les nôtres. Nous serions perdus s'ils étoient assés sages pour savoir se passer des secrets services par lesquels nous les enchainons. C'est ainsi qu'à son tour on se rend necessaire à ceux de qui l'on dépend, et le plus grand malheur qui put arriver à un Courtisan ambitieux seroit de servir un prince raisonnable et juste qui n'aimeroit que son devoir. (2:1029–30)

Such lucid interlocutors are, luckily for Sulpitius, in shorter supply in Rousseau's anachronistic Rome than in the real-life Geneva where his dedication played to mixed reviews among the "reasonable" and "just." Dismissing even Lucretia's "vertu" and "devoir" as the kind of "grands mots" or moral babble to which only a dupe like Pauline would give credence (2:1028), the cynical slave goads his master into action, or rather into neodedicatory speech acts. Sulpitius is so familiar with the territory that he is able to prescribe some refinements that might have stood Rousseau himself in good stead. If Sextus is to avoid becoming his own worst enemy, he must be sure to tone down his "transports indiscrets," even to the point of blurring his agenda: "ce n'est qu'en couvrant vos projets du plus profond mistére que vous pouvez vous flater de les lui faire approuver" (2:1035). Is that what a reckless Rousseau failed to do or an over-cautious Rousseau did too well in the epistle to Geneva? The question is intriguing, if impossible to answer without clearer access to the dedicator's personal and political agenda. But Sulpitius's impromptu advice to dedicators also raises suspicions about the seemingly disinterested moderation of the epistle to Duclos, especially insofar as Sulpitius himself incarnates the insatiable hubris of the minion who would outrank his monarch in all but name.

More disquieting still are the "transports indiscrets" to which, pending desperately needed editorial assistance from Sulpitius, Sextus—madly in love, for all we know, with Lucrèce—continues to give voice. There can be no failing to realize that of the four skeletal characters inherited from Livy, it is not Brutus, Lucrèce, or even Collatin, but foreign interloper, textbook tyrant, and known rapist Sextus whose tirades most closely and consistently approximate the "sentiments" and "hopeless" sincerity of Rousseau's second dedication. Even as he excuses his "égaremens" and "discours insensés" and pledges "docilité" to his editor's "avis," Sextus goes on, in the same breath, to mount a penetrating assault on the object of his "devotion" and on the republic for which she stands: "[T]u me vois enivré d'amour au point que je ne suis plus capable de me conduire. Lucréce est toujours au fond de mon cœur et devant mes yeux, j'entens sa douce voix, ses divins regard[s] sont tournez sur moi; les miens ne peuvent voir qu'elle; mon existence est toute en elle seule, je ne vis que pour l'adorer et toutes les puissances de mon ame aliénée de toute autre objet sufisent à peine aux sentimens qui me consument" (2:1035). So inescapable and sinister are the parallels with Rousseau's likewise all-consuming project of dedication to the later republic of Geneva that the same lines that provisionally "humanize" Sextus tend just as inevitably to make an unmitigated monster of the dedicator. And of dedication they make a more reliable indicator of humanity's darkest, most inhuman depths than, in their measured metaphors, Marmontel and company ever dared dream. Self-knowledge, it turns out, comes just as surely, surprisingly, and revoltingly to the erstwhile dedicator as to his dupes. Not only is Rousseau's Sextus under no illusions when it comes to knowing himself to be "le plus vil des mortels" (2:1045), even in soliloquy, but Rousseau himself must know in what inexcusable and uneditable violence his fellow flatterer's "transports" would have to culminate were he to complete *La Mort de Lucrèce.*

By dint of his ill-advised outpourings, even the villain of the piece ends up making Rousseau sit still for unflattering in figura self-portraiture and keeps the play from finding a clear path back to Brutus's lofty heroism or even to Lucrèce's modest, suspect virtue. More ironies than we could list accrue to the partial identification of Geneva's self-styled citizen with Sextus as heir apparent to an ill-gotten throne. The Roman republic's most overtly declared enemy pays not even lip service to interest in the affairs of state, and "dedicates" his every thought and act to the pursuit of private, criminal passions, to having his say, and to winning back on his own terms what once was his. Fundamental to the uneasiness manifested in *La Mort de Lucrèce* is Rousseau's knowing his dedication to have secretly diverted even other-directed, public-spirited occasional discourse to the Swiss bank account of self-promotion.

There is thus no urgency about acting out the violence of intent and reprisals lurking from the first in the play's seemingly infinite regress of dupery and in the unprecedented infusion of the Lucretia topos with flattery's euphemistic figures. To stage the rape, *bienséances* permitting, would be a redundant, anticlimactic adding of injury to the multiple insults that Lucrèce has already suffered at the hands of the playwright and his conspiratorial surrogates. Physical violence would even detract from the playwright's selective, ill-disguised ventriloquism. Seeming to have mastered only the trick of projecting the modern-day dedicator's voice of (self)-flattery into ancient Rome's every recess, Rousseau does not so much vamp until ready as only, obsessively vamp.

La Mort de Lucrèce thus fulfills, ironically, the *Lettre à d'Alembert*'s prophecy that any nonconforming playwright would end up writing "pour lui-même." Psychodrama serves the erstwhile dedicator as a short course of self-therapy. *In camera* Rousseau can both indulge his unconfessed vice to the hilt and take heart from the *Lettre*'s further assurances that what gets said in the pages of self-styled tragedies has nothing to do with anyone's real life: "Heureusement la tragédie telle qu'elle existe est si loin de nous, elle nous présente des êtres si gigantesques, si boursouflés, si chimériques, que l'exemple de leurs vices n'est guère plus contagieux que celui de leurs vertus n'est utile."[61] Perhaps the tragedy did the trick of abjecting the flatterer in Rousseau and allowing the crisis of *auto-avilissement* to pass on already attenuated to the *Confessions'* stock of hazy, self-serving memories. Julie Kristeva suggests the alternative possibility that "from its place of banishment, the abject [did] not cease challenging its master."[62] The traces of his occasional abjection may have prodded Rousseau into reasserting mastery over the Lucretia topos at the very moment of committing his definitive self-image to the pages of the *Confessions*.

The autobiography implicated in some such scenario surely makes a special point of converting dedicatory losses into autobiographical gains. That means privileging the figure of Lucretia as alter ego and muse and isolating, meta-autobiographically, the moment of an all but unprovoked and unproductive suicide. Using his pen, as she will have used the sword, the Rousseau of Book 8 will finish himself off in anticipation of would-be rapists' dealing a fatal blow to his self-identity or—wherever the palimpsest cannot quite bring itself to obliterate the original of heroic ambitions—to his self-esteem. The still transitive death blow nevertheless resists translation into metaphorical, political terms and becomes, admittedly, solipsistic. Bypassing the detours of ostensibly other-directed flattery, Rousseau will get right down to the business of *auto-avilissement* and leave all the others out of it, except as imagined instigators (his enemies), bystanders recruited from real life for purposes of demonstration (Gauffecourt, Maman, Venture, Palissot, et al.), and the posterity of reader-witnesses to be nonplussed, ideally, by there being nothing more incriminating to say. A Rousseau inspired less by the demise of Lucretia than by the passing of a certain unambiguously exalted way of reading that demise will trade the heroic rhetoric of letters to the republic for a second chance, a chance at "being" in the eighteenth-century Republic of Letters.

There is much more to say. Ironically, even readings like this one that seek to expose and understand the self-protective facticity of Rousseau's occasional antiheroism end up helping to protect the possibility of a self-inscription that under more favorable circumstances might dispense entirely with the distortions of strategic planning. That is the dream of transmissible selfhood that keeps Rousseau writing and, more specifically, keeps the urge to frame occasional messages with selected others in mind from dying gracefully with the second and last *épître dédictoire.* The hope of successfully addressed self-portraiture springs eternal, especially in Rousseau. The *Lettres à Malesherbes,* to name but the most obvious exception to the *Confessions'* eventual rule of damage inflicted for the sake of damage control, culminate in a new instance of devil-may-care dedication to their *destinataire.* And, more discreetly, as we shall see in chapter 3, the *Préface de Julie* reaches out from the margins of another bestseller and from the desert of another self-imposed exile in tacit solicitation of a particular patron and friend.

3

(Without) Naming Names:
The *Préface de Julie*

Le sort fait les parents, le choix fait les amis.

Delille

Cette alternative ne me paroit pas si necessaire qu'à vous.

Rousseau

W ith the superfluous publication of a second preface to his novel *Julie, ou la nouvelle Héloïse,* Rousseau's occasional self-portraiture took an important but tentative step out of margins. The *Préface de Julie* was, on the one hand, freestanding and, on the other, unquestionably devoted to the novel, except insofar as Rousseau distractingly played the prefacer's stock role of "editor" in figura. A prior instance of the exorbitant doubling that gave us two (prefaces) for one (novel) places "editor" R in adversarial and mutually defining tête-à-tête with "man of letters" N, and begs the question of dialogue. Especially when the *Préface* is read against the defiantly monologic "Préface" that had actually headed the novel, the Rousseau between the lines of February 1761 is revealed to have been in a state of considerable agitation and telling ambivalence. In the throes of self-contradiction, he sounds as open as absolutely opposed, and as absolutely opposed as open, to the possibility of discussing his novel with any man of letters. These vacillations between affective extremes can most readily be accounted for by a provisional identification of interlocutor N as erstwhile friend and mentor Diderot, with whom Rousseau had recently, dramatically, and painfully severed all extraliterary ties.

What nonetheless rescues the *Préface* from the banality of a dramatized roman à clef is the fact that Rousseau makes a point of leaving the identification implicit. Operating in the vaguely autobiographical sphere of unmistakable but unconfirmed resemblances gives him the latitude to inscribe N/Diderot in a nebulous but obsessive paradigm of paternity. It remained for the *Confessions* only to appropriate and plot that paradigm as the "true" story and personal myth of a two-stage, paternally engineered fall into reading (Isaac Rousseau) and writing (Diderot).

But even beyond that is the suggestive asymmetry of the R/N dyad. On the one hand, interlocutor R is identified with extraordinary pomp as none other than Rousseau himself and is made, in a remarkable departure from prefatory usage, to pronounce a vow of absolute sincerity. On the other hand, the unnamed N becomes a nexus of mutually aggrandizing fusion between biological fathers and paternal surrogates. Already rehearsing the constitutive autobiographical and referential pacts of the *Confessions,* Rousseau nonetheless hesitates to give up altogether the proven flexibility, irresponsibility, and separate but equal truthfulness of occasional fictions. Poised on the near side of commitment to a more unequivocal brand of life writing, the *Préface de Julie* illuminates the *Confessions'* self-serving partiality. Their reading or "third preface" to *Julie* is an exemplary case in point and gives rise to some still open questions of difference: between autobiographical fiction and autobiography proper, and between inventing autobiography and claiming the patent.

MORE THAN A PREFACE?

"Je me rappelle deux passages*** . . . " (2:25). Rousseau writes at this point in the *Préface de Julie* as though in perfect compliance with the mainstay of prefatory apologetics known as "helpfully" screening the primary text for passages enabling and supportive of whatever interpretation the author wants to urge on the reading public. On this occasion, Rousseau nonetheless has something in mind besides doing his duty as best he can by *Julie.* Not that the novel, which would turn out to be the eighteenth century's most popular and influential, comes in for anything like the slights of commission and omission to which Rousseau had subjected his *Narcisse; Julie* is extensively discussed and just as warmly embraced. Mid-eighteenth-century France qualifies as one of those times and places when, by dint of untold repetition or "une régularité aujourd'hui surprenante,"[1] novel-prefacing in particular had attained "une sorte de perfection technique" and "une certaine absurdité préfacière."[2]

Checklist in hand, we can confirm that, on *Julie*'s behalf, Rousseau left no
well-worn stone unturned. And yet, "Je me rappelle deux passages*** . . . "—what follows the suspension points amounts to a partial
and paradigmatic suspension of prefacing as usual. When the authorial
footnote signaled by Rousseau's three asterisks goes on to locate the two
noteworthy "passages" not within the territorial limits of *Julie*, but in the
preface to *Narcisse* and in the *Lettre à d'Alembert*, the normal retrieval
processes of selective memory are effectively released from exclusive
preoccupation with the prefaced novel. As would any such extraneous
recollections, these two work at disrupting preface-to-prefaced sym-
biosis. The kind of stretching Rousseau had done to echo the First Discourse in the preface to *Narcisse* accedes here to the unambiguous status
of deliberate allusion. Supplementing an inherited intertext with two that
he has freely chosen and clearly identified, Rousseau removes our novel
readers' blinders and reconstitutes the preface of his most recent work as
writing with the more remote and checkered past of a particular individual's curriculum vitae.

His making a pair of philosophical works relevant to discussion of a
mere novel redounds to the advantage of *Julie*. But why should Rousseau
have singled out these two in particular as his intertexts of choice? In
anticipation of tracking down the addendum of content to which the
Lettre à d'Alembert helps to divert *Julie*'s preface, we might first appreciate with what pertinence the footnote formalizes the link between past
and present instances of prefacing. For, with the *Préface de Julie*,
Rousseau's liminary self-indulgence not only compounds the excesses of
the preface to *Narcisse* but inches toward autonomy. The earlier preface
was already too long and too solicitous by far of the reader's undivided
attention to be skipped over lightly as a perfunctory nod to publishing
conventions; the *Préface de Julie* goes on at even greater length, for a full
twenty pages in the Pléiade edition. But this later *Préface* also outdid the
outlandishness of the dedication to Geneva. It was no longer a matter
simply of overdressing a major work for publication, but rather of subjecting liminary space to serious overcrowding. This time, Rousseau all
but signed away his right of recourse to the alibi of prefacing as required
writing: he tendered his *Préface de Julie* as a "brochure"[3] unto itself—
hence, the italics for which the title "Préface" does not normally
qualify—*and* as the second of two published and virtually simultaneous
prefaces to one and the same novel.

Julie already had a perfectly serviceable two-page "Préface" and had been in print for two weeks when the *Préface de Julie* first appeared under separate cover. And, I should add, according to plan: the so-called *seconde préface* or *préface dialoguée* did not respond, as authors' prefaces to subsequent editions sometimes do, to anything that had transpired in the negligible interval of deferment. This second preface is so far from representing a more advanced stage of the author's thinking as to have been published second but written first. Resurrected "as is," at Rousseau's insistence and by pre-arrangement with his publisher, the *Préface de Julie* thus went beyond solicitation to command attention as the next closest thing to an autonomous text in its own right.

Rousseau's contemporaries did take notice. Bypassing the fundamental enigma of its accession to the public domain, they characterized the text itself as "enigmatic." It is to an unabashed Rousseauphile, Mme de Cramer-Delon, that the *Préface* owes its designation as "une maniere d'énigme" (and, incidentally, an enigmatic, unsubstantiated claim to have found the missing *mot*).[4] But Grimm only cast the same findings in a more negative light with his aggressive-defensive dismissal of "en quatre-vingt-dix pages un recueil fort serré de sophismes où la bonne foi est offensée à chaque ligne."[5] The *Préface de Julie* remains somehow opaque and problematical; it is the sort of text that inspires more than the average number of vows to "write an article someday." Recent readings by literary theorist Paul de Man and historian Robert Darnton have validated the widespread intuition that the preface would be worth the effort of a second look.[6]

De Man pays the preface the supreme compliment of making it the high point of intellectual sophistication in *Julie* and, beyond that, the site of Rousseau's acquiring knowledge about the undecidability of reference that would prove vital to his writing of the *Confessions.*[7] The normal preface-prefaced hierarchy becomes subject to reversal when it is suggested that, from an epistemological standpoint, Rousseau's novel is best reconceived as prefacing his preface. De Man thus comes close to instancing the radicalism of Jacques Derrida's move to make a demarginalized, no longer *stricto sensu* prefacing coextensive with any and all writing: "il n'y a que du texte, il n'y a que du hors texte, au total *une préface incessante.*"[8] If the *Préface* is not exactly more than a preface, neither, at this level of abstraction, is any other text we could name. The case for this collapse of difference is conveniently buttressed by what Rousseau himself knew to be a preface too intellectually challenging for mass consumption.[9] But even supposing that the *Préface* had turned out to be less provocatively enigmatic, it would have done its part to raise metaprefatory questions about its own place in the great scheme of texts.

Having been characterized by an introductory "Avertissement" as a "Dialogue ou Entretien supposé" (2:9), the *Préface de Julie* takes up where the prefaced novel had left off. There, Wolmar and Claire had put the finishing touches on epistolary exchange by writing to Saint-Preux over Julie's corpse; here, the editor and a man of letters exchange words over the corpus that includes Julie's letters. The two speakers designated in the margins as R (the editor) and N (the man of letters) get together over a manuscript version of *La Nouvelle Héloïse* that N claims to have finished and to have found not at all to his liking. "Voila votre Manuscrit. Je l'ai lu tout entier," N first says to R (2:11), thereby acting out auspiciously the minimal prefatory gesture of pre*sent*ing or *pres*enting that which is perforce really absent, the prefaced text.[10] The text is in this instance one that N feels should not be published. As N poses his many questions and raises his many objections to the novel and R responds more often than not with questions of his own about N's critical assumptions, the familiar topoi of novel-prefacing are thoroughly, if somewhat haphazardly, inventoried. Arguments associated with all three of the usual lines of prefatory inquiry (Is this book true? moral? interesting?) are rehearsed. They come in eventually for exhaustive enough permutation and combination to warrant N's proposing that the conversation, now nearing completion, be transcribed "pour toute Préface," in lieu of any more conventional preface. Not that the title "Préface" would necessarily cover the "Entretien" in its entirety; N claims only that the "Entretien" would at least cover in *their* entirety the bases of novel-prefacing: "Les éclaircissements nécessaires y sont tous" (2:30).

The conversation will "do" as a preface, but remains free to do and be more than a preface. The distinction is a fine one, and one that might not come to mind if the immediate future did not quite literally hold more in store for R and N. The two pursue their conversation into the margins of the margins and with their microphones down. The exchange actually transcribed extends beyond the region of the text that N had earmarked, as essentially prefatory, for transcription. "Vous avez raison," continues the "editor" (2:30), readily acquiescing at first to the suggestion that he substitute what they have said for what he might have written on his own initiative. R balks only but emphatically at N's further suggestion that, in the eventual transcription, their two roles should be transposed such that the general public would be treated to the spectacle of N's urging publication of *Julie* on a reluctant R and finally conquering his resistance. On the basis of what N says—"Cela sera plus modeste, et fera un meilleur effet"—we third-party readers might easily be tempted to chalk his urgings up to the rhetorical savvy of a man of letters. But R somehow knows better than to believe that N has proposed a harmless exercise of poetic license, or that the proposal has been tendered in a spirit of gracious capitulation and helpfulness to the cause of the novel. The exchange takes a turn for the gratuitously sinister with N's final revelation that, in urging the role reversal, he was in fact only laying "un piege" and for purposes only of catching R out of "caractere" (2:30). With the fate of *Julie* no longer even nominally at issue, the man of letters shows his true colors by putting not the book but its editor to a test of character! And the editor in turn comes through with flying colors by virtue of knowing where to draw the line on principle between such metaphorical exchanges as he absolutely will not brook (N for R) and those (a chat for a preface) to which he *can* subscribe. But can he still? Lapsing into silence at precisely the point where he would have reacted to N's revelation, the metaprefatory coda leaves R's feelings, like Saint-Preux's at *Julie*'s end, unrecorded and unresolved. We can only surmise that, just as the death of Julie had put a damper on her resultant apotheosis, so the exhiliration of successful self-portraiture must be mitigated for R by knowledge of yet another tester's treachery.

TO PUBLISH OR NOT TO PUBLISH? Dialogue at Issue

Rousseau himself wondered what to do with the pseudotranscription whose existence he first acknowledged to publisher Rey in a letter dated almost two years prior to the publication of *Julie*.[11] The *Préface de Julie* had an eventful prehistory, which twentieth-century editions inadvertently suppress by making the second preface readily available for the price of *Julie* and by placing it adjacent to the novel. The twists and turns of that prehistory bear recalling: they suggest an enduring, if ambivalent, investment in the *Préface* on the part of its author. And that ambivalence in turn helps to situate the *Préface* at another pivotal point in the evolution of Rousseau's occasional self-portraiture. The emphasis of inspiration was shifting imperceptibly from literary to existential occasions, in ways that Rousseau leaves unsaid. So do readings of the *Préface* that take either of the extreme positions of considering it only as a gloss on *Julie* or only as a text with the same prospects as any other for standing free and clear on its own perennial intellectual merits of any particular occasion in the author's life.

Writing to Rey that he might call his "écrit sur les Romans" something like *"Préface de Julie,"* Rousseau nevertheless vowed never to affix it to his own novel. Already, he was calling with tantalizing vagueness for permanent separation—beyond separate publication—between the novel and an "écrit" that "n'en doit faire partie *en aucune maniére*" (emphasis added).[12] As publication deadlines for *La Nouvelle Héloïse* came and went, Rey, who had been in possession of the complete six-volume manuscript since 1758, redoubled his excuses. Rousseau was momentarily tempted (2:1342) to distribute the text of the preface as a press release in order to sustain the public's curiosity in a novel (or "manuscrit dont je suis le dépositaire et que je me propose de publier") that had long since been promised by a note to the *Lettre à d'Alembert.*[13]

In the meantime, Rousseau had composed a second version of the preface, the one entitled simply "Préface," which we now know as the *première préface* by virtue of its having been singled out to head the inaugural edition of the novel. From that moment on, the perceived obligation to preface having been fulfilled by another text, the *Préface de Julie* became superfluous, *de trop,* and as difficult to place in practice as in theory. Editors still do not agree whether the *Préface de Julie* belongs at one extreme of the novel or at the other. In the "Pléiade" edition, it follows the "first" preface and directly precedes the novel; in the Garnier-Flammarion edition, it is relegated to an appendix. Neither placement tells the whole story; editors might just as accurately follow the lead of the practically minded Rey, who, in his 1763 printing of *Julie,* used the *seconde préface* to flesh out what he thought to be a too-slim second volume.[14]

For his part, Rousseau contemplated then discarded at least two separate plans for publishing his "digression supplémentaire."[15] The preface was tentatively slated to appear in conjunction first with the illustrations for *Julie*[16] and later with his *De l'Imitation théâtrale.*[17] Once the decision had been made that the preface should appear alone "quinze jours ou trois semaines après la publication du livre," Rousseau hounded Coindet, to whom the manuscript had been entrusted, with almost daily reminders. The anxiety-ridden author wrote on 9 February 1761: "Je persiste à être d'avis que la préface paroisse le Lundi 16"; again (with a proposed change) on the eleventh: "La préface doit actuellement être tirée"; and finally on the fifteenth: "Les exemplaires de la préface ne sont pas arrivés hier; peut-être viendront-ils demain."[18] Even when allowances have been made for some combination of unreliable publishing practices and authorial paranoia, Rousseau betrays a surprising degree of affective involvement in getting out (and getting right) a text that for no apparent reason had so recently and so repeatedly been threatened with permanent suppression. (By contrast, the *Imitation théâtrale,* always an also-ran, would remain unpublished and would later become an unsuccessful candidate for copublication with the *Essai sur les langues* and *Le Lévite d'Ephraïm* [2:1921]). Among other things, we are moved to wonder what could have prompted Rousseau, in the second place, to write the first "Préface."

One way of rationalizing this overinvolvement and inconsistency would be to stage a confrontation between *Julie*'s two prefaces and to ask what would have been lost had the *seconde préface* never been placed into circulation. On the one hand, there is a significant enough carryover of *Julie*-centered content from one to the other to warrant Darnton's approaching the "prefaces" as a seamless document with a single story to tell.[19] The *première préface* is obviously derivative and (mis)quotes liberally from the *seconde*; Rousseau writes in the "Avertissement" to the *Préface de Julie* of having placed it "par extrait à la tête du recueil" (2:9). De Man perceives this process of extraction as having worked to the detrimental oversimplification of the most interesting aspect of the *Préface,* namely its utter refusal to resolve the question of whether *Julie* should be taken for a fiction or for an authentic correspondence.[20] But he does not identify dialogue itself as the single most important source of the *Préface de Julie*'s superior tension. It is only under relentless cross-examination by N that editor R comes off as unmistakably evasive. Tormented by doubt (2:29), N acknowledges his frustration: "Quand je vous demande si vous êtes l'auteur de ces Lettres, pourquoi donc éludez-vous ma question?" (2:27).

The most obvious qualitative difference between the two prefaces is also the most important. What has been lost somewhere en route from the second preface to the first is dialogue. In the process of writing the monological "Préface," Rousseau will have mentally fed himself the questions to which he knows or assumes his readers will want to know the answers; in the *Préface de Julie,* responsibility for actually directing those same questions to R is assumed by a second party, N, who only in retrospect volunteers to speak for any constituency beyond himself: "Tout le monde aura la même curiosité que moi" (2:29). Rousseau himself refers repeatedly to this difference. The subtitle he approved for the *Préface de Julie* reads: "Entretien sur les romans, entre l'éditeur et un homme de lettres" (2:7). Syntactic parallelism with the title of the novel, *Julie, ou la nouvelle Héloïse,* lays the groundwork for a significant distinction. One alternate title, *La Nouvelle Héloïse,* formulates a hypothesis (Rousseau's heroine is a modern-day avatar and spiritual sister of the real-life Heloise) in need of verification by reading; the other, *Entretien sur les romans,* contains an immediately verifiable statement of fact (on whatever subject, dialogue, as signaled typographically, is surely in progress). This business of calling attention to the obvious is carried forward in the "Avertissement," whose first sentence begins by offering a choice (or a happy medium) between the formality of a literary genre with roots in Antiquity ("Ce dialogue") and the informality of loosely focused, everyday conversational exchange ("ou Entretien supposé"). Moreover, this same "Avertissement" later advances the claim that the tête-à-tête to follow has been disqualified from normal prefatory duty on the basis not only of its "longueur" but of its "forme" (2:9).

On rereading in the light of this insistence on the *Préface de Julie*'s idiosyncratic dialogism, the *première préface* begins to look not merely monological, but self-consciously, aggressively, even offensively so. Rousseau's public did take offense: the same contemporaries who would later give the "enigmatic" *seconde préface* mixed reviews were far more unanimous in their distaste for the first. Reporting to Rousseau from Paris on the novel's initial reception, La Condamine got right to the point: "il plait généralement hors la préface."[21] More or less diplomatic in his direct dealings with the author, d'Alembert suggested that *Julie* would be served by "l'adoucissement de quelques phrases de la préface."[22] For Julie Lespinasse, d'Alembert reserved a more critical appraisal: "J'ai trouvé la préface mauvaise; elle m'avoit même un peu prévenu contre l'Ouvrage."[23] Rousseau hardly stood to be cheered by the complicitous reassurance of Mme de Créqui: "Votre prefface est ravissante; on la traduit en ridicule a Paris, mais je le leur fais entendre."[24] Except with this willing exegete, Rousseau's "Préface" could not have gone over as more

off-putting if it had been meant to offend. Perhaps it was. Two-stage publication at close range made comparison with the dialogical original more
or less inevitable. When Mme de Luxembourg was furnished with this
basis of comparison, she seized right away on a singular disparity of tone:
"j'aime bien mieu la grande préface que la petite, la grande dit les mêmes
choses, mais comme c'est plus détaillé cella révolte moins."[25]

Indeed, from the outset of his monological reworking, Rousseau
makes a "revolting" public spectacle of retreat from dialogue: "Il faut des
spectacles dans les grandes villes, et des Romans aux peuples corrompus.
J'ai vû les mœurs de mon tems, et j'ai publié ces lettres" (2:5). The initial
pronouncement is both aphoristic and autoreferential: it repeats and extends to "Romans" the conclusions of Rousseau's own *Lettre à d'Alembert* on the subject of "spectacles." The prefacer is thus established as a
supreme legislator speaking ex cathedra from somewhere beyond the
pale of debate. Nor, in the elliptical follow-up, is there any room for discussion between the two instances of the first-person pronoun: I saw,
therefore I published. Due process is suspended; Rousseau's readers are
condemned to supply the minor premise of their own corruption.

Mme de Luxembourg's point about the monological preface's lack of
details is likewise well taken. As Rousseau proceeds to run apace down a
laundry list of prefatory topoi, he seems to be saying (but with nothing of
Marivaux's good humor[26]), "You people want a preface? Take this . . .
and this . . . and this." Rousseau's coming dangerously close to inadvertent parody of prefacing would account for Mme de Créqui's reports of
public ridicule, and for the otherwise strange pairing of adjectives in
Grimm's review: "La préface qu'on lit à la tête de *la Nouvelle Héloïse* est
déjà assez plate et assez extraordinaire."[27] The author's revolt against
dialogue is at first accessible to us only through these effects of tone and
cadencing. But, as though to appropriate that revolt, Rousseau concludes
his monological reworking with a warning: "Que si, après avoir lû [ce
livre] tout entier, quelqu'un m'osoit blamer de l'avoir publié; qu'il le dise,
s'il veut, à toute la terre, mais *qu'il ne vienne pas me le dire:* je sens que
je ne pourrois de ma vie estimer cet homme-là" (2:6; emphasis added).
The warning comes too late, of course, to prevent the N of the other
preface from approaching the editor, claiming precisely to have read the
novel "tout entier" and rehearsing a litany of reasons why publishing it
would be *blâmable.* But the warning seems to have been framed with
this N in mind. In the first preface, N's former role of discussant is not

merely written out or lost in translation, but emphatically repudiated. All debate with the author has been foreclosed pending a public reunion of the monological and dialogical prefaces. What might have remained a theoretical rivalry for liminary space unable to accommodate both prefaces has been articulated in terms of the specific difference between a one- and a two-man show. The *Préface de Julie* appears to have been published in the name of "Dialogue." And published despite the fact that, on the eve of publication,[28] Rousseau reiterated a personal preference for the monologue, which was nonetheless not permitted to stand alone for long. He wrote as follows, in the eleventh hour, to Mme de Luxembourg: "La préface est unanimement décriée, et cependant telle est ma prévention que plus je la relis, plus elle me plait. Si elle ne vaut rien il faut que j'aye tout à fait la tête à l'envers. Il faudra voir ce qu'on dira de la grande. Il s'en faut bien à mon gré qu'elle ne vaille l'autre. Je la suppose actuellement entre vos mains; pour moi je ne l'ai pas encore. Elle devoit paroitre aujourdhui et je n'en ai point de nouvelles." Dialogue emerges from these thinly veiled expressions of concern for the *préface dialoguée* and from the overall interprefatory confrontation as an emotionally charged issue, one which the Rousseau who made no move to stop the presses chose finally to resurrect but not to resolve.

PACTS OF FRIENDSHIP WITH THE TRUTH

The dialogue form nonetheless provides no guarantees of human warmth or authentic exchange. In fact, on closer inspection, the *Préface de Julie* already engages the figure of the editor in one of Rousseau's characteristic "final" retreats from interpersonal relations into exclusive friendship with the truth. Significantly, Rousseau made a point of displaying on the title page of his "Entretien" the selfsame motto, *vitam impendere vero,* which his R ostentatiously promises to withhold from the title page of *Julie* (2:27, 1336). For, despite this further instance of frustrating N's need to know for sure about the generic status of the novel, R does end up claiming to honor the truth by keeping it quiet (2:28). And beyond that, he vouches for a truth other than *Julie*'s, his own. N's burning question—"Cette correspondance est-elle réelle, ou si c'est une fiction?" (2:11)—and even R's answering silence fall within the bounds of a familiar text-centered prefatory tradition. But no prior novel preface foretells the moment when, as if to compensate for what he will keep secret or undecidable about the novel, R displaces the question and discloses something about himself: "être toujours vrai: voilà ce que je veux tâcher d'être" (2:27).

There is more to this declaration than meets the eye. With remarkable economy, it conflates the substance and the conditions of autobiography. Truthfulness becomes the object of a confessed desire (as it had already in the preface to *Narcisse*). But beyond that, the confessed desire for truthfulness stands ready—as a formal, unequivocal statement of intent—to underwrite an overall autobiographical project. In a theory of autobiography on which his readings of Rousseau's *Confessions* have left an indelible stamp, Philippe Lejeune makes any such autobiographical project contingent on the explicit formulation of a "pacte référentiel,"[29] by which he means that at some point within their texts, would-be autobiographers must make a point of reprising Rousseau's public oath to tell the truth, the whole truth, and nothing but the truth. Or, barring that, they must make clear in what ways they intend to fall short of absolute truthfulness. R cannot say whether his referential intent is susceptible of fulfillment, but he at least goes on record as wanting to try, and at a moment when N wants only and desperately to know about *Julie*. A gratuitous commitment to truth-telling has been hazarded here out of context, or, rather, in partial subversion of a context advertised in advance as prefatory. If Rousseau's version of autobiography calls for a pact, so, conversely, a pact uttered in isolation may cry out for the more congenial surroundings of autobiography. The unspoken, underlying desire to which R attests by simultaneously acting like an autobiographer and presenting his credentials is that the dialogue be decentered and our reading readjusted to allow for the possibility that not only the novel but the preface in progress may in fact be all about R.

This R differs, moreover, from the usual alter egos of in figura self-portraiture in that nothing except a few lines of text stands between the would-be truth-teller and absolute identification with Rousseau himself. Just prior to the skirmish that results in a referential pact, N levels the requisite charges of immorality against the novel and R avails himself of the usual lines of defense, invoking the novel's immanent justice, its fitness to serve as a cautionary tale, and so forth.[30] From there, however, the preface already takes an unanticipated turn toward autobiography: having been advised by N to publish the scandalous letters anonymously, R lets himself be inveigled into volunteering (or confirming) a first installment of vital information about himself:

> N. . . .: Si vous croyez donner un livre utile, à la bonne heure; mais gardez-vous de l'avouer.

> R.: De l'avouer, Monsieur? Un honnête homme se cache-t-il quand il parle au Public? . . .

> N.: Vous vous y nommerez? Vous?

> R.: Moi-même.

> N.: Quoi! Vous y mettrez votre nom?

> R.: Oui, Monsieur.

> N.: Votre vrai nom? *Jean-Jacques Rousseau,* en toutes lettres?

> R.: *Jean-Jacques Rousseau,* en toutes lettres. (2:26–27)

Rather than trust the reader to infer R's identity on the sole basis of an initial or a resemblance to Rousseau, the normally cryptic text twice spells out his name for all to see. The textbook stichomythia of this exchange stands out clearly against a background of paragraph-long, even page-long rejoinders. In Lejeune's terms, a "pacte autobiographique"[31] is sealed here by which a real person, a person known to exist and to write in the outside world, assumes responsibility for all of R's rejoinders and especially for his forthcoming commitment to truth-telling. It is Jean-Jacques Rousseau himself who will have taken time out from prefacing *Julie* to rehearse the preamble to the *Confessions.* The *Préface* would look even more like a full-scale dress rehearsal if the two pacts had followed in greater textual and logical proximity one from the other. Rousseau stops just short, for the moment, of beating the preamble to the punch of overcoming a purported lifelong inability to name himself in conjunction with the expression of his desires and ambitions.[32]

IN MEMORIAM DIDEROTIS: The Interlocutor as Former Friend

There is another way in which the preface hesitates on the brink of the autobiography underwritten just in case by Rousseau's two pacts. That the current performance remains a fiction is borne out by a striking asymmetry in the R/N dyad. The spectacle of R's becoming Rousseau raises expectations that N too will acquire a "proper" name and, by extension, an empirical identity. We can imagine that, were R's interlocutor to be displaced to the *Confessions,* he would become one of the "beaucoup de gens" whose "confessions" Rousseau regrets having to make in conjunction with his own (1:400). As it happens, the mystery man of letters is nowhere named "en toutes lettres." He remains not only anonymous but, by virtue of the inevitable comparison with R, condemned to anonymity. N begs therefore to be treated as the protagonist in some not entirely fictional roman à clef. It is left to the reader to spell out the *mot* of this new *énigme* and to surmise, "à partir des ressemblances qu'il [ou elle] croit deviner,"[33] an identity that Rousseau has chosen not to affirm. Precisely because the pole of autobiography has been so squarely planted in its midst, the "Entretien supposé" gravitates toward that pole, its progress arrested somewhere in the middle ground of "autobiographical fiction." It no doubt comes closer to autobiography proper than does the novel, all of whose protagonists—and none of whom in particular—bear a vague, unconfirmed family resemblance to creator Jean-Jacques Rousseau. "Pas un Portrait vigoureusement peint; pas un caractere assez bien marqué" (2:14), claims N in reference to *Julie*'s referential imprecision. And the Rousseau of the *Confessions,* when he insists on the willful and necessarily approximate nature of his identification with the obvious alter ego of choice, Saint-Preux, and symptomatically divides the hero as lover and friend against "himself," echoes: je m'identifiois avec l'amant et l'ami le plus qu'il m'étoit possible" (1:430).

N becomes the key player in any attempt to fix the respective proportions of autobiography and fiction in the *Préface de Julie.* Whether the preface more closely approximates "Un Portrait" or "un Tableau d'imagination"—the very categories between which N asks R to choose for *Julie* (2:11)—depends on our tracking down an artist's model or models. How closely does N recall a specific character and his dialogue with R a specific scenario in the real-life adventures of Jean-Jacques Rousseau? At least one eighteenth-century reader made a solvable riddle of N's identity and in fact anticipated that the portrait would be modeled on himself. As the only Rousseau intimate to have commented regularly on manuscript versions of *Julie,* the same Charles Duclos to whom Rousseau had dedicated *Le Devin du village* was prepared to assume that the R/N dialogue would take its lead from his own epistolary exchange with the novelist. Upon reading the preface, Duclos was disconcerted to find "himself" transformed beyond recognition. "J'ai été frapé d'une chose, dans votre Seconde préface," he wrote to Rousseau. "L'auteur fait plusieurs reponses que vous avez écrites, mais je ne vous avois certainement pas fait les mêmes objections. Nous causerons de cela et d'autres choses, lorsque nous vous verrons."[34] The writer's memory serves him well: nothing N says even remotely resembles what Duclos had written.

Other letters from the same period promote the less obvious but ultimately more promising candidacy of Diderot. Although Rousseau did write about *Julie* to Duclos, it is with Diderot that he would have liked to talk. It is this "vertueux Philosophe" or—more precisely, and straight to the point of our reading—his "entretiens" that are credited in an early autobiographical fragment with having constituted "la gloire et le bonheur" of Rousseau's life (1:1115). Accordingly, a manuscript containing the novel's first two books had been dispatched to the longtime mentor and received by him in January 1757. In the normal course of events, mentor and protégé would have met soon thereafter to discuss the work in progress. This time, however, there ensued nothing but a series of epistolary feints and parries whose effect was to delay the tutorial indefinitely.

Already in a letter from early March, Diderot uses the conditional to elaborate future projects, as though in anticipation of the fact that no such projects would ever be realized: "J'irois samedi vous prendre a St Denis ou nous dinerions, et dela nous nous rendrions a Paris dans le fiacre qui m'auroit amené. Et ces Jours, scavez vous a quoi nous les employerions? A nous voir; ensuite a nous entretenir de votre ouvrage [*Julie*]; nous Discuterions Les endroits que J'ai soulignés et auxquels vous n'entendrez rien, si nous ne sommes pas l'un vis a vis de l'autre."[35] Rousseau countered, on March 16, with criticism of Diderot's habitual failure to honor his engagements: "Il est vrai que quand vous avez promis de venir, je murmure de vous attendre toujours vainement, et quand vous me donnez des rendez-vous, de vous voir manquer à tous sans exception." By the same letter's end, however, it is Rousseau who not only refuses to discuss *Julie* ("Il n'est pas question de mon ouvrage, et je ne suis plus en état d'en parler, ni d'y penser"), but discourages further talks on *any* subject ("Si vous avez quelque respect pour une ancienne amitié, ne venez pas l'exposer à une rupture infaillible et sans retour").[36] The rift has become so serious that Rousseau directs his reply and the following day's letter to a neutral intermediary. Mme d'Epinay is charged in the earlier missive with stopping the philosopher at any cost—"Surtout que Diderot ne vienne pas"—and later treated to dire predictions about the meeting's outcome were it to be held: "[Diderot] s'excedera pour venir à pied me répéter les injures qu'il me dit dans ses lettres. Je ne les endurerai rien moins que patiemment; il s'en retournera être malade à Paris, et moi, je paroitrai à tout le monde un homme fort odieux."[37] Within a week, the *Héloïse* manuscript had been sent, not carried back to Rousseau. Instead of commenting on the novel, Diderot in his cover letter made excuses for his failure to do so in person: "Je vous renvoye votre Manuscrit, parce qu'on m'a fait assez entendre qu'en vous le reportant, je vous exposerois à maltraiter votre ami." The circle of futility closed with yet another profession of Diderot's willingness to reschedule, if and when: "Si je ne vous chagrine point par ma visite, ecrivez-le-moi, et j'irai vous voir, vous embrasser et conferer avec vous sur votre ouvrage. Il n'est pas possible que je vous en ecrive. Cela seroit trop long. Vous sçavez que je n'ai que les mercredis et les samedis et que les autres jours sont à la chymie. Faites moi signe quand vous voudrez et j'arriverai; mais j'attendrai que vous fassiez signe."[38] For want of any sign from Rousseau, negotiations then lapsed into terminal silence. Without naming Diderot, *Julie*'s first preface echoes the exhortation to Mme d'Epinay ("Surtout que Diderot ne vienne pas") by saying to and about any man who might criticize Rousseau for publishing *Julie:* "qu'il ne vienne pas me le dire" (2:6).

To replace the now legendary falling-out in its epistolary context is to rediscover an enormous investment of time and psychic energy in a single conversation that never took place. The friendship was doomed in larger part than has usually been acknowledged because *Julie* was doomed to publication without benefit of Diderot's collaboration. Residual frustration over life's failure to provide an existential model for the dialogical *Préface de Julie* goes a long way toward explaining why the preface was first written, then reduced to the monological reworking that actually headed the novel, then finally resurrected for separate publication. If the monologue tells it as it really was in the aftermath of relations with Diderot, the dialogue advertised as an "Entretien supposé" shows him (and all the innocent bystanders blanketed by the monologue's vituperation) how it might have been, if only. . .

If only Diderot had consented to play his accustomed role, *Julie* would have passed directly from his hands into Rousseau's. Diderot, not N, would have pronounced the deceptively weighty words: "Voila votre

Manuscrit. Je l'ai lu tout entier" (2:11). The *Confessions* would not bear
the lasting imprint of disappointment at Diderot's failure to make it
through even the first two parts nearly six months after receiving them
(1:460). And though Diderot would surely have raised serious objections
to the novel, he would also have shown N the way to distinguish himself
from the rest of the philosophical establishment. As Masson writes of
Diderot's singular ability to inspire confidence in Rousseau: "C'était, sans
doute, un homme de lettres, mais ce n'était pas un mondain."[39] With the
mutual understanding of adversaries whose begging to differ goes back a
long way, each discussant would have shown signs of ability to complete
the other's thoughts. At some point, Rousseau might have said, "Je vous
suis," and been acknowledged to have followed Diderot's line of reasoning "[p]récisément" (2:11). At another, the roles reversed, Diderot might
have countered with something along the lines of N's "J'aime les vues
utiles; et je vous ai si bien suivi dans celle-ci que je crois pouvoir pérorer
pour vous." And Diderot might have been praised in turn for a job well
done of peroration: "C'est cela même. A quoi j'ajouterai seulement une
réflexion" (2:20–21). No latecomer to discovery of the Rousseau canon,
Diderot would have known enough to jog his interlocutor's memory
about apparent discrepancies between *Julie* and previous works like the
Préface de Narcisse and the *Lettre à d'Alembert.* Making it worth Rousseau's while to respond, such pertinent interventions would have raised
the intellectual level of the discussion above that of the *première préface.*
And throughout, Diderot would have tempered his criticism with an indulgence born of long-standing affection and mutual esteem. Rousseau,
like R, would have been forced to concede: "Votre jugement est sévère;
celui du Public doit l'être encore plus." And Rousseau would have been
sufficiently cheered by that comparison to take a turn, undaunted, at
reading *Julie:* "Sans le [votre jugement] taxer d'injustice, je veux vous
dire à mon tour de quel oeil je vois ces Lettres" (2:14).

The *Préface de Julie* thus improves both on reality and on Rousseau's
prior imaginings. Past sins of omission specifically attributable to the real-
life Diderot are rectified in short order; a fictional dialogue fills the void
left by the cessation of actual relations. At the same time, the preface
departs radically from the scenario for disaster in which Rousseau's letters had earlier cast Diderot as a diabolical figure bent on falling ill and
blaming his illness on Rousseau. In the published version, Rousseau's interlocutor not only shows up spontaneously with his reading done and

feeling civil, but he puts himself entirely at Rousseau's disposal and behaves as though not even chemistry were more interesting and important than discussing *Julie*. Of course, establishing the precise tone of the dialogue or of any single rejoinder depends on paralinguistic factors (positioning of the speakers, body language, tones of voice) to which we readers of a pseudotranscription have no means of direct access. As if to remind us of what we are missing, the "Entretien supposé" repeatedly calls attention to its supposed orality: a note furnishes the correct pronunciation of "Clarens" (2:25); N reads aloud from the inscription to the "septième Estampe" (2:13); N later invites R to catch his breath (2:20), and so forth. Guaranteeing N against too-favorable or unfavorable interpretations, the text makes more initially of his being there and present unto language than of his being.

The change of heart responsible for this somewhat comic revision of Rousseau's worst-case epistolary scenario is not difficult to fathom: after the fact of estrangement, dialogue with Diderot has become more desirable than ever. Like the Geneva of dedication from outside its walls or the master's apples that the *Confessions* place so excruciatingly just beyond the reach of apprentice Jean-Jacques (1:34), this object of desire improves with inaccessibility. Where once he had expected the worst, the autobiographer-in-training now indulges in pseudonostalgia, remembering the best of his own past as better than it ever really was. N's skill in peroration, for example, recasts Diderot's notorious "real-life practice of conversational interruption and appropriation"[40] in a positive light. But beyond that, as though to set a profoundly elegiac tone for the whole, the "Entretien supposé" wastes no time in reaching back beyond the present lives of Rousseau and Diderot to the even longer and more irretrievably lost glory days of dialogue in Antiquity. N and R have barely said two words of unexceptional greeting to each other in the eighteenth-century idiom when they exchange "from memory," without skipping a beat and in the original Latin, a pair of rejoinders from Persius's first satire. What Maurice Roelens has concluded about recourse to "la forme dialoguée" throughout the period of French Classicism takes on added relief on this occasion of Rousseau's ennobling the paradise lost of an "ancienne amitié": "Tout se passe comme si, souvent aux 17e et 18e siècles, la forme dialoguée n'était pas retenue comme un genre mais comme une sorte de signe culturel, forme vide renvoyant à une forme pleine, qu'elle ne désigne que par allusion ou par défaut, dans le lointain inaccessible d'un paradis perdu du dialogue, celui des Grecs et des Italiens."[41] Inscribing a modern-day "Entretien" in the time-honored Classical tradition of dialogue allows Rousseau to avoid the alternative of either naming or silencing his desires. On this, as on so many other occasions, the solution of choice consists in having the objects of desire masquerade as accomplished facts or—for the time being—fictions. N does what he does because Rousseau wishes that Diderot had, but cannot or would rather not say so directly. Recourse to a compensatory fiction makes confession both possible and discreet, more of an inadvertent by-product of the dialogue's *unité d'action* than a speech act assumed by any one speaker.

Publishing that fiction as written, however, amounts to translating the unnamed desire for dialogue into action and to proposing a resumption of rhetorical relations. As R warms to the task of defending *Julie,* N becomes the designated beneficiary of remarks clearly meant to be read by Diderot himself. When Rousseau declared the preface not for everyone, he may have had this singular *destinataire* as firmly in mind as the mental gymnastics that would be required of any readers. For, by placing the preface into circulation, Rousseau renewed the pair's long-standing practice of exchanging personal messages under cover of literary texts addressed to the general public. Jean Fabre has insisted, with good reason, on "le rôle primordial tenu par la littérature dans une querelle où l'on a trop souvent tendance à la négliger."[42] And in a convincing corollary to Fabre's findings, Guy Turbet-Delof has read the novelistic conclusion of Rousseau's *Emile* as harkening back in anger to a note from Diderot's *Deuxième entretien sur le fils naturel.*[43] With the number and virulence of such coded messages increasing in direct proportion to the difficulty of face-to-face confrontation, the *Préface de Julie* joined the intertextual debate close on the heels of Diderot's *Le Fils naturel* and Rousseau's *Lettre à d'Alembert.*

Rousseau had read an indictment of his own self-imposed exile at l'Ermitage into the celebrated *mot* of *Le Fils naturel:* "Il n'y a que le méchant qui soit seul."[44] Such obvious slander could not go unchallenged; a public defense of the solitary life needed to be mounted at the first opportunity. The *Préface de Julie* would do the job even if that meant stretching a point here or there to accommodate arguments having at least as much to do with the novelist as with his novel. R would insist on calling *Julie*'s characters "des Solitaires" (2:14, 16, 22) and N would take the hint (2:18), even though one or the other might just as well have insisted on the social engineering, structural complexity, or internal solidarity of the Clarens community. The *Confessions* go on, in fact, to recognize and exercise these other options by rereading conversions like Julie's to marital fidelity as the cornerstone of "l'ordre social" (1:435). For the moment, however, R arranges to trace the characters' every virtue—from their extraordinarily "natural" language to the heroine's exemplary conversion—to the felicitous fact of their living so far from Paris. N cannot help but misread *Julie* so long as he fails to acknowledge the essential difference from which all the others must follow: "*Dans la retraite* on a d'autres manieres de voir et de sentir que dans le commerce du monde; les passions autrement modifiées ont aussi d'autres expressions; l'imagination toujours frappée des mêmes objets, s'en affecte plus vivement" (2:14, emphasis added).

The same overriding concern for equating goodness with solitude, operationally defined as distance from "la capitale" (2:20), extends to R's discussion of the novel's ideal readers. These happy few are likewise blessed with utter isolation from the Parisian philosophical establishment and cannot be reached by the siren songs of conventional fiction. Pity their less-solitary fellow readers whom alienating novels have lured to the capital city only to ruin their every chance for happiness. At this point, R's zeal gets the better of him: having once depicted novel-reading in graphic detail as nothing short of catastrophic, he catches his breath and launches into a second version of the same cautionary tale. Once provincials have been beckoned to Paris, there is little to choose between one denouement—"une vie infâme," a dishonorable pauper's death, the demise of agriculture, and, for Europe, economic *ruine* (2:20)—and the other—"voilà comment on devient fou" (2:21). The only difference between the two scenarios is that the second makes no pretense of rationalizing the solitary life as conducive to any general good beyond the mental health of "Hermites" (2:18). Melodrama takes over as the erstwhile attorney for the defense of isolationism goes on the attack, twice pointing the finger of blame at the corrupters of solitude, "les Auteurs, les Gens de Lettres, les Philosophes" (2:20). R's moral outrage would not run so disproportionately high with respect to the prefatory task at hand were he not always arguing his case against the would-be perpetrator of Rousseau's own downfall. Just as surely as if Diderot had been named as an unindicted co-conspirator, the apprentice autobiographer here hones his skills of aggressive self-vindication.

The deaf ears of the novel's characters and ideal readers are finally appropriated by the editor himself when he refuses to fall for the alienation of (mis)appropriating N's arguments in the eventual written record of the *entretien*. True to his solitary ways, R/Rousseau triumphantly resists the temptation to cut a more pleasing figure in the eyes of the world according to N. It is in fact for the metaprefatory peroration that the preface reserves the most logically compelling argument of its between-the-lines, impromptu defense. By embracing solitude as both the sign and the enabling precondition of personal autonomy, Rousseau zeroes in on the central irony of a friendship he evidently deems hardly worthy of the name. This friendship subverts its own bases in mutual esteem: one friend makes the resumption of relations contingent on the other's willingness to undergo a transformation so radical as to beg comparison with Rousseau's sitting still for literal abduction to Paris in Diderot's infamous *fiacre.* "Cela sera-t-il aussi dans le caractere dont vous m'avez loué ci-devant?" (2:30) R's rhetorical question lays claim to truthfulness in the form of twofold fidelity to character (I would not be myself if I allowed myself to be another). The question further assumes a metaphorical modeling of male friendship on the metaphorical exchanges of passionate love between the sexes. As the story of Julie and Saint-Preux suggests, there is no falling in love without reciprocity *or* the potential for asymmetrical losses of identity. Once consummated, the relationship thrives at the expense of the fallen female's sense of who she is or used to be; his all-consuming Pyrrhic victory meanwhile restricts the male's availability for the intellectual and social conquests befitting one of his sex. Identifying more closely on this occasion with Julie's loss than with Saint-Preux's, Rousseau blinds himself to the possibility that N might reciprocate his pretensions to identity, and that the other's sense of identity stands to be no less thoroughly compromised than his own by a role reversal that would straitjacket N in the part of a one-note seducer (Please, I beseech you, publish your love story). Seeing only the second-degree seduction, Rousseau stands his ground. Why shouldn't Diderot have made the trip to l'Ermitage or allowed Rousseau to be himself? And N seems to understand: "Non, je vous tendois un piège. Laissez les choses comme elles sont" (2:30). *What* exactly he and the author who fed him the line understand remains unclear, thanks to the inspired indeterminacy of the "choses" in question. Is N referring only to the dead letter of the preface or to the deadlock in relations between the two erstwhile prefacers?

Whether or not Diderot got the message, it was no doubt framed with his inflammatory *mot* in mind. Significantly enough, the *Confessions* would recall Rousseau's having read "cette âpre et dure sentence" not in the main corpus of *Le Fils naturel,* but in "l'espéce de Poetique en dialogue qu'il [Diderot] y a jointe" (1:455). Rousseau's notoriously bad memory for details notwithstanding, the poetic truth of the matter is that one belatedly prefatory and publicly personal *Entretien* deserves another. By responding in kind, Rousseau could pay homage to the acknowledged past master of dialogue and, at the same time, pay him back.

The *Préface de Julie* echoes only faintly the unresolved anger at Diderot that first surfaced in the preface to the *Lettre à d'Alembert:* "J'avais un Aristarque sévère et judicieux, je ne l'ai plus, je n'en veux plus, mais je le regretterai sans cesse, et il manque bien plus encore à mon cœur qu'à mes écrits."[45] And yet, as if to ratify that anger, R goes against prefatory tradition and out of his way to draw the open *Lettre* into the present field of discussion and to stand by its contents. "Souvenez-vous," he reminds N, "que je songeois à faire imprimer ces Lettres quand j'écrivois contre les Spectacles, et que le soin d'excuser un de ces Ecrits ne m'a point fait altérer la vérité dans l'autre" (2:27). But supposing that the truth of the farewell note still holds, so too does the ambivalence attendant on talking to Diderot for the express purpose of declaring an unwillingness to talk. If there is nothing left to say, why say so? If the real purpose is reconciliation, why not say so directly, or at least refrain from saying the opposite? For that matter, repudiating the erstwhile Aristarchus seems more than slightly incompatible with resurrecting him in the person of N, unless, of course, the initial of negation can be construed as a further gesture of repudiation or as a way of striking Diderot's name once and for all from the roster of friendship. A man (made only) of letters is finally no man at all, a no-name, the *nemo* of N's own line from Persius (2:11).

But even if the letter "N" denotes nonbeing, part of the intent may have been to preserve the memory of past dialogue against the eventuality of contamination. In that case, R should have resisted the temptation to use N as a conduit for provocative messages to Diderot. To make the dream of dialogue come true is to run the risk of its turning, once again, into a nightmare. It is to resume against all odds "la recherche, toujours répétée, toujours déçue de l'introuvable Ami, de l'autre partie de soi-même."[46] The chance would have to be taken, however, if Rousseau were ever to find the magical words capable of winning Diderot over to respect for R's point of view. The problem lies, however, in using the selfsame words to clue third-party referees in to the realization that N's is just that as well—*a* point of view, contingent, traceable to a particular "source" (2:14), and finally indefensible. The *Préface de Julie* thus sends out mixed messages to and about Diderot from a Rousseau not quite "[r]evenu de cette douce chimére de l'amitié" (1:727) and imprudently anxious to maneuver the other man into a position of disdain for friendship. "Qu'apprend-on dans la petite sphere de deux ou trois Amants ou Amis toujours occupés d'eux seuls?" asks N (2:14). In the course of its affective vacillations, the preface illustrates both of two diametrically opposed models of friendship made available by eighteenth-century treatises. At one extreme, there is a rational ideal that, as prescribed by Saint-Lambert, seems well worth fighting for: "le philosophe doit fonder l'amitié sur deux . . . besoins: le besoin de la vérité et celui du bonheur." At the other, there is the reality reduced by a disabused Vauvenargues to the lowest common denominator of passionate, egotistical in-fighting for personal supremacy: "En amitié, en mariage, en amour, en tel autre commerce que ce soit, nous voulons gagner."[47] By choosing finally to publish his preface, Rousseau implicitly endorsed the preface's own failure to choose between the extremes of elegy and retaliation. The fact of fulfilling all the requirements for prefatory discourse even as he dabbled in autobiography gave Rousseau the latitude to indulge a gamut of emotions too intense, complex, and unresolved to be named as such.

Interestingly enough, the *Confessions* would pay homage to the "préface en dialogue que je fis imprimer à part" by crediting it with a successful and inadvertent seduction. By simply suspending indefinitely the question of *Julie*'s authorship, Jean-Jacques is said to have won over the "femmes" whom his loquacious silence allowed to go on believing that the novel told the story of his own life (1:547–48). Jean-Jacques thus wins without wooing, as though to compensate Rousseau for a loss of friendship that the *Préface de Julie*'s oblique solicitations will have failed to reverse. But Jean-Jacques's lies of omission do not escape the disapproval of "les rigoristes," a sign of the author's own uneasiness with the kind of victories that come too easily to the protagonist of the *Confessions* from the moment of his reigning as a neonate over the Rousseau family household. Pierre-Paul Clément has convincingly linked this pattern to the real-life Jean-Jacques's lack of opportunity to play out the

Oedipal drama to some decisive conclusion of hard-won personal auton-omy.[48] A further consequence of this hypothetical lack, Rousseau's ten-dency to surround himself with paternal surrogates and to engage them in only imaginary versions of the Oedipal conflict, has special relevance for the *Préface de Julie.* For what dooms friendship within the pages of the preface and keeps R and N from any paradigmatically clinching "étreinte"[49] is an inevitable diversion of the friend and mentor into a developing paradigm of paternity. And it is the particularly defective nature of the paradigm that accounts both for R's avoiding any too overt seduction (for to seduce the father figure would be to diminish his capac-ity to serve as a proper Oedipal rival) and for the dialogue's final degener-ation into an essentially literary version of open warfare. "En vouloir à son père, l'affronter ouvertement, c'est s'engager dans un conflit impossi-ble."[50] The closest Rousseau can come to a full-fledged Oedipus turns out to be a veiled struggle for control not of the mother but of discourse about a text of exemplary maternity.

THE N OF THE FATHER

What sets up the possibility of a father-to-father connection between Diderot and Isaac Rousseau is our recalling to what extent the preface's overall scenario recalls the *Confessions'* primal scene of nocturnal read-ing between widowed father and orphaned son. The *Confessions* are more uniformly elegiac than the *Préface* and less able to besmirch the name of Isaac Rousseau or to bring him far enough down from the ped-estal of idealized paternity to confront him directly and in person. What-ever unspoken ambivalence attaches to the autobiography's biological father surfaces from between the lines and, belatedly, through implicit resemblances between his and the neo-paternal language behavior later ascribed to Diderot. To the *Préface de Julie* goes credit for first recording the resemblances and for working backward through the less remote speech acts of Diderot to a slightly more down-to-earth Isaac than might otherwise have graced the pages of the *Confessions.*

In an entirely other vein, for example, the dedication to Geneva had visualized earliest recorded memories of Isaac in the manner of a willfully sentimental Greuze tableau. In keeping with that occasion of the dedica-tion's New Testament overlay, a father-son couple vaguely reminiscent of the most humble and exalted carpenter of Nazareth and the divine infant entrusted to his care had been removed to the father's *atelier.* And their indirectly reported verbal exchanges had been reduced to the touchingly idyllic dumb show of "les tendres instructions du meilleur des Péres" (3:118). We know for a fact that first Isaac, then Jean-Jacques had up and left this home sweet home. But only insofar as the biblical cast of the memory hints at a revisionary conflation of Jesus's home life with the later scene of precocious intellectual mastery over the elders in the temple does the scene of undying filial dedication yield any inkling of the son's long-range potential for resentment and indocility.

But resentment against the father does surface in the *Préface de Julie*, as the still-accessible idyll recedes into the background of impersonal metaphorics and clearly identified wishful thinking. Metaphorically speaking, while declining to say whether *Julie* is his natural or his adopted brainchild, R vows to conduct himself as an ideal father to the novel, for which he will "answer" without "appropriating" it (2:27). Indeed, by putting "his" *Julie* on a par with N's, R already allows the novel to lead a life of its own in the interstices of their disagreement. By letting the novel breathe for two weeks without benefit of a full-scale prefatorial support system, Rousseau himself thought to attenuate the coercive forces that prefaces (assuming they were read) usually brought to bear on novels and their outside readers: "Il vaut mieux laisser d'abord paroitre et juger le livre; et puis je dirai mes raisons."[51]

With this promise and promising behavior comes R's implicit assurance that *Julie*'s father will not repeat the sins committed by Julie's. The editor's rejoinder that comes closest to pointing an overall moral for the novel contains an unexpectedly scathing indictment of parental tyranny as practiced by the matchmaking Baron d'Etange. It is by an emphatic visiting of sin on their fathers that girls (and boys) like Julie are finally exculpated by R: "Depuis que tous les sentiments de la nature sont étouffés par l'extrême inégalité, c'est de l'inique despotisme des peres que viennent les vices et les malheurs des enfans" (2:24). This interpretation of the novel is more than sustained by the plotting without which *Julie* would risk coming apart at its central seam. That plotting passes the heroine directly from her biological father to his chosen surrogate, Wolmar, at the expense of her happiness and to the near total suppression of her autonomous desiring. Peggy Kamuf's compelling recent discussion of paternal law in *Julie*[52] suggests that Rousseau could certainly have done worse than hold to this preliminary sketch of an interpretation. The fact remains that, by the time he gets around to remaking sense of *Julie* in the *Confessions,* Rousseau has moved so far away from focus on "l'inique despotisme des peres" that the baron is effectively excised from the cast of characters and Wolmar, as though exclusively of Julie's generation and attached exclusively to her, is designated only as "son mari" (1:435). Like all inevitably reductive morals tacked onto complex narratives "for the moment," R's tag line to *Julie* is a good place to look for a sense of the occasion. The outright assumption of paternal tyranny comes well into the debate with N. Paternity has become an emotionally charged issue in the here and now, and in the interval since R first calmly listed the baron among the cast of imperfect but well-intentioned characters who were supposed to distinguish Rousseau's novel from those of Richardson (2:12). Not incidentally, the preface that singles out paternal imperfection to assume a total burden of guilt does double duty as dialogue with an imperfect father.

Intergenerational conflicts are considered, for the moment, to be the root of all evil and unhappiness. It follows, in a Rousseauean universe where the younger generation cannot conceive of winning or wanting to win, that goodness and bliss would be predicated on the absence or avoidance of any such conflicts. No wonder that the "honnêtes gens" who comprise the alternative community of *Julie*'s ideal readership "passent leur vie dans des campagnes éloignées à cultiver le patrimoine de leurs peres" (2:22). In the best of all impossible worlds, fathers would inspire loyalty, and loyalty to their fathers would keep future generations safely at home, out of reach of the fictions that drive real readers wild: "En montrant sans cesse à ceux qui les lisent, les prétendus charmes d'un état qui n'est pas le leur, ils [les Romans] les séduisent, ils leur font prendre leur état en dédain, et en faire un échange imaginaire contre celui qu'on leur fait aimer. Voulant être ce qu'on n'est pas, on parvient à se croire autre chose que ce qu'on est, et voilà comment on devient fou" (2:21). But the irreversible madness projected here onto other unsuspecting consumers of alienating fictions is the same irreversible madness that the *Confessions* will reserve for Jean-Jacques himself. There, Rousseau will derive an entire lifetime of self-delusion, his own, from the primal experience of reading novels. In foretelling the story of his life, the present autobiographical fiction neglects only to incriminate the father who provided those novels and the son who read along, even in the knowledge—such, it turns out, are the "tendres instructions" to which Isaac gave voice—that his place beside the father should naturally have fallen to the dead mother.

We are, of course, condemned in our turn to the madness of prefacing an always elusive something or other. We will never know whether in truth the prefatory fiction here expropriates an autonomous past reality of father-son relations or whether the autobiography will later have appropriated the prefatory fiction as though it were "the story of my life." Which came first, Jean-Jacques's alienation or that of Rousseau's anonymous novel readers? "L'on se plaint que les Romans troublent les têtes," claims R, but on what basis does he add, "je le crois bien" (2:21)? Without presuming to unravel the strands of psychic and textual memory, we can nonetheless comment on the details of divergence between what Rousseau takes it upon himself to name "Entretien supposé" and what he will later, with the stated intention to tell *his* truth, name *Confessions.*

The circumstances of Jean-Jacques's initiation to l'*Astrée* and La Calprenède *are* recalled when R proceeds to involve *Julie*'s ideal readers in a scenario (2:22–23) corresponding detail for detail with the scenario to be enacted on the opening pages of the *Confessions* (1:7–8). In each instance, the readers are two; the couple isolated ("dépourvus de sociétés"); the setting nocturnal ("Durant les longues nuits d'hiver"). In each instance, reading together becomes an avowed substitute for love-making: "la nuit de lecture à la place de la nuit d'amour" is the way Philippe Lejeune puts it with respect to the *Confessions* version.[53] The preface holds out to the co-readers the promise of learning, from *Julie* or from the experience of reading *Julie* together, about "le charme de l'union conjugale, même privé de celui de l'amour." That last stipulation is a tip-off that the two scenes would be identical but for a single difference that makes all the difference: the *Préface de Julie* takes the liberty of (re)casting the real-life father and son as a couple comprised of "deux époux" (emphasis added). The father's guilt does not figure for now in the novel-reading scenario; nor does the son's. The preface holds to a fiction of generational parity and metaphorical interchangeability between co-readers. The name of "époux" to which they answer in tandem suppresses the differential traces of desire and procreation. The fiction reestablishes the (for all we know, childless) bride in her rightful place and strips the husband as potential father of his potentially abusive paternal authority. In the "campagnes éloignées" of what R acknowledges to be his happiest imaginings ("J'aime à me figurer deux époux lisant ce recueil ensemble"), reading together remains an idyll of total intimacy without implications. Ideally, reading *Julie* would do nothing more radically disruptive of the couple's life as lived from time immemorial than put "une face plus riante" on their age-old "état" and "soins." Slipping from the conditional into the future tense, the dream of that perfect meeting of the minds that would or will be the couple's "[e]n quittant leur lecture" remains just out of reach. The name of the Father surfaces as an irretrievable past ideal *and* muffled warning at dream's end. Something will, in fact, have changed overnight: "Ils [les "deux époux"] rempliront les mêmes fonctions; mais ils les rempliront avec une autre ame, et feront en vrais Patriarches, ce qu'ils faisoient en paysans."

The awakening from this impossible dream is ruder when the *Confessions* reunite Jean-Jaques with "true Patriarch" Isaac. To a son barred of necessity from attendance at his own biological conception, the father quickly makes himself known as such by seizing control of verbal creativity. "Jean-Jacques, parlons de ta mere" (1:7), says Isaac, in what Nicole Kress-Rosen has identified as the quintessential paternal speech act.[54] Helpless to disobey the father's command to linguistic performance, the son is further placed in the untenable position of speaking about something—the dead mother—of which he has no firsthand knowledge. He must, then, pass off the other's words as his own. Additional pressure is exerted on the protégé by the exacting mentor's all too obvious investment in the success of the performance; many tears are shed (1:7). Viewed from this perspective, the call to novel-reading becomes an exemplary extension of the father's linguistic dominance. As experienced by the son at the father's behest, l'*Astrée* and La Calprenède do not themselves alienate Jean-Jacques; they only aggravate what is already a catastrophic alienation in language.

The *Confessions* fulfill this prophecy of alienation anecdotally when they subject all-purpose family member Jean-Jacques to the constant costume changes of a vaudevillian bit player. No sooner is he called to tell the mother's story from the matricidal son's point of view ("parlons de ta mere") than he gets a further call to fill in for the mother herself ("rempli le vide qu'elle a laissé dans mon ame"). Yet another call assumes the imperative mode to be already internalized: a father who describes himself as "plus enfant que toi" asks, without saying so, to be fathered by Jean-Jacques (2:7–8). By dint of this literal and logical triangulation, the master of ceremonies clinches his transcendent role of keeper of the Logos; Isaac reconfirms his identity as one of the veritable "*auteurs* de mes jours" (1:7). However scandalous in and of themselves, the specific demands he places on a child of "cinq ou six ans" are only symptomatic. The resultant instability of the child's identity bodes well for the *Confessions'* ability to revisit each vertex of the triangle *en connaissance de cause* and so to exhaust the possibilities of the family drama more thoroughly than most self-centered narratives. But Rousseau cannot completely ignore or accept the more fundamental scandal of the Father's *demanding*. The paradoxical power of the infantile Isaac has nothing at all to do with biology or character; it has everything to do with his privileged relationship to the language that, at the drop of an imperative, a novel, a copy of Plutarch's *Lives,* or even a suggestion, can reduce the son to the nothingness of a character already contaminated by mere words alone.

But if Isaac is named to incarnate the primal instance of this alienation in the *Confessions,* his disappearance by no means restores Jean-Jacques to prelinguistic purity. Nor does a literal demise foretold from the first: "Quarante ans [plus tard], il est mort dans les bras d'une seconde femme" (1:7). Reading and writing will be conceived by the autobiographer as the two stages of a single disaster that is seen to span and transcend whatever welter of experience might have acted in the interval to obscure the metaphorical connection. As written in the *Confessions,* the stage-two disaster of writing dates from a time when Jean-Jacques will already have slipped, with no fanfare or ill effects to speak of, into the writing of poems, plays, a treatise on music, some articles for the *Encyclopédie,* and whatnot. If no one ever reads without writing (back) in the broadest sense of the word, or writes without reading, the commonality of the two activities is neither obvious nor trivial (except now that, through sheer redundancy, it has become the organizing polarity of choice of so many *autobiographies d'auteurs*).

Elsewhere, these two R's converge in the practice of reading cum writing subsumed under the name of "Préface." What do prefaces do besides write for reading their readings of other writings? The job description itself requires that prefacers complete the circuit that other readers and writers remain free to retrace in less obvious ways and as though on an optional basis. Having contracted only to read *Julie,* the two parties to Rousseau's "Entretien" surprise us with a discovery: not that we have been reading a preface all along—we knew that—but that, *in the very process* of their reading *Julie,* they have scripted a preface that now stands complete except for the metaphorical formality of *tran-*scription. What R will eventually write down, what someone must already have written (otherwise we would not be reading) in turn retains the unmistakable character of a reading so self-conscious that at one point R returns the tit of "Relisez mieux . . . relisez aussi" for the tat of N's "Relisez . . . relisez" (2:25).

Whether or not it was by dint of prefacing *Julie* that Rousseau discovered for himself the vicious circle of reading and writing, it was this circle that the *Confessions* would reconfigure as linear, metanarrative progression/regression from one (reading) to the other (writing). And whoever came first (to mind), Isaac or Diderot, the occasion of coming to writing came at some point to call for commemoration under the aegis of a patriarchal man of letters. Diderot would be charged with instigating the further fall away from being that occurs with the transfer of Jean-Jacques's primary linguistic focus from speech to writing: "Il m'exhorta de donner l'essor à mes idées et de concourir au prix" (1:351). Completing the exhortation to speech about the mother is that, more terrible still in its long-range implications—"dès cet instant je fus perdu"—to published discourse on the arts and sciences. Redoubled along the lines of life sentences served concurrently for related crimes, the alienation now named as such becomes the tie that binds writing to reading: "Tout le reste de ma vie et de mes malheurs fut l'effet inévitable de cet instant d'égarement" (1:351). In the dungeon of Vincennes, Jean-Jacques reverts to the posture of filial docility for which the *Confessions*' Geneva nights had so well prepared him. "Je le fis" (1:351)—I did whatever he demanded, nothing more or less. Though its site and specifications have changed, the ancestral stronghold remains intact: henceforth, Diderot will supervise the production of texts, just as Isaac had supervised their consumption. Inordinate hopes once invested in the favored younger son will be reinvested in the genial apprentice on whom Diderot and the entire philosophical community for whom he speaks will count to spread a word that is basically not his but theirs.

It is as though the Father Himself had come back to haunt a perennial man-child. Rousseau's relationship with Diderot gains in obsessiveness through its resemblance to the relationship with Isaac, and vice versa. The *Préface de Julie* operates already on the unspoken assumption of

Diderot's neopaternity, by weaving relevant materials from the father's story into the drama of adult friendship gone astray. Old memories supplement new ones, but also shape them. The preface's subtitle, *Entretien sur les romans,* takes R all the way back to dialogue with the father about the mother's novels and the mother as novel.

Like a latter-day "Susanne Rousseau," *Julie* engages father N and son R in a contest for mastery of the discourse. The entire movement of the *Entretien* can be charted—if only, knowing too much, we think the worst—in terms of what the *Confessions* designate as the most primitive of all generational conflicts. From the moment of R's enjoining N to linguistic performance with the peremptory "je veux un jugement positif" (2:11), the mechanism is set in motion that will wreak the son's revenge on composite father Isaac-Diderot. With a dire prediction—"Ainsi j'arracherai toutes vos réponses avant que vous m'ayez répondu" (2:11)—Rousseau's fictional alter ego turns the tables on the flesh-and-blood *arracheurs de paroles* held accountable for filling Jean-Jacques's head and mouth with "beaux discours" (2:12). In the ensuing rejoinders, everything from the anonymity that makes a *spokes*man of N and precludes him from speaking in his own name to the obstinate mutism that greets his every inquiry into *Julie*'s origins contributes to the same ongoing enactment of poetic justice. Wanting for vital information, the man of letters seems a fool to blather on, embroidering as it were on a void. Grovel though he may in a final flurry of questions, try as he may to trip R up, N comes no closer to the truth of *Julie* than does Jean-Jacques to the truth of his mother.

By the preface's end, this struggle for control of the discourse has become so all-consuming that nothing else matters. Having dropped the pretext of *Julie,* the dialogue turns into metadialogue; "seules comptent les relations entre les deux hommes."[55] In what now looks like a distant echo of Diderot's Vincennes exhortation to seize the occasion, N suggests that the proceedings be published as an occasional text (2:30). R's ready compliance indicates a willingness to retreat from his newfound mastery; despite it all, the role of submissive son, both wanting to please and beholden to the father's essential collaboration, would seem to have retained its original fascination. The fictional adversary proves friendly enough, however, to make a suggestion for role reversal that dredges up persistent rumors of more extensive input by Diderot into the two

Discours than Rousseau will ever want to acknowledge. R gets a chance to foreclose publicly the possibility that one speaker's words might (yet again) be wrongfully attributed to the other. And the fact that he alone will have done the transcribing restores R/Rousseau to a position of relative mastery. Unlike N, the real-life Diderot would have insisted on testifying firsthand to the true nature of relations between the two. (He did so with a vengeance after Rousseau's death, beating the *Confessions* to the punch with his *Essai sur le règne de Claude et de Néron,* "où Rousseau, cette fois-ci, est nommé, il vaudrait mieux dire injurié en toutes lettres."[56]) For now, there can be no transcending Rousseau's refusal at the last to relinquish the possibility of nostalgia or of its polar opposite, revenge: he published the "Préface" *and* the *Préface de Julie.* By rejecting the alternative, the "Entretien supposé" permits its author to write back (as Saint-Preux never did) and to write himself into a paradoxical state of grace. Where else but in a compensatory fiction could Rousseau remain faithful to the memory of fathers Isaac and Diderot while at the same time usurping their prerogatives of paternity?

Fighting with Diderot, losing Diderot, fighting the loss of Diderot— on this *chaude occasion,* the *Préface de Julie* does all three, while purporting to do something else entirely. The loss is all the more acutely felt for having itself been relegated to silence. For sheer poignancy, neither the *Correspondance* nor the *Confessions* can compete with the fiction whose autobiographical dimension they nevertheless illuminate. Without the *Confessions,* feelings left inchoate and unmotivated by the *Préface de Julie* might never have been linked to the pertinent details of Rousseau's biography. But by the same token, without the *Préface de Julie,* those feelings would nowhere be preserved against dilution by the overabundant details and necessary rationalization of straightforward narrative. The *Confessions* replace the "logique . . . surprenante"[57] and irreducible tensions of the preface with the idiosyncratic trivialization to which Diderot's paternal function is subjected in his afterlife as first author of the "plot" to write an unauthorized life of Rousseau. And, even in putting the friendship to rest, the *Confessions* resort to tortuous and faintly patronizing periods: "En rompant avec Diderot que je croyois moins méchant qu'indiscret et foible, j'ai toujours conservé dans l'ame de l'attachement pour lui, même de l'estime, et du respect pour notre ancienne amitié, que je sais avoir été longtems aussi sincere de sa part que de la mienne"

(1:536). All the more reason for subjecting Rousseau to the "*double reading*—of the autobiography with the fiction"—that Nancy K. Miller proposes as "a more sensitive apparatus for deciphering a female self."[58]

AUTOBIOGRAPHY AND AUTOBIOGRAPHICAL FICTION: The *Confessions* as "Third Preface"

There *are* advantages to writing and reading "only autobiographical" fiction or "only fictional" autobiography. Theories of autobiography may tend to overlook or underplay those advantages in deference to their own subject and to a teleology derivable from the fact that authorized autobiographies so often happen at the end of a career. Not that one or the other mode of writing is necessarily more truthful, but autobiography's single-minded commitment to identity, of project and precipitate, exacts a discernible price of "logical coherence and rationalization."[59] Having signed up to tell his truth, R/Rousseau must already keep track of his "caractere," and of his keeping track; unidentified and uncommitted, N remains oblivious to the implications of speaking the other's words or speaking at one and the same time for "Tout le monde" and for "moi." As a minimalist rendering of individuality, N likewise remains open to alternate spellings and to occasional inflections. Once, having turned his back on the N in himself, Rousseau has contracted to do nothing but confess, there will be no turning back. Of course, the autobiographer will continue to tamper with the "facts" and to confuse the "events" of waking life with unconscious desires in ways that are sometimes verifiable, sometimes not, and always suggestive; the writing habits of a lifetime are not so easily broken by a simple statement of intent to write something else.

But, on certain occasions of confessing, Rousseau will perforce take a dimmer view, meta-autobiographically speaking, of anything perceived as a threat to preeminent self-identity. With an investment in who "he was" to protect, Jean-Jacques's self-appointed conservator will do only the kind of reaching out that ritualistic displays of centripetal force can recollect, reconcile, and bring into line with a character established and named "ci-devant" (2:30). That Rousseau's reach is longer and his range of motion more extensive in the *Confessions* than those of many subsequent autobiographers speaks well for the formative years spent hiding out in the recesses of occasional self-portraiture and autobiographical fictions, and just as well for the hubris of the converted zealot's insatiable impulse to make a point of appropriation. At its most stultifying, that impulse would reduce "la forme" of the *Préface de Julie* to a ghost of its former self. The postconfessional reprise named *Dialogues: Rousseau juge de Jean-Jacques* allegorizes the other speaker beyond all chance for authentic otherness in the straw man of "Le François," and replaces *Julie* as textual object of discussion with an objective correlative (Jean-Jacques) of the speaking subject (Rousseau). An author "forcé de parler de moi sans cesse" (1:664) ends up making "égarement" seem a felicitous and productive alternative to the maddening sameness of identity.

The *Confessions* correct the *Préface* in less spectacular but stilll telling ways. R had, for instance, let the question of potentially unreconcilable differences between *Julie* and the *Lettre à d'Alembert* ride on the eventual rereadings of his interlocutor (2:25). The question of incompatibility is still nagging when the *Confessions* revive it: "Mon grand embarras étoit la honte de me démentir ainsi moi-même si nettement et si hautement" (1:434). But the *Confessions* have a plan for rereading *Julie* that has been calculated from the first to "bring it all home." In the service of self-identity, intertextual difference would be reduced to manageable proportions. It is only after Rousseau stretches to unearth the novel's "secret" plot to reconcile "Chrétiens" with "philosophes" that, reconciled in turn to his "fate" of perennial public servant, Jean-Jacques decides to publish *his* novel.

It likewise falls within the *Confessions*' master plan to encode the misreading that *Julie* is destined to overcome in terms of potential resemblances between Jean-Jacques's novel and the "livres efféminés" that he has made a name for himself denouncing (1:434–35). What the autobiographer portrays as a risk of emasculation resides not only in the predictable emphases ("l'amour et la mollesse") of such "livres," but in the very prospect that, in writing one, Jean-Jacques may write himself so far out of character as to fall into a permanent state of unpredictability or *lack* of character: "pouvoit-on rien imaginer de plus inattendu, de plus choquant, que de me voir tout d'un coup m'inscrire de ma propre main parmi les auteurs de ces livres que j'avois si durement censurés?" (1:434–35). It is a feminized difference that scandalizes the, by implication, masculine identity of autobiography and threatens to decontrol that identity by making hard (masculine) incompatible with soft (feminine) writing. Whatever work of reconciliation the autobiography will do in the name of transcendent, androgynous selfhood takes for granted the *Lettres à d'Alembert*'s harsh words or "invectives mordantes" and acts on this premise of "what came before" to harden the "doux coloris" of the *Lettres de deux amans* (1:434–35).

All but confessing here to their own partiality, the *Confessions* protect the identity of Jean-Jacques. But, *self*-protective in the extreme, they also cover over the *Préface de Julie* with a third, more "truthful" preface of their own devising. The *Confessions'* failure to preface the preface means that they have lost sight of one of the most compelling subliminal arguments that could be made in support of the auto-biographical reading of *Julie* that both they and the *Préface* want to urge on the novel-reading public. As Darnton sees it, prefacer Rousseau rein-vents the "truth" of novel-reading. Indeed, R's resistance to N's bad habits effectively releases that truth from the confines of convention and, more precisely, from exclusive equation with what look from here like the red herrings of documentary authenticity and romans à clef. Rousseau's new brand of autobiographical fiction relies neither on the claim that the *lettres* were really sent and received by any real *amans* nor on the ver-ifiability of one-to-one correspondences between characters and discrete real-life individuals. (The *Confessions* point this latter moral by recalling that the novel was already well under way when Jean-Jacques first be-came involved with the "obvious" existential model for Julie, Sophie d'Houdetot [1:431]). Rousseau requires, rather, a "leap of faith—of faith in the author who *somehow* must have suffered through the passions of his characters and forged them into a truth that transcends literature" (emphasis added).[60] But in this instance, nothing better testifies to the author's capacity for suffering and firsthand familiarity with affective ex-tremes than the reprise of psychodrama that coincides, in the *Préface* and in the confrontation between first and second prefaces, with the prescrib-ing of new techniques for autobiographical reading. Not only do R and N come close to extending the emotional vigil at Julie's bedside, but what-ever affectively charged past life they may have shared lurks as close to the surface of their professional exchange as do the former passions of Julie and Saint-Preux beneath the neo-Platonism and theoretical overlay of the new-age Clarens.

The *Préface*, then, resembles the novel as a further case in point of fidelity to primary sources in the author's psychic life. But it is also the specific context of a dialogic preface that allows Rousseau to make a pur-posive spectacle of reinventing and interiorizing the truth that novels tell. His taking the "second nature" of prefatory conventions as an obdurate frame of reference makes it appear that his version of autobiographical writing and reading does not come naturally, effortlessly, or as the only available option. The point of R's straining to avoid easy answers to N's questions and making up autobiographical fiction under the duress of man-to-man combat needed to be made. For Rousseau's move to transcend literature looks considerably less Promethean in the light of recent findings that he was stealing not from the gods but from the poor. What he demanded for himself was the kind of holistically autoreferential reading foisted naturally, offhandedly, and disparagingly on the "livres efféminés" of women writers. The "age-old, pervasive decoding of all female writing as autobiographical" has followed with no fanfare, as Domna Stanton discovers, from the pervasive belief that "women could not transcend, but only record the concerns of the private self."[61] Rousseau's real originality lies in seizing an occasion to choose freely and ostentatiously the fate ascribed by Larnac's *Histoire de la littérature féminine* (1929) to female authors: "In the center of every feminine novel, one discovers the author. . . . Incapable of abstracting a fragment of themselves to constitute a whole, they have to put all of themselves into their work."[62] Fellow novelists like Laclos chose not to follow suit, but saw where Rousseau was going. In an epistolary postface to his anti-Héloïse, *Les Liaisons dangereuses,* Laclos condemns male authors to their own dominant, moralist tradition of scrupulous observation of external realities. And by way of gratuitous countervalorization, Laclos relegates the "modèles" for Mme Riccoboni's fictions to the same "cœur du peintre"[63] where Rousseau had claimed to discover *his* "charmans modéles," Julie and Claire. But it is mind-boggling to consider how differently the critical dossiers of Laclos, precursors like (Pierre) Marivaux, (Antoine-François) Prévost, and who knows what other male novelists of virtually unknown *prénom* might have shaped up if only they had preempted Rousseau's move in the *Préface de Julie* to authorize autobiographical readings. And it is suggestive of Rousseau's knowing to some extent what he was doing that one combatant in the verbal duel of the *Préface* ends up proposing to his fellow man (of letters) a model of reading *Julie* that he has himself appropriated wholesale from none other than the heroine of the novel. "Julie s'étoit fait une regle pour juger des livres: si vous la trouvez bonne, servez-vous en pour juger celui-ci" (2:23). How eloquently a footnote facilitating universal access to the text of Julie's rule works against the pluperfect "s'étoit fait," which, pending formal endorsement by a man of letters, locates that rule just beyond the pale of general relevance. The secret unearthed, endorsed, and promulgated by the *Préface* is one that Julie might otherwise have carried to the grave as an eminently forgettable idiosyncrasy. Tracking down the reference, we make the unsurprising discovery that Rousseau's self-conscious paragon of femininity views whatever books she reads as engaging the entirety of her "ame" or being (2:261). Hers is precisely the kind of wholehearted reading or specular double of his writing that Rousseau, in the person of R, is after and to which he comes after (his) her.

Fathering a tradition turns out to have less to do with reinventing the truth than with claiming the patent. Rousseau did just that in the late 1750s, at a moment when he was already of a mind to bring his narrowly defined and self-protective autobiographical self, "*Jean-Jacques Rousseau en toutes lettres,*" directly into play, but not so exclusively of that mind as to avoid supplementing *Julie* with a further foray into autobiographical fiction. Between R for Rousseau and N for Diderot/Isaac, prefacing *Julie* remains, in both senses of the word, a happy medium, and "truth" a matter of more than logical *conséquence* (2:27). To the good and skeptical friend, a man of letters, who has challenged my provisional reading of N as Diderot on the grounds that "Rousseau wasn't like that," I would answer, with R and N, that the best way to find out what Rousseau was, on occasion, like is to reread. As R puts it, hesitating on the threshold of a more rigid autoreferentiality: "Qui est-ce qui ose assigner des bornes précises à la Nature, et dire: 'Voilà jusqu'où l'Homme peut aller, et pas au-delà'?" (2:12).

If Diderot's did not figure in the list of portraits that Mme de Charrière intended to track down for display in an early edition of the *Confessions,* the portrait of "M. de Malesherbes" did.[64] And for cause. Even as Diderot was receding into the archetypal paternal recalcitrance commemorated and compounded by the *Préface de Julie,* the ambivalent son was looking elsewhere. In the person of Chrétien-Guillaume de Lamoignon de Malesherbes, nine years his junior, Rousseau found the makings of a father figure after an autobiographer's own heart, a father figure of his dreams: a father-confessor. Among the multitudes, male and female, whom the *Confessions'* Jean-Jacques is purported to have pressed into priestly service over a lifetime of compulsive oral confession, Malesherbes stands alone in literary history as the chosen recipient of personal letters that were eventually published as a single confessional opus in four movements. Malesherbes apparently owes this preeminence to having been in the right place (on the author's mind *and* out of earshot) at a time when Rousseau's life and his life story both hung in the balance. But the occasion having so conveniently presented itself, why did Rousseau go so far as to seize it, and what sense would he make of having done so?

4

What the Censor Saw:
Lettres à Malesherbes

---

*Où est-il, où est-il, ce château de Malesherbes que j'ai tant
désiré de voir?*

Rousseau

Our emphasis thus far has been on showing how texts that are surely
occasional are also autobiographical. The *Lettres* that Rousseau wrote to
Malesherbes during the month of January 1762 present the opposite
challenge, that of finding our way back beyond the self-evident fact of the
letters' autobiographical content to a sense of the occasion or "circonstance qui [leur] sert de cadre ou de soutien."[1] The *Lettres* are the only
occasional autobiography from Rousseau's middle period whose claims
to figure in editions of his autobiographical or personal writings have
never been disputed. And the *Lettres* are, not incidentally, the only protohistory that the *Confessions* openly embrace, by calling them "en quelque façon le sommaire de ce que j'expose ici" (1:569). The *Confessions*
further proclaim that, on this basis alone, the letters, which remained
unpublished during Rousseau's lifetime, deserve to be "conservées." But
even as acknowledged sources of the *Confessions,* the *Lettres* stand to
lose by being taken all the way off the support system at their source. The
Confessions are less responsible than the biases of subsequent literary
history for understanding accession to special pre-autobiographical status to be tantamount to release from the stigmatized underclass of "only

occasional" writing. It is the *Confessions'* own lead that we will follow in giving the occasion its due and placing greater than usual stress on the timing of the *Lettres,* on their epistolary context, and especially on the person and persona of their addressee.

In writing back to Malesherbes, the erstwhile author of *La Nouvelle Héloïse* happened for himself on Julie's magic formula of "confessing to a censor." That favorable circumstance accounts for the uncharacteristic ease with which Rousseau recalls pouring his heart out in the *Lettres* and, in the process, unblocking the long-range autobiographical project of which the *Confessions* themselves are the result in progress. Rousseau understood how the choice of a confessor gains in significance in direct proportion to the deinstitutionalization of the act of confession. Making a notable exception to his rule of writing to the Director of the Librairie only on official business was Rousseau's way of self-consciously short-circuiting the usual pathways of literary production in the ancien régime and putting an unprecedented stamp of intimacy and personal sincerity on his impromptu substitute for full-scale memoirs. And it is the letters as residual surplus of extraliterary sincerity that the autobiographer is most eager to incorporate into the prehistory and permanent conceptual sphere of his autobiographical project. To the unspoken advantage of all his other occasional texts, Rousseau uses the *Lettres* to undermine, even invalidate the usually automatic associations of "occasional" with "trivial or insincere writing."[2]

But there are further rewards of reading to be had by taking from the *Lettres* an appreciation of the extent to which Rousseau's Malesherbes personifies the vagaries of institutionalized censorship that were a fact of eighteenth-century literary life. The *Confessions* typically use anecdotal accounts of Rousseau's extensive prior dealings with Head Censor Malesherbes as occasional antecedents for forays in the direction of metaphorical, psychic censorship. Rousseau comes closest to positing the censoring agency within of modern depth psychology in a remarkable passage from Book 11 where the same conceptual apparatus evoked with reference to problems in publishing *Emile* is brought to bear on the immediately ensuing account of Jean-Jacques's likewise censored relations with the ingénue Amélie. It is internalized censorship and not illicit desire or even the desire to confess that momentarily becomes the *Confessions'* most deeply embedded and obliquely revealed secret and, for Rousseau, a point of pride in difference from such disavowed precursors as Montaigne.

A LAST-MINUTE CHANGE IN PLANS:
From Memoirs to Confessions

Unlike Augustine's, Rousseau's *Confessions* did not always go by that name—or so, in hindsight, they imply. Nor did Rousseau have at his disposal the norms or the name of "autobiography." The term wasn't coined until the turn of the nineteenth century;[3] the two traditions of internal self-inspection and anecdotal narration were not yet formally welded into the theoretically daunting but still workable amalgam to which Rousseau's name would in turn be indissociably linked. It is important to keep those facts in mind as we recreate the occasion of Rousseau's coming to write his letters to Malesherbes in January 1762. At that time, Rousseau was still in self-imposed exile from Paris. He anticipated earning enough from sales of his forthcoming *Emile* to set up independent housekeeping and enter into a state of "absolute retirement" (1:517) from society and from literature. In the meantime, he was living with Thérèse at Montmorency as an honored guest of the Maréchal de Luxembourg. There, Rousseau had, at some point, begun making copies of pertinent documents and assembling a dossier with an eye to writing his life story in retirement and having it published after his death. Recalling those initial stages, the story as told in the *Confessions* looks ahead to a finished product not of "confessions" but of "mémoires" (1:516–17).

The term "mémoires" may be meant as a bona fide working title. Or it may simply refer to the project that had been proposed to Rousseau by his publisher, Rey, and that in the Montmorency years remained still nebulous and modestly inscribed in the mainstream eighteenth-century tradition of fictional, "factional," and authentic memoirs. Rousseau chooses, in any event, to remember the work in progress as an exclusive matter of memory. He elects one of Elizabeth Bruss's "[f]aulty or naive" definitions ("autobiography is an act of . . . memory") over the other ("autobiography is confessional")[4] to cover activities anterior to and at least nominally discontinuous with eventual confession. And regardless of whether dramatic irony is intended to enhance the confessional value of the *Confessions* by contrast with what might have been other emphases, the *Confessions* do honor the discontinuity. Making it seemingly unbridgeable, they make it difficult for readers to imagine how Rousseau ever got past the kind of "remembering" that really amounts only to researching, and how he moved on to the business of turning his research to account.

No sense of urgency emerges from Rousseau's retrospective evocations of a systematic, secretive, solipsistic—but, finally, unselfconscious—hoarding of *aide-mémoire.* This apparently passive and unproblematical reunion with bits and pieces of his past remains as uncertainly linked to the actual writing of the *Confessions* as an athlete's or musician's warm-up to the actual playing of a game or symphony. We never see Jean-Jacques in face-to-face interaction with his note cards, formulating or modifying hypotheses, putting together the pieces, sketching an outline. This noteworthy standoffishness brings Rousseau's account into the vicinity of Barrett J. Mandel's contention that unmitigated remembering does not so much enable as interfere with autobiography: "The pictures—part of a survival mechanism—are there to *prevent* self-discovery."[5] There are, of course, abundant traces in the *Confessions'* coherent trip down memory lane of Rousseau's first steps to rescue himself from forgetfulness or from the appearance thereof. In fine memorialist tradition, he would, as planned, make extensive use of his supporting documentation, citing many of the letters he had exchanged with his various correspondents, alluding to others. But he would also insist that on the basis of these raw data alone the *Confessions* did not write themselves.

Book 1 gets straight to the point. Its account of pre-scriptural childhood is unusually long and detailed by the standards of eighteenth-century "memoirs of famous men" and must have been scripted without benefit of much in the way of documentation. Beyond that, however, the author is depicted as willing and wanting to disregard even such documents as he might easily have obtained. First and foremost among those missing pieces is the full text of the (in)appropriately erotic pastorale sung as a lullaby to Jean-Jacques by his loving and beloved aunt: "J'ai cent fois projetté d'écrire à Paris pour faire chercher le reste des paroles" (1:12). But instead of writing to Paris, Rousseau ended up transcribing what he had and what remains readable as a text of forbidden desire despite several missing lines (1:11). The *Confessions* thus make a paradigmatic sacrifice of documentary thoroughness to the end of revealing Rousseau's memories to be in a preferable, even blissful state of incompletion.

Book 10 goes on to provide that sacrifice and Rousseau's leap from remembering to confessing with existential grounds. From where the autobiographer stood, it must have taken the perception of a literal deadline to precipitate a headlong plunge into writing, which he might otherwise have continued, indefinitely, to approach as an asymptote. Having been convinced by a nasty bout with his chronic illness that he would not live to complete the "Mémoires que j'avois projettés" (1:569), Rousseau took exception to his rule of all or nothing and took once again to the margins of literature. He seized another occasion, or, as he puts it in the *Lettres,* "abused" one (1:1142). On the foundations of a long-term professional correspondence with Malesherbes, Rousseau fashioned what would turn out, in the absence of prior long-range architectural planning, to be a makeshift confessional; and he arranged for the performance of last rites.

Although the two men had begun exchanging letters as early as 1755, Rousseau's Letter 1 takes a first step toward confession by locating the terminus a quo of relevancy in a more immediate past. By way of autocontextualization, the letter begins by thanking the addressee for "la derniere lettre dont vous m'avez honnoré" and by alluding, enigmatically, to "ce qui vient de se passer" (1:1130). The events in question are as well known to literary historians as to Malesherbes and accessible through the exchange of letters immediately predating the famous four. Having been drafted by the Maréchale de Luxembourg to help oversee the printing of Rousseau's *Emile,* Malesherbes had become the confidant of delusional fantasies on the part of the ailing author. Fearful that the printing had ground to a halt, Rousseau communicated to Malesherbes as a matter of incontrovertible fact a scenario whereby malicious Jesuits would have seized control of the manuscript. Their plan—or so he assumed—was to suppress it during his lifetime and to thereafter publish in his name a version truncated and falsified beyond recognition.[6] Malesherbes tactfully accorded some measure of verisimilitude to this paranoid plotting, which his firsthand investigation proved to have no basis in fact.[7] Meanwhile, upon awakening independently from his nightmare, Rousseau confessed to having been wrong. Or, rather, backing off from full-fledged confession, he laid the blame for his shameful scenario on a delusional double of whom he claimed to have rid himself once and for all: "je ne prends aucun interest à celui qui vient d'usurper et deshonorer mon nom. Je l'abandonne à vôtre juste indignation; mais il est mort pour ne plus renaittre."[8] (Why Rousseau should have, on this one occasion, voluntarily relinquished the possibility of a plot against him is a not entirely inexplicable curiosity to which we shall return.)

Which brings us to the "derniere lettre" penned by Malesherbes on Christmas Day, 1761. Having assured Rousseau that his secret was safe, Malesherbes, as would any conscientious theatrical confidant, ventured an assessment of his correspondent's mental state. The diagnosis both recalled and revised the philosophical party line. That Rousseau had, by self-imposed solitude, consigned himself to a lifetime of unhappiness was a forgone conclusion, one that Malesherbes did not question. But whereas Rousseau's "enemies" saw him persisting in masochistic folly out of "vanité" or exclusive concern for his reputation as an inveterate eccentric, Malesherbes discerned a constitutional excess of "bile noire," a congenital rather than willful misanthropy. To be pitied for what he could not change, Rousseau also deserved to be admired for living his "true" self to the most logical extreme: "Etant assés malheureux pour voir souvent des horreurs où Démocrite n'auroit vu que du ridicule, il est tout simple que vous ayés fui dans les deserts pour n'en plus estre temoin."[9] Of course, the highly principled persona sketched by Malesherbes uncannily resembles the man of anachronistic moral superiority Rousseau had exhausted himself trying to become in the *Préface de Narcisse.* But then was then, and now was now; there could be no foretelling if, when, or how Rousseau, ever the erratic correspondent, would respond.

He did respond quite promptly in a letter dated 4 January 1762. But the delay is belabored in his salutation: "J'aurois moins tardé Monsieur à vous remercier de la derniere lettre dont vous m'avez honnoré si j'avois mesuré ma diligence à repondre sur le plaisir qu'elle m'a fait. Mais outre qu'il m'en coute beaucoup d'ecrire, j'ai pensé qu'il falloit donner quelques jours aux importunités de ces tems ci pour ne vous pas accabler des miennes" (1:1130). Better late than never—or rather, better late. Opening an interval of deferment and opening that interval to interpretation becomes Rousseau's way of encoding a problem of global misunderstanding (of his "caractére" and "motifs") that he then goes on to address globally. Not that Malesherbes has got Rousseau *all* wrong, but his assessment does err somewhat and, for once, on the high side of the truth. By way of setting the larger record straight, Rousseau wrote back: "Les motifs auxquels vous attribués les partis qu'on m'a vû prendre depuis que je porte une espece de nom dans le monde me font peut-etre plus d'hon-

neur que je n'en merite mais ils sont certainement plus prés de la verité
que ceux que me pretent ces hommes de lettres, qui donnant tout à la
reputation, jugent de mes sentimens par les leurs" (1:1130).

Thus the initial compliment of Rousseau's letter will not have been
turned in vain or as a gratuitous hors d'oeuvre; rather, it sets a precedent
for using the letter's main body to correct whatever errors as to his affect
and motivation Rousseau's silence "to date"—not just since his receipt of
Malesherbes's letter—may have left unchecked. No one but Rousseau
knows why Malesherbes did not hear from him sooner, or, by analogy,
what motive "moins noble, mais plus pres de moi" (1:1131) than the one
hypothesized by Malesherbes really underlies Rousseau's decision to live
far from the madding crowd. The transition from epistolary compliment
as opening gambit to more essentially autobiographical content is easily
made and holds up nicely. Contrary to everyone's assumptions—"Oh!
Monsieur combien vous vous trompez!"—the solitary life is revealed to
be as uniformly pleasurable as receipt of a letter from Malesherbes
(1:1131); avoidance of interpersonal encounters comes off as no less incompatible with humanitarian intentions than failure to reply by return
mail: "Je serois beaucoup plus inutile à mes compatriotes, vivant au milieux d'eux que je ne puis l'etre dans l'occasion, de ma retraite" (1:1143).

Without forcing the analogy, Rousseau also gets away with the pre-
posterous insinuation that in the delayed reaction to Malesherbes's letter
he is likewise saying his piece or telling his side for the first time since
acquiring "une espece de nom dans le monde." It is as though the writer
were utterly oblivious to the marginal notations of aggressive-defensive
self-portraiture we have been reading. Preoccupation with the still em-
bryonic state of his memoirs no doubt explains how Rousseau can pay
Malesherbes the further compliment of granting him exclusive rights to
the heretofore "untold story."

The compliment does, in fact, seem richly deserved. If Malesherbes
had not really made it easier to talk than all the others, the truth-telling
session would not spill over so volubly into the further letters of 12, 26,
and 28 January. It also appears, however, that the charm of breaking past
silence would in turn be broken were the two correspondents to resume
the give-and-take of normal epistolary relations. As though to stave off any
further intervention by the real Malesherbes and to freeze him in the
posture of his Christmas-Day missive, each of Rousseau's letters except

the last concludes with a variation on the warning "to be continued" (1:1133, 1137, 1142).

Meanwhile, the "Monsieur" of direct address becomes, through ritualized repetition, the ubiquitous textual marker of a persona assigned at the outset to the reader in the text. Rousseau's "epanchement" (1:1133) is channeled through the narrowest of openings and depends on the possibility raised by Malesherbes's letter of typecasting then containing him in the role of confessor. Therein lies a most welcome novelty: any response addressed directly to the accusations of the *philosophes* would have had to take the form of yet another outright apology. Malesherbes alone invites confession. His coming close to the truth establishes enough commonality of belief or outlook between the two men for Rousseau to proceed directly, confidently, and with a minimum of posturing or predicating to the specifics of the *cas de conscience* at hand. Better yet, Malesherbes misses the mark only on the side of undue flattery, thus triggering in Rousseau a healthy dose of self-inspection or soul-searching and allowing him to posit the "truth" by subtle opposition with a specific, slightly "too-good-to-be-true" appearance.

In confession, moreover, Malesherbes gives Rousseau an angle from which to come at (or bypass) the mountain of autobiographical materials he had been accumulating with no more clear-cut end than "mémoires" in sight. Left to his own devices, Rousseau's life story might have run the usual risks of enervating over-preparation: "c'est mon ordinaire dans les entreprises que j'ai le plus à cœur, de m'épuiser en belles préparations, et ne rien faire qui vaille quand j'en veux venir à l'execution."[10] Instead, from Malesherbes, our erstwhile memorialist gets the go-ahead to write, as though automatically, "sans brouillon, rapidement, à trait de plume" (1:569)—and documentation be damned! Beyond that, Rousseau gets Malesherbes's tacit permission to come, as ever, from *an* angle—even when, with his "whole life" on the line, some more ceremonial and unprecedented approach would seem to be called for.

Now, if ever, Rousseau is prepared to acknowledge by a prompt act of confession that, however paradoxically, self-presentation flows more easily from the cues and constraints of this or that "occasion" than from any absolute, really paralyzing license to "tell all" whenever and however one wants. The seamless passage in Letter 1 from the prior week's health bulletin to the disappointments and dreams of a lifetime speaks volumes about autobiography's momentary accommodation with the occasional, as does Letter 2's positively charged recollection of writing the First Discourse. No matter that the *Discours* remained the smoking gun of Rousseau's alleged opportunitism, or that, inevitably inexhaustive, the *Discours* had finally managed to conserve not even "le quart de ce que j'ai vû et senti sous cet arbre" (1:1135). What Rousseau commemorates here, precisely because it pertains so well to the work at hand and already well under way, is the incomparable feeling of writing, as though inspired, to the moment: "Si jamais quelque chose a ressemblé à une inspiration subite, c'est le mouvement qui se fit en moi . . . tout à coup je me sens l'esprit ébloui de mille lumieres" (1:1135). What a relief to break the ice once again in an occasional text.

The tacit metamessage from Malesherbes that Rousseau picks up is, in short, a doubly encouraging injunction to confess. On the one hand, keep up the good work of occasional self-portraiture; on the other, rest assured that, however opportunistic, your scaled-down autobiographical project can still be conceived as a one-of-a-kind (i.e., confessional) response to the opportunity of a lifetime. However promptly the *Lettres* retreat into confession's shadow, apology, Rousseau will have begun by announcing a strictly confessional intent and by reducing his hearer's existential heterogeneity to the single function of hearing his confession. For his part, the real-life Malesherbes had graciously presumed to provide the full range of services befitting an all-purpose confidant or professional therapist: "elucidator (where ignorance has given rise to fear), . . . teacher, . . . representative of a freer or superior view of the world," among others. But Rousseau demurred: his unifactorial "Monsieur" is destined from the outset of Letter 1 to specialize as "a father confessor who gives absolution, as it were, by the continuance of his sympathy and respect after the confession has been made."[11] Having recently demonstrated his special aptitude for knowing even the worst of Rousseau's delusions without wavering in his sympathy and respect, Malesherbes has earned the confidence of our once-and-future "penitent"[12] and a right to the whole truth: "Quoique je ne me console point de ce qui vient de se passer, je suis trés content que vous en soyez instruit puisque cela ne m'a point ôté votre estime, elle en sera plus à moi quand vous ne me croirez pas meilleur que je ne suis" (1:1130). In terms of getting the story out, however, it becomes increasingly less important that Malesherbes actually read what he will in any case receive than that he be installed until further notice in a textual confessional. The rhetorical frame suffices to guarantee the ipso facto identity of confession and to keep the letters coming.

BUT *WHO* WILL CONFESS ME? The Lessons of *Julie*

The general cause of putting the life story to paper is thus well served by the occasional cause of Malesherbes's acting in such a way as to pin the telling down to a specific bone of contention and to a particular, confessional mode of telling. Consider, as a further source of urgency, the life-threatening illness on which the survivor's *Confessions* are bound to insist, and it is easy enough to call this convergence of causes to account for the *Lettres* themselves, for the self-satisfaction that Rousseau derives from writing and having written them, and even for the unmitigated cheerfulness with which he acknowledges his opposite number's good offices. Still, what looks, unaccountably, like a surplus of positive affect attaches specifically to Rousseau's depictions of epistolary coupling with his chosen confessor. However good for the soul, confession worthy of the name is supposed to hurt at the time, and to exact a price of shame or difficulty in verbalization. But there would be no guessing that on the basis of the progress reports that a Rousseau in no obvious pain delivers at regular intervals through the *Lettres.* He writes, in the second: "J'ai sûrement bien du plaisir à vous ecrire" (1:1138); expands, in the third: "Quoique j'aime trop à parler de moi, je n'aime pas en parler avec tout le monde, c'est ce qui me fait abuser de l'occasion quand je l'ai et qu'elle me plait. Voila mon tort et mon excuse" (1:1142); and, in the fourth, insists one last time on "le plaisir que je prends à vous écrire" (1:1144).

This undiluted "plaisir" rings truer still when we recall that, several years later and in other circumstances of less than life-and-death urgency, Rousseau proposed an exact replication of the epistolary experiment. "Ce n'est pas d'aujourdhui, Monsieur, que j'aime à vous ouvrir mon cœur et que vous me le permettez," he wrote on 10 May 1766, in what might have been the first of further *Lettres à Malesherbes.* "Laissez-moi donc vous décrire mon état une Seconde fois en ma vie."[13] This surplus and survival of affect make it difficult to hang the *Lettres* so entirely as before on what Malesherbes *did,* on a one-time basis, in his Christmas letter, to elicit confession. We would be moved to ask who this Malesherbes really was, and who he was to Rousseau, even if Letter 4 did not get around to rescuing "Monsieur" from anonymity. On the second-person respectful pronoun, Rousseau finally hangs a surfeit of referents. The letter treats its *destinataire* to a seemingly exhaustive litany of his claims to fame and on the author's affections: "vous né d'un sang illustre, fils du Chancelier de France, et Premier President d'une Cour souveraine; oui Monsieur . . . vous qui m'avez fait mille biens sans me connoitre et à qui malgré mon ingratitude naturelle, il ne m'en coute rien d'être obligé" (1:1145). All the more remarkably, by this belated ennobling of his interlocutor, Rousseau makes Malesherbes as peerless in the microcosm of the *Lettres* as in the venues of everyday life. For, in striking contrast to the name-dropping of most traditional memoirs and of the *Confessions* themselves, the *Lettres* are singularly lacking in secondary characters. The first three letters will have yielded only a passing reference to Diderot (1:1135) and one to Thérèse, who never matters much and who matters less here than Rousseau's faithful pooch (1:1139). It is as though proof of blissful self-sufficiency depended on voiding the life story of all external signs of human life. But Letter 4 ends up making a noteworthy exception to general policy for the other man to whom the proof of self-sufficiency is being, confessionally, addressed. And in bestowing both objective and subjective identities on his interlocutor, Rousseau reminds us of the *destinataire*'s crucial importance in any addressed, but especially in confessed, discourse.

As Stephen Spender puts Rousseau's case in deceptively simple terms: "Confession must always be to a confessor. . . . And the human soul can only be measured adequately if there is an adequate confessor."[14] It has become standard critical practice to classify the *Lettres* by content as "pre-Romantic."[15] But the historical moment that the *Lettres* occupy fully and embrace through their rhetorical frame is also one of crisis in confession. His reaching out to Malesherbes typifies Rousseau's reluctance to extricate himself entirely from a tradition of religious confession that was generally and reassuringly supportive of sustained soul-searching. By the same token, however, Rousseau was loath to inscribe himself wholly as an orthodox penitent within the confines of that tradition, to wit, his going outside religious orders to improvise the ordination of Malesherbes. To be entirely adequate or acceptable in Rousseau's eyes, a confessor would evidently have to fulfill some new version of age-old criteria.

Within the broader context of eighteenth-century challenges to religious orthodoxy, the subversive secularization that made models and metaphors of religious rites and realities extended to displacement of the scene of confession. Even the Pietists among Rousseau's contemporaries participated in this displacement through their practice of exchanging "journaux intimes" epistolarily for the correspondents' "édification mutuelle."[16] But insofar as making the metaphor really involved deinstitutionalizing the office, confession could not meaningfully be removed from the church or from its aegis without some further moves to compensate for the real losses incurred in transition. For, left to its own devices, partial secularization would work especially to *depressurize* the act of confession. By way of putting and keeping the pressure on, the enabling framework of organized religion limits and spells out the penitent's options, making regular attendance at the confessional a prerequisite to full participation in the life of the faith, restricting the choice of confessors to an unambiguously entitled subset of fellow men,[17] and grounding specific choices sufficiently (and secondarily) in such considerations as availability and trust. "The rule requiring confession of sins gives to self-examination a character at once systematic and necessary."[18] Conversely, the decision to confess becomes otherwise remarkable and the choice of a confessor otherwise questionable in the absence (or vague memory) of any institutionalized injunction to confess or institutionally sponsored prelates ready to act by the authority vested in them.

It would take the professionalization of psychoanalysis to put those kinds of pressures back on, to reinstitutionalize the office and the injunctions, to recertify a select number of practitioners, and to redirect confession, with all due formality, toward the new and totally secularized transcendent motivation of mental health in the here and now. From midway between the confession box and the analyst's couch, questions arose with special pertinence in the eighteenth century as to whether the impulse to confess was innate or learned, universal or idiosyncratic. And whatever the answers to those questions, it also bore asking how given individuals might, as private, unordained citizens and on an ad hoc basis, bring out the self-portraitist as "penitent" in a particular interlocutor.

Linguistic usage confirms a necessary displacement of pressure to confess from the institution onto one or both individuals and, in fact, privileges the one who hears, conferring on the secular confessor the function of "tirer des aveux, un secret à quelqu'un."[19] Of course, with the church's blessing and to obviate attempts by the faithful to bypass the institution and speak directly to God, causation has always emanated from the priest's side of the confessional. It is he, not the penitent, whose title of confessor substantivizes the verb "confess." For the priest to "confess," moreover, is really a matter of making the other confess. The fact that court cases today may be thrown out on the basis of a confession's having been coerced belies an ingredient of coercion common and essential to all confession: "The site of confession or self-exposure dramatically reverses power's conventional dynamics: the one who remains silent and listens exerts power over the one who speaks."[20]

If not institutional, at the one extreme, or forcible, at the other, that coercion must be, in some sense, cultural or psychological. With no license specifically to hear confessions, lay priests make confessions happen on the sole basis of what they do (Malesherbes stuck by Jean-Jacques, and overestimated him) or what .they represent (that remains to be seen). Better yet, given the tremendous loss of cultural authority for which restitution needs to be made, doing and being combine in variable proportions to bring the lay priest to the threshold of installation. Of course, a completely internalized coercive force or "voice of conscience" may already be available to assume the confessor's function of drawing out the penitent. In that case, the flesh-and-blood confessor's presence would be a largely ceremonial projection or way of keeping up appearances for old times' sake. Anyone willing to listen would do, with priority accorded, all things being equal, to the confessor presumed to be most closely in tune with the voice of conscience. But even granting that the penitent speaks to quiet that voice, confessed discourse as such remains, and hyperbolically so, addressed. What remains otherwise indeterminate and subject to individual variation is the division of labor between the no fewer than two joint subjects to the verb "confess," and the proximity of the confessional act itself to the institutional model.

But there is more to be said about this partial secularization with immediate relevance to Rousseau's *Confessions* and to the *Lettres à Malesherbes.* Gone the same way as the religious fiat that had made confession mandatory are the institution's reliably dogmatic guidelines as to the contents of confessional discourse. It has become more difficult to know a sin when you see one, and less easy to recognize confession's licit objects as those acts and feelings that some higher authority will have prejudged to be really *il*licit. There is more cause than previously for penitents to fret, upon leaving the confessional, that they may have left something out or, conversely, made much ado about nothing. A possible strategy for overcoming this incertitude of sin is the one adopted by

Rousseau in the *Confessions,* which for great stretches—but not necessarily the same stretches for all readers—seem hardly worthy of the name. That strategy consists in telling all and leaving it up to the confessors to separate mere narrative chaff from the kernel of confession. For more than two hundred years, in an increasingly secularized society and in ever-increasing numbers, readers of the *Confessions* have responded just that way to the challenge of Rousseau's title. The role of confessor has been taken as though it were a sacred mission, despite Rousseau's having conferred it indiscriminately on us all.

But there is a lesson to be learned (and then partially unlearned) from the massive, still accumulating body of sincere attempts at naming Rousseau's real or really important sins (as opposed to the dummy desires he posits and overplays). Each new generation or school of confessor-analysts ends up visiting its own sins (or what pass at the time for sins) on the so-called father of autobiography. Rousseau was sensitive to the implications of confessing to anybody and everybody; he advertised his life story as a "prémiére piéce de comparaison pour l'étude des hommes" (1:3). But critics invested in Rousseau's modernity have perhaps been too quick to seize exclusively on the incipient anthropology of that claim and to discard as quaintly moralizing or pompously defensive the attendant challenge to each of us to compare ourselves with the author on the basis of goodness (1:5). For to accept the challenge or even to contemplate accepting it would be to inquire, as we do self-interestedly at the grocery store: what's good (or bad, or indifferent) today? And to inquire would be to put some distance of mutual illumination between the moment to which Rousseau wrote and the one to which, occasional readers all, we read Rousseau. Take, for example, the recent "discovery" of Rousseau's overriding and presumably guilty desire to make a spectacle of confessing.[21] To what extent, we might ask, does that discovery mirror our own uneasiness with the media confessional mode[22] currently presided over by the electronic-age high priests of radio and television talk shows? Indeed, the parameters of confessional discourse are less and less precisely defined by what priest and penitent both know (because they have it on the same inviolable authority) to follow directly from the axiom "I have sinned." The "confessable" risks becoming identifiable as such only in the confessing or replay of confession, and has more than a little to do with the chosen or accidental confessor.

But Rousseau did not always leave the identity of his confessors to chance. His novel *Julie,* which only slightly antedates the *Lettres,* illustrates one way in which the postorthodoxy penitent can use knowledge of an interlocutor's identity to make a reassuring case for having confessed. With one foot in the old religious and one in the new secular age, Rousseau had penned a pair of deathbed confessions for Julie. During the requisite interview with the man of the cloth, she unburdens herself incompletely and with specific emphasis on her theological heterodoxy (2:727–29). Julie then goes on (thereby compounding that heterodoxy) to confide her deepest, darkest secret to the two men in her everyday life (2:740–43). To be sure, lusting in one's heart for a man other than one's own husband figures to this day on a universally approved list of sins against the patriarchy. But the ultimate meaning of Julie's revelation and our tendency to grant it confessional status derive less from a locution (she has enduring feelings for Saint-Preux) than from the illocutionary— in this instance, epistolary—context. She addresses the text of her letter to Saint-Preux but first submits it for prior approval to husband Wolmar, as he has taught her to want to do; she would not think of doing otherwise.

The thought occurs that, had Wolmar been eliminated from the letter's itinerary, its contents might have taken on an ambiguously confessional or even a decidedly *un*-confessional air: it might have read as a simple declaration of undying love. Instead, what nudges Julie and Wolmar toward the confessional is the presumption of pain to be inflicted by the confidence itself on the person of the confidant. To the loser in love, the message says not only "I have lusted in my heart" but "I don't love *you.*" Lack of certainty that God Himself has absorbed the penitent's sins as so many blows against His own person may call for this added precaution of putting a face on the confessor and making him a truly interested party to that which will surely, in consequence, have been confessed. Following Julie's lead precisely and self-consciously, the Rousseau of our *Lettres* takes care not to make his formal introduction of Malesherbes "himself" without first insulting just about everything Malesherbes stands for: "Je ne puis vous dissimuler Monsieur, que j'ai une violente aversion pour les etats qui dominent les autres, j'ai même tort de dire que je ne puis vous le dissimuler, car je n'ai nulle peine à vous l'avouer, à vous né d'un sang illustre, fils du Chancelier de France, et Premier President d'une Cour souveraine; . . . Je hais les grands, je hais leur etat, leur dureté, leurs prejugés, leur petitesse, et tous leurs vices, et je les haïrois bien d'avantage si je les meprisois moins" (1:1145). On both occasions, "true" confession thus comes to hinge less on the after-the-fact recitation of past offenses than on a speech act of knowingly offending the confessor. If third-party readers would be well-advised to know the confessor, so, it turns out, would the self-styled penitent.

In *Julie*, confession of guilt is thus replaced by what is, in essence, a potentially infinite regress of guilty confession. As Michelet would have it, "La confession conjugale (un sacrement de l'avenir) est l'essence du mariage."[23] Or, rather, that would be the case if the superhuman Wolmar were not really incapable of feeling anything like the pain of a cuckolded husband. "Un mari débonnaire et hospitalier empressé d'établir dans sa maison l'ancien amant de sa femme" (2:13) is the way an incredulous N describes Wolmar in the *Préface de Julie*. Still, Julie's confession is bound to get her first reader "where he lives," if not as M. de Wolmar, then as chief architect of Clarens, the monumental social experiment under which he had intended to bury the novel's former disorder of illicit passion. "[J]'efface un tableau par un autre, et couvre le passé du présent" (2:511) is the way Wolmar describes his own handiwork. It is, in other words, of the metaphorical censor in Wolmar that Julie's final letter makes a perhaps not inadvert mockery. The resurfacing of desire undermines the social architect's attempts to incarnate the censoring agency at its most severe and to extend its activities into the sphere of real-life interpersonal relations. Desire will out. But so too will the possibility, at least, of repression. It is by choice that Wolmar leaves the text of Julie's confession intact and forwards it to its ultimate *destinataire*, Saint-Preux. By leaving the fate of her letter in Wolmar's hands, Julie confirms him to the end in his other role as literal (and permissive) censor of every word ever written by *femme de lettres* Mme de Wolmar.

Julie thus upholds censorship proper, as specifically opposed to unauthorized, dysfunctional, demonically figurative variants thereof. Beyond that, secular confession is to some extent reinstitutionalized as censorship, thanks to Wolmar's wearing the two hats of censor and confessor. It is, however, at the point of resistance to total interchangeability, where the confession-censorship analogy breaks down and one term does not entirely cover the other, that confession to the censor further compensates for the penitent's incertitude of sin. The inviolability of the actual confessional is such that, by definition, the penitent's secrets will

go no further (except instantaneously to an already all-knowing God).
Censorship stands, in contrast, as a provisional way station on the prescribed path of the discourse from writer to intended readers. The sacred
duty of confession translates, in this secular economy of censorship, into
a punctual enactment of desiring. In routing her manuscript through
Wolmar, Julie cannot help but send an implicit metamessage along the
following lines: This, Monsieur (*le Censeur*), is what I desire to say
publicly (about what I have desired). Do I have your permission to
do so?

To the guarantee of confession provided by the penitent's willingness to forgo the self-censorship of ordinary politeness and inflict personal injury on the confessor, written confession to the censor thus adds the
further guarantee of an undeniable, if not necessarily confessed, desire
that the text eventually see the light of day. And when there are ways
around the pseudosacred duty of submission to censorship—supposing,
for example, that Julie could have gotten to the lovers' old mailbox and
posted her letter directly to Saint-Preux—the desire for publication may
be doubled by or predicated on a likewise unconfessed desire for the
prior stamp of approval or legitimacy that only the external censorship
can confer. There is, in this instance, no absolute compulsion to pinpoint
the sin or sins, or to decide on their degree of actual sinfulness, only a
consciousness on the part of the penitent of having committed some acts
of exorbitant and overwhelming desire.

But a delicate balance still needs to be maintained. If the censor-in-
the-confessor were to overshadow the confessor-in-the-censor, the new-
age penitent would be in for new causes of anxiety. Confession is, of
course, beside the main point of literary censorship, which deals indiscriminately with texts of all stripes and degrees of subversiveness. Left to
the exclusive devices of censorship, the writer might, for cause, worry
about the sincerity of texts formulated with the censor qua censor in
mind or not entirely out of mind. A voice of censorship may have so
thoroughly infiltrated and inflected the process of composition as to
make submission to the literal censor a redundant, pro forma gesture, or
what amounts, in fact, to a denial of denial. Has the writer, in fact, "fore-
seeing which passages were likely to be objected to by the censor, . . .
forestalled him by softening them down, making some slight modification
or contenting himself with hints and allusions to what he really wants to

write"?[24] And how does the writer feel about the prospect of complicity with an institution that, unlike institutionalized confession, would seem at best to have the bad name of a necessary evil? For, even as an institution, censorship has almost always required that the political orthodoxy on whose behalf it operates offer at least a pretense of exculpatory rationalization. But then again, the ability to identify a real-life censor "out there" may in fact protect the writer, if not against authorial censorship itself, at least against the intuition that there may be any such thing.

On the other hand, were a secular confessor like Wolmar to be stripped of his concomitant mandate to censor, his reading would serve no transcendent social end. He would read (or not) on his own time, for his own reasons, at his own discretion, and he might, at any time, vacate the confessional or disrupt the confessional process by some move toward resumption of normal interpersonal relations. The exorbitant meta-desire that may or may not accede to consciousness of the penitent has no longer to do with getting the text out and/or approved, but rather with monopolizing the floor and prolonging autoreferential discourse beyond socially acceptable limits.

It is to just such a desire that Rousseau, as author of the *Lettres à Malesherbes,* freely admits in the metaconfessional aside of Letter 3: "Quoique j'aime trop à parler de moi, je n'aime pas en parler avec tout le monde, c'est ce qui me fait abuser de l'occasion quand je l'ai et qu'elle me plait. Voila mon tort et mon excuse" (1:1142). Rousseau does not admit directly to abusing *Malesherbes's* indulgence and liking to write in confidence to *him.* But through the very deviousness of effacing the interlocutor, less becomes more than full disclosure. What the admission leaves largely unsaid and, in consequence, looming large is Rousseau's pleasure in knowing that, with "Monsieur" on the receiving end (and not "tout le monde"), there is little enough reason to fear the worst-case scenario whereby one-sided confession would degenerate into a mutual exchange of confidences. A "Monsieur" named Malesherbes was as unlikely to confide in return as, say, a censor in receipt of an author's unsolicited manuscript. Malesherbes, in fact, came honestly, and more honestly than the self-appointed Wolmar of Rousseau's prophetic fiction, by the title and good offices of censor-confessor. Everyone knew—and no one better than Rousseau—that among the duties that befell Malesherbes in his governmental post as Directeur de la Librairie was that of administering the Parisian Office of Censorship.[25]

THE CENSOR AS BEST OF ALL POSSIBLE CONFESSORS

Censorship was an inescapable fact of eighteenth-century publishing history, and the Librairie was a prominent landmark on the literary landscape. Government regulations called for routine submission to the office of all manuscripts for which authorization was being sought to publish in France. Having been recruited as censors, experts in the field to which manuscripts sought admittance were instructed to scrutinize them for anything libelous or otherwise offensive to church, state, or public morals.[26] These censors could, on the basis of their findings, recommend against publication, make a provisional recommendation for publication pending substantial editing, or authorize publication in one of three ways: by granting an outright *permission,* a *permission tacite,* or a *tolérance.* The last two categories existed in large part for the protection of the censors themselves. In the case of a recognizably important but controversial book, publication could be ensured but not endorsed by a censor's simply looking the other way.[27] And insofar as no individual censor could be expected to catch all instances of libel or heterodoxy, the *permission tacite* was a useful compromise measure. *Permissions tacites* were recorded only in Malesherbes's office (and not in the published books themselves), thus guaranteeing anonymity to censors and protecting the inadvertently permissive among them from eventual prosecution as accessories after the fact to crimes of authorship.[28]

Beaumarchais's ironizing Figaro captures these principles and procedures of the office quite accurately in the process of a bitter denunciation:

> [P]ourvu que je ne parle en mes écrits ni de l'autorité, ni du culte, ni de la politique, ni de la morale, ni des gens en place, ni des corps en crédit, ni de l'Opéra, ni des autres spectacles, ni de personne qui tienne à quelque chose, je puis tout imprimer librement, sous l'inspection de deux ou trois Censeurs. Pour profiter de cette douce liberté, j'annonce un écrit périodique, et croyant n'aller sur les brisées d'aucun autre, je le nomme *Journal inutile.*[29]

It nonetheless bears recalling that individuals living in the vicinity of vigorous censorship tend to make unwarranted generalizations[30] about the institution on the sole basis of their own experience. The unpublished and unpublishable Figaro thus represents the isolated exception to a general rule of variably open, easy, and understandable accommodation with the Office of Censorship on the part of Enlightenment authors. In this business of granting *permissions,* it was hardly a case of hardened lines between "us" and "them." The office frequently employed as censors authors whose own works stood, on other occasions, to be censored—an instance of particularly inspired casting being that of d'Alembert's volunteering to censor and so expedite the publication of Rousseau's *Lettre à d'Alembert.*[31] In whatever political terms one chooses to cast the ancien régime, little happened in its waning moments to refute David Tribe's cool-headed conclusion: "Even in totalitarian countries censorship is usually exercised in a less ham-fisted way than is commonly appreciated, so that most writers are not pure rebels but share some of the interests and prejudices surrounding them."[32]

For his part, Rousseau never opposed literary censorship in principle, although he did, on several occasions, declare himself perfectly capable of doing his own. Out of unwillingness to let the Genevan *Conseil* censor his Dedication to the Second Discourse, Rousseau wrote: "Mon expérience m'a donc fait prendre la ferme résolution d'être desormais mon unique Censeur."[33] And Rousseau did, at times, admit to frustration with the system's inevitable inconsistencies: "Monsieur de Malesherbes m'élève des scrupules sur les sentimens de Julie et de Saint-Preux qu'il n'a point elevés sur les miens propres dans mon discours sur l'inégalité ni même dans ma lettre à M^r d'Alembert."[34] Convinced that Malesherbes's proposals for "retranchemens" in *Julie* added up to a "mutilation . . . choquante,"[35] Rousseau launched a third-person bombastic retort (e.g., "Quoi! Monsieur de Malesherbes veut-il que je renie ma foi?"). The bombast no doubt has something to do with the Head Censor's failure to appreciate what a thorough job of pre-censoring the novelist had already done, in part by thematizing censorship in the character of Wolmar. The Rousseau who railed at efforts on the part of Malesherbes's theologically minded deputies to "convert" Julie[36] was, after all, the author of a "perfectly adequate" conversion already on the books (2:363–65).

Rousseau's conspiracy theory of a Jesuit plot to suppress and later mutilate *Emile* is likewise grounded in the institutional reality of censorship. His wildest imaginings yield a horror story of censorship infiltrated by a seditious fringe element, wrested from the control of the proper authorities, and allowed to run rampant. Evidence we shall turn up later suggests that at some level Rousseau himself knew *Emile* to deserve the dreaded hatchet job of his demonic Censor-Jesuits, "the persecutor always being in some sense the victim's double, if only as a projection effect."[37] But it is also suggestive that, on this singular occasion, Rousseau did get back in touch with reality, precisely by contacting and unburdening himself to Malesherbes, the proper authority. Our own moment in literary history is quite tellingly reflected by the fact that authors' death wishes for their books run toward computer failure or lackluster advertising campaigns. The Jesuit plot theory may be just as illustrative of a former age when authors really dealt, on a day-to-day basis and even in their fantasy lives, with censorship. From too far away, we tend to view that censorship too monolithically and not myopically enough when we alternately deplore and dignify it as our ancestors' special albatross and challenge to greatness.

And, for better or worse, from 1750 to 1763 Malesherbes was the man in charge at the Office of Censorship. For his work there, he earned the grudging respect even of Voltaire.[38] For one of Malesherbes's paraprofessional initiatives, "allowing pages of the manuscript of the *Encyclopédie* to be hidden away from the eyes of the police in his own house," he has since been reductively romanticized as "the Enlightenment's Trojan Horse in the Camp of Authoritarianism."[39] In fact, reflecting in retirement on his experience, Malesherbes would write of having come to view institutionalized censorship as impractical and intellectually undesirable.[40] But, for the duration of his tenure, which included occasional forays into hands-on involvement with day-to-day operations, Malesherbes seems to have exercised his administrative functions as scrupulously, conscientiously, and fair-mindedly as possible. He was more of a "writer's censor" than some, and yet, ever the government's representative.

It was this middle man that Rousseau had in mind when he serendipitously got his letters to the censor in under the wire. In no position to know that Malesherbes would resign his office the following year, Rousseau had every reason to connect, even confuse, the individual with the *charge.* The parallelism of their two careers is so striking that Malesherbes acceded to his post at the Librairie, in 1750, just in time to pass judgment on Rousseau's First Discourse. Symptomatically, thirteen years and countless official encounters later, Rousseau's letter of condolence to the "retiree" evoked the compensations of the private life, to which the writer wrongly supposed the ex-director to be returning: "occupé des charmes de la littérature, vous n'êtes plus forcés d'en voir les calamités."[41] Malesherbes found himself obliged to remind Rousseau that, far from being retired, he still retained his other "charge" (as Premier Président de la Cour des Aides).[42] The opening line of Rousseau's letter of condolence ("J'use rarement, Monsieur, de la permission que vous m'avez donnée de vous écrire")[43] is likewise typical. It salutes in Malesherbes an individual whom Rousseau never quite forgets to be in the business of granting *permissions.* Many among even the most personal of Rousseau's letters to Malesherbes parrot the refrain "Permettez-moi," which had launched their correspondence with a request that the director not allow the Second Discourse to be circulated in France prior to its distribution in Geneva.[44] The correspondence thus illustrates a general truth about autobiographical discourse: "Just as portions of the author's identity may be treated as irrelevant or undistinguished, aspects of the audience's individual or collective identity may be more or less cavalierly neglected."[45] What Rousseau almost never neglects in writing to Malesherbes are the professional bases of their relationship.

In fact, however much he appreciated the occasional warmth of this working relationship, Rousseau was, as a rule, far from wanting "his" Malesherbes for a generic friend or protector. It came as an unpleasant surprise to learn that the Head Censor could forget himself to the point of acting "out of character." To wit, the instructive chapter of their dealings about *Julie.* Having opted for printing in Amsterdam, the penurious novelist proposed that Malesherbes receive the proofs and forward them to him—provided, of course, that "cette grace" not prove too "onéreuse."[46] Rousseau evidently relied too heavily on Malesherbes to understand that he was being provided with an opportunity to do his official duty of censoring. The author could not hide his disappointment at Malesherbes's handling of the request as routine ("Il n'y a aucun homme de lettres un peu connu à qui je ne procure la même facilité")[47] and speeding the proofs along their way unopened. Against the censor's insensitivity and dereliction of duty, the author went on to lodge a formal complaint: "Si malgré nos conventions vous vous faites un scrupule d'ouvrir les pacquets, comment puis-je, Monsieur, ne pas m'en faire un de souffrir qu'ils vous [soient] addressés. Quand M. Rey vous a demandé cette permission, nous avons songé, lui et moi, que puisqu'il faloit toujours que le livre passât sous vos yeux comme Magistrat, vous vous feriez un plaisir, comme ami et protecteur des lettres d'en rendre l'envoi utile au libraire et commode à l'Editeur."[48] It is against this background of resistance by Rousseau to the "decensoring" of relations with Malesherbes that the move to engineer decensored relations by and in the *Lettres* takes on added relief. Not that the *Lettres* ever formally inscribe the censor in his office. It is, rather, the conspicuous censoring of the censor that elevates a fact of biography among others to the status of that which, axiomatically and fundamentally true, would be "needless to say" and does not bear repeating. Given the two correspondents' mutual understanding, there was no need for Rousseau to gloss the possessive in his phrase "Vos gens de lettres" (1:1143). Already, Letter 2's beginnings of a life story had appealed discreetly to Malesherbes the censor in giving a new twist to the primal catastrophe of Jean-Jacques's precocious reading. On this occasion, Rousseau systematically suppresses all signs of personal agency: "A six ans Plutarque me tomba sous la main, à huit je le savois par cœur; j'avois lû tous les romans, ils m'avoient fait verser des seaux de larmes, avant l'age où le cœur prend interêt aux romans" (1:1134). Even the young Rousseau does not but will have read, as though the Fates themselves had dropped a copy of Plutarch into his lap. But this is obviously not what happened; the child must have gotten his hands on the wrong books as a result of someone's dereliction of duty. Where, in Rousseau's hour of need, were those curbs on free expression to which even the most enlightened and permissive societies tend to subscribe, curbs aimed at protecting the "innocence of children"?[49] By tacitly indicting Isaac Rousseau on this single count of failure to censor, the *Lettres* embrace the censor in Malesherbes as fundamentally constitutive of their own more perfect father confessor.

It is, then, as though answering the call for a censor who would have made all the difference in Rousseau's life and who can still exercise a decisive impact on his life story that Letter 4 summons Malesherbes from the wings of discourse and gives rebirth, in the here and now, to a "vous né d'un sang illustre." In the recitation of Malesherbes's indictable existential links to the nobility and political establishment, the title of Directeur de la Librairie is conspicuous by its absence. And rightly so: it is the censor whom Rousseau seeks to take away from all that by ostentatiously disrupting his own syllogism in progress. With major (I hate the high and mighty) and minor (You are one of them) premises firmly in place, the letter veers off. In defiance of formal logic and of the confessional logic that Julie's direct hits on her confessor had raised to an art form, Rousseau's sentence comes to rest on the "mille biens" (1:1145) accorded him by Malesherbes from the time immemorial when the censor only knew of the author and vice versa.

More than anything else, it is this evocation of an impersonal, strictly professional past that allows Rousseau to make an unprecedented "occasion," in the ceremonial sense of the word, of his having happened to confess to the censor. In the normal course of events, personal letters are so obviously extraneous to literature and so unquestionably exempt from censorship, providing no attempt is made at publication, that no one would think to make the point. Only in the particular instance of letters addressed to the censor for his eyes only does the point of deviation from standard literary practice emerge with something like the force of a radical departure or absolute retirement. Even Julie's deathbed letter, which was destined to complete its prescribed trajectory through Wolmar posthumously, does not cover the exceptional case of letters voluntarily dead-ended in the hands of the censor-confessor. What Malesherbes will have received are not merely personal and confidential letters, but letters self-consciously conceived as short-circuiting the process of literature as usual. Omitting Malesherbes's title will have become Rousseau's way of hinting at the relevance of literature as that which an extraordinary rhetorical situation has managed to render uniquely irrelevant.

If, for once, Malesherbes does not censor, but only hears confession, it must follow that Rousseau does not write *mémoires* in any mundane, run-of-the-mill sense of the word. He engages, rather, in the pseudosacred business of making his confession. It is, finally, this chance to knowingly disregard his interlocutor's existential identity that brings out the self-conscious and self-confident innovator in Rousseau. The *Lettres* break new ground. As the first of Rousseau's absolutely freestanding self-portraits, they exit a worst of all possible worlds, one where liminary self-portraiture carried out more or less clandestinely had remained a satellite of real literature and subject to precisely the same guidelines for admissibility to publication. For once, the old rules are momentarily and momentously suspended: Rousseau can, with the other's blessing, move his self to center stage and think to write a life story no less unique than its subject.

To be sure, the *Confessions* would look back on the *Lettres,* "en quelque façon le sommaire de ce que j'expose ici" (1:569), as the kind of by-the-book, unapologetic preface that the *Encyclopédie* recommended and Rousseau himself had attempted when he summarized the First Discourse in the *Préface de Narcisse.* [50] It would even be possible to read the *Lettres* as Rousseau's best extant attempt at dedication to the Maréchal and Maréchale de Luxembourg: Letter 4 tells finally of Rousseau's having been seduced out of solitude to live "au Chateau de Montmorenci" by the exceptional "chaleur de l'enthousiasme" that its "maîtres" inspire (1:1145).[51] But the *Lettres* were never pressed, regardless, into either prefatory or dedicatory service. And the *Confessions* make the point that the *Lettres* were left unpublished, despite Rousseau's having taken all but the final step in that direction. He had made copies of the letters that, on request, Malesherbes returned to sender (1:569), and he had given them the unifying title of a single opus: "Quatre lettres à Monsieur le Président de Malesherbes contenant le vrai tableau de mon caractére et les vrais motifs de toute ma conduite" (1:1131). It was nonetheless only fitting that the *Lettres* should be left just out of the margins and the loop of literature: they thereby remained free to commemorate the occasion on which Rousseau's self-portraiture found a way to leave the (publishing) world behind and to closet itself in the confessional.

Rousseau hastens to make clear that his spiriting Malesherbes away from the prevailing social order should not be construed as a gesture of political subversion. The aim was not to do away with censorship, but merely to liberate a would-be autobiographer from literature. Lest Malesherbes get the wrong idea, Letter 4 closes by relating the recurring "dream" that the Letters themselves fulfill symbolically, but which cannot come true in any real-life context:

> J'ai cent fois supposé dans mes rêves Mr de Luxembourg point Duc, mais [*sic*] Marechal de France, mais bon Gentilhomme de Campagne habitant quelque vieux chateau, et J. J. Rousseau point auteur, point faiseur de livres, mais ayant un esprit mediocre, et un peu d'acquis, se presentant au Seigneur Chatelain, et à la Dame, leur agréant, trouvant aupres d'eux le bonheur de sa vie, et contribuant au leur; si pour rendre le rêve plus agreable vous me permettiez de pousser d'un coup d'epaule le chateau de Malesherbes à demi lieue de la, il me semble Monsieur qu'en rêvant

de cette maniere je n'aurois de longtems envie de me reveiller.
(1:1146)

It is not to promote "J. J. Rousseau" that the dream-come-true de-
motes "Mr de Luxembourg," but specifically to remove literature from
the equation of social inequality. "Point auteur, point faiseur de livres"—
that is precisely the point—Rousseau would not need nor would he
merit so powerful a protector. There would be no call for the specter of
censorship to mediate happy relations with that protector; the protégé
would no longer be obliged to see his lord and lady in the discomfiting
guise of peers of the very realm that censorship normally defends against
bookmakers of his ilk. The censor-turned-neighbor could be added to the
picture at any time, as an "agreable" afterthought and gratuitous embel-
lishment. Asking permission to shove "le chateau de Malesherbes" into
his own vicinity, Rousseau renders appropriately forcible the fait accompli of uprooting the censor and dismantling the three-tiered structure
where censorious middlemen keep authors' wishes in line with political
orthodoxy. For the Letters themselves have done everything in their only
symbolic power to replace that structure with the twin towers of confessional tête-a-tête in a self-consciously transgressive "ton familier"
(1:1133).

EXTENDING THE INSTITUTIONAL MODEL:
The Inside Story of Censorship

Of course—as Freud's dream censor is wont to object when, caught
napping, it must resort to staircase wit—it's only a dream.[52] And Rousseau would live to wake up from his "long rêve" (1:1146). His
Confessions would tell a different story of censorship, if only because
censorship was their own inevitable destination and a subject that, as a
faithful record of waking life, they could not always avoid. Full accounting for the career of any eighteenth-century homme de lettres demanded
discussion of the bureaucratic maneuvering that consumed so much of
the time and energy even of the sometimes desultory Rousseau. The
Confessions oblige, making no secret of Malesherbes's official involvement in Rousseau's attempts to publish his various works, and often going
into considerable detail. Only at the moment of actually evoking the
Lettres do the *Confessions* follow their lead in censoring the censor, but
with different results.

To readers already well versed in the details of Malesherbes's curriculum vitae (and in for quite a few subsequent reminders), it must look suspiciously as though the *Confessions* wished to see the recipient of Rousseau's *Lettres* as having taken his work home and acted the censor even when off duty. Rather than respect the inviolability of the confessional, Malesherbes, as would-be censor in private service to Rousseau, is said to have expressed approval of the letters, shown them around to a broader Parisian public, even—as we know not to have been the case— had copies made himself at the author's behest (1:569).[53] In vague recollection of having inscribed we-know-who in the confines of a private confessional, Rousseau uses the selection and discreet distortion of facts to domesticate the censor as such, to ply the public official over to his side—even, this time around, to thumb his nose in the general direction of the rich and powerful whose interests Malesherbes had been commissioned to protect and at whose pleasure he normally served.

Or, rather, this is one reading to which we are pointed precisely by that (Malesherbes's title) which Rousseau pointedly omits to mention. Then again, the omission may seem pointed only because what we know to be omitted (censorship) is itself a matter of selective omission, and because, once admitted to consciousness, the possibility of censorship runs so rampant through our minds as to infiltrate the environs with an ever-increasing degree of probability. Say the word—or better yet, in a more perfect marriage of form and content—write the word under erasure, and suddenly we find ourselves being pressured into a state of greater than usual vigilance, and into a mode of microscopic analysis. It takes only the vaguest rumor of censorship on the agenda to make us watch an author's words for signs that more may be going on here than meets the eye.[54] Axiomatic foreknowledge of psychic censorship has been the inveterate alibi of symptomatic, "in-depth" reading at least since Freud posited the metaphorical extendability of the institutional model and positioned a censoring agency squarely within the individual psyche. In Rousseau, by contrast, punctual cues do the work of axiomatic foreknowledge. The metaphor is still in the making, always provisional, and always within sight of the institutional base.

A portion of the Malesherbes-Rousseau correspondence dealing with *Julie* illustrates what I mean by a tendency or compulsion to internalize censorship known or surmised to be in the air. There being no legal prohibitions against *contrefaçons* or reprintings in France of books published abroad, Malesherbes offered Rousseau the opportunity of naming his own publisher for the inevitable reprinting of *Julie.*[55] Surprised that the director would even consider granting a *permission* for his novel, Rousseau took Malesherbes to school on "la rigueur de la censure" in France. The director would seem to have forgotten the difference between tolerating foreign imports and permitting domestic publication. To a disconcertingly overpermissive censor, Rousseau proposed the example of his own moral rigor: he vowed to dissociate himself entirely from the French edition and balked especially, "en repos de conscience," at the thought of deriving personal gain from an enterprise detrimental to the interests of Rey.[56] It took every argument Malesherbes could muster to provoke Rousseau's letter of capitulation, which begins as follows: "J'ai fait, Monsieur, tout ce que vous avez voulu, et le consentement du Sr Rey ayant levé mes scrupules je me trouve riche de vos bienfaits. L'intérêt que vous daignez prendre à moi est au dessus de mes remercimens."[57]

But, en route to this resolution, the episode will have brought out and into play the censor within. Why should Rousseau have overreacted to the prospect of receiving a permit for *Julie?* No doubt because he did not or—more precisely—had claimed not to want one. On the occasion of sending Malesherbes an advance copy of the novel for his personal library, Rousseau had added, somewhat gratuitously: "Je vous Supplie, Monsieur, que ce recueil ne Sorte pas de vos mains jusqu'à Sa publication. Alors je suis bien sur que son Succès ne tentera personne de le contrefaire, et bien plus encore que vous ne le permettrez point."[58] Permission being the one thing we never receive without asking for it, or, when it is granted "spontaneously," without the presupposition of an unspoken or deviously spoken (i.e., censored) desire, Rousseau evidently assumed Malesherbes to have made such a presupposition. For the director to pass directly to the details of reprinting meant that an expression of nondesire or *not* of desire by Rousseau must not have been taken seriously. But who or what was to blame if not a malfunctioning of the internal censorship, which must have contented itself with a too transparent translation of desire into its opposite, by allowing the word *permission* to be placed into circulation.

The malfunctioning goes unacknowledged; malaise akin to that of the Freudian dreamer whose wish will have "surprised" the dream censor[59] nonetheless sought relief in two ways: through projection of overpermissiveness onto an external permission-granting agency (Malesherbes would be found remiss, inadequately rigorous), and through a belated public display of self-censorship (Malesherbes would witness a thoroughgoing sacrifice of self-interest to generosity). In Rousseau's letter of capitulation, the lifting of censorship misplaced onto a manufactured desire to profit goes hand in hand with a more adequate "censoring" of the residual desire for permission. "J'ai fait tout ce que vous avez voulu"—the reduction of all desiring to that of an external censor to grant permission commemorates through denial the heretofore unspeakable operations of the imperfectly vigilant internal censorship.

It is to experiences like this one that the *Lettres à Malesherbes* called a temporary, stabilizing halt, by writing even the institutional model out of epistolary relations. The Rousseau of the *Confessions* seems, conversely, to be inching toward a depth psychology featuring something along the lines of literary censorship in a pivotal role. Politically speaking, he had every reason to proceed with caution, lest he surprise himself in the act of having embraced, along with the institution's modus operandi, its institutional loyalties to the high and mighty. That distasteful prospect gives rise to emphatic expressions of denial in the *Confessions* passage that recalls Jean-Jacques's disagreement with Malesherbes over what to do with an aphoristic formula in *Julie* (1:512). Both recognize that the aphorism—"la femme d'un Charbonnier est plus digne de respect que la maitresse d'un Prince"—might be mistaken by the king's mistress, Mme de Pompadour, for a disagreeable allusion to her own status. But Jean-Jacques declares the deed of censorship to be already done, by him, and consciously so: only upon reading his manuscript had he made the connection and so substituted the word "Prince" for the original, more incriminating "Roi." His conscience is doubly clear. To swear that he had no "application" in mind "dans la chaleur de la composition" is to address directly the question of malicious (or censorable) intent, but also to void the creative process itself of internalized pressure from the top to censor along party lines. Guilty of an illicit thought, Jean-Jacques might—perish the thought—have taken unconscious steps to couch it in licit form. His manuscript might have arrived at the Office of Censorship already bearing traces not only of lèse majesté but of the king's censorship and the concubine's pseudolegitimacy.

This brush with unconscious orthodoxy is too close not to call for the extreme measure of projecting the excesses of servile censorship onto Malesherbes. The *Confessions* catch the Head Censor in the act of

deleting the entire sentence and gluing a substitute page "aussi propre-
ment qu'il fut possible" into the copy of *Julie* destined for Pompadour's
perusal. The deed was, however, not neatly enough done to preclude her
detecting this "tour de passe-passe" or sleight of hand. It is from censorship become, in Tribe's words, ham-fisted that Rousseau thinks to dissociate himself by this act of poetic justice. The same moral might,
however, be applied with as much pertinence to the autobiography's
high-visibility "cut" to Malesherbes as to the latter's likewise well-
intentioned, if clumsily executed, cutting and pasting. The excesses of
denial through projection onto the "real" censor so closely mimic those
of a laughably literal, even parodic version of literary censorship as to
suggest that, with the king out of the picture, things might be different
and less defensive. This is not the moment to entertain the possibility
that something like censorship may go on even "dans la chaleur de la
composition." But the more propitious moment *will* come when receipt
of *Lettres* addressed to and not through him will put Malesherbes in the
position of acting not on behalf of the crown but on his own initiative.

Seizing that initiative, the *Confessions* complete their discussion of
the *Lettres à Malesherbes* with a passage that permits of two diametrically
opposite allegorical accountings for the three-stage chronology:
"Mémoires"/"Lettres"/"ce que j'expose ici." Rousseau's relies heavily on
the two-faced concept of *supplémentarité* to leave the question in a state
of indeterminacy: "[P]ar l'esquisse tracée à la hâte dans ces quatre lettres,
je tâchois de suppléer en quelque sorte aux Mémoires que j'avois projettés. Ces lettres qui plurent à M. de Malesherbes et qu'il montra dans
Paris, sont en quelque façon le sommaire de ce que j'expose ici plus en
détail et méritent à ce titre d'être conservées" (1:569). The twice or
doubly supplemental *Lettres* not only take the place of a "vide" called
"Mémoires" but, likewise and otherwise, coexist with the *Confessions* in
the guise of "un surplus, une plénitude enrichissant une autre plénitude,
le *comble* de la présence."[60] These lines, which change meanings of "le
supplément" in mid-course and use the deictic "ici" to formalize thoroughgoing banishment of the *Lettres* to nonpresence, might well have
inspired Derrida's provisional conclusions about supplementarity per se:
"Chacune des deux significations s'efface à son tour ou s'estompe discrètement devant l'autre. Mais leur fonction commune se reconnaît à
ceci: qu'il s'ajoute ou qu'il se substitue, le supplément est *extérieur,* hors
de la positivité à laquelle il se surajoute, étranger à ce qui, pour être par

lui remplacé, doit être autre que lui. A la différence du *complément,*
disent les dictionnaires, le supplément est une 'addition *extérieure'*
(Robert)."[61] The "censored" (and literally condensed) version of the life
story would warrant conserving as an alleged outsider to both the
"Mémoires" and the *Confessions.* It provides documentary counterproof
that neither the remembering nor the confessing has been affected or
infected by the censorship "out there."

But to stop at this point would be to resist knowing that the *Lettres*
qua *lettres* or letters "à ce titre" also serve to underwrite the
"Mémoires"/*Confessions* polarity, investing one pole with the negativity
of absence, the other with the positivity of presence. The *Lettres* lend
substance to a diacritical mark of difference on the basis of which an
unrealized before (of raw materials only) can be distinguished from an
after of "exposure" to the light of day. And in this instance, censorship
can be identified as that extra something without which the *Confessions*
would not be wholly themselves. Rousseau's chronology models the
psychic censorship through whose good graces primal memories and
desires are nowadays universally assumed to emerge from the unconscious and accede to acceptably symbolic form.[62] Earmarking the *Lettres*
for conservation is the *Confessions'* way of remembering, symbolically,
that censorship has underwritten every moment of Rousseau's coming to
confession.

The *Confessions* are as hesitant to affirm as to deny this reliance of
confession on unconscious self-censorship and, in fact, have no business
doing either. To admit directly to self-censorship would be to make a
mockery of the confessional process, whose integrity depends on assurances that the penitent is telling the whole truth and nothing but the
truth as far as he or she knows. But when knowledge of the truth extends
to an intuition of self-censorship, not to say so would in turn be less than
truthful, "en sorte que tout est faute," both avowal and refusal to avow.[63]
In the absence of institutionalized assurances that everyone censors as
much as everyone sins, censorship becomes the most guilty and the least
confessable of sins. The most guilty, insofar as it renders all other secrets,
as formulated, suspect; the least confessable in that suspicion is precisely
what the penitent cannot afford to arouse. Caught in a double bind between the dictates of religious precedent and the murmurs of secular
psychology, the *Confessions* do what they can to be honest with the
autobiographical act.[64] They leave the metaphorical connection with in-

stitutionalized censorship unmade but makeable and, on at least one occasion, use the chronology of their own telling to flee and embrace the occasion of metaphor.

TELLING AND KISSING: An Allegory of Censorship

Time will and will not tell in the suggestive passage from the *Confessions* that begins by establishing a precise temporal frame for a new chapter in Jean-Jacques's adventures entitled "second voyage de Montmorenci de l'année 1760" (1:534). Starting now, and until further notice, we will learn what transpired in the course of the second visit paid by the Maréchal and Maréchale de Luxembourg to the country estate where Thérèse and Jean-Jacques have been installed as permanent guests. As is typical enough of the *Confessions* not to attract undue attention, the relevant memories are then filtered through a second, thematic screen: career developments take their accustomed distance from the private life and, in this instance, take precedence. A first paragraph is devoted in its entirety to developments surrounding *Emile*.

The manuscript having been completed, the issue of the hour is that of where to publish it. A disagreement pitting Jean-Jacques against the Maréchale and her eventual ally Malesherbes turns on the question of whether the Office of Censorship can be counted on to grant a *permission tacite*. An obstinately pessimistic Jean-Jacques second-guesses the king's censorship, as though better qualified to do so than either the professional administrator or the aristocrat. He argues that there is no chance of obtaining a *permission* and that, without one, he absolutely does not want to "permettre . . . l'impression dans le Royaume" (1:534). A long (lost) letter from Malesherbes evidently provided reassurance that "la profession de foi du Vicaire Savoyard," *Emile*'s most outwardly problematical passage, "étoit précisement une piéce faite pour avoir par tout l'approbation du genre humain, et celle de la Cour dans la circonstance" (1:534). Jean-Jacques was at last convinced to let the Maréchale go ahead with arrangements for publication, as though publication per se had ever been at issue. After all, what did Jean-Jacques know about censorship, except that "l'impression d'un livre qu'il [Malesherbes] approuvoit étoit par cela seul légitime" (1:534)?

The permission of an unusually "coulant" (for him) Head Censor thus becomes the necessary, sufficient, and profoundly arbitrary condition of legitimacy. The court's opinion counts for as little as humanity's in a punctual act of legitimization that may very well reflect neither absolute justice nor even its parochial applications "dans le système que le Gouvernement avoit adopté" (1:534). But by a "scrupule" deemed "extraordinaire" Jean-Jacques refuses to back off from his prior insistence on foreign printing (1:534–35). There is no accounting for this scruple, unless Jean-Jacques knows more about *Emile,* censorship, or both than he lets on in this paragraph, which proceeds smartly through a few more minor stipulations to an emphatic conclusion: "Voilà exactement ce qui fut convenu entre Mad^c de Luxembourg et moi, après quoi je lui remis mon manuscrit" (1:535). If the deal is closed, so too is the subject of *Emile;* Jean-Jacques has relinquished the manuscript and claimed to want nothing further to do with it.

The change of subject from literary to real life is easily accomplished. Smoothing the transition to a new paragraph becomes a simple matter of using "Mad^c de Luxembourg" as the antecedent for a subject pronoun and recalling the prevailing temporal frame: "Elle avoit amené à ce voyage sa petite fille Mademoiselle de Boufflers, aujourd'hui Mad^c la Duchesse de Lauzun" (1:535). By more than satisfying the demands of narrative coherence, the text earns the right to forge ahead, to forget, and to lull its unsuspecting readers into forgetfulness of its own immediate past. But rather than exercise that right, the narrative doubles back. And not only at the level of recorded time, whose linear unfolding the pluperfect "avoit amené" already disrupts, transporting the narrative back to the starting line of the "second voyage." Persistent verbal echoes work to bring the publishing story back into play in the course of a supposedly unrelated (or superficially related) domestic drama. Look for "Elle me permit" to revive the issue of "permission," for "ma maussaderie ordinaire" to resurrect "un scrupule extraordinaire," for "je censure" to answer "la censure," for "la Cour" to resurface as "le pouvoir des Rois."

> Elle avoit amené à ce voyage sa petite fille Mademoiselle de Boufflers, aujourd'hui Mad^c la Duchesse de Lauzun. Elle s'appelloit Amelie. C'étoit une charmante personne. Elle avoit vraiment une figure, une douceur, une timidité virginale. Rien de plus aimable et de plus interessant que sa figure, rien de plus tendre et de plus chaste que les sentimens qu'elle inspiroit. D'ailleurs c'étoit une enfant; elle n'avoit pas onze ans. Mad^c la Mareschale qui la trouvoit trop timide faisoit ses efforts pour l'animer. Elle me permit plusieurs fois de lui donner un baiser; ce que je fis avec ma maussaderie ordinaire. Au lieu des gen-

tillesses qu'un autre eut dites à ma place, je restois-là muet, interdit, et je ne sais lequel étoit le plus honteux de la pauvre petite ou de moi. Un jour je la rencontrai seule dans l'escalier du petit Château: elle venoit de voir Therese avec laquelle sa Gouvernante étoit encore. Faute de savoir que lui dire, je lui proposai un baiser que dans l'innocence de son cœur elle ne refusa pas, en ayant receu un le matin même par l'ordre de sa grand maman et en sa présence. Le lendemain, lisant l'*Emile* au chevet de Mad^e la Mareschale, je tombai précisément sur un passage où je censure avec raison ce que j'avois fait la veille. Elle trouva la réflexion très juste, et dit là dessus quelque chose de fort sensé qui me fit rougir. Que je maudis mon incroyable bétise qui m'a si souvent donné l'air vil et coupable quand je n'étois que sot et embarrassé! bétise qu'on prend même pour une fausse excuse dans un homme qu'on sait n'être pas sans esprit. Je puis jurer que dans ce baiser si répréhensible ainsi que dans les autres, le cœur et les sens de Mlle Amélie n'étoient pas plus purs que les miens, et je puis jurer même que si dans ce moment j'avois pu éviter sa rencontre, je l'aurois fait; non qu'elle ne me fit grand plaisir à voir, mais par l'embarras de trouver en passant quelque mot agréable à lui dire. Comment se peut-il qu'un enfant même intimide un homme que le pouvoir des Rois n'a pas effrayé. Quel parti prendre? Comment se conduire denué de tout impromptu dans l'esprit? Si je me force à parler aux gens que je rencontre, je dis une balourdise infailliblement: si je ne dis rien, je suis un misanthrope, un animal farouche, un Ours. Une totale imbécilité m'eut été bien plus favorable: mais les talens dont j'ai manqué dans le monde ont fait les instruments de ma perte des talens que j'eus à-part-moi. (1:535–36)

Thanks to the aforementioned linguistic doublings, a schematic allegory of censorship doubles the narrative proper, as though in defiance of Jean-Jacques's much-protested reluctance at the anecdotal level to test "la censure." The allegorical intertext does not surface without a struggle; on the contrary, by continuing to marshal resistance to the substantive connection between the two paragraphs, the text acts out the very censorship about which it dares not speak directly; "[s]uperficial associations replace deep ones if the censorship makes the normal connecting paths impassable."[65] Indeed, the intent to leave nothing unconfessed both proscribes and prescribes confession to censorship. If the autobiographer is to live up to his word—"je dirai tout, je n'omettrai pas une de mes fautes, pas même une de mes mauvaises pensées"[66]—there can be no omitting the feeling (or "mauvaise pensée") of having lied and continuing to lie by omission. The tracks of censorship must be covered, but also be re-coverable, in both senses of the word. Here, as wherever censorship is not pathological, it will not blot out, but rather compromise at every turn with the returning repressed, which happens, in this exemplary instance, to be a subtext of censorship. At the two levels of *énoncé* and *énonciation,* that censorship will dissimulate its own operations, but only partially.

And so the narrative takes its time and an entire sentence ("Elle s'appelloit Amelie") to reveal the granddaughter's given name, even when the preceding sentence's two titles, "Mademoiselle de Boufflers" and "Mad^e la Duchesse de Lauzun" (*that* Mlle de Boufflers), have established her extratextual identity beyond the shadow of a doubt. It is as though, freed from referential duty, the name "Amélie" were placed into circulation as an approximate anagram for "Emile." The text exchanges one for the other on a regular basis, from the moment of relinquishing the manuscript to Mme la Maréchale and receiving in its stead "sa petite fille." One day Jean-Jacques is kissing Amélie; the next day—and the next sentence, as though by virtue of a cinematic jump cut—finds him rereading the supposedly closed book of *Emile.* Returning tit for tat, a feminine for a masculine, a biological child for a brainchild, the Amélie/*Emile* polarity surreptitiously couples the two paragraphs and installs unspoken censorship at the source of polarization and residual difference. For "Amélie" to become "Emile" and vice versa requires only that letters be scrambled (displacement) and a single letter dropped or added (condensation).

In further testimony to this (in)visible process of linkage, the two poles also exchange properties. The text eventually lets slip a masculine "un enfant" with reference to "Mlle Amélie" and, at the outset, endows the child with the attributes of a work of art. Rousseau's "portrait" does not allow us to see Amélie, but only to see her as a thing of absolute beauty. She is so absolutely self-contained and self-sustaining as to defy misprision by any subjective beholder: "Elle avoit *vraiment* une figure, une douceur, une timidité virginale. Rien de plus aimable et de plus interessant que sa figure, rien de plus tendre et de plus chaste que les sentimens qu'elle inspiroit" (emphasis added). With this objet d'art, moreover, no censor could find fault; there is nothing even remotely corrupting about the influence it exerts—at least until Mme la Maréchale, in unmistakable imitation of Rousseau's Pygmalion (2:1228), tampers with aesthetic perfection and sets about bringing the portrait to life. Amélie as work of art is inspired by the substitution of Platonic categories of good and evil for the unpredictable vagaries of the institutionalized censorship to which her brother *Emile* was subject. Her perfection figures a desire that texts could be wholly virginal, and that desire would reside wholly in the censoring eye/I.

"D'ailleurs, c'étoit une enfant; elle n'avoit pas onze ans." Tipping the balance of the previous period, the text protests too much—but no more than is necessary to rescue the text from unmediated innocence. In anticipation of filling the position of the artist-censor with Mme la Maréchale, the text fills in, censoring by implication the idea that Amélie could be thought of as desirable or desiring and, even as it censors, planting the thought squarely in our minds. Of course, by this point we have begun to wonder what the portrait of Amélie has to do with the story of Jean-Jacques; nothing better serves to arouse our suspicions than a too systematic suppression of the first person pronoun. But by denying subjectivity to the narrator-protagonist, the text points the ghost of an accusatory finger in *our* direction. The text's feigning of ignorance where desire and censorship are concerned only prods us into a state of heightened awareness and blushing self-consciousness: how could we (want to) think "that" of a "me" that has yet to make an appearance in this paragraph? Rousseau obviously knows more about the fear of pedophilia and infantile desire than his later rhetorical question—"Comment se peut-il qu'un enfant même intimide un homme que le pouvoir des Rois n'a pas effrayé[?]"—admits directly. If Freud has it right, the force of a taboo is proportionately and circularly related to that of the (proscribed) desire—and hence, the fear—that the taboo may be violated: "The id says, 'I want it'; the superego says, 'How horrible'; and the ego says, 'I am afraid.'"[67]

Of the three messages, Rousseau's text voices the last, and whispers the others in passing. What it seems to resist more adamantly even than the intuition of transgressive sexuality is knowledge that "le pouvoir des rois" and the power of a child to intimidate should manifest themselves respectively in literary and in psychological censorship, and that the two should have converged in the here and now of a self-censoring text. "Que je maudis mon incroyable bétise"—the exclamation launches a serious attempt at making for cover and diverting the domestic drama toward the *Confessions'* time-honored paradigm of Jean-Jacques's so-called "esprit de l'escalier" or staircase wit. But the diversion is noticeably forcible; the facts do not quite fit: in this instance, "esprit" will have deserted Jean-Jacques especially "dans l'escalier." The very ineptness of the leap from narrative ("qui me fit rougir") to metadiscursive commentary ("Que je maudis") and from an apparent sign of shame to the unexpected signified of foolishness betrays the inappropriateness of the familiar moral to a story that the staircase-wit paradigm cannot entirely domesticate.

Rousseau stretches to recontextualize the Amélie anecdote and to privilege the claims of metaphor (in the guise of Jean-Jacques's character) over those of metonymy or propinquity in the text (to the *Emile* material). But censorship infiltrates even the cover story of staircase wit, which, in this particular rephrasing, places Jean-Jacques in a situation-specific double bind: "Si je me force à parler aux gens que je rencontre, je dis une balourdise infailliblement: si je ne dis rien, je suis un misanthrope, un animal farouche, un Ours." The alternative that pits the inevitable gaffe against dehumanizing silence might be read as positing the equally pathological extremes of totally uncensored and totally censored discourse—that is, if speech itself did not partially censor (the wish not to speak), and silence did not result from a lifting of the censorship on that wish. Symptomatically, anacoluthon had earlier made silence into an attribute of being, rather than a viable alternative to speech: "Au lieu des gentillesses qu'un autre eut dites à ma place, je restois-là." For us speaking animals, there can be no escaping compromise between desire and censorship, except—and on this note, the passage thinks to conclude by exorcising the censor—in those writings where Jean-Jacques will have said what he wants to say and how he wants to say it, and given a "full" accounting of his "esprit."

The distinction between oral and written expression does not, of course, hold up to our scrutiny of the passage in progress. The tongue-tied protagonist has left his mark on a writer whose hands are likewise tied and whose narrative assumes the protagonist's dilemma. What can Mme la Maréchale have been thinking when she "permitted" Jean-Jacques to kiss Amélie? Or, for that matter, when she undertook, notwithstanding her agreement with him, to publish *Emile* in France? Doubly pressing, that line of questioning must, however, be repressed: the discourse cannot afford to question her permissiveness (for fear of exposing hidden desire) or to replicate it too exactly or eagerly (for fear of playing the hoodwinked censor). And yet, displaced, the question stands: what can Rousseau have been thinking at the moment of rendering Madame's injunction or "ordre" to kiss as a speech act of permission?

Censorship eventually, inevitably at issue—when Jean-Jacques "falls," at the Maréchale's "chevet," on a singular passage of *Emile*—is censorship contained and fetishized in a text within the text. "Je censure"—what might pass, out of context, for a bold-faced confession to the censorship presently in progress is inscribed within the pages and the eternal present of another book, an elsewhere "où je censure avec raison ce que j'avois fait la veille." Further blunting the confession and blurring the issue, semantic slippage inherent in the verb "censurer" authorizes translation of "je censure" as "I cen*sure*," or criticize. Does this focus on censure as the simple expression of opinion preclude the other meaning of censorship as the placing of constraints on expression itself? Apparently not: even without tracking down the allusion to *Emile,* we cannot help noticing, in the periphrastic complement "ce que j'avois fait la veille," evidence of inhibiting forces still at work. And no wonder that the *Confessions* talk around the kiss in the staircase, whose implications *Emile* had developed all too pointedly. In fact, what Amélie's grandmother will have unknowingly done is take two pages (4:793–94) out of the book of Sophie's mother, who permits Emile to kiss her daughter only under her own watchful, censoring (and not censorious) eye. "Je ne suis ni farouche, ni prude," the mother explains; "je sais ce qu'il faut passer à la jeunesse folâtre, et ce que j'ai souffert sous mes yeux vous le prouve assés" (4:794). The treatise on education spells out clearly the decisive role of censorship in arbitrarily translating illicit impulses into licit acts. "L'occasion fait le larron"—*et le défait.* Rather than steal a kiss, "Emile . . . tourne un œil suppliant vers la mére, et croyant voir un signe de consentement s'approche en tremblant du visage de Sophie" (4:793). When the young lover, armed with what would amount in literary terms to a *permission tacite,* has gotten his wish, the narrator editorializes: "Quel baiser, s'il n'étoit pas pris sous les yeux d'une mére!" (4:794).

However, in the previous privacy of tête-à-tête with Sophie, Emile had already stolen a kiss (hence, the need to stage this one), and the adult preceptor or Jean-Jacques figure had done nothing to stop him—or to inform his pupil of the crucial difference that censorship makes (4:793). The mother's remedial advice is ostensibly addressed to Emile: "Consultez vôtre ami sur vos devoirs, il vous dira quelle différence il y a entre les jeux que la présence d'un pére et d'une mére autorise, et les libertés qu'on prend loin d'eux en abusant de leur confiance." But that advice cannot help but strike the pedagogue—and the reader-in-the-text at

Madame's bedside—with the force of a "réprimande" (or censure) ad-dressed more to him than to his pupil (4:794).

So much for the rapport of tenuous juxtaposition that the autobiogra-phy's superficial chrono-logic had taken pains to establish between the literary *Emile* and the real-life Amélie. That juxtaposition has been all but supplanted by the new configuration and guilty conscience of an inter-textual *mise en abîme*; a depth dimension has been added to the *Confessions* text that misleadingly appropriates the mother's censorship (and censuring). And more deeply embedded than any other in that text is the guilty secret of unwillingness to know better than Emile or Amélie. Small wonder that negative affect ("je rougis") attaches directly not to the kiss in the staircase but to Mme la Maréchale's expression of approval for a job of censorship well done. It is her indirectly reported direct discourse about censorship ("Elle dit là dessus quelque chose de fort sensé") that makes glaring and shameful the omission or indirection of such discourse in the present text. Of Jean-Jacques's two crimes, stealing a kiss becomes the misdemeanor to which the *Confessions* confess in order to avoid prosecution for the more serious offense of plagiarizing the censor (*proposing* a kiss) without acknowledging the source. The indeterminate status of Amélie vis-à-vis desire matters less, finally, than that the presumed innocence of her "cœur" will have been equated with ignorance of censorship: "elle ne refusa pas, en ayant receu un [baiser] le matin même par l'ordre de sa grand maman et en sa présence."

The narrative proper and the justificatory reprise go to extreme lengths to recapture that lost innocence for Jean-Jacques and, through him, for Rousseau's act of confession. How gratuitous is the explanatory clause that places Amélie on the staircase, unless the circumstance of tête-à-tête between her and Rousseau's respective *gouvernantes* is read as doing what it can to share the child's childishness with him. How labored and yet how purposeful is the period that brackets the question of difference between "ce baiser si répréhensible" and "les autres" en route to declaring Amélie's purity to be at best equal to that of Jean-Jacques. Of course, the avowed basis for comparison favorable to Jean-Jacques consists in "les cœurs et les sens," not in censorship. In Freudian terms, the text tries to take the parental imperative against sensuality more seriously than the (in this case) competing imperative of obe-dience.[68] Better that we should think the worst of our protagonists; bet-ter that Jean-Jacques's desiring should become the bottom line of

willingness to sacrifice the opportunity of seeing—only seeing?—Amélie, than that we should linger too long or too inquisitively at Mme la
Maréchale's bedside.

Censorship and full confession make strange bedfellows. And yet,
were it not for censorship there would be no *Confessions,* or so the
paragraph's barest outlines suggest. The autobiographical trademark of
the first person remains absent from no fewer than seven initial sentences, five of which treat Amélie in isolation, and the first and last of
which pair her with Mme la Maréchale in an exclusive and exclusionary
relationship. The first person accedes to the text belatedly and indirectly,
as the indirect object of a verb of censorship: "Elle me permit." She censored, therefore I am. But when only the other censored, I could not
speak, as anacoluthon makes abundantly clear. And when I only mouthed
the words of the flesh-and-blood, external censor, I still managed to speak
only of other things: "je lui proposai un baiser." I could not, as it were,
kiss and tell. Only now that "je censure," can "je maudis"; only now, says
the text metadiscursively, "je puis jurer . . . je puis jurer. . . ." Propelling
the narrative toward discourse by and about the self, the censorship
moves, always in the direction of greater intimacy, from somewhere out
there (presumably the drawing room) to the transitional staircase, to the
bedroom. Likewise, the paragraph at large gradually absorbs, personalizes, internalizes a chapter in publishing history where the issue of
permissions and, more generally, the desires, interdictions, and fears inspired by censorship, "dans le système que le Gouvernement avoit
adopté," figure prominently. Or rather, what figures prominently is Rousseau's reading of that chapter with reference both to the publishing and
to the text of his own *Emile.* As David Tribe points out: "Apart from
academic specialists, writers on censorship tend to be interested parties.
I do not mean simply that they are interested in removing, reducing or
extending it. Inevitably their experiences are more personal than the
cultural experiences they describe publicly, and from these they make
unwarranted generalizations."[69]

In terms of our barest outlines, the eventual admission of pleasure at
the sight of Amélie is perfectly adequate and rendered with perfect adequacy by parenthetical circumlocution and a restrictive subjunctive
("non qu'elle ne me fît grand plaisir à voir"). Displacement of accent and
affect, the buffering of desire by indirection and irreality[70]—such are
among the essential operations of psychic censorship. And subjectifying

the discourse is in turn the essential desire accommodated by this censorship that, at long last, places Amélie's heretofore objective beauty in
the eye of a particular beholder. In striving after self-consciousness, the
Confessions stop just short of self-conscious censorship. "[S]i dans ce
moment j'avois pu éviter sa rencontre, je l'aurois fait." The referentially
ambiguous phrase "dans ce moment" can be taken to mean "way back
then," but also "just now." The autobiographer hints that he would have
avoided his own "chance" meeting with Amélie had there been any other
way to confess to the constraints on confession. But, in fact, only the
fabrication of an elaborate cover story permits the *Confessions* to commemorate, if not to remember, the conditions of their own elaboration.

Partial, devious, censored confession is preferable to the only alternative, no confession at all. This message is one that the tell-all text can
neither appropriate nor expropriate entirely. It therefore resorts to allegory, both now and when it later enters voluntarily into a relationship of
supplementarity with the *Lettres à Malesherbes*. In flirting with a tripar-
tite scheme of psychic censorship ("Mémoires"/"Lettres"/"ce que j'expose ici"), the *Confessions* place a provisional mark of censorship on the
Lettres. It does not follow, however, that psychic censorship is embraced
or even self-consciously entertained within the missives to Malesherbes.
On the contrary, the real-life censor whom the *Lettres* decline to name
functions as a lightning rod. Censorship known but never acknowledged
to exist beyond the pale of discourse keeps things literal and discourages
the kind of allegorical applications that would—and, in the *Confessions,*
do—depend on formal inscription of the institutional model.

The *Lettres'* final dream of a world without literature is thus challenged by the dream that the more knowing and inevitably literary
Confessions attribute to the young Jean-Jacques. Newly exiled from Geneva, he is about to embark on a lifetime crusade: "Un seul Château bor-
noit mon ambition. Favori du Seigneur et de la Dame, amant de la
Demoiselle, ami du frére, et protecteur des voisins, j'étois content; il ne
m'en falloit pas davantage" (1:45). Glossing this variant of the dream of
displacement, the *Confessions* gently mock the modesty that "limits"
Jean-Jacques's ambitions to something along the lines of a new Coper-
nican revolution or radical reconfiguration of the existing order. From
the margins, the dreamer sees himself advancing disruptively to the center of the microcosm and reducing the remnants of the ancien régime to
the status of constellations. It is, of course, this impossible dream of an

egocentric universe that the *Confessions* fulfill in Jean-Jacques's stead. Revolving around him, the landed nobility ceases to relate primarily to its land: the interloper as "favori" mediates even the coupling of "Seigneur" and "Dame"; as "amant," he differentiates the parental orbit from that of "la Demoiselle" on the sole basis of his desiring. Only the constellation named not young lord (of the manor) but "frére" (of the young lady) retains an attachment other than to Jean-Jacques. An all but imperceptible passage from the feudal to the familial order infuses the dream with a measure of social realism. But, however extraneous to the archetypal fairy tale, the brother's friendship also constitutes the necessary addendum that legitimates the love relationship with "la Demoiselle." Like censorship (literary and psychic), the brother does not so much belong as hold the keys to the castle; it is on his belated approval that the possibility depends of wooing "la Demoiselle" in her father's house. In what might therefore be read as an allegory for the three ages of desire, an archaic wish is delivered to the fraternal censor, and by him into the possession of the present-day consciousness.

Of different orders, the brother-sister team of the Princess and the Censor are nonetheless so inextricably linked as to enter and exit the texts of Jean-Jacques's desiring in tandem. In the fourth letter to Malesherbes, spelling an end to a lifetime of (literature as inscription of) desire thus depends not simply on moving the censor into retirement and down the road, "à demi-lieue de la" (1:1146), but on removing the princess from the castle. No one remains from the original cast but Lord ("Mr de Luxembourg"), Lady ("la Dame"), and neighbors, their number increased by one. When, on the other hand, the Princess and the Censor become uncoupled and Mlle Amélie roams her grandmother's "petit Château" unescorted, the dream's other variant comes to life nightmarishly. Where was friendly neighborhood censor Malesherbes at the time? Right next door, on the facing page, too far and too "coulant" to be of any use in providing Jean-Jacques with the keys to the castle, and yet near enough to facilitate our reading a partially censored intertext of censorship.

What has been missing from analyses of the *Confessions* is not so much the assumption, fundamental to depth psychology, that they are pre-censored and deal in the kind of pseudo-sins we all seem to substitute unconsciously for those harder to admit to consciousness, and to admit. Indeed, it is a still unshaken belief in censorship by the other that gives critical discourse something to say. It is even—and this is where *our* confession becomes difficult—critics' "competitive particularity"[71] or need to say something earthshakingly new that censors our approaches to texts. Not enough attention has been paid, however, to the self-conscious ways in which so much of Rousseau's public and private writing grapples with the knowledge of self-censorship.[72] The *Confessions-Lettres* dyad in particular casts a furtive eye on the potential incompatibility of self-censorship with the will to complete self-disclosure.

When they are acknowledged to be less (pathologically) censoring of censorship, the *Confessions* become more and otherwise truthful than might be supposed, *and* more prosaically literary. Not that "poetry" is precluded once the Jean-Jacques of Volume 2 begins to write in earnest. It is at that point, rather, that poetry begins, increasingly, to take its cues from the day-to-day minutiae of making a literary career. "Point auteur, point faiseur de livres," J. J. Rousseau would not be himself or, at least, not the self whose imagination has been so decisively shaped by repeated run-ins with and end runs around the eighteenth-century version of censorship. Not only would he have had to look elsewhere than to the Château de Malesherbes for alibis and metaphors, but the question of self-censorship might never have occurred. And the "all" that the *Confessions* undertake to tell might not so unabashedly exceed the strictly "confessable" as to intermingle the good and the indifferent. Who knows whether that undertaking does not itself derive or derive value and originality from the specter of really ubiquitous and unpredictable censorship? *Anything* that gets said will have escaped from the infinite category of the potentially "censorable"; relatively speaking, the more scandalous the utterance feels to the speaker, the more dramatic and exceptional the escape he will have thought to make.

In a passage particularly telling of Rousseau's covert moves toward the internally divided self of depth psychology, the *Confessions* recount their own conception and stake their claim to originality. Invoking a distinction since rehearsed impressionistically on countless occasions of criticism, Rousseau indicts Montaigne's *Essais* as inadequately confessional. And on what grounds?—that Montaigne will have balked at delving too deep or, in other words, deep enough. Rousseau's dismissal of the straw man Montaigne would have had only to posit the unconscious to look as though it came straight out of a Freudian primer: "J'avois toujours ri de la fausse naïveté de Montaigne qui faisant semblant d'avouer ses défauts a grand soin de ne s'en donner que d'aimables: tandis que je sentois . . . qu'il n'y a point d'interieur humain si pur qu'il puisse être, qui ne recelle quelque vice odieux" (1:516–17). Over Freud, moreover, Rousseau maintains the ethical advantage of keeping us fully apprised that there is still such a thing as conscious (self-)censorship; we who write to the presumed biases of scholarly journals call it "rewriting" or "editing." And unlike the Freud whom Starobinski credits with "thinking" the "feelings" of Rousseau,[73] the author of the *Confessions* had no theoretical investment to protect one way or the other: the depth psychology that Rousseau eyes furtively seems at the same time to be more real *and* more susceptible of being mocked by some generation still in the future as nothing more than "un long rêve" of Western civilization. In Rousseau, the intimation of self-censorship and the desire to revolutionize discourse about the self by lifting self-censorship more brazenly than ever before by no means preclude nostalgia for real naiveté with respect to its operations and obstinacy. In the vicinity of the Librairie, Rousseau's discourse becomes and remains ambivalent, occasionally anxious, and obsessed. By way of apologizing for the *Lettres à Malesherbes,* the last one concludes by postulating a desire not to usurp the censor's good opinion (1:1147), as though the writer were not already well on his way toward usurping the censor's good offices, and his "calamités."

In the course of wholeheartedly embracing their occasion, the *Lettres à Malesherbes* also serve the *Confessions* to come by making a tentative first pass at drafting the occasional strategy of autobiography. The draft is drably worded; the strategy comes as an afterthought and is modestly intended only for immediate deployment—a far cry from the *Confessions'* fine neo-Malebranchean phrases and self-assured pretensions to universal applicability. But Rousseau was already trying out the thoughts that would eventually crystallize around the still missing term of the occasional. At a loss to explain the inconsistencies of his character, the erstwhile self-portraitist thought to enlist the "facts" of his biography and to lay them out in chronological order: "Quoique je ne puisse resoudre cette opposition [entre une ame paresseuse et un temperament ardent] par des principes, elle existe pourtant, je la sens, rien n'est plus certain, et j'en puis du moins donner par les faits une espece d'historique qui peut servir à la concevoir" (1:1134). Not that he would think of settling for a mere life story, but the story of a soul seemed the next best thing to the uncompromising portrait he now felt to be beyond the means of all but narrative. In the *Lettres,* life comes already, albeit with little fanfare, to the aid of the self.

As we have seen, the "historique" in question begins with the pertinent episode of rebirth through uncensored reading. The *Lettres* leave unconfessed what the *Confessions* will later backtrack to designate as the first and foremost of Jean-Jacques's crimes: killing his mother in childbirth. Nor, in his eagerness to explain and in the provisional certainty of doing something other than literature, does the letter-writer stop to worry that recycling the narrative mode of his theoretical and literary fictions might somehow jeopardize the wished-for fresh start or new beginning of telling his truth. But the autobiographer's literary past would eventually come back to haunt him, as it haunts another recovering fictioneer, Mary McCarthy, in her *Memories of a Catholic Girlhood:* "Can it be that the public takes for granted that anything written by a profesional writer is *eo ipso* untrue? The professional writer is looked on perhaps as a 'storyteller' like a child who has fallen into that habit and is mechanically chidden by his parents even when he protests that *this time* he is telling the truth."[74] In planting this same doubt, *Le Lévite d'Ephraïm* reproblematizes and prolongs the instantaneous wish-fulfillment of our storyteller's extraliterary *Lettres à Malesherbes. Le Lévite* not only rehearses the alleged real-life matricide but provides the *Confessions* with motive, means, and opportunity to do a more thorough job of finishing off their own mother, *littérature.*

5

Ultimate Sacrifices:
Le Lévite d'Ephraïm

Il n'y a pas d'objet ou d'entreprise au nom duquel on ne puisse offrir de sacrifice, à partir du moment, surtout, où le caractère social de l'institution commence à s'estomper.

René Girard

Je ne veux que ces mots pour éloge: Dans les plus cruels momens de sa vie, il fit Le Lévite d'Ephraïm.

Rousseau

Et tout le reste est littérature.

Verlaine

Rousseau's freestanding prose poem *Le Lévite d'Ephraïm* was written during the summer of 1762 and, like the *Lettres à Malesherbes,* remained unpublished during the author's lifetime. The last thing we might expect on the basis of our reading thus far is that Rousseau would end up laying claim to the conventional understanding of occasional writing as perfunctory, impersonal, and strictly literary. And yet the *Confessions* reserve the right to do just that in the case of *Le Lévite,* whose artistic mediocrity they are likewise quick to acknowledge. But there are further ironic twists to the *Confessions'* astounding designation of the fifteen-page *Lévite* as, of all the works in his substantial corpus, the one Rousseau himself persists in holding most dear. His paraphrase of a narrative from the Hebrew scriptures is deemed "précieux" (2:1205) and "chéri" (1:586) for the very reason that it both is and is not the kind of perfunctory, by-the-book writing of which Rousseau ordinarily claims to be incapable. It would have been dismissible as nothing more than a literary exercise had the circumstances themselves not cried out, on this exceptional occasion, for autobiographical writing or no writing at all.

The *Confessions* make a prima facie case for factoring the occasion into appreciations of the text. Jean-Jacques had just been forced to flee into exile amidst rumors that the Parlement de Paris had condemned his

Emile and placed a warrant out for his arrest or *prise de corps.* Under the circumstances, any other man would have understandably wallowed in self-obsession. Assuming that this hypothetical other man could have found the presence of mind to write, he surely would have seized the occasion to bemoan his fate or lash out in some manner of self-defense at his enemies. But Jean-Jacques was evidently not the kind of "any other" man to give in to ire or give voice to the cruel irony of his having counted on proceeds from *Emile* to fund a more orderly "retraite" from Montmorency (1:516). Nor was he the least bit paralyzed by fear. On the contrary, rather than panic or polemicize, our hero chose to while away the leisure of a hastily improvised carriage ride into the unknown by, of all things, drafting the first three of *Le Lévite*'s four cantos. The autobiographer takes lasting satisfaction, in consequence, from the thought of having, for once in his life, turned his back completely on the occasion. It is an exemplary former abstinence from autobiographical activity that the *Confessions* can now invoke, autobiographically, as the surest possible sign of exceptional character or "un cœur sans fiel" (1:586). This time around, self-testing will have occurred without the self's having been brought, except belatedly, into the play of text.

The *Confessions* insist on the unforeseeable suspension of the fleeing Jean-Jacques's autobiographical activities: the would-be memorialist had been obliged to leave his supporting documents behind at Montmorency for triage by the Maréchal de Luxembourg and safekeeping by Thérèse (1:582–83). But we have only to read *Le Lévite* for ourselves to catch the *Confessions* in the act of breaking this suspension. An unmistakable coincidence of superficial detail works to narrow the gap between Rousseau's restrained and affectless account of Jean-Jacques's nocturnal expulsion and his adaption of one of the most gruesome Bible stories ever told. Perversely enough, the intertext reopens the very possibility of autobiography that the *Confessions* proper are working concurrently to foreclose. For its part, *Le Lévite* not only rehearses but belabors and compounds the unspeakably violent reprisals of Judges 19–21. It appears, then, that adapting the Scriptures was, in fact, the fugitive's way of giving vent to the anxieties and "fiel" that really filled his "cœur." In the midst of this barely disguised mutual interference between Rousseau's "autobiographical" and "literary" narratives, the *Confessions* recall that Jean-Jacques had been reading and dreaming about the book of Judges just prior to getting the bad news about *Emile* (1:580). That recollection goes beyond explaining where he got his subject matter to render the dream itself uncannily prophetic. But to interpret the dream only as looking forward to the immediately ensuing events of Jean-Jacques's biography would be to fall for yet another cover story. We would miss out on the chance to appreciate the further, inestimable benefits derived by Rousseau from writing his doubly autobiographical *Lévite*, which also looks back, surreptitiously, to unblock the guilty secret of his mother's death as a result of giving birth to him.

What in fact facilitates Rousseau's emphatic denials that the dream text of *Le Lévite* has anything to do with him is his redeployment in the *Confessions* of the same sacrificial logic entrusted in the prose poem with transposing an original matricide into the reassuring terms of maternal self-sacrifice. The likewise self-serving *Confessions* make a ceremonial display of removing every last vestige of autobiography from *Le Lévite*. The prose poem is thereby prepared for sacrifice, in the name of autobiography, as the quintessential last gasp of literature in Rousseau's lifetime. The difference thus engineered between literary beauty and autobiographical truth makes up in solemnity for what it lacks in substance, and testifies most eloquently of all to the fact and the force of Rousseau's desiring for a difference.

JEAN-JACQUES RELIVES THE BOOK OF JUDGES

"To hear this story is to inhabit a world of unrelenting terror that refuses to let us pass by on the other side."[1] Not even this direst of warnings can adequately prepare us to replicate (in Ostervald's French Protestant version) the reading done by Jean-Jacques on the fateful night of June 10, 1762. Rousseau's own retelling of the biblical horror story appears, at first glance, to relent somewhat. It certainly diverges in some significant ways from its source.

Chapter 19 of the book of Judges briefly recalls a state of political and judicial anarchy—"il n'y avait point de roi en Israël"—and then proceeds to recount how the Levite takes a concubine out of Bethlehem-Judah; how she "commet impureté chez lui" and returns to her father's house; and how, at the end of four months, the Levite journeys there to bring her back. After repeated successful attempts by the concubine's father to detain them for one last meal, the couple finally departs for home, about one third of the way through chapter 19.

Rousseau's entire first canto does not advance beyond this point. In-

stead of launching immediately into the Levite's story, Rousseau begins
with an exordium that is structured as a series of apostrophes, each desig-
nating a new addressee: "Sainte colere de la vertu . . . Mortels . . . O
vous, hommes débonnaires . . . Peuple saint . . . Benjamin, triste enfant
de douleur" (2:1208). These insistent invocations take the place of direct
address to Rousseau's real-life enemies, and serve to propel us back in
time from the future when Rousseau "will tell" the events of a distant past
if the "sacred rage of virtue" heeds his call for inspiration. The text's
eventual readers become the next locus of regression by way of anticipation: we are reminded of our own mortality, only to be taxed with avert-
ing our gaze from the atrocities of Antiquity to be recounted here. Called,
in turn, to witness the most spectacular of those atrocities are the twelve
tribes of Israel or "Peuple saint." But Rousseau's chain of apostrophes will
not have reached its ultimate destination until, at paragraph's end, it
reaches back beyond the outset of the biblical original. It reaches back
even beyond the Exodus named as the extreme limit of the tribes' collective memory by a quotation from that original: "Non, jamais rien de pareil
ne s'est fait en Israël depuis le jour où nos pères sortirent d'Egypte jusqu'à ce jour." Bringing the book of Judges into an emphatically intertextual relationship with that of Genesis, the exordium summons the
criminal whose race now bears his name and perpetuates his violence:
"Benjamin, triste enfant de douleur, qui donnas la mort à ta mére"
(2:1208). In contrast, the self-contained book of Judges never explicitly
entertains this possibility of a genetic link between the latter-day crimes
of Benjamin the tribe and those of Benjamin the individual.

Once Rousseau's Levite has taken up with the concubine (whom he
calls "épouse"), the text lingers over the apparently beautiful beginnings
of a love story. The Levite goes to great lengths to satisfy his beloved,
succeeds paradoxically in boring her, and suffers so intensely in the "in-
fidel"'s absence that he conquers his ambivalence and dedicates himself
to winning her back (2:1209–1210). When her father's unabridged feints
and parries can detain the couple no longer, the invented characters of
the concubine's mother and sisters prolong the tearful farewells; the father's unbearable sorrow would have been greater still had he known
that he would never see his daughter alive again (2:1211).

The remaining two thirds of chapter 19 correspond almost exactly to
Rousseau's "Chant second." Rejoining chapter 19 in progress, we learn
that, rather than stay the night in a city "où il n'y a point d'enfants d'Isra-

ël," the Levite and his retinue pressed on to Gibeah, "qui appartient à Benjamin." No one gives them lodging there, however, until an old man returning from the fields spies them in the street and opens his home to them. A new paragraph recounts how, as "ils faisaient bonne chère," the men of the city ("de méchants garnements") surrounded the house and demanded to "know" the stranger. When the old man's refusal to surrender his guest and his subsequent offer of two (his own virginal daughter and the Levite's concubine) for one meet with resistance, the Levite himself sends out his companion, who is brutalized throughout the night and found at dawn lying on the threshold. When the Levite's exhortation that she get up goes unanswered, he transports what may or may not be her corpse[2] back to his house. There, another new paragraph isolates the ultimate atrocity: "il prit un couteau, et prenant sa concubine, il partagea *son corps* avec ses os en douze parts, et il en envoya *une part* dans tous les quartiers d'Israël." Everywhere it is received, the message provokes the same reaction: "On n'a jamais fait ni vu rien de pareil, depuis que les enfants d'Israël sont montés hors du pays d'Egypte, jusqu'à ce jour. Pensez à cela, consultez et prononcez."

Rousseau deviates less radically here than in his first canto from the narrative outlines of the original. A further apostrophe warns modern readers against taking one city's behavior for the rule of ancient times, when hospitality flourished because it could not yet be bought with "vils métaux" (2:1212). And there are shifts in emphasis, most often involving reassignments of responsibility: Rousseau's Benjaminites have "plotted" in advance their more explicitly sexual attack on a Levite whose youth and "beauté" are stressed (2:1213–14); the host proposes only his own daughter as a surrogate victim and makes the Levite's inviolability a matter not only of his being a guest but of his belonging to the priesthood (2:1214). It is upon waking from a sort of stupor that the Levite himself thinks to offer his concubine in the virgin's stead (2:1214). The horror of gang rape is carried to further extremes of perversion when yet another apostrophe (to the perpetrators) makes it clear that the attack has extended beyond the moment of death (2:1215). Finally, the Levite's obsession with vengeance is named in so many words, as is the inhuman sangfroid of what becomes a surgical operation.

Rousseau's "Chant troisième," like chapter 20, to which it adds little more than a sprinkling of inhuman metaphors for human violence, chronicles the revenge of a united Israel against the tribe of Benjamin. Meeting as one, the nation demands that the Levite tell his story and swears with one voice not to return to their tents and houses until Benjamin has been punished (2:1217). Whereas nothing further is heard in the Bible of the Levite, Rousseau takes time out here to observe his death and public funeral, imagining that he will have spoken dying words of reassurance to his concubine—"Fille de Bethléem, je te porte une bonne nouvelle; ta mémoire ne restera point sans honneur"—and that her corpse will have been reassembled and buried in the same sepulcher as his (2:1216).

Extensive preparations for battle include the choosing of warriors by lot from each tribe, an unheeded request for extradition of the perpetrators, and God's decision that the assault should be led by the injured party of Juda (2:1217). The vastly outnumbered Benjaminites rely on their own ferocity and the sharp-shooting of left-handed (Judges) or ambidextrous (Rousseau) allies to win resounding victories on each of the battle's first two days (2:1217–18). Their ranks decimated, the eleven tribes twice inquire of God whether they should continue to war against their brother Benjamin (2:1218). On the second evening, when the inquiry is prefaced by offerings and sacrifices, He promises them a resounding victory (2:1218). An inspired stratagem indeed enables the Israelites to surround the Benjaminites and to reduce their entire race to six hundred survivors, all adult males (2:1218–19). Chapter 20 ends with the eleven pursuing the remnants of the one into the wilderness and continuing to burn every city in their path; they will not be reported to have wept "larmes en abondance" until chapter 21. In Rousseau's Canto 3, however, remorse follows directly, with no break in the text, from victory (2:1219).

Canto 4, finally, follows the lead of chapter 21 in effecting a reconciliation with Benjamin and finding a way to perpetuate "ce dernier et précieux reste d'une de nos Tribus" without violating the oath that no daughter of Israel shall be given to him in marriage (2:1220). Troops are dispatched to punish Jabesh-Gilead for failure to participate in the war of revenge; all inhabitants of the city are systematically exterminated, except four hundred virgins, whom the Benjaminites are summoned to take as brides (2:1220–21). Rousseau embroiders on the Benjaminites' joyless return, imagining their downcast eyes and faces covered with "shame and remorse" (2:1221). As in the exordium, Genesis is made to speak between the lines of Judges; Rousseau recalls Jacob's prophecy for his youngest son: " 'Benjamin est un loup dévorant; au matin il déchirera sa proye, et le soir il partagera le butin'" (2:1221). The narrator then pauses to consider the situation from the hapless brides' point of view: "Quelles noces pour de jeunes vierges timides, dont on vient d'égorger les fréres, les péres, les méres devant leurs yeux, et qui reçoivent des liens d'attachement et d'amour par des mains dégoutantes du sang de leurs proches!" (2:1221). Out of context, the narrator's apostrophic conclusions would seem to contradict the better known, more misogynic pronouncements of texts like *Julie, Emile,* and the *Lettre à d'Alembert:* "Sexe toujours esclave ou tiran, que l'homme opprime ou qu'il adore, et qu'il ne peut pourtant rendre heureux ni l'être, qu'en le laissant égal à lui" (2:1221).

Context prevails, however. Further bloodshed can be averted only if brides are found for the two hundred members of the vanquished tribe who still have none. The Bible authorizes those Benjaminites to lay traps for the virgins of Shiloh who "sortiront pour danser avec les flûtes" during an annual feast of the Lord. Rousseau does not, however, content himself with reporting the deed to have been done. Rather, he sadistically pictures and prolongs the violence of what amounts, in a radical paradox, to authorized rape: "Les ceps déchirent leurs voiles, la terre est jonchée de leurs parures. . . ." (2:1222). And he deviates just as markedly from his model in personalizing the moment of resolution. For the first time in either this version or the Bible, characters are given proper names. With the throngs of spectators torn between "justice" (for Benjamin) and "pitié" (for their latest victims), it falls to a particular virgin, "Axa, la tendre Axa," to decide the fate of Israel (2:1222). As her beloved fiancé, Elmacin, looks on, Axa's father enjoins her to do her duty and save his face. For, much as he cherishes his hand-picked son-in-law, it is the father himself who has selflessly proposed the collective rape to the Benjaminites (2:1223). It requires only that her glance meet that of her "vénérable pére" for Axa to name Elmacin in a final adieu and fall, half dead, into the arms of his Benjaminite rival (2:1223). Elmacin, in turn, vows to cherish the memory of their innocent love and to dedicate his still pure body and heart to the service of God (2:1223). Swift imitation of Axa's sacrifice by the remaining virgins inspires a collective cry of joy that stands in sharp contrast to the inconclusive conclusion of the biblical original. "En ces jours-là il n'y avait point de roi en Israël, mais chacun faisait ce qui lui semblait bien"—the last verse of chapter 21 echoes the first of chapter 19 and hints that the cycle of violence will really be broken only later, through establishment of a monarchy. "Vierges d'Ephraïm, par vous Benjamin va renaître. Beni soit le Dieu de nos péres! il est encore des vertus en Israël"—in Rousseau's final apostrophe, the future is already near at hand, thanks to the selfless acts of a personal virtue which no measure of violence can have extinguished entirely (2:1223).

But neither can this resolution extinguish our haunting memories of events centered on Rousseau's title character, the Levite. Comparing those events with the *Confessions'* account of Jean-Jacques's activities on the eve of his flight from Montmorency yields a cluster of cross-references that belie protestations of *Le Lévite*'s irrelevance to the author's personal situation. The experience of violent, nocturnal expulsion from what turns out to be an unsafe haven, the house of a host, occupies a central position in both narratives. Like the old man of Gibeah, the Maréchal de Luxembourg has taken in an unmarried couple, Thérèse and Jean-Jacques, on whom the population at large had turned its back. However grateful, Jean-Jacques is said to have reacted with characteristic ambivalence to the hospitality whose essential burden of reciprocity he felt unsuited, by reason of temperament and of inferior social class, to assume (1:517–18). How better to dramatize that ambivalence than through the increasingly importunate demands of the concubine's father that the Levite postpone his intended departure. How better to justify unwillingness to reciprocate than by exposing an unseemly, seemingly pointless rivalry between father- and son-in-law. How better, finally, to absolve Jean-Jacques of pathological punctiliousness than by recalling that, in the second biblical episode of hospitality gone awry, the old man's gesture not only fails to help but even contributes directly to death and disaster. The *Confessions* question only tacitly the sincerity of their host, the Maréchal, who is said to have snatched back with surprising alacrity the garden key tendered him by Jean-Jacques (2:584). Writing the *Lévite* as a kind of wish fulfillment, Rousseau may have wondered why the Maréchal did not go to the same lengths as the old man to defend and detain a guest whom he purported to honor and had (half- or wholeheartedly?) invited to stay on incognito (1:581).

Both of Rousseau's narratives target the nameless "stranger" (the Ephraimite in Gibeah, the Genevan in Paris) as victim of a "plot" to which the Bible makes no allusion. Jean-Jacques doubles, however, as Levite and concubine. To the attenuated violence of a second separation from her family and the concubine's brutal expulsion into the night correspond, in reverse order, the two moments of Jean-Jacques's being summoned from his bed at 2 A.M. and his leaving the château the following afternoon (1:580, 583). Why, if not to reassemble the cast of characters present at his own leave-taking—Monsieur le Maréchal, Madame la Maréchale, Mesdames de Boufflers and de Mirepoix—would Rousseau have thought to endow his concubine with a mother and sisters (1:583)? In what looks very much like a further wish fulfillment, the tearful mother's unmitigated sadness at this "nouvelle séparation" (2:1211) corrects the "air" only "assez triste" of Mme la Maréchale, whose embraces Jean-Jacques finds less passionate than those of a year or two earlier (1:583). In both Rousseau texts, the final, most fond farewells are reserved for a father figure too overcome by emotion to speak; foreknowledge shared by Jean-Jacques and his host that they will never meet again recreates the pathos of foreshadowing in the *Lévite* that the daughter will not live to see the next day's dawn (1:584; 2:1211).

As for the nocturnal expulsion itself, no horde of Benjaminites beats down Jean-Jacques's door. But the illusion of a crowd is created by the densely populated passage that has Thérèse lighting the way for M. La Roche (a valet), who bears a letter from Mme la Maréchale that encloses a further letter, where the Prince de Conti predicts the imminent *prise de corps:* "l'on enverra sur le champ le saisir" (1:580). Rousseau's later speculation will, of course, link Thérèse's "ambassade nocturne" to a "complot" more exactly analogous in its collective hatching and in its perversity with that of the Levite's enemies (1:587–88.) For now, it is already morning; as though violence enough had not been perpetrated by the very light and sound that first dragged Jean-Jacques from "a sort of dream," he is enjoined, like the concubine, to get up and go confer with the Maréchale (1:580).

If the *Confessions* text insists on the experience of expulsion by multiplying instances, so more systematically still does Rousseau's rendition of the biblical narrative. Having been left behind in his own home by his unfaithful consort, the Levite nonetheless experiences his plight, thanks to a corrective image, as that of a player excluded from a childhood game (2:1210). On the return journey from the father's home, he is said, in a second image, to have been as fearful of exposing his beloved to the "injures de l'air" as a mother bringing her child back from the wet nurse (1:1212). To be outside, exposed, whether coming or going, is always to be in mortal danger; to be in danger is, at least sometimes, to be outside, exposed, en route—as when the concubine's attackers are pictured as "un troupeau de loups affamés" attacking "une foible genisse" on her return "de l'abruvoir" (2:1214). A like fate might well have awaited the fugitive Jean-Jacques, whose voyage into the no-man's-land between *asile* and *exil* takes as its starting point the "abruvoir" of Montmorency (1:584).

At every such point of intersection between the two texts, *Le Lévite* invests the *Confessions'* anecdotal account of expulsion with intense anxiety. Simply retelling a biblical tale that forges a metonymic link between the two events of an expulsion and a *prise de corps* makes it unnecessary to choose between or reconcile the available models of birth trauma and castration anxiety. No sooner has the concubine's body crossed the threshold than it is violated. An act in which Rousseau inscribes the several perversities of unwanted homosexual advances, gang rape, and necrophagia gives menacingly literal and nonjuridical meaning to the term *prise de corps,* which English translates simply as "arrest." A narrative chiasmus further reinforces the link between the two traumas: having sent out the concubine to be mutilated by Benjamin, the Levite then mutilates her further—or, as he puts it with chilling matter-of-factness, "j'ai pris son corps" (2:1216)—and sends her back out to the twelve tribes of Israel.

Much remains to be said about Rousseau's uses of this haunting "body in bits and pieces."[3] My point for now is simply that *Le Lévite* not only commemorates but remembers the occasion of Rousseau's flight. At the very least, *Le Lévite* is made by the *Confessions* to look autobiographical. Details, details—upon the fugitive's safe arrival at the way station of Yverdun, Book 11 closes with a meta-autobiographical postface where Rousseau admits to having unselectively recounted everything that he can remember and makes a general rule of "l'importance des moindres détails" (1:587–88). Our reading thus far has acted on his own suggestion that rehearsing "toutes les circonstances" is vital to the discovery of subtexts secretly at work; we have merely substituted, for the subtext singled out by him as "le complot," his own *Lévite d'Ephraïm* (1:587–88). As is often the case, the *complot* surfaces conveniently when Rousseau intuits a patterning of the *Confessions* on some other of his own texts, since to admit that patterning would be to undermine the autobiography's autonomy and singularity of direct access to Jean-

Jacques. In a further "[e]xemple grossier mais sensible" of cross-referen-tiality (1:588), *Le Lévite* makes much of insouciant feasting in the face of imminent disaster. The *Confessions,* in turn, linger over a picnic shared by Jean-Jacques with "deux Professeurs Oratoriens, le Pere Alamanni et le Pere Mandard" on the afternoon preceding his flight. Rousseau goes to otherwise unaccountable lengths to recall that, having forgotten glasses, they used straws to drink directly from the bottle, and insists that Jean-Jacques had never been so "gai" (1:579).

In a monograph devoted to *Le Lévite,* François van Laere cites several of the same uncanny coincidences en route to the conclusion that writ-ing *Le Lévite* must have served Rousseau as an exercise in short-term self-therapy.[4] Closing in progressively on the relationship between Jean-Jacques and Thérèse,[5] van Laere supposes the author to have identified more or less exclusively with his title character and to have worked through ambivalent feelings inspired by his own concubine: love, hate, respect, scorn, guilt at having left her behind, hope that she will decide not to join him, and so forth. Whatever details do not inform this scenario are seen by van Laere as establishing a threshold level of identifiability, or as exceptions to the rule: "Est-il besoin de préciser que l'identification n'est pas absolue? L'on sait en quels termes Rousseau parle du pucelage de Thérèse: on ne pourrait sans ridicule prétendre que c'est à elle qu'il pense lorsqu'il fait dire par son Lévite au père de la concubine: 'Quel autre que moi peut honorer comme sa femme celle que j'ai reçue vierge?' "[6]

In fact, nothing proves less stable in *Le Lévite* than the identities or one-to-one correspondences we are nonetheless encouraged to forge provisionally. As would not occur if he stood everywhere for Jean-Jacques, the Levite plays no part in the scene of parting where the con-cubine herself assumes Jean-Jacques's distress, and her family that of his hosts. Rousseau may really have wished to throw Thérèse to the wolves in his stead, or thought guiltily to have done so by leaving her behind at Montmorency. But the concubine's nocturnal expulsion does not merely project; it also recollects a single moment, that of Jean-Jacques's arousal from "une espéce de rêve" (1:580), which the Levite relives literally and the concubine relives in all its primal, metaphorical terror. Both mem-bers of the biblical couple thus inform the experience attributed by the *Confessions* to a single protagonist. The narrative structure of revenge tends, as ever, toward the dissolution of fixed identities: in "taking the

body" of his concubine, the Levite mimics the gesture of his enemies and
the designs of Jean-Jacques's.

Conversely, a single character in *Le Lévite* may stand for several in
the *Confessions*, as when the biblical protagonist so thoroughly satisfies
his beloved as to bore her. A letter to the Maréchal that postdates the
drafting of *Le Lévite* names Thérèse as the one whose restlessness Rousseau himself fears: "je crains qu'elle ne trouve ma rettraite trop solitaire,
qu'elle ne s'y ennuye."[7] But the *Confessions* also chronicle Jean-Jacques's
efforts to defend against the eventuality of his own boredom and especially against that of Madame la Maréchale's boredom with him. If fears
about Thérèse inspire no specific plan of action, there is more than a little
of the Levite's exquisite sacrifices—love songs, wild roses, golden honey,
a turtledove (2:1209)—in the stratagems devised by a desperate Jean-
Jacques to stave off the displeasure of his demanding hostess. He makes
her the privileged repository of his darkest secrets (1:557) and of *les
avantures de Mylord Edouard* (1:524–25); and he reads to her in discrete doses from *Julie* and *Emile*, like some latter-day Scheherazade
(1:522, 534). In the locus of boredom, as well as in her "ambassade nocturne," Thérèse might be seen as replacing the more terrifying, or just as
terrifying, figure of la Maréchale.

Even without opening the *Confessions*, we can notice how images
deployed within *Le Lévite* make a travesty of identity. Jumping from the
role of excluded child to that of solicitous mother, the Levite transgresses
both generational and sexual barriers. The image that makes his concubine over into a male child being transported home from the wet nurse
establishes the special case of surrogacy—that is, one-way interchangeability of identity—as a general rule and no localized accident
of *Le Lévite*. How could it be otherwise in a text that, propelled by the
contagion of revenge, repeatedly recasts yesterday's victims as tomorrow's avengers and grants no long-term immunity from the indifference
of violence? Van Laere's psychoanalysis of Rousseau through his poem
remains convincing as far as it goes, but, in its rigidity of identification,
cannot hope to go far enough.

A PROPHETIC DREAM OF MATERNAL SELF-SACRIFICE

Freudian psychoanalysis does, however, provide a theoretical model,
that of the so-called "prophetic dream," that accounts more fully for *Le
Lévite* than any attempt to fix identities or assign specific complexes to

the real-life Rousseau. It is from what amounts, after all, to such a dream that the *Confessions* report Jean-Jacques to have been rudely awakened on the eve of his flight. The biblical Levite did not occur to him out of the blue as an appropriate subject for adaptation—rather, it was his long-standing practice to combat insomnia by systematic rereading of the Bible. On the evening in question, greater than usual wakefulness had allowed him to pursue his latest rereading all the way through "le livre qui finit par le Lévite d'Ephraïm." This "affecting" story then formed the basis for the "espéce de rêve" that Thérèse's arrival interrupted (1:580) and that Jean-Jacques might have dreamed on, had he exercised the option, acknowledged in retrospect, to stand his ground and "dormir tranquille-ment la fraîche matinée" (1:588). But in that case, would he have recalled the dream in his own mind, or in his autobiography? Jean-Jacques's penchant for reverie notwithstanding, the *Confessions* almost invariably avoid discussing the content of specific dreams. This avoidance no doubt bespeaks the absence of Freudian authorization to make such dreams a worthwhile topic of discussion and privileged locus of scientific self-knowledge. Rousseau himself asks whether, had he gone back to bed, the same order would have gone out for his arrest. (1:588). Displacing his question, we might wonder whether, had the dream of Judges not to some extent come true, it would have come to consciousness. The Freudian model suggests otherwise.

The question of what to make of the ancient belief that dreams possess the capacity to divine the future recurs at intervals in Freud's *The Interpretation of Dreams*.[8] A response entirely consistent with the author's positivistic pretensions turns up only in a manuscript, "A Pre-monitory Dream Fulfilled,"[9] dated six days after the *Interpretation* had been published. A timely breakthrough thus fulfills the analyst's own wish that "prophetic" dreams might resemble all other dreams in fulfilling some "indestructible wish"[10] of the past. Freud's manuscript analyzes a dream reported to have struck the analysand as premonitory when, on the following day, she had a chance meeting with the individual, Dr. K, about whom she only then remembered having dreamt.[11] The fleeing Jean-Jacques must have been likewise struck to find himself cast out like . . . the Levite's concubine. His thoughts must have settled more understandably than the *Confessions* suppose, not on "tout ce qui venoit de se passer, et le Parlement, et Mad^e de Pompadour, et M. de Choiseul, et Grimm, et d'Alembert, et leurs complots, et leurs complices," but on a "souvenir qui me vint au lieu de tout cela . . . celui de ma derniére lecture la veille de mon départ" (1:586).

To be sure, Rousseau's naming the object of memory as "une lecture" brackets the dream itself and makes it impossible to know how much primary work on the source material had already been done by the sleeping or dozing Jean-Jacques. But the *Confessions'* claim that Jean-Jacques has not consulted his source since that fateful night—that is, not even in writing his text (1:580)—makes the dream's distortions part and parcel of his ultimate referent. Into the contrast between remembered reading and forgotten enemies cataloged exhaustively by name, we might read an intuition of the dream's having functioned precisely to blur identities. Beyond that, there is something intrinsically oneiric about the biblical source, which contains at least one major logical inconsistency. Rousseau shares the perplexity of more qualified biblical scholars as to why, if Levites were exempted from the prevailing marriage laws of endogamy, this particular Levite was precluded from marrying his concubine (2:1209, 1922). And the source derives its highest drama, that of the tribes' spontaneous response to receipt of the concubine's body parts, from an apparent ellipsis: "l'unanimité quasi magique des tribus à la vue de ce prétendu signe est peut-être due à un enchaînement illusoire de cause à effet, une lacune du texte biblique ayant pu nous priver d'un maillon dans les péripéties. . . ."[12] In short, what Jean-Jacques remembers reading was already dreamed, and dream-like.

Freud proceeds to find a natural explanation for his analysand's apparent gift of prophecy in the fact that Dr. K names not only the relatively unproblematic figure whom she did in fact meet, but a second individual with whom she had earlier had a troubled, guilt-ridden relationship.[13] Having opined that, were it not for the chance meeting with the second, relatively benign K, the dream would not have surfaced, Freud concludes: "Thus the creation of a dream after the event, which alone makes prophetic dreams possible, is nothing other than a form of censoring thanks to which the dream is able to make its way through into consciousness."[14] The dream can be remembered because extraordinary circumstances make it possible to forget or disguise what the dream itself remembers. As though once again furnishing us with a key to *Le Lévite* in the guise of a key to the "complot," Rousseau singles out from among the welter of details worth pondering the timing of the "Decret comminatoire" and of the "Decret réel" (1:588). Timing is indeed of the essence if we are to read *Le Lévite* as the report of a dream rendered prophetic by those events of its immediate aftermath that it seems exclusively committed to foretelling. Rousseau knows enough about playing prophetic dreams by these rules to render *Le Lévite*'s own timing impeccable: he holds off on recalling Jacob's prophecy for Benjamin until the moment of its having just been fulfilled. The *Confessions* proceed on the same tacit assumptions. If, in telling Jean-Jacques's story, they half-forget his dream, they also half-forget their reasons for wanting to pin *Le Lévite* down to the there and then of July 1762 at Montmorency. Those reasons have to do with the prophetic dream's unique capacity for covering over the past with the future, for replacing a greater with a lesser source of anxiety, for making a perilous voyage of retrospection appear to be prospective, for looking Janus-faced to the future in order to look back with impunity.

Throughout *Le Lévite,* Rousseau breaks with biblical tradition and alternates narration in the present and in the simple past. This apparently unremarkable recourse to literary convention carries a semantic load: two grammatically incompatible time frames are rendered accessible and pertinent to each other; instantaneous passage can be had, at will, according to no predictable pattern, between the here and now and the long ago and far away. The exordium is more suggestive still of temporal duplicity specific to the prophetic dream. Rousseau's narrator weaves anticipation and retrospection into a kind of future perfect: I will tell (and am in fact foretelling here) the events of that distant past that you who will die (remember your future) have chosen to forget. What the exordium wishes—that the "crimes of Benjamin" be rescued from collective repression—will already have come to pass, thanks to onomastic slippage reminiscent of the two Dr. Ks (2:1208). A *Lévite* more respectful of the integrity of the book of Judges and of the forward march of history would have understood "Benjamin" to name only a tribe and "les crimes de Benjamin" to have commenced with the concubine's rape; a literal exodus would have held firm as the terminus ad quem of collective memory. But Rousseau's text acknowledges this barrier only to transgress it: a second Benjamin is summoned from beyond the pale to answer for what becomes *his* original crime of matricide. The exordium thus stages Rousseau's journey back in time to the moment of his mother's death as a result of childbirth. The *Confessions* would retell that death in strikingly similar terms. For Benjamin, Rousseau coins the epithet "triste enfant de

douleur"; for himself, "triste fruit de ce retour." You who "donnas la mort
à ta mére" will become I who "coûtai la vie à ma mere." In both cases, the
criminal or "self-made orphan"[15] is seen to have suffered for his crimes:
"c'est de ton sein qu'est sorti le crime qui t'a perdu" versus "ma nais-
sance fut le premier de mes malheurs" (2:1208; 1:7).

Tracing an imperfect circle from the crimes of one Benjamin to those
of another, the exordium thus anticipates the movement of the overall
text. A reversal of the same onomastic slippage that has all but named the
birth of the baby Benjamin brings *Le Lévite* to the brink of giving rebirth
to Benjamin the tribe. If the prose poem's definitive title, *Le Lévite
d'Ephraïm,* corresponds roughly to the prophetic component or cover
story of Rousseau's dream, the discarded alternative, *Les Benjamites,*
bears witness to its component of regression: Rousseau looks ahead to
the resurrection of heretofore suppressed traumas dating from the time
immemorial of his own biography. The all-embracing storyline that prob-
lematizes the birth of Benjamin significantly displaces the unspoken, unfulfilled desiring of the biblical source for a monarch. Rousseau's *Lévite*
rejoices in the imminent satisfaction of a different desire: that Benjamin
should live; that the community without exception should desire and
authorize him to live; that the mother's death (or swoon) should result
not from matricide but from the ultimate maternal self-sacrifice.

The path to this denouement is strewn with thwarted attempts at
return to the womb. Each successive displacement of the Levite and his
concubine approximates such an attempt: from their retreat to the
"côteaux du mont Hébal" and repeated descents "dans les vallons de
Sichem" to her misguided attempts at flight back to the bosom of her
family, to his retrieval of her from the arms of the wet nurse, to her
metaphorical return as heifer from the drinking trough and literally falling short on the host's threshold (2:1209, 1210, 1212, 1214, 1215). In
each case, the return is either failed or short-lived; a new instance of
violent expulsion inevitably follows. Nor can Axa find permanent refuge
in the arms of her mother, to whom she flees from her Benjaminite captor
(2:1222). Only Benjamin will be welcomed back into that oft-cited
"sein" of Israel from which the other tribes first think to expel him
(2:1217–18). But the womb must first be made over into a truly safe
haven; there will be no going back for good until it is no longer possible
for the children of Israel to be massacred "chacun dans son habitation"

(2:1219). In the interval, the house of a host remains no more secure than a public square and, in effect, less secure.

No imagery could more drastically call into question the notion of the womb as refuge than that of the tribes' instructions to the brideless Benjaminites: "Allez, et mettez des embuches aux vignes: puis quand vous verrez que les filles de Silo sortiront pour danser avec des flutes, alors vous les enveloperez, et ravissant chacun sa femme, vous retournerez vous établir avec elles au pays de Benjamin" (2:1221). In the story's penultimate paroxysm of violence, rape is figured as entrapment or envelopment in makeshift wombs. It makes no difference that the rapists are really male, or the victims female. The call to violence is worded as a call to violate sexual identity more systematically than ever before. The Benjaminites are enjoined to arm themselves with "embuches" in which to ensnare virgins endowed with the "flutes" suggestive of male sex organs. In an apostrophe to the virgins, the narrator insists on the impossibility of escape from this omnipresent, all-devouring womb: "Jeunes beautés où courez-vous? en fuyant l'oppresseur qui vous poursuit vous tombez dans des bras qui vous enchaînent" (2:1222). Benjamin's "return" to the womb as refuge is thus predicated on forcing the virgins to return to the womb as trap. But this episode only dramatizes a principle self-consciously at work throughout the text: wherever violence needs the nourishment of renewed impetus, new wombs are improvised. The Levite's own revenge depends on his ability to inscribe the Benjaminites' crimes within the broader matrix of Israel as corporate body and on his seeing to it that the public embraces and swallows up his private story.

The "desirable and terrifying, nourishing and murderous, fascinating and abject inside of the maternal body"[16] thus becomes the inescapable locus of crimes committed in a text-long crisis of indifferentiation. The "crise sacrificielle" that René Girard postulates as the necessary and sufficient cause of recourse to the legitimating violence-to-end-all-violence of sacrifice comes about with and through such denials of difference.[17] In *Le Lévite,* this crisis of indifference manifests itself in symptoms ranging from the localized ambidexterity of the Benjaminites' allies to the global ambiguity of innocence and guilt; from the apparently benign reciprocity of hospitality to the obviously malignant reciprocity of mutual recriminations; from the positively charged pole of "un amour partagé" (2:1209) to what the text sees as the perversion of homosexuality; from the boring sameness of ritualized love-making between the Levite and his concubine to the mortal sameness of repeated massacres; from the literary use of animals to figure human violence to the literally indiscriminate slaughter of "tous les habitans, hommes et femmes, jeunes et vieux, grands et petits, jusqu'aux bêtes" (2:1219). In the process, there is a further leveling of differences between the local and the global, the positive and the perverse, the benign and the malignant, the boring and the mortal, the literary and the literal. Rousseau's text seizes on the lack of respect for difference that was inherent in his source and carries chaotic anarchy to new and more emphatic extremes. Paradigmatically, the Benjaminites continue their assault on the concubine beyond the no longer operative limit between life and death.

In this, as in any crisis of indifference, violence breeds violence and will continue to do so until a mechanism is devised for reasserting difference by projecting the totality of indifference onto a "guilty" party. One symptom must be singled out as the carrier of contagion; violence must be traced, arbitrarily but such that the community remains blind to this arbitrariness, to a single source.[18] As I have already suggested, *Le Lévite* targets sexual indifference as symptom and the womb as source. The very fact that any site in the text can be outfitted as a female inner space means that the womb has lost its material specificity. But as the locus of nondifference between mother and child, that space can—arguably, if not necessarily—be voided of any specifically female or benignly positive connotations. Our matricidal dreamer's peace of Israel and peace of mind depend on reading those vaguely encouraging signs of indifference to mean that the sum total of the text's violence can and must be recontained in a literal womb. In order to short-circuit the violent reprisals to which his biblical source gives full rein, Rousseau will thus tap into the archetypal resonances of his personal prehistory. *Le Lévite* replaces the truism that violence begets violence with the original, originating tautology that violence *is* begetting and begetting violence. "Fear of the archaic mother turns out to be essentially fear of her generative power."[19]

Preparations are under way from the outset of the poem for the supreme moment of scapegoating when the womb of Axa, mother-to-be as sacrificial victim, will have been made available to assume the totality of violence within the text. No sooner has the initial charge of matricide been entered against Benjamin than he is in turn endowed with uterine space: "c'est de ton sein qu'est sorti le crime qui t'a perdu" (2:1208). Metaphorical matrilinearity recasts the erstwhile father of his race as the monstrous source *and* victim of a new matricide. Only divine intervention saves the tribes of Israel from playing out the same dual role to its logical conclusion: "ton peuple . . . périra-t-il pour vouloir ôter le mal de son sein?" (2:1218). However much Benjamin the tribe is said to suffer from shame and remorse for *his* crimes, this version of Israel's collective death wish is closer to suicide than to matricide and so already approximates the really desired outcome of maternal self-sacrifice. From the anxious son's perspective, there is further cause for reassurance in the knowledge that the Levite's sacrificial gesture of delivering his/her child to the enemy was imperfectly executed (and, in fact, no sacrifice at all since he later yielded to the temptation of revenge).

In preparation for the other, more desired and desirable sacrifice, *Le Lévite* misses no opportunity to feminize its many instances of violence. The apostrophe to the concubine's rapists, earlier designated as "loups affamés," masculine animals with gaping jaws, concludes as follows: "Barbares, indignes du nom d'hommes; vos hurlemens ressemblent aux cris de l'horrible Hyene, et comme elle vous devorez des cadavres" (2:1215). The evocation of an animal whose name has no masculine form, the "elle" that establishes the "Hyene" herself as an absolute referent, the implied interchangeability of her devouring with forthcoming burial in "mother" earth—all tend toward obscuring the biological identity of the apostrophe's addressees. Man (*vir*) versus woman replaces man (*homo*) versus animal as the passage's operative polarity. The attackers' homosexual intent is thus realized as a kind of lesbian lechery with overtones of infanticide.

Earlier, a gratuitous digression on ancient hospitality had produced the assurance that in those days, "l'homme avoit des entrailles" (2:1212). That assurance might, in some other text, have given rise to no other reading than the metaphorical, platitudinous "human beings had feelings." It looks suspiciously here like a literal key to reading this text's metaphorical subversion of sexual difference. In these days of biblical revisionism, men have wombs. This same aside grounds the phenomenon of ancient hospitality in blissful ignorance of exchange mediated by "vils métaux," thereby condensing Rousseau's well-known equation of metallurgy with catastrophic descent into Mother Earth's nether regions.[20] A feeling humanity would not violate its common mother; in this admitted exception to the rule, men with wombs do repeated violence to whatever mothers they encounter. Even the most literally hypervirile violence is recorded through obsessive recourse to feminine articles and pronouns: "Mais les Benjamites étant sortis en bon ordre l'attaquent, *la* rompent, *la* poursuivent avec furie, *la* terreur les précéde et *la* mort les suit" (2:1217). (The referent, whose name comes to matter less than its gender, is not in this instance the concubine, but rather "l'armée d'Israël.") The fields of Rama are likewise strewn with cadavers "comme les sables d'Elath se couvrent des nuées de sauterelles qu'un vent brulant apporte et tue en un jour." (Another exclusively feminine animal name, "sauterelles," has the further advantage of already containing the feminine surrogate *elles.*) And all this on a day when no actual females took part in the Benjaminites' killing of twenty thousand men with the aid of allies brandishing slingshots in both hands, as though in testimony to their hyperbolic masculinity (2:1217).

The doubling which will eventually make a difference to the text's outcome is that of the female. Provisional pairings between virginal daughter and concubine, mother and surrogate mother, Benjamin's mother and Benjamin as mother point ahead to the possibility of a single female's occupying simultaneously the two poles of subject and object in the enactment of self-sacrificial violence. This condition of efficacy is graphically recalled by the made-to-order name of Axa, A times a. Rousseau's twice, even exponentially feminine heroine can be named as the common denominator of violence, thanks to the femininity that factors twice in her name.

The person of Axa likewise freezes the wide-ranging vacillation of the Levite's feelings toward his concubine in an untranscendable ambivalence. The virgin who must be defiled in order to be deified is the eighteenth-century commonplace for what Girard describes as the dual nature of any sacrificial victim: "Il est criminel de tuer la victime parce qu'elle est sacrée . . . mais la victime ne serait pas sacrée si on ne la tuait pas."[21] The anarchical violence that has made a travesty of difference between innocence and guilt now fixes itself, arbitrarily but unanimously, on the solitary figure of Axa. Transposition of the dreamer's life story into the sacrificial register dignifies the commonplace and reduces his anxiety, by rendering moot the question of "real" innocence and guilt. It follows instantaneously from the ceremonial punishment of the innocent-but-guilty mother that the child whose life derives from her death can and must worship her.

"Sexe toujours esclave ou tiran, que l'homme opprime ou qu'il adore, et qu'il ne peut pourtant rendre heureux ni l'être qu'en le laissant égal à lui." The narrator's lucid and surprisingly sympathetic outburst recognizes the feminine condition per se to be inscribed within a sacrificial order to which equality as the political analog of sameness is, sadly, anathema (2:1221). But this unseasonable editorial handwringing goes nowhere; a lone voice of dissent speaks up too late to produce any substantive inflection in what has by now emerged as the universally endorsed plot line of sacrifice. There can be no two ways about it, except in the initial stages of a dream that, en route to choosing the sacrificial order over the disorder of equality, promiscuously intermingles the two. Nowhere do the aspirations of the dream text contradict themselves more blatantly than in the purple prose of the Levite-concubine romance:

> Là, coulant une douce vie, si chere aux cœurs tendres et simples, il goûtoit dans sa retraite les charmes d'un amour partagé; là, sur un sistre d'or fait pour chanter les louanges du Très-Haut, il chantoit souvent les charmes de sa jeune épouse. Combien de fois les côteaux du mont Hébal retentirent de ses aimables chansons? Combien de fois il la mena sous l'ombrage, dans les vallons de Sichem, cueillir des roses champêtres et gouter le frais au bord des ruisseaux? Tantôt il cherchoit dans les creux des rochers des rayons d'un miel doré dont elle faisoit ses délices; tantôt dans le feuillage des oliviers il tendoit aux oiseaux des pieges trompeurs et lui apportait une tourterelle craintive qu'elle baisoit en la flattant. Puis l'enfermant dans son sein, elle tressailloit d'aise en la sentant se débatre et palpiter. Fille de Bethléem, lui disoit-il, pourquoi pleures-tu toujours ta famille et ton pays? Les enfans d'Ephraïm n'ont-ils point aussi des fêtes, les filles de la riante Sichem sont-elles sans grace et sans gaîté, les habitans de l'antique Atharot manquent-ils de force et d'adresse? Viens voir leurs jeux et les embellir. Donne-moi des plaisirs, ô ma bien-aimée; en est-il pour moi d'autres que les tiens? (2:1209–10)

In its telling from the Levite's point of view, with him as the only active participant, this "amour" would appear to be anything but "partagé." The promise of reciprocity is broken from the initial moment of the erstwhile priest's indulgence in idolatry. He makes a goddess of the woman whom he will later recall having "taken" as a virgin. A text desirous of having it both ways tenuously links this violation with the later rape, only to write out original violence by using a reciprocal reflexive to declare, romantically, "ils s'unirent" (2:1209). The same refusal to choose invests the entire series of images that both repeat sexual initiation as profane event and ritualize it as sacrifice. Read "literally," the images tell of simulating an original violence, of offering Nature's children to the lover-goddess in order to keep her and the violence she incarnates at a safe distance. Read as images, they tell of literal lovemaking, as predicated on a desire for human intercourse where her desire would return and replicate his own. On whose womb, Mother Earth's or his partner's, did the Levite visit his violence? Did he merely stage sacrifices and observe them voyeuristically, or cast himself in the lover's role? Did he pick flowers for, or deflower, the concubine? mine golden honey for her, or ejaculate? Does the turtledove's trajectory mimic that of a sacrificial victim, or that of the male member in repeated coitus? Even when this final image is taken only for a euphemistic depiction of sex (and not intentionally sacrificial) acts, it underscores and displaces confusion between the sacred and the profane: masculine self-sacrifice becomes the necessary condition and concomitant of romantic love between the sexes. In a surrender that amounts to attenuated autocastration, the male fashions wombs ("pieges trompeurs") for himself and sees his member reduced to equivalence with yet another exclusively and emphatically feminine animal, "une tourterelle craintive."

The appropriately redundant expression "pieges trompeurs" bespeaks the essential aim of sacrifice, "ce trompe-violence."[22] But it also exposes the cross-purposes at which the Levite works when he both seeks to ward off violent reprisals by doing the violence of autocastration to himself and desires that his partner return the favor. The only reciprocity the Levite really knows to demand is reciprocity of sacrifice. And reciprocity of sacrifice is something the female lover could not deliver even were the notion of reciprocal sacrifice not intrinsically oxymoronic. In the aftermath of half-forgotten sacralization, she has nothing of value left to give him; gods must be worshiped from afar if they are to keep "their" violence to themselves. The Levite's enterprise fails for lack of a single focus, not so much because a really insatiable goddess no longer smiles on his efforts as because he seeks to worship and be worshiped by a supposed goddess. The concubine does pay him back for his violence and for the passivity to which Rousseau's text has relegated her. Repayment does not, however, take the form of self-sacrifice; it comes, rather, in the form of an autonomous human desire, which matches his own, for safe return to the womb of her parents' house. What was never really perfect happiness thus disintegrates into an unavowed rivalry that will be played out to the death, and beyond: one or the other of the two "lovers" must be expelled from the house of the host. As though to punish her desiring no less than the Benjaminites', the Levite will cold-bloodedly dismember the one who has made his own exhausted member palpate.

There is something suggestive, as well, about the fact of the concubine's desiring to be *with* the mother, rather than *be* the mother of Rousseau's dream. That desire erupts at the very moment when the wriggling turtledove in her womb (or at her breast) might just as well be a love child as a sex organ. Foreclosing this possibility, the text depicts her, at the moment when she expels the Levite into solitude, not as a mother but as "other"—that is, equal—"children" (2:1210). The text will not be prodded into naming the second use of the concubine's duplicitous womb until such time as the Benjaminite rapists move to "desecrate the act intended for procreation" (2:1214). The concubine remains radically unsuited for the role of sacrificial victim as specified by the text of Rousseau's desire. She cannot be "the one" of maternal self-sacrifice. The residue of her romance guarantees that she will, at best, approximate that role, and only for the fleeting instant before the Levite's exorbitant gesture of mutilation implicates her body in the perpetuation of violence.

Romantic, emasculating love having been rendered incompatible with thoroughgoing, exclusive sacrifice of the female, the denouement takes care to discriminate between the two instances of Axa. The mother of Benjamin will make a point of having nothing more to do with the lover of Elmacin. This fourth canto was written at a further temporal remove from Rousseau's dream than the others; as we might expect, it is less tolerant of contradictory wishes or, at least, more mindful of getting its priorities straight. Accordingly, in *Le Lévite*'s lone instance of directly recorded female speech, Axa names Elmacin as the object of an autonomous desire, which she renounces immediately by falling into the arms of her Benjaminite captor (2:1223). Baby Benjamin will have her all to himself; nothing remains of the lover or of reciprocal love in the victim charged with putting an end to reciprocity.

Elmacin has been added to the cast precisely so that he can be eliminated, and as a corrective to the Levite's indulgence in revenge of and against his concubine. But Elmacin has a further role to play in saving *Le Lévite* from noncompliance with the normal requirements of sacrifice. A true sacrificial victim would die, not merely swoon; she would remain metaphorically sterile, that is, utterly insusceptible of provoking reprisals;[23] and her death would herald a community's metaphorical rebirth. But what a Rousseau in personal crisis needs instead is the fertile womb of a surviving mother. That *Le Lévite* addresses this need with single-minded intensity is suggested by a letter that Rousseau wrote during the same week to the Maréchale de Luxembourg: "Je dois pourtant vous dire qu'en passant à Dijon il fallut donner mon nom, et qu'ayant pris la plume dans l'intention de Substituer celui de ma mère, il me fut impossible d'en venir à bout; la main me trembloit si fort que je fus contraint deux fois de poser la plume."[24] Axa, the mother whose name *can* be written, will have absorbed the son's violence and survived to bear literal fruits. But that requires of Elmacin that he spontaneously retire from the locus of revenge *and* assume the sterility that should otherwise have fallen to Axa.

Only then can the text's final apostrophe proclaim the glad tidings of Benjamin's return to the womb, or, more precisely, to the even more ideal state of being on the brink of birth. Neither expelled from the womb nor engulfed by it, Benjamin is still together with the mother and already separate enough from her to know the value of that togetherness. The autobiographer Rousseau would become can only look back on what *must have been* paradise; Rousseau the dreamer can look back on that paradise *and* live it. In this magical equilibrium of difference and indifference, even the Levite's wish for reciprocal sacrifice would seem to be susceptible of fulfillment. The original Benjamin's perverse repayment in kind—Rachel gave birth to him; he "gave her death" (2:1208)—is rewritten in a major key. The denouement's Benjaminite rapist reserves for Axa an otherwise precious gift, a child so nearly identical to himself as to bear his own name. The onomastic slippage that we posited as the enabling condition of Rousseau's prophetic dream brings a further desire to fruition: he who gives (a facsimile of) himself to the mother can neutralize the anxieties of fatherhood and sonship by becoming, in essence, his own father.

It is precisely "on the brink" that the *Confessions* place Jean-Jacques on what would stand as the afternoon of his greatest "gaiety." About to be expelled and seized, he picnicked. Having forgotten to bring glasses, he and two harmless "fathers" of the church improvised with the largest "chalumaux de seigle" (1:579) they could find and playfully engaged in the contained rivalry of a drinking contest. Taking their distance, the *Confessions* parody the more profound pleasures of rewriting his own birth that the same evening's dream held in store for Jean-Jacques.

SACRIFICING *LE LÉVITE* (AND ALL THE REST) AS LITERATURE

"[J]e coûtai la vie à ma mere" (1:7). The Book 1 narrative that recounts Jean-Jacques's crime against maternal generosity in mercantile terms likewise testifies to a partial dismantling of the sacrificial apparatus that had brought the crime to consciousness. Readers have always managed to appreciate Jean-Jacques's lifelong quest for maternal surrogates and repeated failure to sustain normal relations with women without knowing *Le Lévite.* Book 11 deviates, however, from the *Confessions'* established practice of attempting to settle issues of innocence and guilt without recourse to the sacred. Rousseau returns to embrace *Le Lévite*'s preoccupation with the anxiety-reducing properties of sacrifice per se. In the telling of Jean-Jacques's hour of doom, sacrificial gestures are as tightly woven into the fabric of everyday life as in Old Testament times.

Amidst deafening rumors of problems with the publication of *Emile,* it is the prospect of being elected to "suffer for truth" (1:579) that explains a singular lack of anxiety and action on Jean-Jacques's part. Notwithstanding appearances of laziness, passivity, even willingness to let his book burn in his stead, Jean-Jacques quite simply has no choice once he has been designated as a sacrificial victim. This sacrificial reflex is exercised anew when it comes to denying the apparent cowardice of flight from Montmorency. The honor of being sacrificed to truth will in turn be sacrificed to the honor and tranquility of Jean-Jacques's hostess; conversely, Mme la Maréchale must not be made to suffer for *his* crimes (1:580). Her "blindness" to the heroism of this project, failure to discourage him from leaping onto the altar, and general "indifférence" (1:581) suggest that "sacrifice" has by now become, largely, a question of semantics.

In support of Jean-Jacques's nomination as a kind of all-purpose sacrificial victim, *Le Lévite* is eventually summoned to provide documentary evidence. A "normal" individual would have sought immediate reprisals against the violent excesses of his tormentors. But not the Jean-Jacques

who, as though putting an end to some latter-day *crise sacrificielle,*
declares himself "stérile de vengeance" and "characteristically" vacates
the locus of recrimination into which circumstances have placed him:
"Naturellement emporté j'ai senti la colere, la fureur même dans les prémiers mouvemens, mais jamais un désir de vengeance ne prit racine au
dedans de moi" (1:585). Of course, sacrifice, in this instance, imperfectly
masks what van Laere aptly names the "vengeances à rebours"[25] of using
a display of perfect calm to frustrate his enemies' desire to get a rise out
of him. "Il n'y a qu'une seule chose audessus de leur puissance, et dont je
les défie: c'est en se tourmentant de moi, de me forcer à me tourmenter
d'eux" (1:586). The pointed absence from this sentence of any reciprocal reflexive belies the subject's less than total retreat from reciprocity. Like the Levite himself, Jean-Jacques straddles the fence between
the sacred and the profane.

But if the temptation to rivalry proves irresistible, the *Confessions*
will provide it with a forum or "champ clos" for controlled reenactment.
At the historical midpoint between prophylactic rituals and the modern
judiciary, Girard situates "les aménagements et entraves à la vengeance,
comme les *compositions,* duels judiciaires, etc., dont l'action curative est
encore précaire."[26] In this spirit, Rousseau proposes a storytelling contest whose outcome, were he to enter *Le Lévite,* would be a foregone
conclusion: "Qu'on rassemble tous ces grands philosophes, si supérieurs
dans leurs livres à l'adversité qu'ils n'éprouverent jamais, qu'on les mette
dans une position pareille à la mienne, et que dans la prémiere indignation de l'honneur outragé on leur donne un pareil ouvrage à faire: on
verra comment ils s'en tireront" (1:587). The mere fact of having written
Le Lévite permits Rousseau to account for his in-flight activities, and
would attest to extraordinary powers of self-discipline if he were not
really more eager to promote a simply extraordinary self. Whatever secret resentments he might be suspected to have harbored even as he
wrote are further supposed to have left no trace in his text.

Lest we object that Rousseau has mistaken transparent projection for
abstinence, the remnants of the sacrificial apparatus come once again to
the rescue. The biblical source is named as *the* source of a violence that
Rousseau's revisions will have done everything in the power of pastoral
overlay (a "style champêtre et naïf") to attentuate (1:586). The *Confessions* radicalize and essentialize a difference for which no profane
reading of *Le Lévite* can take their word. Their account of the poem's

composition takes as its starting point "un sujet si atroce," and as its destination the "véritable" idyll whose "douceur de mœurs" and "antique simplicité" will have been achieved "malgré l'horreur du sujet, qui dans le fond est abominable" (1:586). Cutting off lines of communication between the biblical and writing subjects, the *Confessions* echo the poem's original, originating call for sacrifice: "Sainte colere de la vertu, vient [*sic*] animer ma voix" (2:1208). There will be no writing *Le Lévite* until the explicit externalization of violent inspiration establishes the poem's authorial voice as "essentially" violence-free. No wonder that Rousseau makes a point of not having reread the book that only to the best of his recollection "est le livre des Juges" since the night of his dream (1:580). Sacrifice run rampant renders untouchable whatever victims it designates—including, inevitably, *Le Lévite* itself.

We have come to the point of no return, where the long arm of sacrifice reaches out to tap the poem per se. It is precisely this possibility of sacrificing *Le Lévite* that explains why the author of the *Confessions* both holds it so dear *and* goes to such lengths to deny its autobiographical content. "Jamais," writes Rousseau of *Le Lévite,* just prior to announcing the storytelling contest, "je ne l'ai relu, jamais je ne le relirai sans sentir en dedans l'applaudissement d'un cœur sans fiel qui loin de s'aigrir par ses malheurs s'en console avec lui-même et trouve en soi dequoi s'en dédomager" (1:586–87). Readers denied direct access to *Le Lévite* thus join in progress a series of ritualistic rereadings, which are presumably derivative of some forgotten original reading. The possibility foreclosed is that the usual violence of interpretation might, at some future date, produce a significant deviation from that original. Rousseau rereads *Le Lévite* not to learn from it, but rather to reproduce the affective experience most dramatically rendered by the metaphor of the clapping heart. This new *touchant-touché*[27] or impossible fusion of hand and organ instills mere being (which would be figured as a *beating* heart) with value, and implicates *Le Lévite* in the sacred business of putting Rousseau in touch with himself. To what extent and in what way will by now have been forgotten; the content of the prophetic dream is evacuated from the structure that places *Le Lévite* at the intersection of past— "Jamais je ne l'ai relu"—and future—"jamais je ne le relirai." In an experience of identity that yields a single kernel of character, "un cœur sans fiel," *Le Lévite* plays a privileged role by its exclusion. Nonreflexive pronouns referring to the text give way at the appropriate moment to a cascade of reflexives, subject-object relations to metaphorically onanistic orgies. From beyond the ceremonial circle, we ethnographers look on as *Le Lévite* is served up to the whole race of Rousseaus past and future. By way of preserving their "community" against internal dissension, they use the sacrifice of *Le Lévite* to predicate their collective identity on an absence of rancor.

That the autobiographical yield is singular in both senses of the word invests Rousseau's ritualistic rereadings with a further urge to commemorate the birth of autobiography per se. What the *Confessions* have long since promised—that Jean-Jacques will retire from "littérature" and devote himself to "mémoires" (1:514–17)—presupposes a polar opposition between two discrete activities, consecutive in time and carried out in different geographical sites. In coding the two by respective times and places, Rousseau avoids the issue of a substantive difference. And yet, he seems so sure that "littérature" and "mémoires" will never meet in some murky middle ground of "literary autobiography" or "autobiographical literature" that the *Confessions* make the distinction without betraying a moment's hesitation or anxiety. In forging the distinction, Rousseau's letters of confession to the censor Malesherbes were a start, but finally less of a step in the right direction than a one-time leap outside the purview of literature as usual. In fact, if the *Confessions* can make axiomatic an antithesis that continues today to preoccupy talk of "autobiography," it is thanks to *Le Lévite d'Ephraïm*. The *Confessions* use *Le Lévite* to render transition as violent disruption, to ground the birth of autobiography in nothing less than the death of literature, to observe that death and so make it observable.

For the difference between a literary before and an autobiographical after to accede to the status of the sacrosanct requires that sacrifices be offered in the name of autobiography. That much is already implicit in the account of Jean-Jacques's activities on the morning of his flight from Montmorency: "Depuis que j'avois résolu d'écrire un jour mes mémoires, j'avois accumulé beaucoup de lettres et autres papiers, . . . Une partie de ces papiers déja triés, furent mis à part, et je m'occupai le reste de la matinée à trier les autres, afin de n'emporter que ce qui pouvoit m'être utile et bruler le reste" (1:582). This project of triage and burning remains unrealized at the level of anecdote: "nous ne pumes achever dans la matinée, et je n'eus le tems de rien bruler." The project will find deferred fulfillment, not in violence inadequately focused on random non-autobiographical letters, but in a forthcoming (mis)reading that prepares *Le Lévite* for sacrifice as the quintessence of literature.

The timing could not be more right for a final, finalizing fling: an unforeseen literary postscriptum will reopen the book on literature so as to close it more emphatically and self-consciously than could anything written in ignorance of autobiography already "in the works." Nor can a heavy dose of chance—Jean-Jacques only happened to read the book of Judges, to complete it, to leave when he did, to remember his dream, and so forth—help but enhance *Le Lévite*'s attractiveness as a sacrificial victim. Violence would be done to a party really and solely guilty as charged (and not merely available) at the expense of the desired sacrificial dimension. That dimension is already underwritten by Rousseau's insistence on the generic duality of his "poeme en prose." *Le Lévite* is thereby set up to cover all conceivable instances of literature in Rousseau, from the most youthful poems to the recent treatise on education. Even *Le Lévite*'s avowed lack of literary values serves to qualify it for forcible valorization on other grounds. The enactment of sacrifice will have simultaneously translated intrinsic mediocrity into infinite worth; autobiography will owe everything to *Le Lévite d'Ephraïm.*

But the work of preparation for sacrifice has only just begun: in addition to his biblical "lecture," the fleeing Jean-Jacques will have fortuitously recollected "les *Idylles* de Gessner que son traducteur Hubner [*sic*] m'avoit envoyées il y avoit quelques tems" (1:586). The possibility of pastiche occurs and takes hold: "Ces deux idées me revinrent si bien et se mêlerent de telle sorte dans mon esprit, que je voulus essayer de les reunir en traitant à la maniére de Gesner [*sic*] le sujet du *Lévite d'Ephraïm*" (1:586). What was once a life-and-death occasion has become doubly, even wholly literary. Embracing a perceived challenge to literary mastery, the *Confessions* proceed to tell the whole story of *Le Lévite*'s composition as the triumph of indifference over apparently irreducible difference between the biblical and Gessnerian inspirations. By virtue of commingling the sacred and the profane, the ancient and the contemporary, the abominable and the idyllic, and more and less recent readings, *Le Lévite* comes to share in the quintessence of any sacrificial victim. It can be declared different only and precisely as the carrier of an indifference that it carries to the point of blatant contradiction. Symptomatically, several lines after confessing to the "facilité" with which he rendered his ideas, Rousseau takes credit for the "mérite" of "la difficulté vaincue" (1:586). Self-congratulation is, purportedly, in order on the (to us) dubious bases of *Le Lévite*'s virtuousness and virtuosity: "je suis sur de n'avoir rien fait en ma vie où régne une douceur de mœurs plus attendrissante, un coloris plus frais, des peintures plus naïves, un costume plus exact, une plus antique simplicité en toute chose, et tout cela, malgré l'horreur du sujet, qui dans le fond est abominable" (1:586). These doubly distortional lines misrepresent both the text at hand (or at arm's length) and the lifetime of literature that preceded it. On the one hand, they postulate an all but unrecognizable *Lévite,* made good (touching, fresh, naïve, exact, simple) in memory/anticipation of the good it will have done. And on the other hand, however much *Le Lévite* really does to defy (advantageous) comparison with much of anything else he ever wrote, the writer forces it to epitomize his "vie" synecdochically, as more and most of same.

In the fabrication of a literary text to end all literary texts, Rousseau's original contributions are limited to superior craftsmanship, and by the fact of his having imitated Gessner. What the *Confessions* conveniently fail to remember is that Rousseau first encountered Gessner not as the author of *Idylles* but as an unabashed Rousseauphile and precursor in biblical paraphrase.[28] Unavowed similarities between *Le Lévite* and Gessner's *Der Tod Abels* extend beyond the obvious "epic pretensions" and "division into cantos."[29] There is the more profound commonality of ambivalent fascination with the all-devouring womb. It may appear that "love" is exuded everywhere in Gessner for "sheltered, enclosed spaces."[30] But that does not stop his Cain from being driven to fratricide by a prophetic nightmare where he foresees that his own proudly virile race will be swallowed up by the violent "mollesse" of Eve's younger son.[31] Recognizing the smouldering misogyny of *La Mort d'Abel* and imagining how gratified Rousseau must have been by the popularity and docility of his self-styled disciple make it easy to see how Gessner came to mind at a moment when the traumas of violent disapproval and actual violence had invaded the safe haven of Montmorency.

These biographical and neo-biblical connections are nonetheless suppressed by the *Confessions*, which pick their spots and use the Gessner of the Hellenic *Idylles* to make Rousseau's *Lévite* a matter of derivative artistry. The sacrificial order converts even this apparent minus into a plus. With respect to his inviolable biblical source, the would-be *littérateur* occupies the precise position that Girard recalls Aristotle's having reserved for the tragedians of Classical Antiquity: "le bon auteur ne touche pas et ne doit pas toucher aux mythes, parce que tout le monde les connaît; il doit se contenter de leur emprunter des 'sujets'."[32] It is, arguably, the essence of art to embellish or, as Gessner puts it in his preface to *La Mort d'Abel,* to inventory "la nature" for the "multitude d'images dont il orne artistement son objet chéri."[33] And the Rousseau who "confesses" to doing nothing more or other than embellish gains the right to call himself the quintessential artist. His modesty, like Gessner's, attests indirectly and somewhat prematurely to the narrow specialization in matters aesthetic that was the fate just beginning to be reserved for literature by the incipient rise of modern science. But beyond that, naming Gessner and advertising his indebtedness allows Rousseau to contain the business as usual of imitative rivalry within the confines of literature. The territory of autobiography is, by implication, set aside as still virginal. It can be (re)discovered, as though for the first time, when the preamble to these same *Confessions* proclaims their absolute originality: "Je forme une entreprise qui n'eut jamais d'éxemple, et dont l'exécution n'aura point d'imitateur" (1:5).

This preamble comes back to mind when Rousseau as proud author of *Le Lévite* challenges all comers to a storytelling contest on the model of Gessner's pastoral "concours de chants." Striking parallels between Rousseau's two challenges, to outdo the autobiographer and to write a better story than *Le Lévite,* confirm the two paradigms of literature and autobiography in the wished-for relationship of non-interference. But by the same token, these parallels confirm *Le Lévite*'s privileged rôle in founding and formalizing difference. Only the deviations of sacrificial logic from everyday thought processes can, in short, explain why the autobiography makes so much of *Le Lévite*'s preciousness. The *Confessions* would have us read *Le Lévite* not as a companion piece or even as a "source" in the normal sense of the word, but as an enabling precondition of their own and Jean-Jacques's self-identity. In Girard's terms, the consummate oeuvre d'art will have been not only fetishized "sous le rapport de la beauté," but "radicalement niée et émasculée . . . posée en antithèse imaginaire de l'inflexible et désolante vérité scientifique."[34] In the *Confessions*' embrace of this "antithèse imaginaire," *Le Lévite* serves the cause of sending *littérature* out of Rousseau's life not with a whimper but with a bang. The prose poem is charged with figuring the many moments of beauty in Rousseau's career to which the *Confessions* will oppose a single, autobiographical moment of truth.

BODIES IN BITS AND PIECES: Sacrifice and Synecdoche

Multiple rereadings are purported to have taken place without provoking the slightest hesitation as to the validity of this scenario. Even such clues as the *Confessions* plant about attention to detail and timing send us off in hot pursuit not of the mother's womb but of a phantom plot. Rousseau's readers have, for the most part, followed the lead of his rereadings. Jean Lecercle takes the *Confessions* at their word and goes them one better, by obligating *Le Lévite* to an even greater profusion of literary sources: "La Bible, Homère, Fénelon, Gessner sont là, et malheureusement les derniers plus que les premiers. Rousseau n'y est pas. Il ne lui convenait pas de faire de la littérature."[35] On the other hand, Thomas Kavanagh's convincing reading of *Le Lévite* in relation to major works like the *Social Contract* challenges the pertinence of Lecercle's pejoratively (and anachronistically) narrow definition of *littérature*. And despite a misleading over-emphasis on the men of *Le Lévite,* Kavanagh is nonetheless struck by the subject's special fascination for "a man whose life was marked by the death of a woman."[36]

Such defections from the ceremonial circle of Rousseau's authorized rereadings were bound to happen someday. An extant text differs from traditional sacrificial victims by its potential ability to talk back and, in this instance, to make its own case for inclusion under the rubric of "autobiography." Still, if Rousseau did not publish *Le Lévite,* neither did he burn it. And his having left us more to go on than the word of the *Confessions* is not necessarily the undoing of his, albeit wishful, sacrificial scenario. Actual encounters with selected regions or bits and pieces of the prose poem can still work wonders; there is more than one way to isolate a *Lévite* that, as though inspired by Axa, all but asks to be sacrificed as the ultimate in literature.

Take, for example, the fourth and last canto, whose deferred composition mimics in miniature the overall *Lévite*'s belated literariness. Not only does Rousseau fictionalize here to a degree unprecedented in the earlier cantos, but his imaginary characters—Axa, her father, Elmacin—link *Le Lévite* to one of Rousseau's earlier fictions. A father who handpicks his son-in-law and may even be accused of using his own daughter to mediate male friendship; a daughter who, even as she takes the Father's word for divine fiat, suppresses her own desire imperfectly and names its object on her deathbed; a lover who retreats voluntarily into the posture of Platonic adoration, contenting himself with memories and vowing never to know another woman—where else have we heard something very like this story, if not in the pages of *Julie?* It is only fitting that the "maniére de petit poeme en prose" (2:1205) earmarked for equation with literature should recall the "espéce de Roman" (1:434) that constitutes the real summum of literariness and literary success in Rousseau's oeuvre. Moreover, en route to sacralization, *Le Lévite* as palinode is systematically stripped of *Julie*'s impurities. *This* father will eventually sacrifice his daughter to a higher cause than ego gratification; *this* daughter will come to her husband's embrace as a virgin; equally virginal, *this* lover will cherish his memories *and* preserve his beloved against temptation by entering the priesthood. It is as though *Julie* had undergone purificatory rites and emerged, ripe for sacrifice, as *Le Lévite.* A further point of commonality occurs: Julie's plunging into the canal to save her son from drowning, which critics have tended to dismiss as a plot device or only occasional cause of her death, reasserts its claim to preeminent causality through the univocal, unequivocal celebration of Axa's parallel sacrifice.

But the *Confessions* want to hide the sacrificial mother behind the sacrificial *Lévite* and to package the imminent birth of Benjamin/Rousseau as that of autobiography. In support of this enterprise, *Le Lévite* permits of an allegorical rereading where excesses of femininity might be used to figure those of literature. Rousseau's violation of his biblical source most often comes in the form of metaphors, which in turn work most often to subvert identity, especially sexual identity. "Forced" metaphors, contradictory, even self-contradictory metaphors, metaphors that singly and en masse call into question the most sacred categories of being—all tend toward "identifying" metaphor as the inherently violent mother of all violence. Assimilation in *Le Lévite* does not so much reconcile opposites as breed rivalry and reprisals, and assimilation occurs whenever metaphors come into play. What Rousseau's metaphors of violence end up proving is the violence of metaphor. On several occasions, literal and metaphorical instances of the same terms cohabit close quarters of the text. Having been abandoned among the "roches brulantes" of Gelboa, the Levite "burns" to rejoin his concubine (2:1210). Later, as the Benjaminites likened to the wolves of "[l]es Alpes glacées" prolong their attack, the narrator asks, rhetorically: "comment cette beauté mourante ne glace-t-elle point vos feroces désirs?" (2:1214–15), and so forth. Making a spectacle of making metaphors lays bare a crime of appropriation that would otherwise go undetected. Caught in the act of stealing from nature, metaphor beats down the door between the human and the inhuman and assumes the semantic burden of "man's inhumanity to man." We have already traced the Levite's troubles to his "improperly" diverting the name of God onto his concubine and seen how indeterminacy between the literal and the figural plays havoc with a love affair that metaphors would seem at first glance only to "embellish." But to embellish is already, for the goddess-concubine, to preside, if she will, over the games of local athletes (2:1209) and, for goddess-metaphor, to preside over the deadly serious play of language and the dissolution of difference in the text.

There is no such thing as an innocuous metaphor in *Le Lévite*; violence is as indissociably linked to figurative as to female beauty. And "beauty," in turn, is the name reserved for Rousseau's variation on the theme of Judges from the moment of the exordium's enjoining us mortals to respect not only "les mœurs" and "l'hospitalité" but, first and foremost, "la beauté" (2:1208). The moral thus pointed is extraneous to the biblical narrative and prepares us for the moment when the Levite's "beauté" and not the Levite himself will be designated for use as a sacrificial victim; "que sa beauté," demand the rapists, "nous paye le prix de cet azile" (2:1213). If beauty feminizes the Levite, then it is of beauty that he must rid himself; beauty must be objectified, fetishized, projected, made other. Exit the concubine, the soon-to-be "beauté mourante" whom the further violence of metaphor will transform into the personification of the Levite's physical "property" (2:1214). Throughout the host's harangue on hospitality, the Levite remains immobile; he leaps into action only when his inviolability is further predicated on his being not merely a guest but man of God (2:1214). Had he been secure in that identity, he could have witnessed a sacrifice of the other man's daughter as confirming the feminine in its otherness. But since he is really threatened in that identity, he must begin by externalizing the feminine other in him. The situation demands not a sacrificial victim in the narrow sense that Girard reserves for the already marginal beings who figure in the ritualistic recreation of original violence, but a bona fide *victime émissaire* on whom to wreak that original violence.[37]

He cannot stop there, however: the Levite whom Rousseau's "poeme en prose" beautifies is himself an aesthete and a poet. He first places his "true" identity in jeopardy by worshiping a graven image; his sacrilegious practice takes the form of inveterate image-making: "sur un sistre d'or fait pour chanter les louanges du Très-Haut, il chantoit souvent les charmes de sa jeune épouse. Combien de fois les côteaux du mont Hébal reten-tirent de ses aimables chansons?" (2:1209). If love emasculates the lover, literature emasculates the author in the text with whom Rousseau so identifies as to make him the eponymous hero of a story from which he disappears halfway through. Like *Le Lévite*'s author, the Levite as alter ego and poet-priest traces a route to reclamation of his singular priesthood that takes him through a final, finalizing paroxysm of poetry: he dismem-bers his concubine and sends her body to the tribes of Israel.

By way of illumination and contrast, we might recall Rousseau's ear-lier evocation of that act in the *Essai sur l'origine des langues:*

> Quand le Lévite d'Ephraïm voulut venger la mort de sa femme, il n'écrivit point aux tribus d'Israël; il divisa le corps en douze pièces, et les leur envoya. A cet horrible aspect, ils courent aux armes en criant tout d'une voix: *Non, jamais rien de tel n'est arrivé dans Israël, depuis le jour que nos pères sortirent d'Egypte jusqu'à ce jour.* Et la tribu de Benjamin fut exterminée. De nos jours l'affaire, tournée en plaidoyers, en discussions, peut-être en plaisanteries, eût traîné en longueur, et le plus horrible des crimes fût enfin demeuré impuni.[38]

What this passage states more directly than *Le Lévite* is Rousseau's understanding of the surgical operation as essentially scriptural: body parts were sent in lieu of letters; the Levite *wrote* with the corpse of his concubine. *Le Lévite* makes the same point more subtly: however un-precedented in the history of Israel, the decisive dissection nevertheless has a precedent in Rousseau's story. In the process of exhorting the Ben-jaminite rapists to cease and desist, his narrator breaks the victim's body down into its component parts: "Voyez ses yeux déja fermés à la lumiére, ses traits effacés, son visage éteint; la pâleur de la mort a couvert ses joues . . . elle n'a plus de voix pour gémir, ses mains n'ont plus de force pour repousser vos outrages: Helas! elle est déja morte! . . ." (2:1215). A text that will already have realized the death by dissection that it then reports its protagonist to do goes a long way towards establishing the Levite's gesture as not only essentially but paradigmatically scriptural. In a redoubling of synecdoche, one part stands for the textual as for the bodily whole. The Levite, "le barbare" (2:1215), does not so much substitute violence for writing as realize to the fullest and with maximal efficacy the violence that *is* writing. Insofar as the Levite replicates Rousseau's writing of *Le Lévite,* the poem rejects emphatically the alternative presupposed by the *Confessions* to be that of revenge, on the one hand, and writing, on the other; Rousseau did not choose writing over revenge, it would appear, but revenge through writing.

But the parallels with his role model go deeper still, to the heart of Rousseau's career as a writer and philosopher of writing. A prevailing plot economy of one-for-one, eye-for-eye, and tooth-for-tooth reprisals makes the Levite's mysterious "projet" exorbitant, and conceivable only in the aftermath of its realization. Writing in the text is thus endowed with appropriately violent origins and devious intentionality. The vengeful Levite's recourse to dissection as dissemination and to epistolarity as deferral and disappropriation literalizes the logic whereby writing as renunciation of being is credited with leading circuitously to its reclamation. Beyond that, the use of (a human) being as a metaphor for writing hazards a scandalous reversal of priorities, in hopes that re-reversal will be forthcoming. Derrida summarizes thusly the logocentric credo at the root of the writer's calculated risk-taking: "L'acte d'écrire serait essentiellement—et ici de manière exemplaire—le plus grand sacrifice visant à la plus grande réappropriation symbolique de la présence."[39]

Dreaming of or as the Levite, Rousseau experiences immediately the immediacy of writing's return to being. He reverts to blissful ignorance of what the *Essai* had acknowledged to be the profane alternative to sacrificial circularity. Oneiric teleportation to patriarchal times allows him to turn his back on the "plaidoyers," "discussions," and "plaisanteries" that typically bog down modern-day writing in the potentially infinite linearity of deferral and in eventual death through dissipation of energy. Endowing the Levite's story with a proper denouement, where the concubine's body will have been reassembled and reunited with his, fulfills doubly the wish of perfect, timely restitution. There is, of course, the nagging imperfection of the corpse's having, in the interval, become a corpus of letters. The text does its utmost, however, to divert attention from this trace of epistolarity and to re-humanize the concubine. The Levite addresses the still-scattered body parts as "Fille de Bethléem" and reappropriates not merely her being as such but the even more precious truth and value thereof: "ta mémoire ne restera point sans honneur" (2:1216).

From the central episode of the biblical Levite, Rousseau thus abstracts a familiar scenario: the containment of writing per se and conversion of scriptural into salubrious violence. Emphasis nonetheless falls, in this variant, on the containment/conversion of specifically figural language. The poet-priest did not merely write but wrote imagistically. In its retelling by Rousseau, the perverse fetishism of dissection comes to fetishize whatever "embellishing" the latter-day prose-poet will have done to his source. Dissection not only replicates in (more) graphic terms the rapists' violation of bodily integrity but rivets the reader's gaze on the scandal of synecdoche.

It is already unnerving to have to admit that the body parts can speak more eloquently and efficaciously than would the concubine's body in assembling and exciting the wrath of a united Israel. As Derrida puts it: "Que le signe, l'image ou le représentant deviennent forces et fassent 'mouvoir l'univers', tel est le scandale."[40] It is precisely this scandalous state of affairs that the overall *Lévite* produces by using imagery as the virtually exclusive means to radical displacement of biblical emphases: poetic "padding" changes the narrative's shape; meaningful metaphors force it into compliance with the indestructible wishes of Rousseau's own past. But why privilege synecdoche, if not as the quintessential image, as the root of all figurative evil, and good? No mere metaphor among others, synecdoche instead founds metaphor by that necessary division into component parts or "properties" that underwrites the perception and proclamation of commonality. Synecdoche leaves little doubt, moreover, as to its being a figure; unlike the metaphors (or what *may* be the metaphors) of the Levite's lovemaking, for example, synecdoche cannot be (mis)read literally, insofar as it always leaves something but not quite everything to the imagination. Or rather—and this is the supreme scandal—that "thing" that synecdoche bids us imagine consists not in the absent whole itself, but in the unnameable act of severing, in that which will have constituted the whole only by separating the part. The Levite's letters "refer" less fundamentally to the concubine than to the rape of the concubine, less fundamentally to that rape than to the letters' own fabrication. It is to violence of unknown origin, violence without origin, inconceivable violence *as* origin that the tribes react in the only way possible: "Non, jamais rien de pareil ne s'est fait en Israël depuis le jour où nos pères sortirent d'Egypte jusqu'à ce jour" (2:1208). They deny, cannot name, render external to human history the writing writ large that alone makes possible distinctions such as those between history and pre-history, the human and the inhuman.

But synecdoche can also epitomize the restorative powers of figural language. "Alors j'ai pris son corps, je l'ai mis en piéces, et je vous l'ai envoyé à chacun dans vos limites" (2:1216). Reporting on his activity, the Levite mentally puts together the still-scattered pieces; a singular pronoun ("je vous l'ai envoyé") names as a reconstituted whole that which each tribe, individually, will have received. Synecdoche's residual violence is not so easily short-circuited or circumscribed, however: in the same report, the communal whole ("vous") disintegrates into the parts ("chacun dans vos limites") that only the amputation of Benjamin will reassemble into a new community. Only the idolater's return and re-dedication to the recognized sacred order rehabilitates synecdoche as that figure of sacrifice that, by forcing the part (Benjamin) to stand for (the unrecognized violence of) the whole (Israel), permits the new whole minus one to believe in its immunity from violence.

In fact, the writing of letters is but one part, the first, of the Levite's two-stage "projet." Had he but written, Benjamin would not have been sacrificed, even imperfectly. In its highly motivated insistence on the second stage of oral confession to the tribes, *Le Lévite* deviates tellingly from the *Essai sur l'origine des langues.* Taking ellipsis to new lengths, the *Essai* had suppressed everything, including the confession, which happens in Judges 20 between the gathering of the tribes and the extermination of Benjamin. The point the essayist wanted to make about the efficacy of the Levite's gesture benefits from this dramatic foreshortening, but so too does the polarity he was in the process of establishing between gestural and oral language.[41] The *Essai*'s Levite emblematizes the former and does not engage at all in the latter: he writes, the tribes speak. There are traces in *Le Lévite* proper of the *Essai*'s further theoretical investment in tracing gestural language to needs and orality to passions.[42] As though mindful of how sorely the *Essai*'s "dispassionate" dissector had strained credibility, the prose poem does what it can to void his vengeance of the signs of passion and to view him as doing "d'un œil sec et sombre" and "sans hésiter, sans trembler" only what "needs" to be done (2:1215).

But *Le Lévite*'s deeper, more heartfelt investment is in making the gestural/oral polarity work to the advantage of difference between literature and autobiography. That requires a minor but meaningful improvement on the biblical source. No sooner desired than done; dreams formulate wishes primarily through their fulfillment. Once the tribes' oral expressions of initial shock have been removed without a trace to the exordium, Rousseau's third canto is left with two complete, discrete linguistic moments. Israel will not speak here about the unspeakable, Israel will only buzz inarticulately "like bees" (2:1216) until the time is right for speaking. In a first, scriptural moment, movement provokes only movement; the tribes gather in response to the Levite's letter. Their declaring war on Benjamin is, in turn, contingent on the erstwhile poet's speaking first and, more specifically, on his making his oral confession. Having written in (literally, with) the third person, he now tells—simply, straightforwardly, in strict chronological order—a story whose high incidence of first-person pronouns makes it unmistakably his:

> Je suis entré dans Gabaa ville de Benjamin avec ma femme pour y passer la nuit; et les gens du pays ont entouré la maison où j'étois logé, voulant m'outrager et me faire périr. J'ai été forcé de livrer ma femme à leur débauche, et elle est morte en sortant de leurs mains. Alors j'ai pris son corps, je l'ai mis en piéces, et je vous l'ai envoyé à chacun dans vos limites. Peuple du Seigneur, j'ai dit la vérité; faites ce qui vous semblera juste devant le Très-Haut. (2:1216)

Whereas the poet had counted on the overwhelming power of a single image, the priest counters by letting or seeming to let the facts speak for themselves. So sober is his prose that it does not even editorialize through the use of connectives. Metonymy takes over for metaphor to the point of mitigating even the most obvious cause-effect, tit-for-tat relationship between rape and mutilation. Of course, we know the Levite to have blatantly misrepresented his own violence toward the concubine: he was in no way "forced" but rather inspired to throw her to the wolves. But our looking on as the Levite "gets away with murder" renders all the more decisive whatever impression his narrative creates among the unquestioning tribes of his having told the truth, the whole truth, and nothing but the truth. In fact, the distinctions we have just drawn between the Levite's letter and his confession are, at best, impressionistic; they owe more than a little of their apparent "truth" to the fact of being grounded in the gestural/oral polarity that the *Essai* had proclaimed to be logically and chronologically absolute. *Le Lévite* recontextualizes the polarity, forging new associations between the literary and the scriptural on the one hand and between confession and orality on the other. A Rousseau already contemplating the *Confessions* separates the two moments of literature and autobiography and makes the second dependent on but essentially different from the first. The violence of writing is thus written out of autobiography, which tells of that writing in the past tense.

The erstwhile poet no longer has anything to fear from the effeminacy of literature: he has learned since Canto 1 to postpone his worship of beauty for the aftermath of its utter desecration by him. Indeed, the Levite who, without risk, rejoins the concubine in death acts in accordance with a personal agenda—the emasculation/sacralization of literature—that remains distinct from that of the tribes and more pertinent than theirs to that of the dreamer. How suggestively Rousseau elects to unite the buzzing bees of Israel around their "King" (2:1216). There is a poetic truth to this violation of the laws of zoology. For the Levite both joins the tribes in unswerving orthodoxy and worship of the one true God *and* harbors a secret feminocentric cult on whose objects—the concubine goddess and goddess literature—a more straightforwardly truthful text would rightly have bestowed the title of "Queen."

The Levite's "confession" and its unanimously favorable reception no doubt fulfill the perennial wish of a tongue-tied author for successful self-defense before a jury of his peers. (The Parlement de Paris is the particular jury that comes to mind on this occasion of their having condemned *Emile.*) And it must have done Rousseau's heart good to rewrite the Levite's use of synecdoche to inscribe his personal story within the sacred history that narrowly averts the sacrifice of a younger son and consummates that of a willing mother. These necessary and sufficient sequels to the Levite's story facilitate regression and gratify survival instincts. But this focal point of Rousseau's dream also has a properly "prophetic" dimension: it is only after writing *Le Lévite* that Rousseau will be able to confess in his own name and glory in the indisputable fact that when *his* enemies did violence to him, he too did nothing but write literature. The *Confessions'* authorial first person will have adapted the Levite's misleading confession to his own needs. The literary text thus predicts but also undermines what the *Confessions* proclaim about *Le Lévite*'s being, always and forever, only literature.

The literature/autobiography polarity collapses in part because there is so much overlapping, even outright duplication, of autobiographical content between *Le Lévite* and the *Confessions*. But the literary text also knows better than the autobiography about the facticity of fetish, the arbitrariness of sacrifice, the fiction of a fine line between "good" and "bad" violence. The narrator of the *Confessions* chooses to ignore the blind spot (of sacrifice) at which his counterpart in *Le Lévite* takes direct aim: "Malheureux humains qui ne savez ce qui vous est bon, vous avez beau vouloir sanctifier vos passions; elles vous punissent toujours des excés qu'elles vous font commettre" (2:1220). From the "unhappy" autobiographer's exorbitant recourse to sacrificial models, we learn less about the difference between autobiography and literature than about the excesses of his desiring that they *should* differ. Wherever it occurs, writing is, after all, always writing and always violent. Nothing Rousseau writes can prevent our choosing to read *Le Lévite* and the *Confessions* profanely and intertextually.

Still, as spectators to the dramatization of that desire for difference, we can speculate less idly than before about how much Rousseau may have known and chosen not to reveal with regards to autobiographical source materials in the other occasional texts we have read. In this, their last, most sustained direct engagement with an occasional antecedent, the *Confessions* bring the issue of indebtedness to the fore and into focus through the sheer volume, force, and single-mindedness of their denials. A question occurs: is it really the whole catch-all category of literature that the *Confessions* will have attempted, with mixed feelings and results, to silence through *Le Lévite?* Or does Rousseau's less controversial insistence on the fact of *Le Lévite*'s occasional status count for enough to train a more realistic version of the *Confessions'* ambivalence on the body in bits and pieces of his occasional corpus? In any case, *Le Lévite* alone prods the autobiographer into making a priority of responding to an occasional text's prior claims on autobiography. Previously, we have seen avoidance of the issue (when the "Préface" to *Narcisse* is credited only with advancing Rousseau's ideas), displacement of the issue (when the *Préface de Julie* is acknowledged to have fostered autobiographical readings of *Julie*), projection of the issue (when the Genevans' misreadings are blamed for initiating discussion of the dedicator's self-image), and haste to declare a non-issue (when the *Lettres à Malesherbes* are singled out as a précis and first draft of the *Confessions*).

What we see for the first time through the *Confessions'* thorough-going (mis)treatment of the most highly cherished *Lévite* is a self-conscious grappling with the less than utter otherness of an other text. That revelation provides a real basis for generalization, and a warning against taking generalization too far. The same *Confessions* to which it occurs to deal sacrificially with an intrinsically sacrificial text will have played out their previous denials of indebtedness on a case-by-case basis. In each instance, by showing the way to the means and meaning of its own partial suppression, the occasional antecedent becomes part and parcel not only of the *Confessions'* "untold story" but of their likewise untold storytelling operations. From the "Préface" to *Narcisse,* the *Confessions* learn about playing autobiography off against self-portraiture; from the tactical errors of the Dedication to Geneva, they learn to make a strategic necessity of playing the fool. They are inspired by a second, overlong preface to *Julie* to write a third that is even longer and more self-serving; and, by the *Lettres à Malesherbes,* they are inspired to essay a more lastingly truthful accommodation between confession and censorship. If the unconscious dimension of Volume 2 turns out to be primarily textual and less singular than serial, neither can any one member in the series be reified as that which, written out, would have made no lasting contribution to the protean processes of writing. Time and again, we have known the *Confessions* to divert the adventures of Jean-Jacques into an allegory play of their own inscription, each of whose acts is a product of collaboration with the occasional text of the hour.

In the debate that pits evolutionary against "big bang" theories of autobiography, Book 11 of the *Confessions* nevertheless comes down hard on the side of the big bang. To the extent that he can blind himself to the arbitrariness of his choice, Rousseau will have wreaked the perfect revenge on his enemies. Rather than allow him to slip prosaically, imperceptibly into retirement and incidentally into the writing of memoirs, they will have choreographed the one step back into literature that can propel him once and for all into the great beyond of confession. If the fleeing Jean-Jacques is reported to have handed over the key to the castle housing his document collection at Montmorency without the slightest reluctance (1:584),[43] it is no doubt because Rousseau knows the keys to the *Confessions* to lie elsewhere, in other texts. Whether or not *Le Lévite* really spells the end of literature and founds a new age of confession, there is a holiness of purpose in and about the sacrificial text that surely differentiates the memoirs we might have read from the *Confessions* we do read.

Conclusion

Theorizing the Practice
of Occasional Autobiography

Ici commence l'œuvre de tenebres . . .

I t is one thing to make a practice of occasional autobiography, as Rousseau surely did with increasing frequency and self-consciousness during the years 1752–62. And it is something else again to conceptualize autobiography per se as the written record of a past life governed in its entirety and entirely explainable by a neo-Malebranchean interplay of general and occasional causes. This latter move was hinted at, haltingly and improvisationally, in the *Lettres à Malesherbes.* But it was fully realized, tautly formulated, and properly named only in a discarded draft of the *Confessions* themselves.[1] Getting from the side of practice to the other side of theory poses a problem of some difficulty and present urgency. Barring a leap of faith in metaphor, there are existential and/or conceptual gaps to be closed between this "occasional" and that one.

The "Ebauches" do not, strictly speaking, offer an ex post facto theoretical accounting for the autobiographical adventure that began in the margins of *Narcisse* and continued episodically, intermittently, more or less clandestinely, even past the point of preliminary work on the *Confessions.* Nowhere does Rousseau think to extrapolate and expose the overall goals and methods of *that* adventure. Nor does he formally reassemble an occasional corpus on the basis of whose persistent features and impulses and in spite of whose apparent heterogeneity such generalities could be made. Nor, finally, does he take even the half-step toward theory that would have produced an autobiography of the autobiographer or narrative account of autobiographical activities predating the *Confessions*. Rather, what the "Ebauches" propose, in lieu of a theory of occasional autobiography, is a theory of autobiographical realism in which occasional causes figure prominently but not exclusively, and to the precise extent that they will have figured throughout the life to be recorded.

Some sort of pathway needs, therefore, to be traced between these two instances of the "occasional" in Rousseau, lest the term itself be suspected of bearing the full weight of an only nominal commonality. It might well be, for example, that "autobiography" is the really operative term whose place "the occasional" would be charged with holding down, metonymically and provisionally, only until such time as the better name unavailable to Rousseau could be coined. The "Ebauches" and the *Confessions* themselves, in the episode of encounter with Mme de Warens, may have trotted out the *causes occasionnelles* of Malebranche's metaphysics as a mildly satisfying, uninsistent afterthought. The "why" of it all might really be a matter of "why not." Momentary recourse to the ready-made formula may be less of a theoretical necessity than a vaguely formalistic gesture of solidarity with whatever else in Rousseau's corpus has "something to do" with occasions. This apparent confessing to connectedness nonetheless falls short of articulating connections; parallel metonymies run the risk of never meeting at any one point.

The conclusions we can derive from our readings of the occasional autobiographies will lead us in the general direction of a more substantive connection. Rousseau's punctual acts of seizing occasions for self-inscription *do* inform his eventual vision of a parallel universe where the sum total of empirical subjects and events would function as the no less than absolutely essential occasions of transcendent selfhood. There is something to go on already: both descriptions, mine of his praxis and his of the planet, proceed by suspenseful indirection to a surprise of self that literary history has since managed to render thoroughly unsurprising. The word is out; shoulders are shrugged. Even in the eyes of knowing nonreaders, the *Confessions* alone provide proof enough of Rousseau's quasireligious commitment to the Word and Word-Made-Flesh of selfhood, as sometimes reduced to the case-clinching lowest common denominator of his abandoned offspring. Rousseau is rightly fabled and frequently faulted for this commitment, which nonetheless continues to leave a mark and exercise a magnetic attraction on even the self-proclaimed skeptics and would-be heretics among us.

Rousseau remains the personification of choice of whatever excesses of now orthodox self-worship are deemed, at the moment, to be in need of pruning. *Un certain Rousseau* has been pressed into service as the simple-minded bogeyman of deconstruction's joining forces with a sadly wiser Rousseau to expose human self-identity and selfsameness in general as perennially wish-fulfilling myths of Western civilization. The specter of Rousseau likewise haunts feminists' recent moves to remap the corpus of autobiography and open its "I" to an otherness that would nonetheless steer clear of reversion to pre-Rousseauist self-irradiation. It is against everything that Rousseau can be made to stand for that feminist readings of autobiography have countervalorized the reality and recording of interpersonal relations, as left by the *Confessions* in a state of considerable and dangerously normative neglect. Indeed, the impulse to illustrate his theoretical splitting of the "I" into occasional and general instances does lead, in the *Confessions* and wherever else they are taken as a model, to the elaboration of a primary, sometimes exclusionary relationship between *moi* and *soi,* subject and self.

We know, however, from the clumsy gestures of texts like the *Préface de Julie,* that Rousseau did not give up without a fight on finding some accommodation between preeminent selfhood and genuine intersubjectivity. As amply demonstrated by the *Préface,* the dedication to Geneva, and *Le Lévite d'Ephraïm,* he simply lacked the tools to *conclude* his well-intentioned forays into intersubjectivity otherwise than by sacrificing the others in his life to the precarious cause of self-identity. All the more reason not to dignify the deficiencies of the *Confessions* as quintessentially autobiographical. We are certainly not required to make a virtue for all times and places of what was, in part, one man's pathological necessity—and, even by his standards, a particularly aggressive-defensive espousal of that necessity.

But the legend has outstripped and obscured the textual bases of Rousseau's multiple comings to a place of selfhood from which we now have the option and the luxury of wanting to strike out in new directions. What our review of the protohistory to the *Confessions* will allow us to put into perspective is the constancy of his solitary cult, its essential component of adaptability to varying sites and changing circumstances, and its gradual evolution in the years just prior to his spelling out the articles of what became in consequence a universally accessible faith. The hypothesis I want to hazard is that Rousseau's theory of autobiography in the "Ebauches" is not so much an explanation as an extension, a further instance, one more case of his inveterate practice. The intuitive lessons of his experience count for something, even if he does not say so. Rather than explain or take exception to what he has been doing all along, the Rousseau of the "Ebauches" keeps on doing it, this time, as it happens and for cause, by theorizing. Once we have abstracted the history and theory of occasional autobiography he never wrote from the corpus of occasional texts he never regrouped as such, we will be positioned at least to appreciate the poetic justice of an eventual recourse to theory.

But it is from somewhere on the near side of absolute certainty, without having managed to produce either a seamless narrative or a mathematical proof, that we will turn back one last time to the *Confessions* and put our nagging question of the two "occasionals" to Rousseau himself. His answer is waiting and, significantly, wanting. In the celebrated opening lines of Book 12, he sets out his own assessment of what can and cannot be done about rationalizing autobiography's essential connections among text, life, and self. Those connections are revealed to have been as intuitively sound and intellectually fragile for him as they remain for us. A hauntingly eloquent text of paranoid projection exposes the limits of Rousseau's ability to theorize and barely disguises the insights and anxieties of a frustrated meta-autobiographer. "Je me perds . . . ," he writes; go on without me. We readers are treated to the excruciatingly painful spectacle of a momentarily impotent pedagogue.

That spectacle looks all the more perversely self-revelatory when we consider how profoundly pedagogical is the impulse that drives all of Rousseau's occasional autobiographies except the first. By this, I do not mean only or primarily that the author poses as a teacher, recruits a pupil or pupils, and indulges in explicit pedantry, although after the "Préface" to *Narcisse* that is invariably the case. Whenever the potential for a specifically teacher-student coupling is inherent in the rhetorical frame, it is exploited: the Genevans will be taught to know and love their lot, Malesherbes will learn to know and esteem the real Rousseau. Absent an extant coupling, the text invents one. Co-prefacer N has barely arrived on the scene when he is being instructed by R on the right and wrong ways to read a novel. And, in what becomes a striking incursion on the immediacy of a dream text, the narrator or teacher-turned-high-priest of *Le Lévite d'Ephraïm* resorts early and often to his right of apostrophe, sermonizing right and left and dispensing all manner of sanctimonious, doom-laden advice to encoded readers and characters alike.

Only the prefacer to *Narcisse* passes up the opportunity to sit some textually encoded pupils down and set them straight about something or other. Not incidentally, the journey of self-discovery on which that prefacer embarks following his formal retreat from rhetorical relations is the most daringly open-ended and perilous to the self-concept of any undertaken in Rousseau's occasional autobiographies. But our only means to confirming this has been to tag along in the guise of uninvited guests or unofficial auditors. Epistemological sophistication holds sway, but only for the moment, over pedagogical demonstration. That is not to say that the two are mutually exclusive, or that the "Préface" to *Narcisse* marks the beginning and the end of Rousseau's stretching to learn new and different things through occasional autobiography. But the subsequent parade of teachers-in-the-text attests symptomatically to Rousseau's having learned selectively from prefacing *Narcisse* to divert his occasional writing toward a primarily pedagogical vocation. He seems to have been more struck by the preface's tour de force of self-centering and takeover of liminary space for the self than by any intellectual challenges the text had gone on to pose to his intuitive sense of self-identity. Or perhaps it was his need to silence those very challenges that dictated a shift in emphasis. Teaching came to be of the essence, and a matter of externalizing the bases of inner assent to selfhood. Whatever the specific curriculum of the hour, the general lesson to be learned and relearned remedially as often as necessary was this: the self exists—still ubiquitous, still resilient, still transcendentally intact, and still incapable of not making a difference or leaving a mark.

Each of Rousseau's comings to autobiography thus rehearses a reconquest of the cogito: part of me is here, therefore I am. Regardless of where "here" happens to be, demonstration entails staging one or more surprises of self at the level of manifest content. In the "Préface" to *Narcisse,* "moi-même" bursts onto the scene all but unannounced. Likewise, the first person of the dedication to Geneva immediately shrugs off reductive identification as the author of the Second Discourse and lays claim to thirty years of unswerving lived (not literary) dedication. And, in a later incarnation, he ostentatiously yields to the temptation of solipsistic reminiscence on the Genevans' time. The two closely related, mutually reinforcing metamessages are these: there is more me here than you or I expected, and there is more to the me we expected to find here than meets the eye (or pronominal I). As a further case in point, consider the courtroom melodrama of R's falling slowly but surely, rejoinder-by-tense-rejoinder, for defiant autonomination as "Jean-Jacques Rousseau, en toutes lettres." Under the circumstances, pleading the fifth would have been a perfectly normal, honorable, and understandable response to N's relentless cross-examination. Once again, more me than anticipated intrudes on surroundings clearly earmarked as inhospitable or ill-equipped to accommodate more than a shadow of the writer's self.

Sometimes the good news of the surprise of self is not broadcast in so many words. It may be reserved for the author himself, pending the ability of some wider audience to reconstruct the context of unfavorable circumstances. At the prompting of this or that fresh attack of anxiety, the *autodidacte* in selfhood was well prepared to counter with refresher courses designed primarily for his own benefit. The self that would be submitted to the Censor in lieu of a mere manuscript rose to meet the challenges of imminent death and a mutilated *Emile.* The traps of patronage were narrowly averted by a self that through dedication not to Louis XV knew itself to be beyond the contingency of class distinctions. And the one of its skins that was under threat of a *prise de corps* was shed by a self for whose life as Benjamin thousands, including his own mother, would gladly lay down their lives.

Rousseau never wavered in keeping his third-person distance from Benjamin and from the Levite. But that was only the last and most emphatic of his stands against confirming unmistakable resemblances to textual alter egos as hard-and-fast identities. In *Le Lévite,* a dream-aided fuzziness of identification comes to epitomize a career of in figura self-portraiture that also stands the message of selfhood in good stead. Rousseau's version of in figura self-portraiture functions as a necessary corrective to unwanted appearances of irreversible incarnation. It guards against the possibility of misreading the surprise of self to go hand in hand with a cutting down to size or threat to transcendence. In this complementary encoding, the subliminal cogito reads: whatever you may just have been led to believe, I am because I am *not* Narcissus—or, for that matter, Echo or Socrates or Brutus or Lucretia or Saint-Preux or Julie or a mere "faiseur de livres." I am all of the above rolled into one, and then some. Each of these figures captures and conveys some of who I am or may be at any given moment. But I am beyond the powers of any one of them to pin my whole self down to earth. As proof of that last point, Rousseau could invoke the record of a singular capacity for virtually simultaneous identification with each (Narcissus and Echo) or all (Lucretia, Brutus, Sextus, Collatinus) of the known antagonists of whatever classical drama his Olympian self had been moved to revisit. Nor, arguably, would he dare linger so long in the mirrors of antiheroism and villainy if that were tantamount to forfeiting his right of pulling back into transcendence. On the contrary, he is perfectly capable of demonstrating the difference between strategic self-images and bona fide selves.

The brunt of that last demonstration nevertheless falls on the *Confessions.* Most notably, Book 8's virtuoso variations on the theme of Lucretia go to expose *auto-avilissement* as a contingent possibility and strategic compromise with modern mores to which the self does not, however, give its full, unqualified assent. This self-serving disengagement stands in sharp contrast to the more myopic, self-embroiling intuitions of the unfinished occasional tragedy *La Mort de Lucrèce.* There, Rousseau seems convinced of his utter inability to get beyond or transcend a no longer optional *auto-avilissement* at the very core of his being. The usual reserves of self appear to have been thoroughly depleted; Rousseau cannot stage a reversal of *auto-avilissement* but can only abandon the play after two acts. For the interminable moment when baseness resonates in his characters' every word and suffocates the voice of virtue, he knows himself to be irredeemably tainted by the abject. *That* he is provides small consolation, given the demonstrated monstrosity of *what* he is.

In insisting on transcendent selfhood as the pedagogical bottom line of Rousseau's in figura self-portraiture, I do not mean to cheat these relatively unguarded moments of rediscovered vulnerability out of their intermediate epistemological values. Knowing who he is and keeping up to date with the *quality* of his self do matter, always and desperately, to Rousseau. And it is never too late to supplement or touch up the static official portrait compiled by scholarship on the sole basis of the major works. We owe it to Rousseau and to ourselves to let the specific centrifugal forces of each occasional text lead us to new and unexpected qualities. I have been surprised, for instance, to discover the dyed-in-the-wool homme de lettres whom Rousseau does not normally embrace as part of his public persona. The liminary texts betray an acute, well-informed sensitivity to the exploitable nuances of literary convention; the *Lettres* and other letters to Malesherbes reveal an imagination that has been not merely touched but profoundly shaped by the reality of eighteenth-century publishing practices. Shock better describes my reaction to being introduced in *Le Lévite* to a Rousseau who had it in him (and not just in his biblical source) to blow the lid right off his family romance and off the *locus amœnus* of the patriarchal Golden Age.

To be sure, the austere Genevan's version of giving in to the impulse of the literary moment rarely comes close to approximating Montaigne's pose of devil-may-care drunkenness; hence, Rousseau's expressions of wonder at the ease with which the First Discourse and letters to Malesherbes "wrote themselves." His counter-impulse to self-control and airtight coherence of corpus were not born with the *Confessions.* Even the "Préface" to *Narcisse* remembers to reinvest the here and now of exploratory writing in the possibility of long-term gains for self-identity. But livening up the autobiographer's model by acknowledging its capacity for change is precisely what is called for by an early "Enigme" that Rousseau wrote as though at the behest of "le portrait":

> Enfant de l'Art, Enfant de la Nature,
> Sans prolonger les jours j'empêche de mourir:
> Plus je suis vrai, plus je fais d'imposture,
> Et je deviens trop jeune à force de v[i]eillir (2:1133).

By no stretch of the imagination will the imposters of Rousseau's occasional self-portraits ever become too young to be true—or intellectually engaging. With the portraits as a point of departure, we can work backwards to add to our firsthand knowledge of biblical and Classical topoi, sideways to gain a more realistic view of the eighteenth-century literary scene, and ahead to the psychoanalytical theories that Rousseau seems, uncannily, to anticipate. Paradoxically, the portraits' having grown old gracelessly enough to keep us interested derives in part from the fact of there being so much more to them than mere me alone, and so many other foreign places embedded in the ones Rousseau appropriates for the self. In fact, Rousseau himself appears to have grasped the irony of how fundamentally his project of full-scale *Confessions* was advantaged by his already proven ability, as an original thinker, to stimulate and captivate the thoughts of others. Whereas he starts out in the "Ebauches" to justify the autobiographical project by recommending the qualities of his pre-Romantic thinking *and* feeling soul, he ends up all but imperceptibly reverting to a neo-Cartesian equation of soul and mind: "Dans quelque obscurité que j'aye pu vivre, si j'ai pensé plus et mieux que les Rois, l'histoire de mon ame est plus intéressante que celle des leurs" (1:1150). The prediction, as borne out by subsequent literary history, is that the lure of intellectual adventure will cover a multitude of sins, foremost among them the excrescence of presumptuous selfhood or Idea behind the ideas to which all who set foot in the *Confessions* will necessarily be exposed.

Indeed, the experience of sheer, unmitigated excrescence had been a further key to conversion of the doubters since the earliest occasional autobiographies. Rousseau's twofold boast of thinking "plus et mieux" says it all: quantity of soul counted no less than quality at a historical moment when it was still as much a question of postulating and promoting the self as of defining or refining it. Above and beyond their respective contributions to qualifying the subject of their self-portraiture, Rousseau's occasional texts go en masse to show an irrepressible surfeit of what (we are encouraged to assume) can only be the self. The pedagogical impulse is not content with staging punctual incarnations and escapes from incarnation. Rather, it shows up unfailingly in the form of sheer numerical excess and overabundant textuality. Liminary texts that have no business being so long clearly overshoot the mark. But so too do the four letters of response to Malesherbes's one and a second preface (with a second prefacer) to *Julie* that, unless it is really more than a preface, has no reason for being in the public domain. The *épîtres dédicatoires* overdo it just by being. Rousseau seems to have misheard the *philosophes'* warnings against any dedication whatsoever to mean that there is no use dedicating to any single citizen when there is an entire republic out there just waiting to be harangued. And, for the Bible's three chapters, the "paraphraser" who has more to say on the subject than God Himself substitutes four cantos.

But assuming Rousseau to be behind all this excess is not something we readers need to do on our own initiative. The task of provoking that assumption falls to the personified textual markers of selfhood that we have already caught in flagrante delicto of being somewhere that they alone do not belong. Suspicion is thereby cast on the self, which "must be" the prime mover or general cause or only available explanation for unmitigated excrescence in the environs. Wherever we have caught a glimpse of the creator, recognition of its overabundance is prompted by the signs of an overabundant creation. On the basis of the accumulated evidence, teacher and pupil have due cause to reconfirm that there is more to me than (directly) meets the eye, and to speculate that there is a lot more of me where that came from.

Falling short of the mark is a further, if sparingly exercised, option. In the dedication to Duclos, the terse two-line excuse for a main body that is sandwiched between the fulsome formulae of salutation and complimentary closing hints at a disproportionate withholding of self from heartfelt participation in the dedicatory enterprise. But when Rousseau's stated intentions are factored in, overshooting the mark can just as easily lead to a tell-tale falling short, most dramatically in the flattering overkill-as-suicide of the dedication to Geneva.

What remains constant, through thick texts and thin, is the derisory new meaning lent by Rousseau's occasional autobiographies to the Classical and neoclassical ideals of rising promptly, smartly, and precisely to the occasion. Rousseau has evidently discerned the threat posed to discernible selfhood by any wholehearted preoccupation with rising just as far and no further than would be required by circumstances or common consent. And, on this score, Rousseau's ideas have certainly taken hold. If we still share the remnants of the Classical ideal with him, we also share his fear of pursuing it too exclusively or successfully. Meeting only requirements and only as necessary is nowadays assumed to exact a sometimes prohibitive price of self-immolation. Our contemporary, the Rousseau of the occasional autobiographies, went to illuminating extremes to avoid paying that price under any circumstances. Even when it would have been easiest and most excusable to stick to commonplaces or remain silent (e.g., pocket the dedication to Geneva or keep his partly guilty dream of Judges to himself), he established a characteristic pattern of excrescent, all but uncalled-for responses. Repeatedly disrupting and disequilibriating the smooth flow of text, an overdetermined increment of excrescence went a long way toward developing and substantiating the sense of self with which Rousseau came already converted and forearmed to write the *Confessions.*

One way of picturing the swerve on the rising to the occasion for which Rousseau is at least partially responsible would be to contrast a pair of icons of the goddess OCCASIO. In the first, that of Ausonius's Classical epigram, a strangely configured head or hysteron-proteron of OCCASIO seems at first to back through the poet's field of vision. She presents no distinct features, no tell-tale signs, but only the unrecognizable aspect of a face covered with hair. It is for hindsight that the epigram reserves the shock of baldness "at the back of thy head."[2] By the time there is something there to see, there is nothing left to seize, except the fact of the poet's having unselfconsciously deployed a second figure where the head of OCCASIO stands for the opposite extreme of the female torso. The figure works subliminally to essentialize her otherness and to model the occasion to which he will have failed to rise on that of a potentially perfect heterosexual coupling.

From a Rousseauist vantage point, however, the slow-witted Ausonius is to some extent well rid of *that* OCCASIO. For, in what might easily have become the stranglehold of the other's too perfect embrace, the poet stood to lose by losing sight of himself. Interestingly enough, the *Encyclopédie* makes a point to certify the linguistic accident of OCCASIO's femaleness: "Les Romains en firent une déesse, parce qu'en latin son nom est féminin."[3] Indeed, that femaleness becomes a transparent ruse in more recent versions of the icon. Rather than celebrate unselfconscious fusing with the occasion as an end in itself, these versions domesticate otherness and more nearly approximate the Rousseauist ideal of using the occasion to hold a mirror up to the self. It is far easier for the male subject to see *his* self in OCCASIO when Ausonius's deceptive pubic thicket is replaced by the single lock ("une longue tresse de cheveux par devant")[4] or hair of the proverbial expression, "L'occasion n'a qu'un cheveu."[5] Replicating the male anatomy as closely as possible, this OCCASIO sometimes brandishes "un rasoir,"[6] the better to keep him fully apprised of threats more relevant to his sense of self than to hers. Rousseau's paradigmatic trajectory in the occasional autobiographies consists to a significant degree in forcing and finessing the first OCCASIO into closer conformity with the second. His victories of partial self-mirroring look to be all the more resounding because the territory— whether of a bad play written in a former lifetime or of an anonymous biblical horror story—looked, to begin with, so defiantly alien.

It is as though Rousseau were out to prove that, at least where he is concerned, there can never be any such thing, strictly speaking, as an occasional text. From the first moment of refusal to do his prefatory duty by *Narcisse,* he makes a point of declining the eighteenth century's open invitation to do a perfunctory, selfless job of fulfilling the basic requirements for publication. And he later makes a point of extending the same invitation (and possibility of declining) to the freestanding texts he explicitly brands as "occasional." But the presumption of occasionality is invariably a rallying cry in response to which the self shows up in force, the implication being that the self will show up whenever or wherever the writer puts pen to paper. The argument for infinite extendability is supported by the fact that criteria for admission to Rousseau's potentially all-inclusive occasional corpus supersede the usual considerations of genre and manifest content. His ad hoc category of occasional writing gradually moves out of the margins and stretches the envelope of œuvres de circonstance. Cutting across generic boundaries, uniform labeling levels differences between prefaces and dedications, between personal letters and belles lettres, and between liminary and freestanding texts. The lowest common denominator of occasionality comes to herald the highest (and only other) common factor of autobiography, as if to proclaim: part of me is in more places than you ever imagined I could be—here, for instance, and beyond that, who knows?

The question of how much proof is proof enough is intriguing. Rousseau may have had any number of reasons for limiting his occasional canon by and large to the texts we have read here. The antecedent narcissistic wounds that we have been able to attach to each of these texts[7] may have been the added impetus he needed to do a more pointed and vigilant than usual job of self-enhancement. There was a danger, moreover, in expanding the required reading list beyond these few well chosen, tried-and-true examples: everyone who writes prolifically knows the experience of reading back something that looks utterly perfunctory, something in which they do not at all recognize themselves. The same goes for all the infinite gestures of daily life that, following the democratization of history, are now open for consideration as potential occasions. Since the self cannot possibly be perceived to give its all at all times, the subject has the option (and every reason) to subjectivize as occasions the selected words and events on the basis of which he or she wants the self to be known and judged.

Rousseau's supreme instance of naming and claiming a literary occasion involves *Le Lévite d'Ephraïm.* This version of riveting attention on the occasion is a twofold investment in playing it safe while shooting for the stars. At the very worst, autobiography will out: the self will be discovered, as usual, to figure through partial, prismatic incarnations in the body of the text; Rousseau will be recognized to have lent his fears, fixations, and "fiel" to Levite, Benjamin, and concubine alike. But, better yet, if Rousseau can make us believe that there is no autobiography in *Le Lévite,* the self will overwhelm us by the infinitude and infinite serenity of its absence from the neo-biblical recriminations. That self will exist and preside just as surely as the God of the Old Testament without benefit of incarnation. Having reascended into the stratosphere of uncompromising selfhood, Rousseau's "cœur sans fiel" will appear only but unmistakably in the mind's eye of the true believer.

And yet, in order to feel that absence as extraordinary and explainable only as a function of an extraordinary self, we need first, as Rousseau reminds us, to get a good feel for the occasion. In fact, there can be no moving the doubters to perceive the great beyonds of self without a clearly defined frame of reference, a horizon of expectations, some preconceived notions as to what would amount under the circumstances to a self's perfectly decorous and unremarkable intervention. The illuminating irony of *Le Lévite* is that, all things being relative, making violent reprisals against his enemies would, in this instance, have been the only normal and "decorous" thing for Rousseau to do. In the context of Rousseau's overriding desire to confer absolute value on the perception of selfhood, *Le Lévite* is the apparent exception that proves the methodological rule of relativism and promotes that rule to a new level of abstraction. To the extent that his pedagogy is grounded in spectacular failure to rise only to the occasion, disproportionality and deviation from norms are his indispensable teaching tools.

The disproportionalities in his liminary autobiographies are easy to spot. Any experienced reader knows when a preface or dedication has dragged on too long for the good of the primary text or primary audience—or, conversely, when a suspiciously slapdash job of prefacing has been done (e.g., Mme de Luxembourg's reading of the first preface to *Julie*). On the other hand, the horizon of expectations concerning correspondences was considerably more hazy: real letters might say however much they had to say in tones ranging from ultra-formal to familiar. In writing to Malesherbes, Rousseau thus makes a point of naming his two transgressions of excessive length and undue familiarity. The pertinent norms of their professional correspondence are invoked through the writer's almost incredulous avowal of deviation from them. And, more generally, whenever deviations risk sneaking by unperceived, Rousseau takes this added precaution of reinscribing the norms. That means, for example, getting N to remind us out loud that eighteenth-century novel prefacers almost always settled, as R eventually will not, for the minimalist in figura incarnation of editor.

Whether this positing of the self by explicit opposition with norms of relative selflessness says anything about the self's existing and being known to exist in a real world outside the realm of occasional autobiographies remains indeterminate. The tacit by-product yielded by the autobiographies' pedagogy of selfhood is not a detailed, generalizable metaphysics, but a fledgling theory of text production. The point, as proven under the controlled conditions of a discrete corpus, is not that there is no such thing as an occasional text, but that there is no such thing as an *only* occasional text. All texts both are and are not occasional. A confluence of circumstances and expectations solicits the writing self and lays down certain of the parameters of its writing. Circumstances and expectations do not, however, go so far as to determine absolutely the process or end product on which the self in its own right leaves an indelible stamp. It is this mark that, by throwing some of the circumstances into high relief, Rousseau seeks to render even more highly and unmistakably visible. The beauty of putting this plan into action in texts like the "Préface" to *Narcisse* is that the nonself (i.e., play to be prefaced and conventions of prefacing) is clearly identifiable and distinguishable from what can be calibrated in consequence as an increment or surplus of self.

Through his periodic returns to write at this conjuncture of isolatable occasional and general causes, Rousseau may have hoped to exorcize residual fears concerning the occasional—or only occasional?—text that had launched his career. To be sure, the "Préface" to *Narcisse* alone addresses the precise challenge of putting more self than Rousseau's critics would grant him into his response to the Dijon Academy. It nonetheless bears recalling with what persistence the First Discourse kept cropping up, like some perennial touchstone or threat of the only occasional, in our discussions of the later autobiographies. It figures, in chapter 2, as his manifesto of Herostratan envy; in chapter 3 as the stakes of Diderot's catastrophic rise to neo-paternalism; and, in chapter 4, as a precedent for the guilt-free automatic writing (to Malesherbes) in which Rousseau could again indulge once he had assumed himself to be dying. Significantly, Rousseau comes closest to making his peace with the *Discours* in the same *Lettres à Malesherbes* where he most fully embraces what feels, for the moment, less like the sterile bipartite causal mechanism that had been known to require vigilant readjustments than like a miraculously dis-inhibiting fusion of occasional and general inspirations.

The more ambivalent *Confessions* would brandish the Academy's flyer as occasional catalyst and culprit of the *Discours.* So too, even those of the occasional autobiographies that are not liminary take at least some of their cues from an immediate and certifiable textual antecedent. Rousseau writes directly back to the Head Censor, and he later paraphrases the Scriptures with more and different help from Gessner than he admits. At its most elegantly schematic, the prevailing economy of text production can thus fill the available slots of general and occasional causality with the self and the already written. *Within* our texts, however, there is an unobtrusive move afoot to complicate the occasional by removing it from the exclusive purview of the antecedent text or texts. The "Préface" to *Narcisse* fetishizes *Narcisse* and detextualizes the ideas of the First Discourse by removing them to the heart of the prefacer. The dedication to Geneva likewise evokes the occasion of meditating on the idea of inequality without letting on that this meditation has resulted in a Second Discourse. The value-charged message would seem to be that Rousseau's self is not moved by text alone. And when the *Préface de Julie* makes its solo flight into publication, that message may be accompanied by a pertinent question: if not *Julie,* then what or who is behind this text? "[C]e qui vient de se passer" is explicitly acknowledged (along with Malesherbes's Christmas Day letter) to share in responsibility for Rousseau's response. Events have crept onto the scene as pretenders to occasional causality. And it is precisely the causal role of events that the *Confessions* will go to such lengths to assert vis-à-vis the *Lettres* (The threat of death alone moved me to write) and to deny in the case of *Le Lévite* (The threat of a *prise de corps* moved me not at all—except, physically, to flee). The always excessively and obligingly literary *Lévite* is, in fact, used to reaffirm the minimalist pre-text/self dyad: a simultaneously maximal indebtedness is proclaimed to influential textual sources and to an absolutely superhuman self.

For the occasional autobiographies themselves, there is no urgency about settling these disputed claims to occasional causality. To the precise extent that (except for the *Lettres*) the autobiographies are not primarily referential, they are not preoccupied with referential understanding of the way things work out there in the real world. Nor do they articulate a full-blown theory of text production, although they hint that mounting such a theory would be a tall order. For purposes of staging their microcosmic moments of truth, it suffices to introject enough self into the passage from one text to another to preclude misapprehension of a too seamless *texte-à-texte.*

To summarize, then, the various ways in which we have seen that aim to be fulfilled in the occasional classroom: through its unexpected incarnations in a wide range of venues, the self reveals its ubiquity and ecumenical spirit; through the reversible incarnations of in figura self-portraiture, it reveals its transcendence; and through the qualitative and quantitative excesses for which it is the only conceivable accounting, it asserts its claims to be privileged as a general cause or prime mover. Moreover, in this business of simulating the inner assent of Rousseau's clapping heart, quasiscientific proof comes to the aid of faith. Measurable excess and unexpectedness emerge, gradually or instantaneously, against a backdrop of reinscribed norms, circumstances, and expectations. A prior sense of the occasion becomes crucial to engineering an absolute sense of self.

These lessons have all been thoroughly internalized by the Rousseau of the "Ebauches," who offers the following accounting for the work in progress:

> . . . j'écris moins l'histoire de ces éve[ne]mens en eux-mêmes que celle de l'état de mon ame, à mesure qu'ils sont arrivés. Or les ames ne sont plus ou moins illustres que selon qu'elles ont des sentimens plus ou moins grands et nobles, des idées plus ou moins vives et nombreuses. Les faits ne sont ici que des causes occasionnelles. Dans quelque obscurité que j'aye pu vivre, si j'ai pensé plus et mieux que les Rois, l'histoire de mon ame est plus intéressante que celle des leurs." (1:1150)

Supposing that the fundamental commitment to demonstrable selfhood still holds, we can further assume that successful demonstration hinges on the ability to deliver more self than normally anticipated or required under the circumstances. From Rousseau's dismissal of "éve[ne]mens en eux-mêmes" as the least of his concerns, we can infer that the norm that he has mentally re-created and taken for his point of departure is the genre of memoirs. And to the usual strategies of exorbitant selfhood, that norm poses some paradoxically daunting challenges through its very proximity to the enterprise at hand.

Incarnation in the two first persons of narrator and protagonist is entirely consonant with the memoir tradition and, however insistent, cannot necessarily go to prove that there is more me here than you expected. But beyond that, what is to be feared is that a surfeit of incarnation will multiply, normalize, and fetishize the incarnated self to the point of conflating the visible part with the invisible whole. Rather than suggest that there is more here than meets the eye, the memorialist's text may be reduced to implying that what you see is all there is. And the chances of reversing incarnation by the usual means appear slim once Rousseau has endorsed the memoir tradition's referential claims and strict standards of biographical truthfulness. By those standards, the kind of in figura self-portraitist who ignores his contemporaries to go rummaging around in the costume box of Antiquity stands already disqualified from consideration on grounds of mythomania.

As for sheer textual excess, it will be hard to prove and hardly clinching. Some of the longest memoirs on record are also, thanks to their secretarial scrupulosity, the most impersonal. It would appear that, for the time being, Rousseau will have to content himself with thematizing textual excess through the frequent allusions to his "papers" that end up endowing the archives, if not the archivist, with monumental proportions. The really striking moments of self-induced textual excrescence will come later, when it turns out that the *Confessions* will not have exhausted the autobiographical materials or impulse to autobiography. The *Dialogues* and *Rêveries* have since proven to everyone's satisfaction that there *is* a lot more of me where that came from.

But, in the meantime, the present situation of the "Ebauches" can also be salvaged emblematically. Part of Rousseau's purpose in evoking and poising himself on this precipice of potentially self-defeating memoirs is to set the stage for yet another refresher course in selfhood. I want to suggest, by glossing this one, that such mini-courses proliferate throughout the infinitely divisible *Confessions*. We need only look beyond the referential cover story's corollary concern for the quality of self to discover some exquisitely discreet variations on the familiar pedagogical theme of staging the axiom. Indeed, what makes the passage I have extracted from the "Ebauches" particularly emblematic is its apparent obsession with identifying qualities on the basis of which the past records of selves can be ranked with respect to their fitness for autobiographical treatment.

If we look closely at the passage, we will note that it revolves around a pair of closely related but not entirely synonymous incarnations. Rousseau starts out ("j'écris") in what becomes the guise of a writer once he has left it behind for the other guise of thinker ("j'ai pensé"). By way of widening the gap, the writer is clearly reinscribed in the reportorial docility of the memorialist as scribe. He is said to be telling the two stories of Jean-Jacques exactly as they happened. For the moment, of course, he is telling nothing at all—a warning of the exorbitant further splitting of the pronominal *je* for which the predicate of thinking will supply the implied referent of philosopher. The changing of the guard actually occurs as a direct, yet in no way predetermined or predictable, result of the doctrinaire memorialist's unspoken presupposition that the special circumstance of whole-life writing calls for referential realism or for the holding up of a mirror to real life—whatever that may be. From the in figura writer's perspective, the requirement of realism is so binding that the consequences of that realism for his writing—"Les faits ne sont *ici* que des causes occasionnelles"—must follow automatically, with no mediating causal connection, from the "reality" sketched in the preceding lines of text. In the interim, however, what began as a simple description of work in progress has been diverted through a controversial metaphysics that only passes for reality.

It is certainly significant, in terms of enhancing the illusion of reality, that what follows the "or" of imprecisely oriented digression skips over the possibility of backing up to posit the self. Instead, Rousseau proceeds directly to the politico-textual ramifications of selfhood's quasireligious universal accessibility. But this telling of selfhood as a fait accompli is doubled and, indeed, overshadowed by a showing. One of the helpful suggestions of the Malebranchean subtext is, in fact, that there can be no depositing the "ame" in a textual body without precautionarily testing its capacity for an afterlife of release from bondage.

And so, before our eyes, that soul takes flight. The tell-tale markers of the thinker in the text and the quotation from Malebranche point to excrescent new heights of philosophy from which some *je* above and beyond the indentured slave of past reality and realistic writing practices must be responsible. The narrator who intends (and pretends) to subscribe and even the protagonist who, for purposes of demonstration, has been limited to thinking "better and more" are left in the dust of incarnation by a transcendentally disincarnate philosopher. Even as the first "I" writes, the philosopher thinks daringly, systematically, and all but inconceivably to reorder God's universe.

And in this he is only following the lead of the occasional autobiographers. The trajectory of upward displacement to the "thinking big" of philosophy had already been traced—to an extraordinary degree, given their limited maneuverability—by the prefacers of *Narcisse* and *Julie.* The latter-day metaphysician has something else in common with them, with the correspondent who erected a makeshift confessional in the midst of a professional correspondence, and with the paraphraser who moved Genesis into the midst of Judges. Like all the occasional autobiographers, Rousseau remains committed to the project (or implied necessity) of reconfiguring and personalizing whatever "ici" the self is obliged to call home for the moment. Only now, that place happens to be a simulacrum of reality or single-story house of external events to which, for purposes of accommodating his self, Rousseau thinks to add a second story. From somewhere above and beyond the lèse majesté of the encoded philosopher's taunting comparisons with "les Rois," the text retransmits the first lesson of Rousseau's occasional pedagogy: the subject is also a self.

What the "Ebauches" do not provide, however, is a satisfactory answer to our question of the two occasionals. Their theory of autobiography wants to be a metaphysics to which writing would be tacked on for good measure and without changing anything. We are left with that applied metaphysics, on the one hand, and, on the other, with the vaguely suggestive theory of text production that can be abstracted from the occasional corpus. Between the two systems, there is agreement about the end product of an autobiographical text and about the notion of self as general cause. It may well have been his prior experience that prompted Rousseau to formalize his declaration of selfhood along with his formal declaration of autobiographical intent. But whereas the rule of thumb of occasional practice inevitably gave priority in filling the place of occasional causality to prior texts, the *Confessions* will have unhesitantly reassigned that priority to "facts" and "events."

We have already noted how, in the general spirit of logocentrism's low regard for writing, the occasional texts made some momentary passes at supplementing their textual with existential antecedents. In this, they anticipate the *Confessions'* more emphatic desiring for transparent referentiality. But we have also seen to what degree the eventual shape and substance of the occasional autobiographies remain text-dependent. The hypotheticals are mind-boggling. What if Rousseau had had a play by some other name than *Narcisse* not to preface? What if he and Diderot had not corresponded about *Julie* and traded barbs in *Le Fils naturel* and the *Lettre à d'Alembert?* What if Malesherbes had seconded the diagnosis of the *philosophes* or failed to hazard any diagnosis whatsoever? What if Rousseau had read only Gessner's *Idylles* and not his *Death of Abel?*

There is no escaping the answer: other texts of self-inscription could have been penned in response to other solicitations of the self, but not the selfsame autobiographies of Rousseau's occasional corpus. The most haunting legacy of that corpus in the *Confessions* may, in fact, be a united front of resistance to letting the would-be autobiographer-as-applied-metaphysician close his mind or his text to the nagging question of text production. To the discarded draft's wishfully simple understanding of things and words, the occasional autobiographies oppose not only their own example of unmistakable text-dependency, but the further thoughts that occur by extension. For significant stretches of Volume 2 of the *Confessions,* memories of one or the other of the occasional autobiographies may be standing between Rousseau and Jean-Jacques. And, for those same stretches, the muffled cries by which the autobiographies urge Rousseau on to allegory and meta-autobiography may be the "only occasional" stimuli standing between the *Confessions* that are and the Memoirs that might have been. Even if Rousseau does not recognize these thoughts for what they are, a censored version of them eventually breaks into the consciousness of the *Confessions.* Leaving behind the existential "obscurité" in which the draft's Jean-Jacques "may have lived," let us then venture into the theoretical darkness or "effrayante obscurité" (1:598) of the exordium to Book 12: "Ici commence l'œuvre de tenebres dans lequel depuis huit ans je me trouve enseveli, sans que de quelque façon que je m'y sois pu prendre il m'ait été possible d'en percer l'effrayante obscurité."

The "reference" is, of course, to the ongoing "complot," as would quickly become evident even if the *Confessions* were opened at random to this page. Rousseau imagines himself to be buried in an impenetrable crypt of darkness, tortured by blows of unknown origin, and accused of crying out (from his broken heart) for no good reason. He goes on for more than a page to create the atmosphere of unremitting existential and epistemological terror that we have since learned to call Kafkaesque. But a dire new twist would seem to have provoked this particularly extended and evocative update. In the interval since Rousseau's last bulletin, his enemies have gone public with their version of his life and character and somehow managed to be met with unquestioning acceptance: "les auteurs de ma ruine ont trouvé l'art inconcevable de rendre le public complice de leur complot sans qu'il s'en doute lui-même et sans qu'il en apperçoive l'effet." The three vertices of "œuvre," "auteurs," and "public" alert us to the fact that the brunt of this latest assault will necessarily fall on the *Confessions* themselves. Either as intended victims or as innocent bystanders, they have been preempted, perhaps irrevocably. No wonder that Rousseau hesitates to resume his real story: it may be too late; it may be no use.

But on these same grounds of metaphorical exchangeability between his book and their plot, we can also appreciate that a reversal of paranoid projection would catch the *Confessions* trying and failing to make sense not of the "complot" but of themselves. "Here beginneth the work of gloom. . . ." It is, after all, the tell-tale "ici" of self-portraiture's preoccupation with the textual here and now that launches the discourse and lingers on, even after a belated anchoring in time ("depuis huit ans") has partially rescued the text for referential narration. Recognizing where we are in the *Confessions* remains at least as important as situating ourselves on the timeline of a past life, which has, in any event, become indissociable from the present of narration. And where we are is at the precise point where, having brought Book 11 to the ceremonial endpoint of sacrificing *Le Lévite,* the *Confessions* suddenly find themselves to be at loose ends. Having depleted their stock of occasional interlocutors, they are left to fend for themselves. Old dependencies do not die easily; addicts whose support systems have been cut off invariably panic.

Indeed, it is with enormous trepidation that the autobiographer faces up to a prospect he can name only as that of being reduced to countering his enemies' best-selling masterplot with the isolated and imperfectly understood facts of their plotting. But there is another way of naming the profoundly disarming prospect of having nothing to tell, nothing on his side but "tout ce qui m'est arrivé." It is precisely now that his autobiographical sources have dried up that he will, for the first time since Book 7, have to go it alone, with nothing but the recalcitrant "faits" of Jean-Jacques's biography or "evenemens qui me regardent." Looking those events straight in the eye rather than through the magic prism of regenerative prior writing strikes Rousseau with a panic fear of the unknown. It is, literally speaking, not even he who does the looking, but they, all of them, that stare him down, from somewhere outside himself, into a state of helpless victimization. In this place of sudden deprivation, the *Confessions* come closest to acknowledging the decisive role of occasional mediation in some of their encounters with Jean-Jacques. And they further hint at the bad faith and undesirability of identifying "facts" and "events" as the *only* only occasional causes of Rousseau's new brand of life writing.

It would be tempting to conclude that, despite himself, the Rousseau of the *Confessions* ends up seeing the light of the occasional autobiographies' theory of text production. But that would be to shut out the deeper, more unspeakable darkness of this text's challenge even to the dream of demonstrable selfhood that the theory of text production shares with the autobiography-as-applied-metaphysics of the "Ebauches." For the benefit of any "generous" readers who might still think to give the *Confessions* a chance, the disadvantaged Rousseau of nothing but facts provides whatever hints he can to help offset his enemies' head start and monopoly on plotting. Rereading of the earlier *Confessions* is recommended, insofar as all the data necessary for recreating the "complot" as coherent system, all the interlocking parts of the philosophical war machine, are said to have been exposed "dans les trois precedens livres." The fact that these are also the books of the *Confessions'* intermittent *texte-à-texte* with occasional autobiographies reinforces the suggestion that what the reader is really being invited to devise in the author's stead is a theory of autobiography as text production or systematic way of accounting for the way those books came to be.

For some sort of tacit promotion of occasional text to occasional cause, we might, on this basis, have been prepared. But it is otherwise disconcerting to see our champion of selfhood go on to name whatever it is—plot elements or elements of autobiography—that lurks in the latency of Books 8–11 as "[c]auses *primitives*" (emphasis added). Of course, the cover story takes "primitives" to refer simply to the earliest in date of the plotters' machinations. In terms of our alternative reading, however, the epithet resonates with intuitions of a specifically textual unconscious and with doubts concerning the metaphysical hegemony of the self as first or general cause.

The complexities of an "other" plot protect Rousseau against knowing this irony of the occasional texts' belated challenges to preeminent selfhood and to the enabling simplicity of Malebranche's bipartite scheme. But the plot does not prevent a confession of pedagogical impotence or momentary inability to mount one of Rousseau's patented demonstrations of selfhood. Inner assent is not lacking; what is lacking is a plan for bringing readers all the way through a newly complex and chaotic welter of causes to the source of sources behind it all: "qu'ils remontent d'intrigue en intrigue et d'agent en agent jusqu'aux prémiers moteurs de tout, je sais certainement à quel terme aboutiront leurs recherches, mais je me perds dans la route obscure et tortueuse des souterrains qui les y conduiront" (1:588–89). Nor can the plot explain away the even more overwhelming loss of self that is not simply told but shown and played out by the page of text that appropriates *his* autoreferentiality to tell *its* story and symptomatically encodes the "complot" (and all the world) as text.

It is a measure of the text's despairing that it emphatically blocks the familiar pathways of escape from incarnation into the demonstrable transcendence of philosophy. The supreme torture or cosmic retribution conceived with an eye to Rousseau's former exploitation of those pathways is the perceived reduction of the erstwhile meta-autobiographer to the status of mere fact-obsessed memorialist. What the text proclaims loud and clear is that there is something that can be known about Rousseau's life story that Rousseau himself cannot know. The business of separating out and putting back together the various roles of text, event, and self in the production of an autobiography turns out to be more of a mystery than he bargained for. And it is precisely on that mystery or "core of darkness at the center"[8] that I have shed some light by extending my reading of Rousseau's occasional autobiographies into his *Confessions*. This is of necessity and by design a different book than the systematic "history and theory of my *Confessions*" that Rousseau's "generous readers" would have written. Beyond a certain point, my readings give up on diagramming the profuse vitality and overdetermined interconnectedness of his autobiographical corpus. But they also give the last word to the surprise of self that Rousseau manages to engineer from the depths of a darkness that puts the whole of Books 8–11 into the new perspective of transcendable contingency. The failed philosopher-in-the-text emblematizes an escape from the lure and prestige of philosophy into pantheistic suffusion of a literary creation too vast and varied to know except firsthand. Perhaps that is why, when it came time to name what Rousseau had wrought, the three terms of *autos, bios,* and *graphē* were simply laid out end to end.

Notes

INTRODUCTION

1. Michael Sprinker, "Fictions of the Self: The End of Autobiography," in *Autobiography: Essays Theoretical and Critical,* ed. James Olney (Princeton: Princeton University Press, 1980), p. 326.

2. Jean-Jacques Rousseau, *Confessions, autres textes autobiographiques,* vol. 1 of *Œuvres complètes,* ed. Bernard Gagnebin and Marcel Raymond (Paris: Gallimard, 1959), p. 3. All subsequent references to this edition of Rousseau's complete works will be noted in the main body of my text.

3. Georges May, *L'autobiographie* (Paris: Presses Universitaires de France, 1979), pp. 18–19.

4. Francis R. Hart, "Notes for an Anatomy of Modern Autobiography," *New Literary History* 1, no. 3 (1970), p. 486.

5. Pierre-Paul Clément, *Jean-Jacques Rousseau: de l'éros coupable à l'éros glorieux* (Neuchâtel: Editions de la Baconnière, 1976), p. 346.

6. Elizabeth Bruss, "Eye for I: Making and Unmaking Autobiography in Film," in Olney, p. 298.

7. Sidonie Smith, *A Poetics of Women's Autobiography: Marginality and the Fictions of Self-Representation* (Bloomington and Indianapolis: Indiana University Press, 1987), pp. 145, 174.

8. *Ibid.,* p. 12.

9. Sprinker, p. 326.

10. Olney, "Autobiography and the Cultural Moment: A Thematic, Historical and Bibliographical Introduction," in Olney, p. 22.

255

11. Georges Gusdorf, "Conditions and Limits of Autobiography," trans. Olney, in Olney, p. 39.

12. Olney, "Some Versions of Memory/Some Versions of *Bios:* The Ontology of Autobiography," in Olney, p. 241.

13. Sprinker, p. 326.

14. *The Autobiography of Giambattista Vico,* trans. Max Harold Fisch and Thomas Goddard Bergin (Ithaca: Cornell University Press, 1944), p. 200.

15. Madeleine Anjubault Simons, *Amitié et passion: Rousseau et Sauttersheim* (Geneva: Droz, 1972), p. 76.

16. Decimus Magnus, *Ausonius,* trans. Hugh G. Evelyn White, 2 vols. (Cambridge: Harvard University Press, 1949) 2:175.

17. "Occasion," *Encyclopédie ou Dictionnaire raisonné des sciences, des arts et des métiers,* ed. Denis Diderot, 35 vols. (Paris, 1751–79; rpt. Stuttgart-Bad Canstatt: Friedrich Frommann Verlag [Gunther Holzboog], 1966–67), 11:331.

18. *Ibid.*

19. Ronald Grimsley, *Jean-Jacques Rousseau* (Sussex: Harvester Press, 1983), p. 179.

20. "Malebranchisme," *Encyclopédie,* 9:942.

21. James Frederick Naify, "Arabic and European Occasionalism: A Comparison of Al-Ghazali's Occasionalism and Its Critiques by Averroes and Malebranche's Occasionalism and Its Criticism in the Cartesian Tradition" (Diss., University of California at San Diego, 1975), p. 99.

22. Pierre Maurice Masson, *La "Profession de foi" de Jean-Jacques,* vol. 2 of *La Religion de J. J. Rousseau* (Paris: Hachette, 1916), p. 120.

23. Bruss, p. 318.

24. Thomas M. Lennon, "Philosophical Commentary," in Nicolas Malebranche, *The Search after Truth,* trans. Thomas M. Lennon and Paul J. Olscamp (Columbus: Ohio State University Press, 1980), p. 860.

25. Clément, p. 268.

26. Robert Ellrich, "Rousseau's Androgynous Dream: The Minor Works of 1752–62," *French Forum* 13, no. 3 (1988), pp. 319, 321.

27. Ronald Grimsley, *Jean-Jacques Rousseau: A Study in Self-Awareness* (Cardiff: University of Wales Press, 1969), p. 237.

28. *Autobiography of Giambattista Vico,* p. 113.

29. Louis A. Renza, "The Veto of the Imagination: A Theory of Autobiography," in Olney, p. 287.

CHAPTER 1

1. I build here on the term coined by Christie V. McDonald in "Jean-Jacques Rousseau: The Biographfiend's False Friend," *Romanic Review* 66 (1975), pp. 296–311.

2. Stendhal, *Henry Brulard,* cited in Marcel Raymond, *Jean-Jacques Rousseau: la quête de soi et la rêverie* (Paris: José Corti, 1962), p. 191.

3. Michel Beaujour, *Miroirs d'encre: Rhétorique de l'autoportrait* (Paris: Seuil, 1980), p. 9.

4. Beaujour attributes this panic to Artaud, in *ibid.*

5. *Ibid.,* p. 10.

6. Jacques Prévert, "Je suis comme je suis," in *Paroles* (Paris: Gallimard, 1949), p. 96.

7. In a letter written the morning after to the actor La Noue, Rousseau might have gone into the same dramatic details as do the *Confessions.* Instead, he claimed only to have *somehow* confessed to authorship of *Narcisse:* "J'ai appris, Monsieur, que quelques personnes vous attribuoient la petite Pièce qui m'a tant ennuyé hier à la Comedie, et je me suis hâté de me nommer afin que vous ne portassiez plus la peine de vôtre amitié pour l'auteur. D'ailleurs, je ne gardois l'incognito que pour éviter les complimens qui me sont insupportables, et cet inconvénient n'est plus à craindre." See "To Jean-Baptiste-Simon Sauvé, dit de La Noue," letter 188 (19 Dec. 1752), *Correspondance complète de Jean-Jacques Rousseau,* ed. R. A. Leigh, 47 vols. (Geneva: Institut et Musée Voltaire [vols. 1–14]; Oxfordshire: Voltaire Foundation [vols. 15–47], 1965–89), 2:207. Nor does the "Préface" itself venture into the autobiography's all-important "caffé de Procope," although the *Anecdotes dramatiques* of Clément and La Porte (1775) do recount that Rousseau did. See Leigh's note, *Correspondance complète,* 2:208. In the preface, the playwright leaves the theater already applauding himself for his indifference to the play's lack of success: "Ma Pièce a eu le sort qu'elle méritoit et que j'avois prévu; mais, à l'ennui près qu'elle m'a causé, je suis sorti de la représentation bien plus content de moi et à plus juste titre que si elle eût réussi" (2:973). But these "omissions" are only logical: the autobiography's café recreates the scene of the preface, or, rather, remembers the preface *as* scene.

8. Beaujour, p. 40.

9. *Ibid.,* pp. 40, 53–66.

10. *Ibid.,* pp. 63–64.

11. *Ibid.,* p. 64.

12. Jacques Scherer, "Notes" on *Narcisse* (2:1864).

13. Grimm, *Correspondance littéraire,* 15 Feb. 1754, cited in Leigh, *Correspondance complète* 2:344.

14. Jacques Borel, "Narcisse écrit-il?", *La Nouvelle Revue française* 257 (May 1974), pp. 22–30.

15. Reuben Fine, *Narcissism, the Self, and Society* (New York: Columbia University Press, 1986), p. 20.

16. Philippe Sollers, "Littérature et totalité," in *L'écriture et l'expérience des limites* (Paris: Seuil, 1968), p. 70.

17. Lester G. Crocker, *Jean-Jacques Rousseau: The Quest (1712–1758)* (New York: Macmillan, 1968), p. 238.

18. Beaujour, p. 15.

19. "Préface," *Encyclopédie* 13:280.

20. Elzbieta Zawisga has shown how simultaneous commitment to these

two contradictory ends precluded novel prefacers from elaborating a coherent theory of the novel: "Le paradoxe essentiel de la préface consiste en ce que le même sujet parlant aborde le discours critique et le discours romanesque à la fois, que le même sujet juge et défend, et, en tant qu'observateur et défenseur—il est obligé de regarder diversement le même objet, c'est-à-dire son propre roman." See "Sur le Discours préfacier dans les romans au XVIIIᵉ siècle," *Acta Universitatis Wratislaviensis* 319 (Wroclaw, Poland: Romanica Wratistaviensia, 1977), p. 103.

21. Voltaire, "Auteurs," *Dictionnaire philosophique,* in *Œuvres complètes* (Paris: Garnier, 1878), 17:498.

22. "Préface," *Encyclopédie* 13:280–81.

23. Philippe Lejeune, *Le pacte autobiographique* (Paris: Seuil, 1975), p. 14.

24. Julia Kristeva, *Powers of Horror: An Essay on Abjection,* trans. Leon S. Roudiez (New York: Columbia University Press, 1982), p. 65.

25. Béla Grunberger, "Study of Anal Object Relations," in *Narcissism: Psychoanalytic Essays,* trans. Joyce S. Diamanti (New York: International Universities Press, 1979), p. 147. Grunberger quotes "a patient of Abraham's."

26. Roland Derche, "Narcisse," in *Quatre mythes poétiques* (Paris: Société d'Editions d'Enseignement Supérieur, 1969), p. 73.

27. Beaujour, p. 40.

28. Louise Vinge, *The Narcissus Theme in Western European Literature up to the Early 19th Century* (Lund, Sweden: Gleerups, 1976).

29. "Narcisse," *Encyclopédie* 11:23.

30. Beaujour, p. 64.

31. *Ibid.,* pp. 113–31.

32. Luce Irigaray, *Speculum de l'autre femme* (Paris: Les Editions de Minuit, 1974), p. 116.

33. Jean Starobinski, "Jean-Jacques Rousseau, Reflet, Réflexion, Projection," *Cahiers de l'Association Internationale des Etudes Françaises* 11 (May 1959), p. 217.

34. I shall expand in chapter 4 on the ways in which chrono-logic censors associative logic in the *Confessions,* by reading a passage that all but knowingly allegorizes this persistent phenomenon. See pp. 173–82 below.

35. Du Maunoir, cited in Leigh, *Correspondance complète* 7:317.

36. Sigmund Freud, "On Narcissism: An Introduction," in *The Standard Edition of the Complete Psychological Works of Sigmund Freud,* trans. James Strachey (London: Hogarth, 1957), 14:89.

37. Paul Zweig, *The Heresy of Self-Love: A Study of Subversive Individualism* (Princeton: Princeton University Press, 1980), p. vi.

38. Masson, *La Formation religieuse de Rousseau,* vol. 1 of *La Religion de J. J. Rousseau,* p. 167.

39. Beaujour, p. 40.

40. Ronald Grimsley, *Rousseau's Religious Quest* (Oxford: Clarendon Press, 1968), p. 142.

41. Cited by Scherer in his notes on *Narcisse* (2:1862).

42. "Préface," *Encyclopédie* 13:280.

43. André Green, "le narcissisme moral," in *Narcissisme de vie, narcissisme de mort* (Paris: Les Editions de Minuit, 1983), p. 182.

44. *Ibid.,* p. 187.

45. Du Maunoir, cited in Leigh, *Correspondance complète* 7:317.

46. George Sandys, *Ovid's Metamorphoses Englished* (New York: Garland, 1976), p. 105.

47. Louis Corman lists "rigidité d'identification" among the symptoms of narcissistic withdrawal. See *Narcissisme et frustration d'amour* (Brussels: Dessart et Mardaga, 1975), p. 76.

48. "Préface," *Encyclopédie* 13:280.

49. Beaujour, p. 153.

50. Sandys, p. 106.

51. "Préface," *Encyclopédie* 13:280–81.

52. Grunberger, "Observations on Orality and Oral Object Relations," in *Narcissism,* p. 132.

53. Beaujour, p. 40.

54. Kristeva, p. 63.

55. Grunberger, "Preliminary Notes to a Topographical Study of Narcissism," in *Narcissism,* p. 115.

56. Grunberger, "Introduction," in *Narcissism,* p. 17.

57. Sandys, p. 106.

58. Beaujour, p. 13.

59. Zweig, p. vi.

60. Beaujour, p. 13.

61. "To Suzanne Dupin de Francueil, née Bollioud de Saint-Julien," letter 157 (20 Apr. 1751), *Correspondance complète* 2:142.

62. "Préface," *Encyclopédie,* 13:280.

63. Ovid, *Metamorphoses,* trans. Frank Justus Miller (London: William Heinemann, 1928), 1:149.

64. Ovid, p. 151.

65. Irigaray, p. 461.

66. Pierre Carlet de Chamblain de Marivaux, "Préface" to *La Voiture embourbée,* in *Romans,* ed. Marcel Arland (Paris: Gallimard, 1949), p. 3.

67. Daniel Defoe, "Preface" to *Colonel Jack,* cited in *Novel and Romance, 1700–1800,* ed. Ioan Williams (New York: Barnes and Noble, 1970), p. 63.

68. William Congreve, "Preface" to *Incognita,* cited in Williams, p. 27.

69. Green, "Un, autre, neutre: valeurs narcissiques du même," in *Narcissisme de vie,* p. 51.

70. Marivaux, p. 3.

71. I borrow the echo/allusion distinction from John Hollander: "In contrast with literary allusion, echo as metaphor of, and for alluding, does not depend on

conscious intention." See *The Figure of Echo: A Mode of Allusion in Milton and After* (Berkeley: University of California Press, 1981), p. 64.

72. To this textual construct, Juliet Flower MacCannell has assigned the name of the "post-fictional self." She reads its status as a corollary of the text's discovery about the simulacra of self-portraiture in the works of the fallen philosophers. See "The Post-Fictional Self," *Modern Language Notes* 89 (1974), p. 585.

73. Michel Foucault, *The Archaeology of Knowledge,* trans. A. M. Sheridan Smith (New York: Random House, 1972), p. 221.

74. Hélène Cixous, "Sorties," in Cixous and Catherine Clément, *La jeune née* (Paris: Union Générale d'Editions, 1975), p. 162.

75. Grimm, cited in Leigh, *Correspondance complète* 2:344.

76. Cixous, pp. 173, 169.

77. Beaujour, p. 131.

CHAPTER 2

1. Clément, p. 196.

2. Aristides, quoted in *Dedications: An Anthology of the Forms Used from the Earliest Days of Book-Making to the Present Time,* ed. Mary Elizabeth Brown (New York: G. P. Putnam's Sons, 1913), p. 1.

3. Marivaux, *Romans,* p. 3.

4. Bernard le Bouvier de Fontenelle, quoted in Emile Littré, *Dictionnaire de la langue française,* 7 vols. (Paris: Gallimard, 1961), 2:1439.

5. Jean de La Fontaine, *Fables choisies* (Paris: Larousse, 1965), 1:34.

6. Voltaire, p. 497.

7. Brown, p. 6.

8. Voltaire, pp. 497–98.

9. Condorcet, quoted in Littré, 2:1439.

10. Tore Janson, *Latin Prose Prefaces: Studies in Literary Conventions* (Stockholm: Almquist & Wikell, 1964), p. 125.

11. Pierre Bayle, quoted by Brown, p. 2.

12. *Encyclopédie,* 5:821.

13. *Ibid.,* 822.

14. *Ibid.*

15. Jean Starobinski, "Sur la flatterie," *Nouvelle revue de psychanalyse,* no. 4 (1971), p. 144.

16. Anthony Ashley Cooper, Earl of Shaftesbury, and Diderot, quoted in Vinge, pp. 282–84.

17. *Encyclopédie,* 5:822.

18. Kevin Guinagh, introduction to *Praise from Famous Men: An Anthology of Introductions,* ed. Guy R. Lyle (Metuchen, N.J.: Scarecrow Press, 1977), p. ix.

19. Herbert J. C. Grierson and Sandys Wason, *The Personal Note, or First and Last Words from Prefaces, Introductions, Dedications, Epilogues* (London: Chatto & Windus, 1946), p. 2.

20. Brown, p. 4.

21. Eustache Le Noble, for example, seizes the opportunity of a dedication to the Duc de Bourgogne to remind the so-called "Aiglon" about the "Aigle invincible," Louis XIV, "dont le Sang coule dans vos veines." See Le Noble, *Contes et fables* (Amsterdam: Geroges Gallet, 1700), p. iii.

22. Clément, p. 20.

23. "Jean-Louis Du Pan à Rousseau," letter 303 (20 June 1755), *Correspondance complète* 3:136–37.

24. *Ibid.*, p. 137.

25. *Correspondance complète* 3:xxi.

26. Luke 15:18–19 (in the J. F. Ostervald or eighteenth-century French Protestant version that Rousseau would have known).

27. Kenneth E. Bailey, *Poet and Peasant: A Literary Cultural Approach to the Parables in Luke* (Grand Rapids: William B. Eerdmans, 1976), p. 181.

28. Dan Otto Via, *The Parables: Their Literary and Existential Dimensions* (Philadelphia: Fortress, 1967), p. 171.

29. Bailey, pp. 183, 87.

30. Grunberger, p. 32.

31. Zweig, p. 65.

32. Masson, *La Formation religieuse de Rousseau*, p. 222.

33. Voltaire has great fun with this conventional practice of piling up titles: "Plusieurs personnes trouvent mauvais qu'une compilation dans laquelle il y a de très-beaux morceaux soit annoncée par *Monsieur*, etc., ci-devant professeur de l'Université, docteur en théologie, recteur, précepteur des enfants de M. le duc de . . . , membre d'une académie, et même de deux. Tant de dignités ne rendent pas le livre meilleur." See "Auteurs," p. 497.

34. Gregory L. Ulmer, *"The Legend of Herostratus: Existential Envy in Rousseau and Unamuno* (Gainesville: University Presses of Florida, 1977), p. 27.

35. *Ibid.*, p. 32.

36. *Ibid.*, p. 15.

37. *Ibid.*, p. 34.

38. *Correspondance complète* 3:64.

39. Ulmer, p. 17.

40. *Ibid.*, p. 21.

41. *Ibid.*, p. 39.

42. *Ibid.*, p. 34.

43. Madeleine B. Ellis has amply illustrated Rousseau's discreet use of friends and acquaintances to incarnate or double facets of his own life and personality. See *Rousseau's Venetian Story: An Essay upon Art and Truth in "Les Confessions"* (Baltimore: Johns Hopkins University Press, 1966), p. 174.

44. *Lettre à M. d'Alembert sur son article "Genève"* (Paris: Garnier-Flammarion, 1967), p. 69.

45. Ian Donaldson, *The Rapes of Lucretia: A Myth and Its Transformations* (Oxford: Clarendon Press, 1982), pp. 85–86.

46. Ellrich, p. 327.

47. Rousseau may well have seen the artist's renderings of Titian and Tintoretto during his stint in Venice as secretary to the French ambassador, although the *Confessions* account of this period is strangely devoid of allusions to the physical and cultural landscape. See Ellis, p. 41.

48. Augustine, quoted by Donaldson, p. 29.

49. *Ibid.,* p. 34.

50. *Ibid.,* p. 37.

51. Livy, *The Early History of Rome: Books I–V of "The History of Rome from Its Foundations,"* trans. Aubrey de Sélincourt (Baltimore: Penguin Books, 1960), pp. 80–85.

52. Voltaire, "Discours sur la tragédie," *Théâtre* (Paris: Firmin Didot Frères, 1856), pp. 69–71.

53. Donaldson, p. 128.

54. Simons, p. 10.

55. Kristeva, p. 4.

56. *Ibid.,* p. 11.

57. Cited by Leigh, note to letter 346, *Correspondance complète* 3:227.

58. Partially disputing Rousseau's recollection, Leigh writes: "En réalité, l'étude des documents montre que Stanislas n'avait pas bronché pendant la représentation de la pièce, qu'il se fit tirer l'oreille pour condamner Palissot, et qu'il tâcha de ménager la chèvre et le chou." See *Correspondance complète* 3:199.

59. "Jean le Rond d'Alembert à Louis-Elizabeth de La Vergne, comte de Tressan," letter 356 (26 Dec. 1755), *Correspondance complète* 3:242.

60. Charles-Louis de Secondat, baron de La Brède et de Montesquieu, *Considérations sur la grandeur et la décadence des Romains,* in *Œuvres complètes,* ed. Edouard Laboulaye, 7 vols. (Paris, 1875; rpt. Kraus Reprints, 1972), 2:118.

61. *Lettre à d'Alembert,* p. 92.

62. Kristeva, p. 2.

CHAPTER 3

1. Georges May, *Le Dilemme du roman au dix-huitième siècle: étude sur les rapports du roman et de la critique, 1715–1761* (Paris: Presses Universitaires de France, 1963), p. 106.

2. Jacques Derrida, "Hors livre," in *La Dissémination* (Paris: Seuil, 1972), p. 21.

3. "To Hippolyte-Lucas Guérin," letter 1222 (18 Jan. 1761), *Correspondance complète* 8:11.

4. "From Claire Cramer, née Delon," letter 1250 (31 Jan. 1761), *Correspondance complète* 8:46.

5. Friedrich Melchior, Freiherr von Grimm, *Correspondance littéraire,* cited in J. G. Prodhomme, *Vingt chefs-d'œuvre jugés par leurs contemporains: opin-*

ions, critiques, correspondances choisies et annotées (Paris: Stock, 1930), p. 126.

6. Paul de Man, *Allegories of Reading: Figural Language in Rousseau, Nietzsche, Rilke and Proust* (New Haven: Yale University Press, 1979), pp. 197, 198, 202–10, 217, 237, 296; Robert Darnton, *The Great Cat Massacre and Other Episodes in French Cultural History* (New York: Basic Books, 1984), pp. 227–34, 241–49. For a more comprehensive discussion of their readings, see Susan K. Jackson, "Text and Context of Rousseau's Relations with Diderot," *Eighteenth-Century Studies* 20, no. 2 (1986–87), pp. 195–219.

7. De Man, p. 296.

8. Derrida, "Hors livre," p. 50.

9. "To François Coindet," letter 1118 (Oct. 1760), *Correspondance complète* 7:254.

10. Derrida, "Hors livre," p. 13.

11. "To Marc-Michel Rey," letter 788 (14 Mar. 1759), *Correspondance complète* 6:45.

12. *Ibid.*

13. *Lettre à d'Alembert,* p. 205.

14. Daniel Mornet, ed., *"La Nouvelle Héloïse" de Jean-Jacques Rousseau* (Paris: Hachette, 1925), 1:184, 207.

15. Derrida, "Hors livre," p. 34.

16. Letter 1118, p. 254.

17. "To Hippolyte-Lucas Guérin," letter 1201 (21 Dec. 1760), *Correspondance complète,* 7:364.

18. Letter 1222, *Correspondance complète* 8:11; "To François Coindet," letter 1268 (9 Feb. 1761), *Correspondance complète* 8:68; "To François Coindet," letter 1279 (11 Feb. 1761), *Correspondance complète* 8:80; "To François Coindet," letter 1293 (15 Feb. 1761), *Correspondance complète* 8:106.

19. Darnton, pp. 228–29.

20. De Man, p. 196.

21. "From Charles-Marie de La Condamine," letter 1255 (3 Feb. 1761), *Correspondance complète* 8:52.

22. "From Jean le Rond d'Alembert," letter 1276 (10 Feb. 1761), *Correspondance complète* 8:76.

23. Cited in Anna Attridge, "The Reception of *La Nouvelle Héloïse,*" *Studies in Voltaire and the Eighteenth Century,* no. 120 (1974), p. 232.

24. "From Renée-Caroline de Froullay, marquise de Créqui," letter 1249 (31 Jan. 1761), *Correspondance complète* 8:45.

25. "From Madeleine-Angélique de Neufville-Villeroy, duchesse de Luxembourg," letter 1301 (18 Feb. 1761), *Correspondance complète* 8:129.

26. See above, p. 58.

27. Cited in Prodhomme, p. 126.

28. "To Madeleine-Angélique de Neufville-Villeroy, duchesse de Luxembourg," letter 1294 (16 Feb. 1761), *Correspondance complète* 8:108.

29. Lejeune p. 36.

30. For a catalog of these defenses, see May, *Le Dilemme du roman*, pp. 106–36.

31. Lejeune, p. 33.

32. Clément, p. 160.

33. Lejeune, p. 25.

34. "From Charles Pinot Duclos," letter 1357 (12 Mar. 1761), *Correspondance complète* 8:247.

35. "From Denis Diderot," letter 479 (10 Mar. 1757), *Correspondance complète* 4:168.

36. "To Denis Diderot," letter 484 (16 Mar. 1757), *Correspondance complète* 4:178, 180.

37. "To Louise-Florence-Pétronille Lalive d'Epinay, née Tardieu d'Esclavelles," letter 486 (16 Mar. 1757), *Correspondance complète* 4:183; "To Louise-Florence-Pétronille Lalive d'Epinay, née Tardieu d'Esclavelles," letter 488 (17 Mar. 1757), *Correspondance complète* 4:187.

38. "From Denis Diderot," letter 491 (21 or 22 Mar. 1757), *Correspondance complète* 4:191–92.

39. Masson, *La Formation religieuse de Rousseau*, p. 143.

40. Ellrich, p. 330.

41. Maurice Roelens, "Le Dialogue philosophique, genre impossible?: l'opinion des siècles classiques," *Cahiers de l'Association Internationale des Etudes Françaises*, no. 24 (1972), p. 49.

42. Jean Fabre, "Deux frères ennemis: Diderot et Jean-Jacques," in *Lumières et romantisme* (Paris: Klincksieck, 1963), p. 42.

43. Guy Turbet-Delof, "A propos d'*Emile et Sophie*," *Revue d'Histoire Littéraire de la France* 64, 1 (1964), 44–59.

44. Denis Diderot, *Le Fils naturel*, in *Œuvres complètes*, ed. J. Assézat (Paris: Garnier, 1875), 6:66. Darnton has also found in the *Préface de Julie* a "reply to Diderot's terrible phrase" (p. 231).

45. *Lettre à d'Alembert*, pp. 49–50.

46. Simons, p. 67.

47. Frédérick Gerson, *l'Amitié au XVIIIe siècle* (Paris: la Pensée universelle, 1974), pp. 107, 115.

48. Clément, p. 319.

49. Simons, p. 106.

50. Clément, p. 39.

51. "To Chrétien-Guillaume de Lamoignon de Malesherbes," letter 1152 (5 Nov. 1760), *Correspondance complète* 7:300–301.

52. Peggy Kamuf, *Fictions of Feminine Desire: Disclosures of Heloise* (Lincoln: University of Nebraska Press, 1982), pp. 97–122.

53. Lejeune, p. 100.

54. Nicole Kress-Rosen, "Réalité du souvenir et vérité du discours," *Littérature* 10 (1973), p. 26.

55. Mikhaïl Bakhtine, *La Poétique de Dostoïevski,* trans. Isabelle Kolitcheff (Paris: Seuil, 1970), p. 342.
56. Alexis François, "La Correspondance de J. J. Rousseau dans la querelle littéraire du XVIIIᵉ siècle," *Revue d'Histoire Littéraire de la France,* no. 33 (1926), p. 367.
57. Derrida, "Hors livre," p. 13.
58. Nancy K. Miller, "Women's Autobiography in France: For a Dialectics of Identification," *Women and Language in Literature and Society,* ed. Sally Mc-Connell-Ginet, Ruth Borker, and Nelly Furman (New York: Praeger, 1980), p. 270.
59. Gusdorf, p. 41.
60. Darnton, pp. 233–34.
61. Domna C. Stanton, "Autogynography: Is the Subject Different?", in *The Female Autograph: Theory and Practice of Autobiography from the Tenth to the Twentieth Century,* ed. Domna C. Stanton (Chicago: University of Chicago Press, 1987), p. 4.
62. Cited by Miller, p. 270.
63. Pierre Choderlos de Laclos, *Œuvres complètes,* ed. Maurice Allem (Paris: Gallimard, 1951), p. 688. Also see Susan K. Jackson, "In Search of a Female Voice: *Les Liaisons dangereuses,*" in *Writing the Female Voice: Essays on Epistolary Literature,* ed. Elizabeth C. Goldsmith (Boston: Northeastern University Press, 1989), p. 167.
64. "To Jean-Pierre de Chambrier d'Oleyres," letter 674 (12 Dec. 1789), in Isabelle de Charrière, *Œuvres complètes* 3 (Amsterdam: G. A. van Oorschot; Geneva: Slatkine, 1981), 167.

CHAPTER 4

1. Predrag Matvejevitch, *Pour une poétique de l'événement: La Poésie de circonstance, suivi de L'Engagement et l'événement* (Paris: Union Générale d'éditions, 1979), p. 67.
2. Thom Gunn, *The Occasions of Poetry: Essays in Criticism and Autobiography,* ed. Clive Wilmer (London: Faber & Faber, 1982), p. 106.
3. Elizabeth Bruss, *Autobiographical Acts: The Changing Situation of a Literary Genre* (Baltimore: Johns Hopkins University Press, 1976), p. 7.
4. *Ibid.,* p. 1.
5. Barrett J. Mandel, "Full of Life Now," in Olney, p. 51.
6. "To Chrétien-Guillaume de Lamoignon de Malesherbes," letter 1548 (18 Nov. 1761), *Correspondance complète* 9:245–47.
7. "From Chrétien-Guillaume de Lamoignon de Malesherbes," letter 1591 (16 Dec. 1761), *Correspondance complète* 9:323–38.
8. "To Chrétien-Guillaume de Lamoignon de Malesherbes," letter 1605 (23 Dec. 1761), *Correspondance complète* 9:348.
9. "From Chrétien-Guillaume de Lamoignon de Malesherbes," letter 1610 (25 Dec. 1761), *Correspondance complète* 9:355.

10. "To Chrétien-Guillaume de Lamoignon de Malesherbes," letter 6986 (8 Mar. 1773), *Correspondance complète* 39:135.

11. Sigmund Freud, "The Psychotherapy of Hysteria," in Joseph Breuer and Sigmund Freud, *Studies on Hysteria*, trans. James Strachey (New York: Basic Books, 1957), p. 282.

12. I use this noun, for want of a better, more affectively neutral alternative, to identify a party to a speech act, and without making any assumptions about that speaker's state of mind.

13. "To Chrétien-Guillaume de Lamoignon de Malesherbes," letter 5195 (10 May 1766), *Correspondance complète* 29:188. It is likely that this letter was never mailed.

14. Stephen Spender, "Confessions and Autobiography," in Olney, p. 121.

15. See Rousseau, *Lettres à Malesherbes*, ed. Gustave Rudler (London: Scholartis Press, 1928), pp. 12, 18; and L. A. Bisson, "Rousseau and the Romantic Experience," *Modern Language Review*, no. 37 (1942), p. 49.

16. Jacques Voisine, "De la confession religieuse à l'autobiographie et au journal intime: entre 1760 et 1820," *Neohelicon* 2, no. 3–4 (1974), 339.

17. This subset is not even necessarily coextensive with the priesthood. "Ce prêtre ne confesse pas" means, in an absolute sense, that the priest in question is not institutionally *empowered* to hear confessions. See Paul Robert, *Dictionnaire alphabétique et analogique de la langue française* (Paris: Société du Nouveau Littré, 1965), 1:886.

18. Gusdorf, p. 33.

19. Robert, 1:886.

20. Foucault, quoted by Smith, p. 49.

21. See, for example, Paul de Man, "Excuses (*Confessions*)," in *Allegories of Reading*, pp. 278–301.

22. Fred Davis, *Yearning for Yesterday: A Sociology of Nostalgia* (New York: Free Press, 1979), p. 127.

23. Jules Michelet, *La Femme*, quoted in Robert, 1:886.

24. Sigmund Freud, *A General Introduction to Psychoanalysis*, trans. Joan Riviere (New York: Washington Square Press, 1952), p. 146.

25. To be sure, Malesherbes eventually returned the favor, making Rousseau privy to intimate feelings inspired by the suicide of Mme de Malesherbes in 1771. Even then, Malesherbes worried—needlessly, as his occasional confidant would seem to have burned them—that the unusually personal letters would be published by Thérèse as part of Rousseau's complete correspondence: "je luy ai écrit plusieurs fois sur des choses qui me concernent moy et ma famille et je serois très fâché que tout cela fut divulgué." See Pierre Grosclaude, *Malesherbes: témoin et interprète de son temps* (Paris: Fischbacher, 1961), pp. 554–56.

26. Malesherbes, *Mémoires sur la librairie et sur la liberté de la presse*, ed. Graham E. Rodmell, North Carolina Studies in the Romance Languages and Literatures (Chapel Hill: U.N.C. Department of Romance Languages, 1979), pp. 119–35.

27. *Ibid.,* pp. 31–34.

28. *Ibid.,* p. 39.

29. Pierre Auguste Caron de Beaumarchais, *La Folle Journée, ou, le mariage de Figaro* (Paris: Editions Sociales, 1956), p. 182.

30. David Tribe, *Questions of Censorship* (New York: St. Martin's Press, 1973), p. 12.

31. See "Jean le Rond d'Alembert to Chrétien-Guillaume de Lamoignon de Malesherbes," letter 663 (3 July 1758), *Correspondance complète* 5:105.

32. Tribe, p. 11.

33. "To Jean Perdriau," letter 250 (28 Nov. 1754), *Correspondance complète* 3:59.

34. "To Chrétien-Guillaume de Lamoignon de Malesherbes," letter 1303 (19 Feb. 1761), *Correspondance complète* 8:134.

35. *Ibid.,* pp. 132–33.

36. "To Chrétien-Guillaume de Lamoignon de Malesherbes," letter 1304 (19 Feb. 1761), *Correspondance complète* 8:137.

37. Naomi Schor, *Breaking the Chain: Women, Theory, and French Realist Fiction* (New York: Columbia University Press, 1985), p. 153.

38. George Armstrong Kelly, *Victims, Authority, and Terror: The Parallel Deaths of d'Orléans Custine, Bailly, and Malesherbes* (Chapel Hill: University of North Carolina, 1982), p. 227.

39. Rodmell, p. 37.

40. Tribe, p. 229.

41. "To Chrétien-Guillaume de Lamoignon de Malesherbes," letter 3638 (11 Nov. 1764), *Correspondance complète* 22:43.

42. "From Chrétien-Guillaume de Lamoignon de Malesherbes," letter 3716 (8 Dec. 1764), *Correspondance complète* 22:189.

43. Letter 3638, p. 43.

44. "To Chrétien-Guillaume de Lamoignon de Malesherbes," letter 293 (5 May 1755), *Correspondance complète* 3:125.

45. Bruss, p. 13.

46. "To Chrétien-Guillaume de Lamoignon de Malesherbes," letter 953 (6 Mar. 1760), *Correspondance complète* 7:54.

47. "From Chrétien-Guillaume de Lamoignon de Malesherbes," letter 956 (10 Mar. 1760), *Correspondance complète* 7:56.

48. "To Chrétien-Guillaume de Lamoignon de Malesherbes," letter 970 (17 Apr. 1760), *Correspondance complète* 7:72.

49. Tribe, p. 293.

50. See above, pp. 35–40.

51. Planning, in 1765, an *"Edition générale de ses Œuvres,"* Rousseau may in fact have thought to make a third exception to his rule of abstinence from dedication. A few surviving lines suggest that "ce monument de mon respect et de mon attachement pour vous" would have been presented as an "hommage de mon cœur" to "M. et Mad^c la Mareschale" (2:1320, 1956).

52. Sigmund Freud, *The Interpretation of Dreams,* trans. James Strachey (New York: Avon, 1965), p. 527.

53. After Rousseau's death, Malesherbes expressed the opinion that Rousseau had always intended for the *Lettres* to be published. See "Chrétien-Guillaume de Lamoignon de Malesherbes to Oliver de Corancez," letter 7477 bis (18 Feb. 1779), *Correspondance complète* 43:147.

54. Watching Freud's moves at the moment of "discovering" dream censorship, we might for example note the care he takes to dissociate delight at having found the answer to a theoretical riddle from what might otherwise be construed as approval for the answer as such. How interesting that he writes of the "censor to whom we have had to attribute such a powerful restricting influence upon the form taken by dreams" (*Interpretation of Dreams,* pp. 543–44). Moreover, this is one of several instances where the Freudian text personifies the agency of censorship, as though in partial admission of the author's personal investment in having us believe that psychic censorship exists quite independent of any desire on his part that it should. Paradoxically, it is on the term "censorship," self-consciously and steadfastly employed in preference to whatever "special technical names" ("Psychotherapy of Hysteria," p. 261) his peers may have coined, that Freud relies to protect his investment. How better to prove himself right about the nature and force of resistance by the ego to incompatible ideas than by knowingly provoking resistance to just such an idea. We are bound to find what we wish no less objectionable than the way we make our wishes known: by censoring, and, until this resistance can be overcome by the master's soothing analogies, no more apt to proclaim "I don't want *that,*" as to pretend "I don't want *like* that; I don't censor, *they* do."

55. "From Chrétien-Guillaume de Lamoignon de Malesherbes," letter 1133 (29 Oct. 1760), *Correspondance complète* 7:269–70.

56. "To Chrétien-Guillaume de Lamoignon de Malesherbes," letter 1152 (5 Nov. 1760), *Correspondance complète* 7:298–300.

57. "To Chrétien-Guillaume de Lamoignon de Malesherbes," letter 1273 (10 Feb. 1761), *Correspondance complète* 8:73.

58. "To Chrétien-Guillaume de Lamoignon de Malesherbes," letter 1126 (22 Oct. 1760), *Correspondance complète* 7:261.

59. Freud, *Interpretation of Dreams,* p. 301.

60. Jacques Derrida, *De la grammatologie* (Paris: Minuit, 1967), p. 208.

61. *Ibid.,* p. 208.

62. Freud, *Interpretation of Dreams,* p. 177.

63. Maurice Blanchot, *La Part du feu* (Paris: Gallimard, 1949), p. 251.

64. Renza, pp. 287–88.

65. Freud, *Interpretation of Dreams,* p. 569.

66. "To Charles Pinot Duclos," letter 3875 (Jan.-Feb. 1765), *Correspondance complète* 23:100.

67. Calvin S. Hall, *A Primer of Freudian Psychology* (New York: New American Library, 1954), p. 66.

68. *Ibid.*, p. 68–69.

69. Tribe, p. 12.

70. Freud, *Interpretation of Dreams*, p. 509.

71. *Communications Control: Readings in the Motives and Structures of Censorship*, ed. John Phelan (New York: Sheed & Ward, 1969), p. 103.

72. Suggested further high-intensity reading on censorship in Rousseau: a sentence fragment from the chapter "De la censure" of *Du contrat social*. There, in the process of applauding the operations of the Spartan censorship agency or Tribunal des Ephores, Rousseau belabors to the point of censoring several times over an untold dirty joke: "Certains ivrognes de [Chio] souillerent le Tribunal des Ephores" (3:459), for which historical accuracy alone (could have) provided a perfect alibi. I know, having tried and abandoned the attempt, that pages on end of analysis cannot do justice to the convolutions of the inside/outside metaphor to which this one line, aided and abetted by two versions of an "explanatory" footnote (3:1497–98), gives rise, at one point laying censorship provisionally on the doorstep of the French language itself.

73. Starobinski, *Jean-Jacques Rousseau*, p. 142.

74. Mary McCarthy, *Memories of a Catholic Girlhood* (New York: Berkeley Medallion Books, 1963), p. 9.

CHAPTER 5

1. Phyllis Trible, *Texts of Terror: Literary-Feminist Readings of Biblical Narratives* (Philadelphia: Fortress Press, 1984), p. 65.

2. Unlike the Greek text, which pronounces her dead, the more ambiguous Hebrew leaves open the awful possibility that she is still alive. See *ibid.*, p. 79.

3. Jane Gallop, *Reading Lacan* (Ithaca: Cornell University Press, 1985), pp. 79–81.

4. François van Laere, *Jean-Jacques Rousseau, du phantasme à l'écriture: les révélations du "Lévite d'Ephraïm"* (Paris: Lettres modernes, 1967), p. 12.

5. *Ibid.*, pp. 39ff.

6. *Ibid.*, p. 67.

7. "To Charles-François-Frédéric de Montmorency-Luxembourg, maréchal-duc de Luxembourg," letter 1879 (17 June 1762), *Correspondance complète* 11:93.

8. Freud, *Interpretation of Dreams*, pp. 38–39, 97, 129, 659–60.

9. *Ibid.*, pp. 661–64.

10. *Ibid.*, p. 660.

11. *Ibid.*, p. 661.

12. *La Bible*, ed. Edouard Dhorme, cited by van Laere, p. 61.

13. *Interpretation of Dreams*, p. 663.

14. *Ibid.*, p. 664.

15. James M. Cox, "Recovering Literature's Lost Ground Through Autobiography," in Olney, p. 142.

16. Kristeva, p. 54.

17. René Girard, *La Violence et le sacré* (Paris: B. Grasset, 1972), pp. 63–101.

18. *Ibid.,* pp. 118–22.

19. Kristeva, p. 100.

20. See Derrida, *De la grammatologie,* pp. 211–14.

21. Girard, p. 13.

22. *Ibid.,* p. 17.

23. *Ibid.,* p. 35.

24. "To Madeleine-Angélique de Neufville-Villeroy, duchesse de Luxembourg," letter 1882 (17 June 1762), *Correspondance complète* 11:99.

25. van Laere, p. 38.

26. Girard, pp. 38–39.

27. Derrida, *De la grammatologie,* p. 227.

28. "Michel Huber à Rousseau," letter 1598 (20 Dec. 1761), *Correspondance complète* 9:336–37.

29. John Hibberd, *Salomon Gessner: His Creative Achievement and Influence* (Cambridge: Cambridge University Press, 1976), p. 132.

30. *Ibid.,* p. 51.

31. Salomon Gessner, *La Mort d'Abel* (Paris: A. A. Renouard, 1802), pp. 143–52.

32. Girard, p. 109.

33. Gessner, p. 34.

34. Girard, p. 283.

35. Jean-Louise Lecercle, *Rousseau et l'art du roman* (Paris: Armand Colin, 1969), p. 362.

36. Thomas M. Kavanagh, *Writing the Truth: Authority and Desire in Rousseau* (Berkeley: University of California Press, 1987), p. 110.

37. Girard, p. 147.

38. Jean-Jacques Rousseau, *Essai sur l'origine des langues où il est parlé de la mélodie et de l'imitation musicale* (1838; rpt. Paris: Editions Stock, 1979), pp. 162–63.

39. Derrida, *De la grammatologie,* p. 205.

40. *Ibid.,* p. 211.

41. See *ibid.,* p. 338.

42. Rousseau, *Essai sur l'origine des langues,* pp. 160–67.

43. Freudian readings of castration anxiety to the contrary. See *Interpretation of Dreams,* p. 389.

CONCLUSION

1. See pp. 6–12, 185–86 above.

2. *Ausonius* 2:175.

3. "Occasion," *Encyclopédie.*

4. "Occasion," *Littré* 5:914.
5. "Occasion," *Larousse du XXe siècle,* 1932 ed.
6. "Occasion," *Encyclopédie.*
7. See pp. 44–45 above.
8. Roy Pascal, quoted by Miller, p. 269.

Index

Alexander the Great, 80, 94
Antiheroism, 58, 76, 81, 83, 103
Antiquity, 241; biblical, 190, 191, 205, 211;
    classical, 23, 58, 65, 72, 88, 94, 98, 121–
    22, 217, 239
Aristides, 58
Aristotle, 217
Aubonne, Paul-Bernard d', 42–45
Augustine, Saint, 76, 83, 85, 144
Ausonius, 7, 240
(*Auto*)-*avilissement* (self-abasement), 75;
    attribute of dedicatory epistle, 58, 59,
    60, 61, 65, 66, 68, 73, 82–83, 102; auto-
    biographical strategy, 15, 58, 73, 78, 79,
    83, 87, 94, 95, 102–3, 236; fact of life,
    87, 89, 92, 93, 94
Autobiographical fiction, 105, 117, 129,
    130, 135, 136, 138, 139; Rousseau's pat-
    ent on, 140
Autobiographical pact, 105, 116
Autobiographical reading, 138–40, 227
Autobiography, 27, 56, 132, 172; coming
    to, vii–viii, 13–14, 215; contrasted with
    self-portraiture, 21–25, 26, 29–31, 35–
    36, 54, 228; female writing as, 139; his-
    tory of, 1–3, 144, 155; in *Confessions,*

232; in *Lettres à Malesherbes,* 142; in
    Lévite, 188–89, 194–97, 213, 242; in
    Préface de Julie, 117; occasional, 2, 149,
    227, 230, 231, 233, 234, 239, 241, 244,
    248, 249, 251; opposed to literature,
    144, 165–67, 186, 187–89, 214–15,
    217, 226, 227, 228; related to fiction,
    91, 117, 126, 129, 130, 136; Rousseau's
    corpus of, 2, 11, 12–18, 232, 240, 248,
    252–53; Rousseau's theory of, 6–7,
    230–31, 233, 247–48, 250–52; theories
    of, 2–6, 28, 54, 132, 163, 172, 214, 228,
    231, 232. See also (*Auto*)-*avilissement;*
    Occasional strategy of autobiography

Bailey, Kenneth E., 75
Barbeyrac, Jean, 70
Bayle, Pierre, 60
Beaujour, Michel: *Miroirs d'encre,* 21, 22,
    23, 30, 40
Beaumarchais, 160
Benjamin: individual and alter ego, 17,
    201–2, 209, 210, 219, 235; son of
    Rachel, 190, 192, 201–2, 204, 206, 210;
    tribe of Israel, 190–94, 196, 201–6,
    209, 219, 221, 224, 225

273